Customer Centered Six Sigma

Linking Customers, Process Improvement, and Financial Results

Also Available from ASQ Quality Press

Customer Satisfaction Measurement and Management
Earl Naumann and Kathleen Giel

Analysis of Customer Satisfaction Data
Derek R. Allen and Tanniru R. Rao

Measuring Customer Satisfaction: Survey Design, Use, and Statistical Analysis Methods, Second Edition
Bob E. Hayes

Improving Your Measurement of Customer Satisfaction: A Guide to Creating, Conducting, Analyzing and Reporting Customer Satisfaction Measurement Programs
Terry G. Vavra

Measuring and Managing Customer Satisfaction: Going for the Gold
Sheila Kessler

Statistical Quality Control Using Excel®
Steven M. Zimmerman, Ph.D. and Marjorie L. Icenogle, Ph.D.

Root Cause Analysis: Simplified Tools and Techniques
Bjørn Andersen and Tom Fagerhaug

Value Leadership: Winning Competitive Advantage in the Information Age
Michael C. Harris

Improving Performance through Statistical Thinking
ASQ Statistics Division

The Desk Reference of Statistical Quality Methods
Mark L. Crossley

To request a complimentary catalog of ASQ Quality Press publications, call 800-248-1946, or visit our website at http://qualitypress.asq.org .

Customer Centered Six Sigma

Linking Customers, Process Improvement, and Financial Results

Earl Naumann and Steven H. Hoisington

ASQ Quality Press
Milwaukee, Wisconsin

Customer Centered Six Sigma
Earl Naumann and Steven H. Hoisington

Library of Congress Cataloging-in-Publication Data

Naumann, Earl, 1946–
  Customer centered Six Sigma : linking customers, process improvement, and
financial results / by Earl Naumann, Steven H. Hoisington.
    p. cm.
  ISBN 0-87389-490-1 (alk. paper)
    1. Customer services. 2. Customer services—Quality control—Statistical methods.
I. Hoisington, Steven H., 1953– II. Title.

HF5415.5. N327 2000
658.8'12—dc21

00-063975

10 9 8 7 6 5 4 3 2

ISBN 0-87389-490-1

Acquisitions Editor: Ken Zielske
Project Editor: Annemieke Koudstaal
Production Administrator: Shawn Dohogne
Special Marketing Representative: David Luth

ASQ Mission: The American Society for Quality advances individual and organizational
performance excellence worldwide by providing opportunities for learning, quality improvement,
and knowledge exchange.

Attention: Bookstores, Wholesalers, Schools and Corporations: ASQ Quality Press books,
videotapes, audiotapes, and software are available at quantity discounts with bulk purchases for
business, educational, or instructional use. For information, please contact ASQ Quality Press at
800-248-1946, or write to ASQ Quality Press, P.O. Box 3005, Milwaukee, WI 53201-3005.

To place orders or to request a free copy of the ASQ Quality Press Publications Catalog, including
ASQ membership information, call 800-248-1946. Visit our web site at www.asq.org or
http://qualitypress.asq.org .

Printed in the United States of America

 Printed on acid-free paper

American Society for Quality

Quality Press
611 East Wisconsin Avenue
Milwaukee, Wisconsin 53202
Call toll free 800-248-1946
www.asq.org
http://qualitypress.asq.org
http://standardsgroup.asq.org
http://e-standards.asq.org
e-mail: authors@asq.org

Table of Contents

PART I Why Six Sigma?

PART II Capturing the Voice of the Customer

List of Illustrations

Acknowledgments

Writing a book is always a challenging process that would be impossible without the support of a variety of people. The team at ASQ Quality Press has been great to work with, particularly Roger Holloway, Ken Zielske, and Annemieke Koudstaal. Tricia Behnke, at Shepherd, Inc., did a great job as project editor.

The team at Naumann & Associates picked up the slack, allowing Earl time to write. Special thanks to Sharmaine Aulbach, Dan Matoske, and Kathy Walker, who put the whole manuscript together.

Colleagues and friends at both Johnson Controls, Inc., and IBM provided Steve with expanded knowledge and examples that are shown throughout the book. These individuals are to be commended on leading efforts that produced these results. A special thanks is due Dr. Sam Huang and Judy Wasser at IBM, as well as Ken Bailey, Hugh Hudson, Bob Zastrow, Bob Galaszewski, and Gloria Frigerio at Johnson Controls. A special thanks is also due Brian Stark, Dale Lueck, and Tom Gannon for encouraging and facilitating Steve's ability to coauthor this book, as well as to John Cairo, Jay Bayne, Mark Duszyski, Tom Buckley, and Jerry Okarma for providing technical support and background on Johnson Control's history in quality, customer satisfaction, and Six Sigma. Finally, a special word of gratitude is due Steve's son Lenny for asking tough questions during the editing process that made the book more robust, reader friendly, and useful.

Preface

Current thinking in business suggests that organizations must continuously improve their products and services, their processes, and their people. Failure to improve in all three areas leads to stagnation and the decline of any business. Firms have pursued a variety of strategic initiatives in an attempt to keep pace with the increasingly competitive business environment.

According to a survey of CEOs of multinational corporations, becoming more customer centered is the major challenge facing large corporations. Therefore, a variety of strategic initiatives typically surround becoming customer centered. A common strategic initiative is process improvement. More recently, process improvement has evolved to a higher improvement standard, the concept of Six Sigma. The process improvement initiative usually has a goal of cost and cycle time reduction. Unfortunately, these two initiatives are typically viewed as separate, distinct activities.

The purpose of this book is to show how these two initiatives can be linked and integrated. Customer feedback should be used to identify where an organization needs to improve. This usually involves some type of process improvement. Process improvement efforts of all types, including Six Sigma, should address the impact of process changes on the customer. The two initiatives should be dovetailed into a single strategic effort.

We, the authors, attempt to show how to efficiently and objectively capture the voice of the customer. Then we show how to link the customer data to Six Sigma initiatives. We do not attempt to show the reader everything possible dealing with capturing the voice of the customer. That would take at least 800 pages. Nor do we attempt to address every aspect of the concept of Six Sigma. That would be another 800 pages. We do attempt to provide enough detail so that the reader will see how things could or should be done to link customer-centered initiatives and Six Sigma initiatives. Separately, both initiatives can produce results. Together, they can be amazingly powerful and the centerpiece of corporate strategy.

All of the data and examples presented in this book are real or based on real situations and organizations. In some cases, it was necessary to disguise the data for proprietary reasons. Our belief is that actual data is richer and more realistic than made-up data. Where possible, the actual names of organizations are included, but, in some situations, that simply was not possible.

We considered using a company that has a well-developed Six Sigma program as an integrating case study, but we chose not to do so for two reasons. First, most students of

Six Sigma have probably read all that they want to see about companies such as Motorola and General Electric. The second reason for not using one of these leaders is that the problems and challenges that they are now facing are far different from those that a firm faces when just starting a Six Sigma initiative, and many more firms are now beginning Six Sigma initiatives.

The firm that was selected for the integrative case studies is Johnson Controls. Since the Controls Business of Johnson Controls, Inc. is two years into its Six Sigma initiative, it provides good examples of issues that must be addressed early on. Not all of the case studies illustrate world-class performance. It may take Johnson Controls several more years to achieve world-class Six Sigma performance. But the case studies illustrate how one firm applied some of the concepts in the chapters. Johnson Control's Six Sigma initiative is simply a work in progress.

This book is divided into four parts. Part 1 contains two chapters. The first of these address why the concept of Six Sigma emerged. Six Sigma represents a natural evolution of several disciplines but most notably quality management. The second chapter addresses the financial payoff of being customer centered and applying Six Sigma concepts. This chapter is included since managers must sell the benefits to senior management for approval and support.

Part 2 of this book focuses on how to capture the voice of the customer. The five chapters in this section provide an overview of the major approaches that can be used to solicit customer feedback. Each approach has its own set of advantages and disadvantages, and each approach would tell us something different about the customers' attitudes. Therefore, we recommend that firms conduct an audit about how customer input is currently gathered and develop a comprehensive, integrated strategy.

Part 3 of this book includes three chapters that address the issues that must be faced in simply getting ready to start a Six Sigma initiative. There must be a good deal of leadership and planning at all levels of the organization. The right processes must be selected for initial implementation efforts, and the teams must be carefully selected and trained.

Part 4 addresses the more technical issues involved in linking the voice of the customer to Six Sigma initiatives. The customers' needs and expectations must be matched with processes and process metrics. The processes must be mapped and problems or potential problems identified. Recommended solutions must be integrated into a new process design and an implementation plan developed. Process capability and sigma performance levels must be tracked and calculated. Finally, the concept of continuous improvement must be institutionalized throughout the organization.

We trust the readers will share our belief that the integration of customer feedback and Six Sigma continuous improvement holds a great deal of potential for improving organizational performance. Integrating both initiatives provides a much more holistic approach than pursuing each independently.

Part I

Why Six Sigma?

Part 1 of this book consists of two chapters. Chapter 1 discusses why the concept of Six Sigma has emerged. Very simply, the rapidly changing business environment has created a need for an organized, structured way to foster innovation and creativity. A Six Sigma initiative is a way to stress continual innovation and improvement in products, services, processes, and behavior. Six Sigma itself is not a radical breakthrough concept. Six Sigma is the result of a natural evolution that has been taking place for the past 20 years.

Chapter 2 addresses the financial impact of customer-centered Six Sigma. Very often, executives need to be sold on the financial impact of increasing customer satisfaction and pursuing Six Sigma. This chapter summarizes many studies that address the significant financial impact of building continuous improvement around the customer.

1

Becoming Customer Centered Is Not a Choice

This is not a book about quality, at least not in its traditional meaning. This is a book about corporate strategy or, a bit more specifically, a book about a specific strategic initiative, Six Sigma. A Six Sigma strategic initiative must be founded in corporate strategy and mixed with healthy doses of concepts from marketing, quality, finance, accounting, and human resources. If Six Sigma is viewed as primarily a *quality* initiative, it will probably fail miserably. If Six Sigma is viewed as a *strategic* initiative, it will require years of hard work to be successful. The Six Sigma initiative will need to be adapted and modified to fit the organization's culture. Six Sigma definitely is not a quick-fix tactic, but the rewards from a Six Sigma strategic initiative can be tremendous.

Although this book discusses a high-level view of basic statistics, statistical tools and techniques, and the concept of Six Sigma itself, it is not meant to teach everything about a true Six Sigma initiative. It is meant to provide a basic understanding and to really emphasize the consideration and implementation of customer input throughout the entire process. The reaffirmation of *customer input* into the concept of Six Sigma is what sets this book apart from the others.

The simplest definition for Six Sigma is to eliminate waste and to mistake proof the processes that create value for customers. Yes, there is a good deal of discussion about statistics required to understand Six Sigma. The discussion of the statistical analysis comes later in this book. However, a Six Sigma initiative is more about managerial innovation than about statistical process control. In essence, a Six Sigma initiative leads to a culture that strives for continuous improvement of products, services, processes, and behaviors.

Before delving more deeply into Six Sigma, examining why Six Sigma has emerged is important. Six Sigma emerged as a natural evolution in business. It is not a radical break-through idea. While the term *Six Sigma* is catchy and fresh, most of the tools and techniques associated with Six Sigma have been in existence for many years. Six Sigma emerged because of the current business environment. The current business environment now demands—and rewards—innovation more than ever before.

WHY SIX SIGMA?

There are a wide variety of factors that work together to force businesses to innovate. These factors are not independent of one another; each is synergistic. In total, the factors have created a business environment far different than 10 or 15 years ago.

Customer Expectations

Customers, both businesses and consumers, are dynamic, always changing. As individuals, we expect new products to be better, faster than previous models. We expect better service and technical support. We do not expect products to fail, but, if they do, we expect the company that made the product to stand behind their products and take care of us. Our expectations are continually moving upward. We, as consumers, do not expect product capability and service to decline; we expect it to get better for virtually all suppliers. To meet these rising expectations, businesses must continually improve and innovate at a rate at least equal to the increase in customer expectations.

In a recent survey of CEOs of the Fortune Global 1000 firms, the 1000 largest firms in the world, CEOs were asked to identify the major challenges facing their organizations. The major challenge identified by CEOs of firms based in North America and Europe was to become more customer focused and to better satisfy customer needs. Becoming more customer focused was the second most frequently identified issue by CEOs of Asian firms.

Technological Change

The rate of change in technology continues to accelerate. No longer are there *high-technology* businesses; all businesses are directly affected by rapid technological change. Customers expect a new personal computer to have a bigger hard drive, more speed, more RAM, a higher resolution monitor, and better software. These expectations flow across almost all product and service industries. While still in its infancy, the Internet has changed the way business and support services are conducted. And there are certain to be big changes in the consumer use of the Internet when Web-TV becomes more widespread. The only thing certain is that there will be new, currently unavailable, technological advances that will be in widespread use in five years.

In the survey of CEOs, the second most critical issue in North America and Europe was dealing with rapid technological change. This was the most frequently identified issue in Asia. The issue of technological change included both rapid change in products as well as underlying productive systems. The implication is that functional life cycles have become shorter and shorter. For example, an old 486 computer with a Windows 3.1 operating system may still perform as well as it did in 1995, but it surely has been functionally obsolete for years.

Global Competition

The rate of growth of international trade among industrialized economies has been twice the rate of domestic economic growth for years. The implication is that customers have a wide array of products and services from around the world from which to choose. Country of origin is less and less of a concern to customers and is often unknown. In fact, many *foreign* products have a higher domestic value added content than traditional *domestic* products. Customers select from the products of the very best global suppliers, guaranteeing tough, global competition in all major economies.

The demonstrations at the World Trade Organization (WTO) meetings in Seattle in December 1999 clearly demonstrate this trend. Environmentalists demonstrated against shifts in jobs to countries with weak environmental standards. Human rights groups demonstrated against harsh working conditions (compared to the United States) and the use of child labor in developing countries. Unions demonstrated against the loss of jobs to countries with lower wage rates. But, in spite of the demonstrations by various special interest groups, world trade continues to grow because consumers and customers want to buy products and services that deliver good customer value. This trend has been in place for over 40 years, and there is no reason for it to abate.

Market Fragmentation

The mass markets have shattered, causing suppliers to produce more customized products that fit a customer's specific needs. As the market segments have become smaller, firms have been forced to change their productive processes to become more flexible and adaptable. There are many more *niche* markets to which larger firms have trouble adapting. Economic order quantities are not driven by a formula in an Economics book; production levels are driven by customer demand that can change quickly. Even large firms, such as Hewlett-Packard, have reorganized into smaller business units, each with a high degree of autonomy. At Hewlett-Packard, the goal is to foster *intrapreneurship,* and posters abound touting the *principles of the garage,* where Hewlett-Packard was founded.

Workforce Changes

Workforce issues are a major challenge for most businesses. Low unemployment rates and the mediocrity of education systems make hiring and keeping good workers difficult. The industrialized economies all have aging populations, with many countries significantly older than the United States. Employees are working and living longer. Older employees expect and often demand a different work environment than younger employees. But the rapid technological changes often result in equally rapid knowledge obsolescence, resulting in the need to create new skill sets among employees. Continual learning is an often overlooked or underestimated factor in employee development, and the issues of workforce diversity never seem to go away.

Complicating all of this is that productivity improvements, particularly in manufacturing of all types, have lead to a dramatically reduced workforce for most businesses. Stated simply, it takes fewer people to produce more products and services. An individual's career track may change direction frequently during a lifetime, with many more job changes. But finding those people has never been more challenging, as workers shift across industries. The current shortage of computer professionals has caused firms in the United States to import workers with the needed skills. Collectively, these and other environmental changes present a major challenge for all business. The old adage of "manage change or change management" has never been more true. Unfortunately, most organizations and people do not deal with change particularly well.

ORGANIZATIONAL CHANGE

Most large organizations manage change through periodic reorganizations or restructuring. Many organizations may restructure themselves every 12, 18, 24, or 36 months. Once they change, the new structure and behaviors settle for a period of time while everyone gets accustomed to the new structure. This *stepwise approach* to change is depicted by the stepping stone line in Figure 1.1. Gradually, the changes become more and more frequent and larger and more radical, or the organization will become less suited for the business environment. But, since the environment, collectively, is acknowledged to be changing exponentially (the curved line in Figure 1.1), such an approach will always lag behind the ideal situation; and employees are sure to be frustrated by the tumultuous, periodic changes.

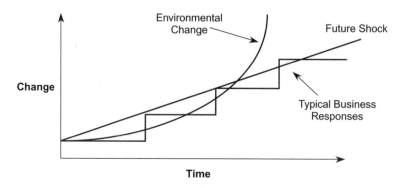

Figure 1.1 The Change Curve—Elements of Change.

Another approach to change is *continuous,* depicted by the straight line in Figure 1.1. Perhaps an organization views the useful life of its technological base as 10 or 15 years and depreciates and replenishes the technological base accordingly. Perhaps an organization invests in a week or two of training each year and relies on this amount of training to keep employees "up to speed." Perhaps an organization relies on a marketing strategy of "milking" mature products rather than one of rapid product innovation. All of these views will lead to a constant rate of change of 10 percent to 15 percent per year. This rate of change is guaranteed to eventually lead to mediocre organizational performance, at best, that significantly lags behind the business environment.

If the environment is changing exponentially, an inescapable fact, and organizations are changing more slowly in a stepwise or gradual fashion, facing future shock is inevitable. Often the shock takes the form of a merger or acquisition. Sometimes the future shock takes the form of corporate bankruptcy. In some cases, the future shock takes the form of radical downsizing to hang on to one or two *core competencies.* And, often, the future shock is marked by a significant decline in stock price as investors lose confidence in a firm. But, if an organization pursues an appropriate strategy, the future shock may never happen.

Responses by World-Class Companies

There have been numerous studies that have attempted to identify the responses of *world-class* companies to the changing environment. The logic behind these studies is that, if the strategies of the very best firms can be identified, the strategies should be transferable to other firms. The extension of this logic is that other firms would enhance their success by mimicking the strategies of world-class leaders. Rather than adopt the conclusions of any particular study, we have tried to synthesize the results of many studies. In doing so, six key organizational responses consistently emerged (Table 1.1).

Customer-Driven Continuous Improvement.   Linking customers to continuous improvement of products and services is a key response by world-class companies. Customer-driven product and service improvement is a result of the recognition that the customer is the ultimate judge of quality. Customers can easily identify what aspects of an organization's performance need improvement. And, for many firms, customers are an excellent source of ideas for technical product innovations. For example, when laser printers were early in their product life cycle, Hewlett-Packard found that many of the ideas for innovation in product features originated with the end-users of the product.

- Customer-Driven, Continuous Improvement
- Closer Relations with Suppliers, Customers
- Supporting Structure, Systems, and Culture That Encourage Innovation and Creativity
- Global, External Orientation
- Clear Vision of Core Competencies
- Emphasis on Developing and Harnessing the Intellect of Human Assets

Table 1.1 Strategic Responses by World-Class Companies to the Rapidly Changing Environment.

The more recent development is to use customer input to drive the improvement of *processes,* not just products and services. The improvement of products and services usually focuses on *what* the customer needs and expects. The improvement of processes focuses on *how* value is created. This concept is explored in more detail in chapter 9.

The needs of customers are satisfied by delivering specific product and service features. The features are created by a firm's processes. Accurate invoices are created by the billing process. Technical support is created by a call center process. Getting the product to the customer is a result of a product delivery process. To improve product features and, especially, service features, a firm's processes must be improved to better meet the customer's expectations.

Closer Relationships with Customers and Suppliers.   The unit of competition in many industries has shifted from individual firm against individual firm to value chain against value chain. The reason for this is quite simple. Few firms create 100 percent of the value that customers expect. Most firms rely on a supply chain to create value in the form of inputs to a firm's key processes. Often, over 60 percent of the value of a product is created by suppliers. A firm will then add value to the inputs provided by suppliers. There also may be a series of value-added resellers who add additional value before the product reaches the end-user.

To create value efficiently for the end-user, all members of the value chain must work closely together. This is achieved by a more fully integrated series of relationships. The first step in this integration is the elimination of average or below average suppliers. In the manufacturing industries, 70 percent to 90 percent of the traditional suppliers are eliminated. Only the world-class performers, or those with potential to become world class, remain as suppliers. The relationships with the remaining suppliers become much closer and deeper so that alliances and partnerships are formed. The goal of the whole value chain becomes to fully satisfy the needs of the end-user.

This implies that the whole value chain knows and understands the needs and expectations of the end-users. Each member of the value chain must know its role in creating value for the end-user. In order to gain this level of knowledge, end-user and downstream customer expectations must be known better than ever. This requires a variety of approaches to capture the voice of the customer and translate the voice into actionable data. Then the data must be shared throughout the value chain.

Innovation and Creativity.   A third characteristic of world-class organizations is a culture and supporting systems that encourage innovation and creativity of all types. The innovation is not restricted to product innovation but also includes innovation in services, strategies, and business practices. All employees in the world-class organizations—not just the management—are encouraged to offer ideas for improvement.

The systems to encourage innovation do not focus only on sources internal to a company's own organization, such as employees. The systems that encourage innovation should also look to sources such as competitors, other industries, and other countries. All sources of innovation are pursued, and the resulting culture is the antithesis of the "not invented here" philosophy. Good ideas are seized, modified, and applied quickly.

For example, the division of Motorola that produces pagers worked for a year to develop a new product. Within two weeks of the new product's market introduction, a Taiwanese competitor had bought the product, reverse engineered it, identified all of the best performance features, and built those features into its own products. The Taiwanese firm had developed a clone that was at least as good as the Motorola product and reached market introduction in slightly over two weeks. Hewlett-Packard has had the same situation occur with a 30- to 60-day time frame for printers. Innovations, particularly technological innovations, spread rapidly around the world.

Global, External Orientation.   World-class organizations pursue a global, external orientation for most activities. These companies search for *best-in-class* practices of all types, wherever they might be found throughout the world. The search for best practices includes all types of initiatives. Recently, Six Sigma has emerged as one of the initiatives adopted by an increasing number of world-class companies. World-class companies are beginning to take notice of this initiative because of the successes that a Six Sigma strategy has demonstrated. Stock markets are also beginning to reward Six Sigma initiatives, as is discussed in detail later.

Core Competencies.   A fifth characteristic of world-class companies is a focus on their core competencies. World-class companies identify what they are very good at and concentrate on improving and extending these core competencies. All aspects of continuous improvement, innovation, and creativity are intended to strengthen the core competencies. None of the world-class firms pursue a strategy of diversification to minimize risks.

If new opportunities require skills beyond the core competencies, the companies develop partnerships or alliances with other firms who possess the necessary skills as a core competency. Thus, these firms pool their talents to create strategic synergies. This characteristic is in direct concert with supply chain integration, in which world-class companies rely on and develop other partners and suppliers in the supply chain to deliver aspects of value creation that are not core competencies of the company. It is also in line with emphasizing innovation, where the world-class company recognizes the importance of the additional core competency in delivering value to the customer but does not have to innovate or develop the competency on its own.

Human Intellect.   A final characteristic of world-class companies is an emphasis on harnessing the intellect of all employees. This is normally manifested in the recruitment of the best possible employees. Then, a wide variety of training and development programs are made available to all employees. The employees are given the opportunity to use their new skills on the job. And, perhaps most important, employees are involved in a wide variety of decision-making opportunities. In some organizations, all employees are expected to be involved in at least one process improvement effort each year. This is the experience of Six Sigma deployment at General Electric in which, according to Jack Welch, nearly every employee in the company is trained on the use of Six Sigma tools and is expected to assist in the identification and improvement of their own work processes.[1]

To briefly summarize these characteristics, world-class companies form closer relationships with customers and use customer input to continually improve products, services, and processes. World-class companies enlist the support of the very best suppliers to create better value for end-user customers. World-class companies actively encourage innovation and creativity among their workforces, developing and harnessing the intellect of all employees at all organizational levels. Finally, world-class companies monitor the best practices of firms, including competitors, anywhere in the world. All of this leads to a broader discussion of Six Sigma.

Each of these common characteristics of world-class companies should also be a characteristic of a successful Six Sigma initiative. Admittedly, some well-known companies have focused primarily on the cost-savings benefits with a very substantial disregard for the customer. However, it could be easily argued that a focus purely on cost reduction would have dire long-term market consequences in most industries. For example, General Electric was forced to reset its Six Sigma initiative during its second year of implementation because customers stated they did not see the value or benefit to them.

THE CONCEPT OF SIX SIGMA

The unique contribution of the concept of Six Sigma is the development of a uniform way to measure and monitor performance and to set extremely high expectations and improvement goals. The measuring and monitoring performance issue deals with a variety of statistical applications, but all of the statistical analysis has the goal of managing and reducing variation and waste in productive processes. A Six Sigma level of performance means that there will be only 3.4 defects, or less, per million opportunities for error.

However, there is a good deal of subjective judgment involved in applying Six Sigma in service activities. Taking this page as an example, is an *opportunity for error* a single word, a sentence, a paragraph, or the whole page? Is a *defect* a grammatical error, a punctuation error, a spelling error, or all of these? Since there is a good deal of stylistic license allowed in the English language, whose interpretation will be used?

These types of decisions emerge in most Six Sigma projects in one form or another. The inherent subjectivity of service activities is precisely why Six Sigma service projects are often more challenging than manufacturing applications. But the subjectivity of service activities also holds the potential for substantial benefits, since the subjectivity usually leads to higher variation in the way activities are performed.

A firm that has adopted a Six Sigma initiative may find itself struggling with the definition of *opportunities for error* and discover that the organization is more focused on increasing the number of error opportunities as opposed to reducing the number of defects. This is not a customer-focused approach and serves as a caution in implementation. This is exactly what happened early in IBM's implementation of Six Sigma.[2] For instance, IBM measured the number of defects in a system shipped to a customer. Let us say for simplistic reasons that the definition was 1 defect per 100 computer systems or a defect rate of 1 percent. If each computer contains, on average, 1000 parts, then the opportunities for error increase from 100 to 100,000 (100 computer systems times 1000 parts per system). Suddenly, the defect rate improves to 1 defect per 100,000 opportunities for error, or 0.001 percent. However, from a customer's perspective, the defect rate has not changed. The customer is still concerned with the number of defects per computer, but IBM would have developed a different performance standard.

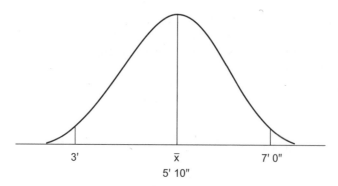

Figure 1.2 A Normal Distribution.

Normal Variation

Almost every activity or characteristic is subject to *variation*. If we were to take a large random sample of U.S. males and measure their height, we would probably find a range from 3 feet to over 7 feet. Perhaps the sample mean would be 5 feet 10 inches, and around this mean would be a normal distribution. If we measured the weight of the same sample of males, the sample mean might be 160 pounds with a range from 70 pounds to over 400 pounds.

If the sample had a perfectly normal distribution, about half of the males would be 5 feet 10 inches or taller, and the other half of the sample would be under 5 feet 10 inches. This normal distribution is depicted in Figure 1.2. This concept of a normal distribution for an activity or characteristic is the foundation of most types of statistical analysis and of the concept of Six Sigma. The shape of a sample distribution is the primary indicator of the amount of variation in an activity or characteristic. The greater the variation in a population, the wider and flatter the distribution will be. The smaller the variation, the narrower and taller the distribution will be. The greater the variation in an activity or a characteristic, the greater the probability of an error occurring.

There is one other important issue in addition to the amount of variation in the population, and that is the *mean* of the population. If we had taken a sample of U.S. males during the 1860s, the mean height would have been about 5 feet 5 inches and the weight would have been about 140 pounds. On average, U.S. males are 5 inches taller and 20 pounds heavier than they were 140 years ago. It also is interesting to note that the biggest changes in both height and weight have occurred in the past 30 years. In other words, the characteristics in question—height and weight—have both had significant shifts over time, so the mean of the population has changed. A characteristic's mean for most populations is not stable and will shift over time.

There are two fundamental objectives of Six Sigma that deal with variation. The first is to stabilize the mean of an activity or characteristic around a target value. The second is to reduce the variation in the activity or characteristic.

Basic Statistics

In order to delve into the statistics that underlie Six Sigma, it is necessary to review some basic statistical concepts. A *population* is the universe being studied. A population could consist of all invoices sent to customers, all customer inquiries seeking technical support, or a production run, for example. A population's central tendency can be measured by a population *mean,* which is an average of the total population. A population's *median* is the numerical midpoint of the population where exactly half of the population is above the median and half of the population is below the median. In a perfect normal distribution, the mean and the median are very close to one another. Less frequently used is the *mode,* which is the most frequently obversed value for a characteristic.

A population's *dispersion* is indicated by its variance. *Variance* is calculated by first calculating a population mean μ (pronounced *mu*). Then μ is subtracted from each observation in the population. The difference between μ and each observation is squared (multiplied times itself). All squared differences are summed and divided by the number of observations in the population. This results in the variance. Pragmatically, the variance is the average squared distance of each observation from the population mean. The more variation, or heterogeneity, in a population, the larger the variance.

To illustrate, let us assume that a computer store is tracking the number of computer sales made each day. Over a period of 20 days, the daily sales ranged from 1 to 12 with a mean of 4.35. By calculating the difference between 4.35 and each day's sales, squaring the individual differences, summing the squared differences and dividing by 20 (the population), the variance is determined to be 7.33.

If we calculate the square root of the variance, we can obtain the standard deviation of the population. In our example, the square root of 7.33 ($\sqrt{7.33}$) is 2.71. The notation for the standard deviation is the Greek symbol σ (pronounced *sigma*). Hence, a sigma denotes the population's standard deviation.

All of the preceding discussion deals with a total population. However, when a population is large, we usually use sampling to make estimates of the population mean and standard deviation. For example, a firm might survey 400 customers each quarter out of a total customer base of 10,000. Or a production manager may sample every thirtieth item being produced. The sample mean $\bar{x}$ (pronounced *x bar*) is an estimate of the population mean μ. The sample standard deviation Sx is an estimate of the population standard deviation σ.

The only thing that we can be sure of is that the sample does not exactly represent the true population mean and standard deviation. A sample will always have some degree of error associated with it. This is typically referred to as *sampling error.* A small sample has more potential for sampling error than a large sample. The amount of sample variation is referred to as *precision.* For example, a sample of 360 usually has a precision of about ± 5 percent. This means that the sample mean is within ± 5 percent of the true population mean.

Process Variation

Once again, every process, activity within a process, or process output will have some variation. In some proportion of cases, the variation will cause performance to vary from the design specifications or from the customer's expectations. Reducing this variation is the major challenge for any improvement effort. There are typically two major sources of variation in productive processes. These sources are *common-cause variation* and *special-cause variation.*

Common-cause variation is the variation that is always present in the process. If *only* common-cause variation is present, the process is stable and predictable. For example, Figure 1.3 shows a process with only common-cause variation. The sample

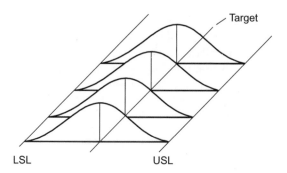

Figure 1.3 Common-Cause Variation.

means are all right on target, and the complete distribution falls between the lower specification limit (LSL) and the upper specification limit (USL). This process is stable, because the shape of the distribution is constant, and capable, because all observations are within the acceptable range. To improve this process, the focus would be on changing the process itself so that the shape of the distribution is changed. In other words, the relatively flat distribution depicted in Figure 1.3 would become narrower and taller as each activity or characteristic becomes more and more consistent with others being produced.

Special-cause variation is caused by unusual or external events that cause variation. Special-cause variation is unpredictable and must be addressed as it occurs. This is illustrated in Figure 1.4. On successive samples, the mean is sometimes above and sometimes below the target value. As the sample mean varies, a portion of the observations fall beyond the upper or lower specification limits. This process is not stable because the sample mean varies. The process is unpredictable because the sample mean varies both above and below the target with no apparent pattern. The process is not capable because some observations fall beyond acceptable limits. To improve this process, the operator would have to take responsibility for making adjustments as special causes occur. Special-cause variation is corrected by ensuring that the means for activities or characteristics are more closely aligned with the target value. This might require, for example, dealing with a sole supplier that produces very consistent quality.

Dr. Deming* estimated that 80 percent to 95 percent of quality problems are related to common-cause variation and are, therefore, the responsibility of management. Specifically, management must take responsibility for improving the process to reduce variation. The remaining 5 percent to 20 percent of problems are due to special-cause variation, and detection is the responsibility of the individual performing the activity. The individual must monitor for the special causes or improve his or her own performance. This normally occurs through traditional statistical process control (SPC) techniques.

Six Sigma Goals

The goals of Six Sigma are to minimize the special-cause variation that causes a sample mean to shift from the target and to reduce common-cause variation, or the standard

---

*Dr. W. Edward Deming is considered by most to be a pioneer in defining and using quality management tools to improve a company's performance. He is often credited for improving quality in products produced in Japan.

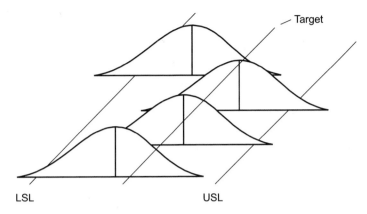

Figure 1.4 Special-Cause Variation.

deviation of the distribution. Since the vast majority of problems are caused by common-cause variation, that is addressed further here.

If a good deal of variation exists in a process activity, that activity will have a very large standard deviation. As a result, the distribution will be very wide and flat. This is illustrated in Figure 1.5. All distributions have exactly the same mean value, $\bar{x} = 50$. The top distribution *(a)* has a large standard deviation. This distribution will result in very inconsistent performance levels and a large number of defects.

As we move from *(a)* to *(b)* to *(c)*, the distribution becomes much more consistent due to a progressively smaller standard deviation. The bottom distribution *(c)* could have a shift in the sample mean of 1.5 σ and it would still be able to produce at acceptable performance levels. This is precisely what Six Sigma performance is all about.

We know that a population mean will vary by some amount. Motorola's research found that it was very unusual for a population mean to shift by more than 1.5 σ. A shift of 1.5 σ would typically be due to a special cause and would be detectable by the person performing the activity.

The goal of Six Sigma is to reduce the common-cause variation so that the population has a very small standard deviation. Pragmatically, this means that everyone performing an activity knows clearly what is expected and performs in a very consistent manner, time after time. By reducing common-cause variation, the process mean could shift and the outer tails of the performance distribution would still be within acceptable limits.

Therefore, if a process is designed to produce very consistent results and perform at Six Sigma quality levels under normal conditions, the process is virtually defect free when the mean is on target. There is less than one defect per million opportunities. If the process mean were to shift by 1.5 σ, only 3.4 defects would be produced per million opportunities for error.

Since most products do not consist of only a single activity, the possible sources of a defect are many. For example, a television set has about 1000 opportunities for error. These 1000 opportunities include both materials and activities that must be performed. If the process means for all materials and activities are on target or close to target and the firm is operating at Six Sigma quality levels, all television sets would be defect free. If some of the process means shift away from target by up to 1.5 σ, there is a very slight chance of a defect being produced. If all of the process means for all 1000 activities shift,

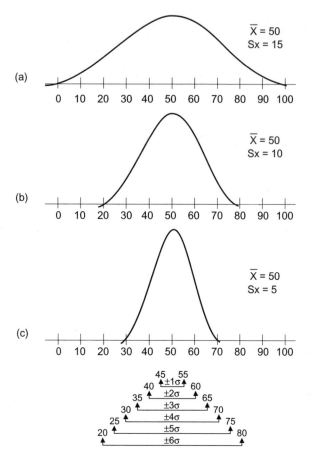

Figure 1.5 Reducing Common-Cause Variation.

each television would have less than 0.4 defects, on average. The likelihood of all process means shifting by 1.5 σ undetected is obviously very unlikely.

SUMMARY

There are many who view the concept of Six Sigma as a radical, new breakthrough concept. Put simply, it is not. All of the tools that are used in achieving Six Sigma have been in existence for years. The unique contribution of Six Sigma is the development of a common performance metric that demands extremely high performance levels. Achieving Six Sigma performance often requires an extremely rigorous and critical self-evaluation that results in innovations in products, services, and processes.

The forces demanding change and innovation are not just internal, improvement initiatives. Evolving customer expectations require innovation. Rapidly shifting and emerging technologies require innovation. Increasing global competition requires innovation. Six Sigma initiatives are simply a formalized, organized, strategic approach to identify and apply opportunities for innovation in products, services, and processes.

CASE STUDY

BECOMING CUSTOMER FOCUSED

The goal of this book is to present concepts and provide specific examples to assist with understanding as well as aid in implementation of a Six Sigma initiative. A case study is presented at the end of each chapter to provide an additional example of the concepts in the chapter. The case studies focus on just one company, Johnson Controls, Inc., because of the maturity and depth of its quality management system. Further, the case studies focus on the Controls Business of Johnson Controls, Inc., one of two major business units. This does not mean that there are not better examples elsewhere, but the case studies emphasize how the concepts were used in a real-life situation and allow you to see how a single company has addressed many of the issues that you may face.

Johnson Controls, Inc., is a publicly traded company with over a 115-year history of excellence. Johnson Controls, Inc., is traded on the New York Stock Exchange under the symbol *JCI*. Financial performance of the company through 1999 includes $16.1 billion in sales, 52 years of consecutive sales increases, 23 successive years of dividend increases, 8 consecutive years of net income increases, and dividends paid consecutively since 1885. Johnson Controls, Inc., is 126 on the Fortune 500 list as of 1999, and has over 95,000 employees at nearly 500 locations worldwide. The headquarters for Johnson Controls, Inc., is in Milwaukee, Wisconsin. Johnson Controls, Inc., has been selected as one of the top 25 places to work and has been awarded the 1999 Energy Star Buildings Ally by the U. S. Environmental Protection Agency (EPA).

Johnson Controls, Inc., contains two major business areas: the Controls Group and the Automotive Systems Group. The Controls Group is the world leader in supplying, installing, and maintaining systems to control heating, ventilating, air conditioning, lighting, security, and fire management for buildings and, through its Integrated Facilities Management Business, provides total management of an organization's facilities.

The Automotive Systems Group is the global market leader in seating and interior systems (seats, door panels, overhead systems, instrumental panels, etc.) for every major light vehicle and passenger automobile manufacturer in the world including BMW, Daimler-Chrysler, Ford, General Motors, Honda, Mazda, Mercedes-Benz, Mitsubishi, Nissan, Renault, Rover, Toyota, and Volkswagen. The Battery Business is the world's largest automotive battery manufacturer in the world and provides aftermarket batteries for Auto Zone, Sears, Interstate Batteries, Wal-Mart, and Costco, among others, as well as OEM batteries for DaimlerChrysler, Ford, Honda, Nissan, and Toyota.

Johnson Controls, Inc., has expanded remarkably since Professor Warren Johnson founded the company to manufacture his invention, the room thermostat. Since its start in 1855, Johnson Controls, Inc., has grown to a multibillion dollar corporation with world-wide leadership. Fundamental to this success is the Johnson Controls, Inc., mission to "continually exceed customers' increasing expectations." The company and its employees believe that if they go beyond what customers expect, customers will return again and again, asking Johnson Controls, Inc., to further contribute to their success.

That is why, over all its businesses, Johnson Controls, Inc., is doing more for its customers than it did just a few years ago. Automakers, for example, outsource their seating requirements to Johnson Controls, Inc., to improve quality and reduce costs. They look to the company not just to manufacture a complete seat or component; they also look for Johnson Controls, Inc., to design it, engineer it, integrate it with surrounding parts, and deliver it globally. By offering automotive interior innovations that "surprise and delight" customers, Johnson Controls, Inc., helps automakers improve vehicle comfort and convenience. Integration of electronics into vehicle interiors is one of its specialties, ranging from global positioning systems to digital compasses and Homelink®. The company is continuously developing new products and holds more patents than any other automotive interior supplier. The Automotive Systems Group was selected as *the* number one supplier for General Motors in 1999.

With more than 115 years of experience in the controls industry, Johnson Controls, Inc., understands buildings better than anyone else. That is why tens of thousands of commercial, institutional, and government building owners and managers around the world turn to Johnson Controls, Inc., to improve the quality of buildings' indoor environments by maximizing comfort, productivity, safety, and energy efficiency. The company engineers, manufactures, and installs control systems that automate a building's heating, ventilating, and air conditioning, as well as lighting, security, and fire safety equipment. Its Metasys® Facility Management system automates a building's mechanical systems for optimal comfort levels while using the least amount of energy; it monitors fire sensors and building access, controls the lights, tracks equipment maintenance, and helps building managers make better decisions.

Building systems at many companies are critical to achieving their corporate missions. In the pharmaceutical industry, for example, the failure of a building's equipment or staff to maintain the proper laboratory conditions could mean the loss of years of new drug research and development. In a bank's data center, the failure of cooling equipment could shut down computer systems, delaying millions of dollars in transactions every minute. For these kinds of mission-critical requirements, customers turn to Johnson Controls, Inc., for integrated facility management. The company furnishes full-time, on-site staff and management to handle all of a building's operating and maintenance services. Johnson Controls, Inc., employees manage more than 1.2 billion square feet of commercial building space around the world, providing customers with unmatched technical expertise.

The case studies in this book illustrate specific examples of the Controls Business of Johnson Controls, Inc., because of this organization's breadth and maturity. The case studies are not meant to represent all of Johnson Controls, Inc., whose businesses are managed and run independently of one another. A Six Sigma strategy is part of the Controls Business' overall quality initiatives and part of its overall continuous improvement philosophy.

2

Linking the Customer, Customer Satisfaction, and Six Sigma Results to Financial Performance

S enior executives in organizations are becoming more and more reluctant to accept information, changes, or new challenges without understanding the value it will have on them or the bottom line of the business. Managers want to know what's in it for them or their organizations, the WIIFM (what's in it for me) factor. Increasingly, managers are being asked to document the financial impact of their decisions. This is especially true for activities such as quality or customer satisfaction improvements that are hard to associate with bottom line financial results. For example, in a recent survey of vice presidents of quality, 75 percent were challenged to document the financial results of their quality improvement efforts. These executives had to calculate the return on their investments in continuous quality improvement. As more companies make similar demands, the significant financial impact of becoming customer centered is becoming more apparent.

There are at least five direct financial impacts of becoming customer centered. Market share tends to go up. Customer loyalty increases. Share of the customer's pocketbook increases. Process improvements reduce costs while increasing customer satisfaction. All of these impacts work together to improve the organization's financial performance such as stock price.

In order to make these calculations, a variety of information is necessary. Some information is *perceptual* in that it is data from surveys that measure customer perceptions. Examples of perceptual data are *overall satisfaction* scores and *value for the money* scores. Some information is *behavioral* in that actual customer behavior is monitored. Examples would be market share, defection rates, and share of pocketbook. Some information is financial such as cost savings, revenue growth, and stock price. Calculating the financial impact of being customer centered requires the use of a variety of these measures.

A number of firms have already stepped up to the challenge of determining the financial impacts of quality and customer satisfaction actions. Several of these studies are explained throughout this chapter. The use of actual customer behavioral data can be very shocking to an organization that has not been used to associating actions or internal measurements with how customers actually react, as demonstrated through their pocketbooks. Some of the data and examples presented here can be used to sell the concept within an organization, but these cannot be a substitute for a company's own data and results. Sometimes it is advantageous to provide an internal view of your own company's results with an external view of another company, maybe even a competitor. In any case, you may not have to chart new ground when looking for ways to link financial performance with quality or customer satisfaction actions. All of the following examples are based on actual firms and data, although a few have been disguised for proprietary reasons.

MARKET SHARE

There is a strong relationship between customer attitudes and *market share*. While measuring customer attitudes can be done very accurately, measuring market share is more ambiguous. To determine market share, a firm must be able to clearly define both *market* and *share*. Since market share data is often gathered by an outside, independent organization, that source may use different definitions for both *market* and *share*.

For example, market share data can be gathered through warehouse withdrawals for some types of products. The withdrawal of products from a warehouse can be analyzed on a product basis, by product lines, or as a general category. These categories may not exactly fit what the company defines as its market, so inherently there is some subjectivity. Or a firm may not operate in all geographic areas served by a warehouse. The firm may have high share in one area and none in another. Quite often, market share data ignores market segmentation. If the market segments are defined differently from one source to another, the data may not accurately match up. A firm might "own" a niche, having a 70 percent share in that niche, but have only a small share in a more broadly defined market. The key issue here is that market share data is inherently subjective in most cases, and it is seldom precise unless applied to a very clearly defined product. If a firm studies the relationship between customer attitudes and market share and finds no relationship, it may be due to ambiguous market share data.

When calculating the impact of customer perceptions on market share, a firm should use long-term tracking between customer-perceived measures and actual market share data. Both types of data could be gathered monthly or quarterly. To make these types of calculations, it is necessary to compare measures over an extended time of at least 10 to 12 time periods due to the requirements of statistical techniques. This would be 10 to 12 months or 10 to 12 quarters depending upon the type of data that is available in the organization. Because of the time lags between changes in customer attitudes showing up in market share, quarterly data is usually better. To conduct statistically accurate quarterly surveys, approximately 3 or 4 years' worth of data is needed to identify trends.

There are a variety of attitude measurements that can be used in this type of study. Some companies use *overall satisfaction,* some use *value for the money,* some use *willingness to recommend,* some use *repurchase intent,* and some companies develop an index that is a composite of several different measures. The two most commonly used measures appear to be *value for the money* and *overall satisfaction.*

Using 10 years' worth of data, IBM Rochester was able to determine, through multivariate statistical analysis, extremely strong correlation between factors of Employee Satisfaction, Productivity, Cost of Quality, Customer Satisfaction, and Market Share.[3] The technique used, along with the results of the study, are shown in Appendix A.

Another illustration is the relationship between customer perceptions of value and market share at AT&T. This example focused on business telephone systems (Figure 2.1). On this graphic, the dotted line represents the top box scores (a 5 or excellent response on a 5-point "Excellent—Very Good—Good—Fair—Poor" scale) for value on quarterly customer satisfaction surveys. This line tracks the customer's perception of value over a period of about four years. The solid line represents market share. The time lag between

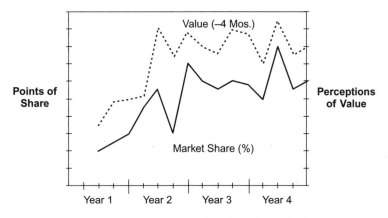

Perception of value mirrors market share 4 months later.

Figure 2.1 Perception of Value versus Market Share at AT&T for Business Telephone Equipment.

changes in value perceptions and changes in market share is four months. AT&T measured value first, and then, four months later, their market share changed. The time lag for other companies could be two, three, four, five, or six months, depending on the purchase pattern for products. Federal Express (Fed Ex) has found that changes in customer attitudes will result in changes in market share in only 48 hours. FedEx customers have a very short purchase cycle.

It is typical for a firm to try different time periods and different survey questions to determine the combination that gives the best fit for the data. At AT&T, it was found that customers' value perceptions were the best single predictor of market share. *Value* produced a better relationship than *satisfaction, price,* or *repurchase intent,* for example. In other organizations, a different variable may have good predictive power.

LOYALTY

In the past few years, the issue of *loyalty* has emerged as very important. Sometimes referred to as *customer retention,* it is important because it has a direct financial impact. Nortel, formerly Northern Telecom, studied the relationship between customer attitudes and customer loyalty. Nortel found much the same thing that AT&T did, a strong correlation between customer perceptions and loyalty. However, for Nortel, the overall satisfaction question produced the best results. The satisfaction rating at Nortel was based on an overall satisfaction question that used a 10-point response scale. Nortel found a marked difference in loyalty between a customer that gave a 9 or 10 rating for overall satisfaction and the person that gave a 4, 5, or 6 (Figure 2.2). Customers that gave a 4, 5, or 6 were not very loyal at all, while the customers that gave a 9 or 10 were far more loyal. Nortel concluded that only delighted customers, those giving a rating of 9 or 10, are truly loyal.

Nortel also found that highly satisfied customers tend to use only 1 or 2 suppliers (Figure 2.3). As customer delight went up with a particular supplier, the probability of multiple suppliers went down considerably. This meant that Nortel would capture a larger portion of the customer's expenditures for telecom equipment and services.

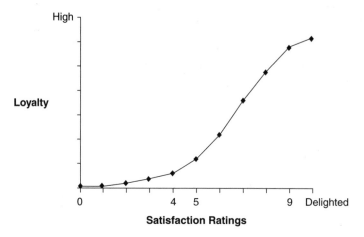

Figure 2.2 Customer Delight Drives Loyalty.

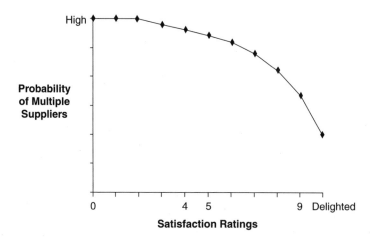

Figure 2.3 Customer Delight Drives Customer Share.

Taking these two observations together, it appears that a highly profitable relationship is based on delighted customers (Figure 2.4). In this case, Nortel would be one of only a couple of suppliers, and their customers would expect to do business with them for a long period of time. Nortel's customers are looking for a long-term business relationship, are less price sensitive, and more concerned with the overall relationship.

When conducting customer loyalty analyses, several types of information are necessary. One type of necessary information is an estimate of the customer defection rate, as in the Nortel example. It is imperative to know how many customers are leaving an organization each year. If the actual defection rate is unknown (and most organizations do not know), an estimate will need to be made. The average amount of revenue that each customer spends must also be determined. By multiplying the defection rate times the amount of revenue per customer, the dollar impact of customer defection can be calculated.

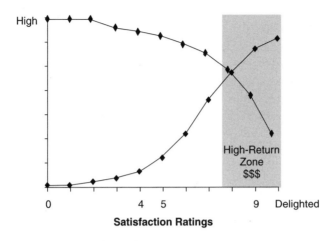

High-Return
Zone
$$$

Satisfaction Ratings

0   4 5   9   Delighted

Figure 2.4 Creating Profitable Relationships.

Score (5-Point Scale)	Retention Rate (1 Year Later)
5 Very Satisfied	92%–97%
4 Satisfied	80%–85%
3 Neither	60%–65%
2 Dissatisfied	15%–20%
1 Very Dissatisfied	0%–5%

Table 2.1 Average Retention Rates.

In many organizations, the defection rates, or the number of customers that leave, are unknown. Commonly, 15 to 20 percent of a firm's customer base turn over each year for an average firm. That is, they take their business elsewhere. Ironically, many firms do not know which customers have defected until much later. When conducting customer satisfaction research using a sample frame of current customers, it is not unusual to find respondents who say, "I haven't been a customer of that firm for three years." Yet the customer's name showed up on the internal customer database as a current customer. The implication is that databases often do not accurately reflect current customer relationships.

Since retention rates are often unknown, Table 2.1 provides some approximate retention rates for an overall satisfaction question that used a 5-point scale. These defection rates have been validated in numerous business to business research projects by Naumann & Associates. When using a 7- or 10-point scale, the retention rates are more dispersed, but the results are similar. As indicated in the graphic, if the customer gave a *very satisfied* rating, or a 5 on a 5-point scale, 92 to 97 percent of those customers would still be with the supplier one year later. Unfortunately, if a person gave a *dissatisfied* rating, or a 2, only 15 to 20 percent of those customers will remain a year later. If there is no actual retention data in your organization, these figures closely approximate what occurs in most industries. If the industry is highly competitive, the retention rate may be lower. If it is not as

Satisfied Customers 5, 4		Not Satisfied Customers 3, 2, 1	
Total Customers	80,000	Total Customers	80,000
Percent Satisfied	82%	Percent Dissatisfied	18%
Total Satisfied	65,600	Total Dissatisfied	14,400
Customer Defection Rate	10%	Customer Defection Rate	50%
Total Lost Satisfied Customers	6560	Total Lost Dissatisfied Customers	7200

Table 2.2 Revenue Impact of Customer Loyalty at Controls Business of Johnson Controls, Inc.

competitive, the retention rate may be higher. For example, in an electric utility, there are not as many choices for residential consumers. Even if they give a low rating, they do not have many alternatives to go someplace else, but they could switch to another energy source such as natural gas.

The following example is based on actual data from the Controls Business of Johnson Controls, Inc. This unit had revenue of nearly $3 billion and a diverse customer base of about 80,000. These figures are several years old and are not current. Dividing 80,000 customers into the total revenue of $2.9 billion results in a per-customer-revenue average of $37,223. Of the 80,000 customers, 82 percent were viewed as *very satisfied* or *satisfied,* as indicated by a 5 or 4 response on a 5-point survey scale. That meant there were 65,600 satisfied customers (Table 2.2). Of these, about 10 percent would probably leave during the year based on the retention rates in Table 2.1. The estimate of 10 percent was reached by averaging the defection rate of customers who rate their satisfaction at 5 (approximately 5 percent defection rate) and those who rate it at 4 (approximately 15 percent to 20 percent defection rate). This equated to 6560 satisfied customers that were potentially lost each year.

Conversely, if the business unit had 82 percent satisfied customers, that implies it also had 18 percent dissatisfied customers. Therefore, it had a total of 14,400 dissatisfied customers. The defection rate here is much higher, and this was estimated at 50 percent, which was roughly an approximation of those 3, 2, and 1 scores from Table 2.1. Multiplying the defection rate times the dissatisfied customers, it was estimated that there would be 7200 lost dissatisfied customers. Adding together the estimates for all lost customers, approximately 13,700 customers would be lost. Subsequently, it was found that the estimate of 13,700 was within 500 of the actual defection rate in that year. The bottom-line implication was that almost 14,000 customers defected. By multiplying the per capita revenue times the number of customers defecting, the total lost revenue can be calculated (Table 2.3). This business unit was losing a total of $512,188,480 annually due to customer defections. This meant that the sales force had to acquire $512 million in new revenue just to keep total revenue even.

If the satisfaction level could be improved from say 82 percent up to a 90 percent, there would be a dramatic impact on customer loyalty and retention. An 8-percentage-point improvement from an 82 percent satisfaction level to a 90 percent satisfaction level was worth $95 million in additional revenue through reduced customer defection. In other words, a one-point shift in customer satisfaction was worth something on the

Satisfied Customers 5, 4		Not Satisfied Customers 3, 2, 1	
Total Lost Satisfied Customers	6560	Total Lost Dissatisfied Customers	7200
Multiplied by Per Capita Revenue	$37,223	Multiplied by Per Capita Revenue	$37,223
Lost Revenue	$244,182,880	Lost Revenue	$268,005,600
Total Lost Revenue: $512,188,480			

Table 2.3 Revenue Impact of Customer Loyalty at Controls Business of Johnson Controls, Inc.

magnitude of $10 million to $11 million. Each point of customer satisfaction has a very significant impact on profitability. IBM Rochester determined that a one-point improvement in customer satisfaction increased revenue by an additional $257 million over five years.[4]

Another consideration in terms of customer loyalty deals with the occurrence of a merger or acquisition. Very often when a merger occurs, an assumption is made that all customers are going to be satisfied and there will be synergies that develop as a result. Unfortunately, this is not always the case. A client of Naumann & Associates recently studied how many customers remained with the firm one year after an acquisition. The assumption was that there would be synergies resulting in increased revenue over time that would be beneficial to the acquiring firm. In reality, 31 percent of customers left in the first year. The customers were not highly loyal to the previous firm, and the merger did not include a plan to transition the new customers smoothly to the acquiring firm. As a result, the customers became very frustrated with the acquisition and switched to a competitor at that point. The acquiring firm did not anticipate such a high defection rate and, as a result, overpaid for the acquisition by a relatively significant amount. Had the acquiring firm known that they would have a significant customer loss, the purchase price would have been much lower. This firm wasted a lot of money by not calculating the probable defection rate.

SHARE OF SPEND

When customers are highly satisfied with a supplier, they tend to spend a larger proportion of their budget with that supplier. Think of the purchase patterns of a typical consumer. If a consumer is satisfied with a restaurant or a department store, they tend to go back to that establishment much more frequently. The revenue aggregates throughout the year and adds up to be significantly larger than the consumer's second or third favorite store or restaurant. The same implication applies in most supplier-customer relationships.

As firms are moving toward supply chain management, the supplier base is reduced by eliminating suppliers with lower performance. The reduction in the number of suppliers is often in the range of 70 percent to 90 percent. The suppliers that do remain are the higher performing firms. These suppliers are rewarded by capturing a larger portion of the customer's expenditures.

As an example, Nortel found that customers who gave an overall satisfaction score of 5 (a response of *very satisfied* on a 5-point scale) had twice the annual revenue growth rate of customers that gave them a 4. Although the top two box scores (4 and 5 on a 5-point scale) are the most commonly used indicators of customer satisfaction, Nortel's research indicated that the top box score (5 on a 5-point scale) was far more valuable in terms of revenue growth and financial impact than a second box score.

To illustrate how the share of spend can be calculated, data from the following example from the Controls Business of Johnson Controls, Inc., is used again. This company's revenues were about $2.9 billion at the time. Based on responses from customers, the share of spend for this company was estimated at 40 percent. About 60 percent of the average customer's budget was being spent on other, competing suppliers. By doing a simple algebraic equation, if 40 percent of the customer's budget generated $2.9 billion, then 50 percent of the customer's budget would generate $3.7 billion and 60 percent of the customer's budget would generate $4.4 billion. The potential revenue among the existing customer base was quite significant. However, the strategy to capture a larger portion of existing customer's expenditures is quite different from a customer acquisition strategy. Capturing a larger portion of an existing customer's budget is accomplished by being more customer centered.

In most organizations, the existing customer base has a good deal of potential for revenue growth. If existing customers can be satisfied more fully, customers will probably spend more money with that supplier. Total revenues for a firm will go up simply because of the increased purchases by existing customers. In another study by IBM Rochester, it was determined that customers behave the way they say they will behave regarding repurchase intentions (see note 4). In other words, if customers say that they will repurchase IBM equipment, they usually do. This study, shown in Figure 2.5, also shows that as customer satisfaction levels improve, loyalty and share of spend improve as well. Customer loyalty for very satisfied customers (5 response on a 5-point customer satisfaction survey scale) is twice that of a satisfied customer (4 response on a 5-point customer satisfaction survey scale).

A few interesting questions for many organizations emerge from this approach. What is happening to the share of spend among customers? Is a firm getting a larger portion of the customer's budget? Is it staying the same, or is it decreasing? Unfortunately, many firms cannot answer these questions. There are some firms that are growing through a merger and acquisition strategy, even though the individual customers are decreasing their annual purchases. This action masks a very precarious situation. If customers tend to be dissatisfied and continually reduce the amount they spend with the firm, the long-term implications on revenues, market share, and share of spend are very negative. Revenues ultimately begin to match satisfaction levels and decline. It is important not only to look at the existing share of spend but also to track what is happening to it.

For example, a firm studied the purchase patterns of its customers. The firm bracketed its customers into three categories: those who increased year-to-year revenue by more than 10 percent, those who stayed within 10 percent from the previous year, and those who reduced year-to-year revenue by more than 10 percent. The firm found that slightly over 50 percent of its customers were reducing revenue by more than 10 percent. About 35 percent of the customers remained approximately the same. Only 15 percent of customers increased revenues by more than 10 percent. But the firm's total revenues were increasing due to an aggressive acquisition strategy. Revenues were increasing because they were acquiring more customers, not because they were getting more share of spend

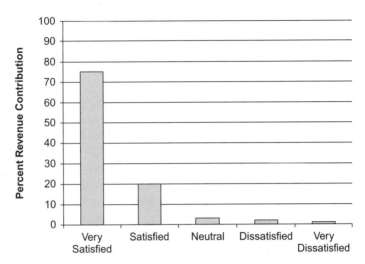

Figure 2.5 Correlation between Customer Loyalty and Revenue to Customer Satisfaction Levels at IBM Rochester.

from existing customers. IBM Rochester conducted a study in 1990 that found that it cost 5 times more to gain a new customer than to keep an existing one and 12 times more to regain a customer it had lost (see note 4). Therefore, even though a company is increasing revenues, its margins may be decreasing because sales expenses are increasing. A company needs a balanced approach to increase its share of spend from existing customers, as well as gaining new customers.

PROCESS IMPROVEMENT

One of the best sources of ideas for process improvement is the customer. In fact, the issue of customer-driven process improvement is one of the characteristics of high-performing organizations around the world. Most of the more innovative firms explicitly stress the idea of having customer-driven process improvement in which they are trying to improve their processes and, even more broadly, improve their products and services based on customer input.

Some process improvement initiatives in organizations improve customer satisfaction and do not have an impact on cost structures. Some improve internal communication and coordination. Some process improvements reduce cost and, in some cases, very significantly. Some improve satisfaction, improve coordination, and reduce cost simultaneously. It is more common to have all three of these work together than it is to have one effect alone. When examining the benefits of process improvement, sometimes it is difficult to identify the actual cost savings because they may not be very significant. There could be very significant improvements in customer satisfaction or some other measure that has an indirect impact on the financial position of the firm.

To use the customer as a driver of process improvement, it is important to identify which elements of value or satisfaction are most critical to the customer. The processes that deliver the key drivers become the focus of improvement initiatives. The first step within this effort is to identify those processes and then map them very carefully. Next, benchmarking of those key processes will help identify ways to improve. The goal is to identify what other firms, preferably competitors and world-class organizations, are doing very innovatively and bring those ideas back into your own organizations. This typically will occur through the use of Six Sigma process improvement teams. Additional discussions on linking process parameters to customer satisfaction attributes are presented in chapter 11.

GTE Directories, a Baldrige Award winner based in Dallas, Texas, found that cost savings and better service simultaneously resulted from most of their process improvements. The average annual cost reduction of process improvement was between 3 to 5 percent. That may not seem to be very significant, but this organization had been improving the processes for an extended period of time. When firms first begin the process improvement initiatives, the savings are normally much larger than that. With some firms, there have been savings in the magnitude of 30 percent of their process cost. GTE found that they could respond faster and more effectively to their customers by streamlining their processes. As a result, customer satisfaction increased while cost went down. General Electric credits Six Sigma for boosting earnings and estimated that the return on investment from Six Sigma process improvements was more than $1.5 billion in 1999.[5]

Cost savings from process improvements can be calculated most easily if a firm utilizes an activity-based-cost (ABC) accounting system. This allows the improvement in activities within a process to be documented clearly and quickly. In the absence of an ABC system, a manager should plan for how the financial impact will be calculated. This often requires work sampling. There are many areas for potential savings. The concept of ABC accounting is further discussed in chapter 9.

Labor savings are often significant since cycle time reduction of major activities within a process is a common goal. However, labor savings can be achieved through more than just cycle time reductions that remove unproductive activities. Employee absenteeism and turnover are often reduced, as are training and learning curve expenses for getting newly hired employees up to speed. Job descriptions and procedures are usually updated and clarified, thus improving employee productivity. On-the-job safety rates also improve, resulting in a reduction of lost time due to injuries. Employee downtime due to poor maintenance is reduced. Labor devoted to rework of defective products is also reduced. Collectively, all of these contribute to higher levels of employee satisfaction. Again, IBM Rochester determined a direct correlation between employee satisfaction, productivity, cost of quality, customer satisfaction, and market share, described in Appendix A (see note 3). This is one study that demonstrates a clear correlation of employee satisfaction on financial performance of a company.

Since product defectives are reduced, there are also often substantial materials savings. Having fewer defectives reduces the amount of scrap. Materials savings can also come from lower carrying cost by reducing in-process inventory levels and shrinkage rates. Reduced cycle time usually results in lower finished product inventory levels since a firm is more responsive to customers and needs less safety stock. Materials costs can be reduced by partnering with key suppliers to harmonize value-creating processes in both firms.

Many firms experience a fixed asset reduction through process improvements, thus improving economic value added. This could come through automation or improved material handling equipment. As the amount of invested capital in a process decreases, the return on investment improves.

In addition to the improvements in labor costs, material cost, and fixed assets, there are other *soft* benefits that are somewhat more difficult to quantify. There are improvements in employee morale due to more involvement and participation in decision making. This contributes to increased customer satisfaction along with the actual process improvements. Employees have increased participation in suggestion programs and are a better source of managerial, product, and service innovations. There are normally reductions in overhead charges and improvement in sales efficiency as well.

Collectively, these benefits can be quite substantial. Since customer-centered improvement is at the heart of the Malcolm Baldrige National Quality Award, state and industry quality awards, and Six Sigma strategies, there is broad research support for improved profitability. This improved profitability leads directly to increased stock market performance.

STOCK PRICE

A number of studies have provided a direct link between customer attitudes and the price of common stock. These studies have occurred in individual organizations and also in broader studies that include several hundred organizations. The studies very consistently show a correlation between customer attitudes and stock price. Before looking at the results, it may be helpful to see how the relationship actually develops.

The most logical relationship between customer satisfaction and stock price includes a number of intermediate steps (Figure 2.6). Improved customer satisfaction is linked to increased loyalty among customers, which is linked to market share. Market share is directly linked to profitability, which drives stock price. For instance, increased customer satisfaction increases referrals from existing customers and makes more customer acquisition easier. Having highly satisfied customers who are loyal means losing fewer of those customers. These aspects of satisfaction, and particularly loyalty, work together to drive market share. Market share in turn has been linked directly to profitability for quite a number of years through the Profit Impact of Market Strategies (PIMS) studies and other research. Market share is an excellent predictor of profitability in most industries and most

Figure 2.6 The Relationship between Customer Attitudes and Stock Price.

Correlation of Very Satisfied to Share Price: 0.88

Figure 2.7 Relationship between Stock Price and Customer Satisfaction at Nortel.

organizations. Profitability, in turn, is the primary driver of stock price. With the expectation that profitability will increase comes a raise in stock price.

This relationship has been demonstrated in a number of organizations. The relationship between Nortel's top box satisfaction scores (a 5 or very satisfied response on a 5-point customer satisfaction survey scale) and the share price of common stock is presented in Figure 2.7. As the percentage of customers who are very satisfied goes up, the share price also increases. The correlation between very satisfied scores and share price was 0.88, an extremely high correlation. Nortel determined that satisfaction among their customer base was very visible to investors either directly or indirectly. Some companies may view these results as an anomaly, based on just one company. But there is much broader support.

The American Customer Satisfaction Index (ACSI) is a national program jointly sponsored by the American Society for Quality (ASQ) and the Social Research Center at the University of Michigan. This program conducts quarterly satisfaction surveys of about 14,000 individuals. Research has encompassed several major industries and a variety of firms within each of these industries, so the scope is quite large. Tracking of this data has been going on since the fourth quarter of 1994, providing a substantial history of data for the American Customer Satisfaction Index. The ACSI discovered that firms or organizations that have a high ACSI (customer satisfaction) score, on average, showed a positive improvement in stock price of 4.6 percent. For those firms with low ACSI scores, changes in stock price, on average, were negative and declined 0.4 percent.[6] The results are summarized in Figure 2.8.

The Customer Satisfaction Index is not just a top box score as Nortel used, but a combination of factors. The Index pools several overall concepts of customer attitudes. For this study, the firms included in the survey were tracked with respect to their changes in their particular customer satisfaction indexes. Those firms were then tracked for their stock price in equivalent periods. The researchers found that there was a one-quarter lag between the changes in the Index and changes in the Dow Jones average (Figure 2.9). The graphic shows a very strong correlation with the exception of the second quarter of 1997 during the start of the Asian financial crisis. The change in the Index did not show up as strongly at that point. The correlation here is not 0.88 as in Nortel's research, but it is certainly very strong. Clearly there is a strong relationship between customer satisfaction and stock price

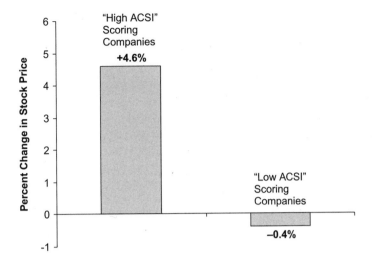

Figure 2.8 Stock Price Performance of High versus Low ACSI Scoring Companies.

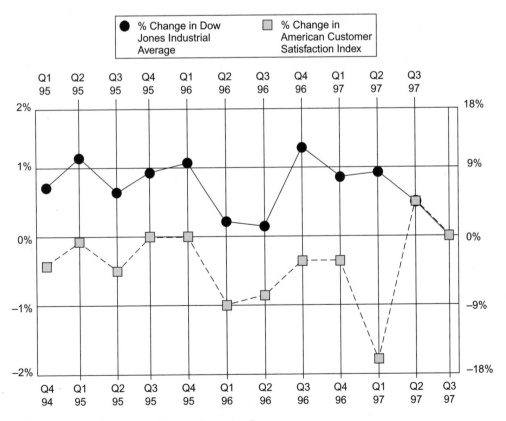

Figure 2.9 As Customers Go, So Goes the Dow.

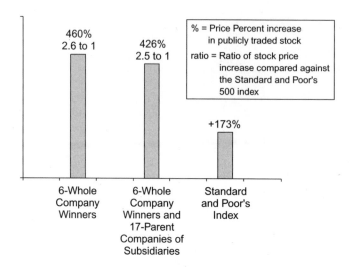

Figure 2.10 NIST Baldrige Winners Stock Performance Index.

when viewed either individually or in aggregate. The firms included in this study from the American Customer Satisfaction Index are included in Appendix B.[7]

There have been several other studies that examine the stock market performance of quality award winners. The evaluative criteria for the quality awards are much broader than customer satisfaction. For example, the Malcolm Baldrige National Quality Award examines seven performance areas, including one on customer relationships and satisfaction. Additionally, being customer centered is one of the Award's core values that runs pervasively throughout the Award criteria.

The U.S. Department of Commerce, National Institute of Standards and Technology (NIST) that administers the Malcolm Baldrige National Quality Award (MBNQA) developed a *Baldrige Index,* a fictitious stock fund. The fund is made up of the publicly traded companies that have won the Baldrige Award since its inception in 1988. Results are published each year at its website (www.nist.gov) and are summarized in Figure 2.10. The fund includes all winners of the Baldrige Award but segments whole company winners from divisions or subsections of larger companies. For instance, IBM Rochester, a 1990 MBNQA winner, is a division of the IBM Corporation and does not issue its own shares of stock. Also, a number of the small business award winners are privately held, so they are excluded from the fund. The stock price was tracked from the first day of the month after the award was announced. In 1999, the Baldrige Winners Index that included the 6-whole company winners achieved a 460 percent return on investment compared to a 175 percent return for the Standard and Poors (S&P) 500 Index. The whole company winners outperformed the S&P 500 by a ratio of 2.6 to 1.[8]

NIST also tracked the performance of all firms that won the award as a whole firm or as a division or subsidiary of a larger parent company. Thus, the parent company performance of division winners was considered. This group of firms had a return on investment of 426 percent, outperforming the S&P 500 by a ratio of 2.5 to 1.

In addition to the actual award winners, there were other firms that were selected for site visits based on highly rated applications. The site visit firms outperformed the S&P

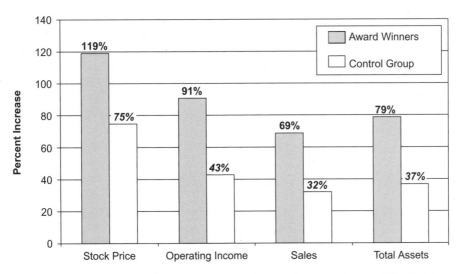

Figure 2.11 Quality Award Winners Outperform Control Group in Areas of Stock Price, Operating Income, Sales, and Total Assets.

500 by a ratio of about 1.5 to 1. While this group's stock performance was lower than award winners, it was still quite good.

Robinson Capital Management, an investment company located in Minneapolis, Minnesota, has formed a real stock fund composed of companies that have a strong focus on quality and have demonstrated strong quality results. The fund has significantly outperformed the S&P 500. Craig Robinson, president of Robinson Capital Management and the stock fund manager, says this is one of the strongest funds in the company's portfolio of funds.[9]

Another study was conducted by Dr. Vinod Singhall of Georgia Institute of Technology that examined the stock market performance of any quality award winner, not just Baldrige winners. The awards included industry awards, state awards, and the Baldrige Award, but all the awards were for quality performance.[10] About 600 award winners were identified with about 75 percent coming from manufacturing industries. The stock performance was examined for a five-year period before winning the award and a five-year period after winning. To control for industry differences, a control group was also developed. Each winner was paired with a firm from the same SIC classification and was the closest in size to the winner based on the book value of assets.

There was no difference in performance measures or stock price in the five-year period before winning an award. However, that changed rather dramatically after an award was received or won.

The award winners outperformed the control group by a ratio of 2 to 1 in changes in operating income, sales, total assets, number of employees, return on sales, and return on assets. The stock return for the award winners was 114 percent compared to 80 percent for the S&P 500. The award winners outperformed the S&P 500 by almost a 1.5 to 1 ratio. The results of this study are summarized in Figure 2.11.

IBM Rochester has demonstrated a very strong correlation between IBM stock price and the overall customer satisfaction score (see note 4). This study spanned more than seven years. The results of this study are summarized in Figure 2.12.

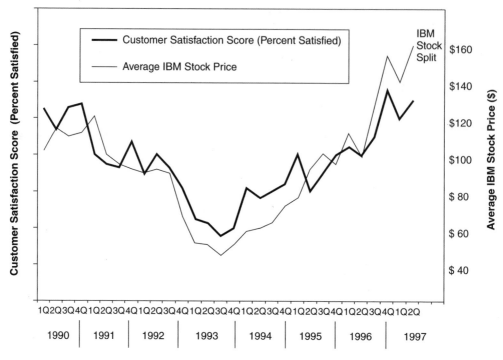

Figure 2.12 Correlation between IBM Stock Price and Customer Satisfaction.

VA³

The previous portions of this chapter have demonstrated some of the specific linkages between customer attitudes, quality, and financial performance. However, the discussions focused on outcome measures rather than the managerial strategies necessary to achieve the improved financial performance. This portion of the chapter presents a framework to integrate the various strategies.

An organization creates wealth for shareholders by performing successfully in three major areas. First, an organization must develop its employees by creating people value added; secondly, an organization must manage its financial decisions well, by creating economic value added; and lastly, an organization must create added value for its customers. These three components form the *VA³ model* (Figure 2.13).

All three of the components interact with one another rather than function independently. For example, changes in customer value added will certainly influence employees and financial performance. If an organization performs poorly in any of the three areas, overall performance will suffer.

Customer Value Added

The major drivers of a customer's perception of value are product quality, service quality, price, image, and relationship. These collectively create customer value. When a firm delivers a good value proposition, high levels of customer satisfaction, loyalty, share of spend, and market share result. Also, a firm's overall image is enhanced among customers.

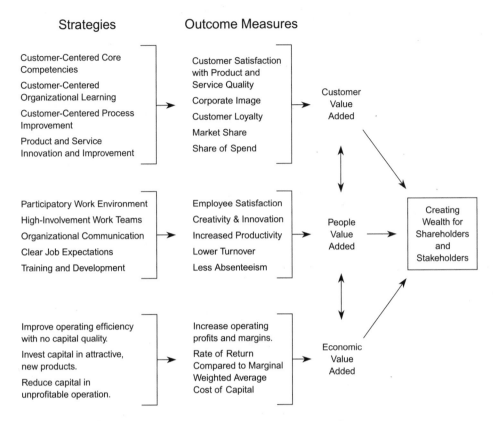

Figure 2.13 VA³ Model.

The six chapters in Part 2 of this book address how the customer's voice, expectations, and perceptions can be captured and measured in a variety of situations. Yet, the issue of what strategies lead to the positive outcomes must be addressed.

Firms must have clearly defined core competencies. A firm must know what it is good at and what it is not good at. These core competencies must be aligned around the needs of the most critical customers, specifically, and other secondary customer segments more generally. Organizational learning should focus on improving the core competencies and on gaining a better understanding of the customer. This requires a strong commitment to the training and development of employees. Because customer expectations are continually increasing, a firm should strive for innovation and improvement of products and services and the primary value creating processes. Centering these activities on the customer is enhanced through people value added.

People Value Added

There is a strong correlation between the satisfaction level of employees and customers. It is difficult, if not impossible, for disgruntled employees to deliver good customer value. The breakdown in the value delivery system normally occurs in those dimensions of service quality that personally touch customers. For example, Nortel found that area offices that had higher employee satisfaction also had higher customer satisfaction scores. If the assumption is made that employee satisfaction does influence customer satisfaction, then the challenge for a company is to identify and manage the key drivers of employee satisfaction.

There is a huge body of literature that examines factors related to employee satisfaction. Summarizing all of the literature is beyond the scope of this discussion. However, there are some consistent concepts that are positively related to employee satisfaction. Again, IBM Rochester demonstrated a very strong correlation between employee satisfaction and customer satisfaction, among other variables. The results and techniques used are described in Appendix A (see note 3).

Employees are more satisfied when a participatory work environment exists. Participatory means that employees are substantively involved in the decision-making process and have input into organization improvement. Closely related to this is the fact that employees in high-involvement work teams tend to be more satisfied. While it takes time to develop an open, trusting team environment, the results can be impressive.

Organizations that have high levels of communication also tend to have more satisfied employees. This means that communication among all parts of the organization, from top to bottom, is open, creating a *no secrets* environment. At the job level, good communication ensures that employees know what is expected of them, that job expectations are clarified. A firm that will remain anonymous conducted an employee satisfaction survey and discovered that the major issue impacting employee satisfaction was poor communications throughout the organization. Not surprising, the major issue impacting customers from customer satisfaction survey results was a lack of communications by the company with its customers.

Finally, organizations that place an emphasis on training and development tend to have higher employee satisfaction. The allocation of resources to employee development allows employees to gain new skills and grow personally and professionally. The personal growth creates higher levels of intrinsic satisfaction, which, in turn, leads to higher overall job satisfaction. The IBM Rochester correlation study between employee satisfaction and customer satisfaction, among other factors, identified the most critical factor that influenced employee satisfaction as having the right skills for the job.

Economic Value Added

The third major component of the VA[3] model is economic value added. Economic value added addresses the efficient use of financial resources. There are three operating strategies to improve financial efficiency. First, a firm can improve operating efficiency with no additional capital outlay. This is normally achieved by pursuing customer-centered process improvements that often simultaneously improve efficiency and reduce cost. The second strategy is to invest capital in attractive, new products. To do this, a firm must have a clear understanding of the customer's needs and expectations. These new products often have substantially higher profit margins than more mature products. The third strategy is to reduce capital in unprofitable operations where returns are below the fully allocated cost of capital. This strategy is closely related to the idea of customer-centered core competencies, or focusing on those performance areas in which a company is strategically focused.

The VA[3] model provides an integrative framework for the strategies that must be pursued to achieve high wealth creation for shareholders, specifically, and stakeholders more generally. If a firm excels in all three areas, revenue growth and profitability are the likely outcomes.

SUMMARY

There are numerous direct, clearly identifiable financial impacts of integrating the voice of the customer into Six Sigma improvement efforts. When starting out, the examples in this chapter, all based on real firms and data, can be used to illustrate the financial impacts. The data becomes more powerful to an organization when estimates are made based on a firm's own customer data, sales revenue, and profitability. The data becomes even more powerful when based on documented results instead of estimates.

Therefore, it is absolutely critical to plan for exactly how customer metrics, internal performance metrics, and financial performance will be used to track the impact on the bottom line. If financial impact cannot be documented, senior management support for customer-centered Six Sigma initiatives will fade. When the financial results are clearly stated, customer-centered Six Sigma can become a unifying strategic initiative.

CASE STUDY

LINKING CUSTOMER SATISFACTION RESULTS TO FINANCIAL PERFORMANCE

A good deal of research has been conducted by the Controls Business of Johnson Controls, Inc., to understand customer satisfaction and buying behavior. Chapter 2 cited numerous examples of this analysis including the facts that

- A one-point improvement in customer satisfaction will yield an additional $10 million in sales.

- More than $500 million was being lost annually due to customer defections to other competitors.

- A 10 percent gain in the spend of share per customer would yield an additional $800 million in sales.

This analysis is not being repeated here. An extension of these analyses led to further information about customer buying behavior that is shown in Figures 2.14, 2.15, and 2.16.

The Controls Business of Johnson Controls, Inc., looked at actual repurchases by customers over a two-year period of time. They discovered that satisfied customers have a much higher propensity to repurchase or do business again with Johnson Controls, Inc., than a customer that is not satisfied. In fact, 91 percent of customer renewals are from customers that are satisfied or very satisfied (Figure 2.14). And, a very satisfied customer is twice as likely to repurchase from Johnson Controls, Inc., than a satisfied customer. They also discovered that the more satisfied a customer was, the more they spent with them. A very satisfied customer spent nearly twice the amount with Johnson Controls, Inc., than a satisfied customer (Figure 2.15). In fact, a very satisfied customer contributed 327 times the revenue of a very dissatisfied customer. The final interesting fact about this study is that the average contract price for a very satisfied customer was

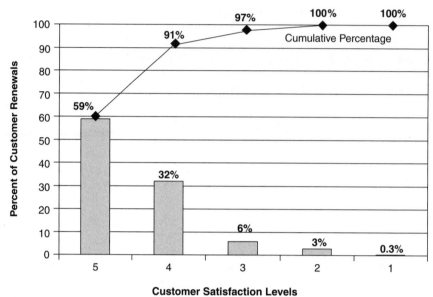

Customer Satisfaction Levels
(5 = Very Satisfied, 4 = Satisfied, 3 = Neither, 2 = Dissatisfied, 1 = Very Dissatisfied)

Figure 2.14 Percent of Customer Renewals by Customer Satisfaction Level.

significantly higher than that for a satisfied customer by nearly 20 percent (Figure 2.16). The more satisfied customers are, the more likely they will repurchase your products and the more money they will spend with you.

With this data in hand, the Controls Business of Johnson Controls, Inc., can now not only identify ways to eliminate causes for dissatisfied customers, but also identify ways to move customers from being just satisfied to being delighted. These actions will have a more significant impact on increasing revenues.

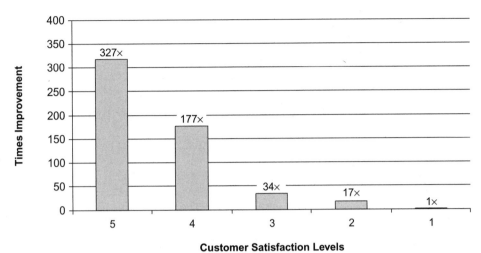

Figure 2.15 Amount of Revenue Improvement by Customer Satisfaction Level, Beginning with Very Dissatisfied = 1×.

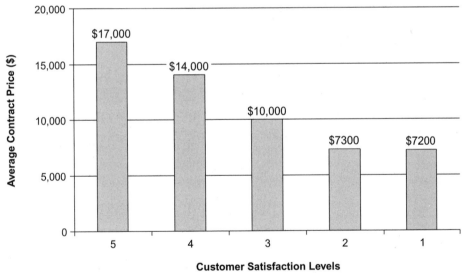

Figure 2.16 Average Contract Price by Customer Satisfaction Level.

Part II

Capturing the Voice of the Customer

Part 2 of this book addresses how to capture the voice of the customer. In order to center a Six Sigma initiative around the customer, the customer's needs and expectations must be understood. There is a very wide array of techniques that can be used to capture the voice of the customer. This part of the book focuses on the five most common and beneficial techniques.

Chapter 3 addresses the use of large-scale, global customer satisfaction surveys. These surveys are usually conducted periodically and have a large sample size. Chapter 4 addresses the use of transaction surveys. Transaction surveys are event driven, consist of relatively short questionnaires, and generate a continuous flow of customer feedback. Chapter 5 addresses lost customer analysis. Studying lost customers quickly identifies what performance factors caused a customer to defect. Chapter 6 addresses customer complaint management. A customer complaint should be viewed as an opportunity to dazzle the customer through outstanding recovery behavior. The last chapter in this section, chapter 7, addresses how to build better relationships with key accounts. Most organizations have key customers who are critical to their success, and merely surveying these customers is simply inadequate.

Each of these approaches provides a somewhat different view about customer preferences. Therefore, the argument could easily be made that a firm should be using all of these techniques. Many world-class firms do just that. But all approaches share the common goal of providing customer feedback so that customer expectations are well known.

3

Global Customer Satisfaction Surveys

A *global customer satisfaction survey* is a large-scale survey of customers. The term *global* is used because the survey should measure all five components of value: product quality, service quality, price, image, and relationships. Several of the five components may have many subareas that address very specific attributes. The global survey should measure the customers' perceptions and attitudes from very broad conceptual issues down to very detailed activities. As a result, global surveys usually have between 40 and 100 questions, most of which are quantitatively scaled.

Global surveys can be administered quarterly, semiannually, annually, or even biannually. The frequency of administration is largely dictated by the ability of the organization to change and by cost. If a firm can change employee behavior and processes quickly, more frequent surveying will provide valuable feedback. If significant change is culturally difficult for a firm, less frequent surveying may be more appropriate. The more constrained and limited the financial resources, the less frequent the surveying tends to be.

These global approaches are very valuable in measuring a customer's perceptions for several reasons. First, the relative importance of each attribute, or small group of attributes, can be accurately and reliably determined through the development of value models. This allows the identification of what is really important to the customer, the sifting out of the wheat from the chaff. These key drivers of value are where management must focus energy and resources if meaningful improvements are to be made.

The second benefit is that these global approaches can also provide a comprehensive competitive profile. A firm can measure its own performance using a global customer satisfaction measurement (CSM) program. But competitors' performance can also be measured by surveying the competitors' customers. In this way, a manager will know how the competitors' performance compares to the organization on each attribute. In many cases, a firm can learn more about its competitors than the competitors know themselves. This has obvious marketing and sales benefits.

The third benefit of these global approaches is that they are good at tracking performance over time. Global surveys usually utilize a sample size of 300 to 2000 customers. Samples of this size are usually statistically reliable and stable. Therefore, the global surveys can be linked to compensation systems such as incentive pay, gainsharing, or balanced scorecards. The global results can also be used for performance evaluation at the individual, department, or business unit level.

While the benefits are significant enough that virtually every firm should have a global customer satisfaction survey, there are some limitations. The primary limitation is the lack of actionability. There are usually two reasons for the lack of actionable data. One is timing, and the other is the level of detail.

If global surveys are completed annually or biannually, the feedback is often too infrequent to really motivate employees. This is particularly true for customer contact employees at lower levels in the organization who may feel that they are far removed from the high-level surveys. Quarterly or semiannual surveys are probably frequent enough to have motivational value, provided they overcome the other weakness.

Due to some very practical research constraints, global surveys can lack real detail. The most common method of administering a customer survey is by telephone. The upper time limit for a telephone interview, the point at which respondents become bored or annoyed, is approximately 15 minutes, and getting shorter. A 10- to 12-minute survey is preferable. Depending upon the type of questions and response choices, around 50 to 60 questions can be asked in a normal interview. Of these, 5 to 10 are usually demographic characteristics of the individual or organization, 3 or 4 of the questions are overall global measures, and several are open-ended questions; so the remaining questions, perhaps 40, are specific attribute questions. These 40 questions must cover product quality, service quality, price, and image. The result is that each performance area may have only 2 or 3 questions. For example, there may be only 2 or 3 questions each for billing, customer service, installation, technical support, or sales. These 2 or 3 questions may not provide sufficient detail to guide the continuous improvement efforts in those specific areas. Both of the major limitations of global surveys can be overcome through the use of *transaction surveys*. Transaction surveys are discussed in chapter 4.

THE CUSTOMER SATISFACTION MEASUREMENT PROCESS

Designing a customer satisfaction measurement (CSM) program is best thought of as a sequential process. The CSM process has 10 sequential, although iterative, steps (Figure 3.1). Decisions made at each step can influence other decisions. No CSM program is perfect; virtually all can be improved. Therefore, a good CSM program is dynamic, evolving, and always improving. These 10 steps provide a good framework to discuss the characteristics of world-class CSM efforts.

Step 1: Define the Objectives

For global CSM surveys, there should be clearly stated, fully supported objectives. The purposes of the objectives are twofold. First, the nature of the objectives will dictate many aspects of the research effort. For example, an objective may require the development of a competitive profile. This objective will influence virtually every aspect of the program from questionnaire design to sampling to data analysis. Establishing objectives early in the process also enhances behavioral support and involvement by those who will actually use the data.

In general, the objectives should answer a variety of questions: "Why are we doing this?" "Who will use the data?" "What form must it be in to be usable?" Objectives should not be developed by just one individual in most cases. Objectives should be designed and supported by the internal customers or managers who will use the data. Many managers are skeptical of data that evaluates their performance if they have played no part in designing the measurement process.

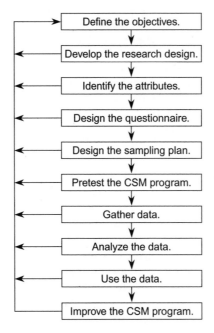

Figure 3.1 The Customer Satisfaction Measurement (CSM) Process.

Unfortunately, not having objectives is a common flaw in CSM programs, as the following example illustrates. A consultant (one of the authors) was asked by a senior executive in a Fortune 200 firm with revenues over $5 billion to evaluate the firm's CSM program. The program had been in place for several years. The conversation went something like this:

Consultant: I'd be happy to evaluate the quality of your CSM program, but first I need to know what you are trying to accomplish. Let me see your objectives, then I'll tell you if your program is effective.

Vice-President: That's an interesting question! I've never really thought of that before. We don't have any objectives. We just started gathering customer satisfaction data a few years ago because the CEO said to. And part of my incentive compensation package is based on it. We just hired a high priced, name brand marketing research firm to gather data. They never asked what the objectives were so we haven't ever developed any.

Consultant: Well, if you don't know what you are trying to accomplish, then the current program is completely adequate.

An organization's CSM objectives can take many forms. Boise Cascade Corporation had an overall goal of "We will meet or exceed the expectations of 97 percent of our customers." Eastman Chemical had a goal "to be the world's preferred chemical supplier and to be rated number one by 75 percent of our customers." IBM Rochester's vision was "to become the undisputed leader in customer satisfaction."[11] While these are lofty goals, they are too general to be of much value in the design of a CSM program. The more specific the objectives, the more valuable they will be.

- Fully Supported by Top Management
- Addresses Issues That Are Important to Our Customers
- Unbiased
- Statistically Reliable
- Assesses Strengths, Weaknesses, and Competitive Advantages
- Determines Relative Importance of Key Performance Measures
- Comparable across Business Units
- Consistent over Time
- Backed Up with Corrective Action

Table 3.1 Milliken Objectives.

Milliken Corporation, a Baldrige Award winner, manufactures a variety of products such as carpets and floor coverings. Milliken has nine detailed objectives for its CSM program (Table 3.1). These objectives have very clear implications for the design of a CSM program. For example, the second objective requires that either depth interviews or focus groups be conducted. The fourth objective influences sample size. The fifth objective requires that competitors' customers be surveyed. The sixth requires that a value model be developed. The seventh and eighth objectives require that the CSM program be standardized across business units. As the subsequent steps are discussed, the role of the objectives will become even more apparent.

Step 2: Develop the Research Design

Research design is a description of how you are going to actually gather the data from customers. There are five different alternatives to choose from, and each has its own unique advantages and disadvantages. The five choices are mail, telephone, personal interviews, computer (Internet or Intranet), and interactive voice response. However, telephone and mail remain the most common. In most cases, the research objectives will dictate the type of design. If a firm wants to "drill down" and understand customers better by asking open-ended questions, then telephone or in-person approaches are necessary for interviewer-respondent interaction.

Each research alternative has its own unique characteristics. For example, telephone surveys are shorter in length, use simpler wording and simpler scales, and can have many sorting and routing patterns. Conversely, mail surveys can be longer and use more complex response scales but should not have many routings. In-person surveys need to be far less structured than telephone or mail surveys and create a conversational relationship. The implication is that the research objectives need to be carefully developed since they will drive the choice of research design.

When the customer base is large, mail surveys are a relatively low cost alternative. But response rates are often very low, less than 25 percent. As a result, the data is usually less reliable, since most of the customers are not responding for some reason. It is not unusual for mail surveys to have a bipolar response pattern. This means that customers who are very happy or very upset tend to respond more than the average customers. Therefore, drawing firm conclusions from the data is difficult. Any time a response rate is below 50 percent of the sample, a manager should have concerns about nonresponse bias.

Telephone surveys are more costly and labor intensive, but the quality of the data is better because the interviewer can screen for the best respondent. Telephone surveys also allow the capture of qualitative data. Personal interviews are particularly good for key accounts as they enhance the relationship. Personal interviews are quite good for capturing qualitative data, but this approach is more costly than mail when sample sizes are large.

Computer applications such as Internet or Intranet surveys are emerging as an interesting alternative. These approaches have a significant up-front cost for design and programming of customer websites but have a very low marginal cost for each interview. When using Internet surveys, respondents are not always representative of the whole customer base. Internet respondents tend to be younger and better educated. Intranet surveys are particularly appropriate for internal use within an organization. Even when used internally, response rates are often only in the 40 percent to 50 percent range. Also, response rates tend to be lower when used on external customers. Since these electronic surveys have some potential bias associated with them, the results need to be carefully evaluated.

Interactive voice response surveys in which the customer phones in on an 800 number and responds to recorded questions using the phone pad are good for short, simple surveys. But these too have a higher design and set-up cost. Customers must be provided with some incentive to participate. For example, Pizza Hut gives their respondents a $4 discount on their next purchase if they complete the survey. McDonald's included a survey on the back of a $1 discount coupon, which had to be completed before it could be redeemed.

It is not unusual for a firm to combine several of these research design alternatives in a single CSM program. There are actually some advantages to doing so. But there are a variety of considerations that must be evaluated.

If a firm wants very unbiased, valid, and reliable data, then high *data control* may be necessary. Data control means that the correct person responded and thoughtfully considered each question. Often, telephone surveys provide this. If very precise results are needed ($\pm$ 1 percent to 2 percent), large sample sizes are required. This may require a combination of alternatives. National Cash Register (NCR), Inc., partitions its customer base into several groups. NCR surveys all of its critical customers, about 20 percent of the total customer base. Four respondents are surveyed in each firm; a senior executive, the top information technology executive, the manager in charge of billing and invoicing, and the manager in charge of using the equipment. Each of these four groups has a different questionnaire that contains between 67 and 100 questions. NCR predominantly uses a telephone methodology but supplements that with mail and personal interviews. For the remaining 80 percent of the customers, a telephone survey is conducted. Many firms adopt a mixed research design such as this.

Perhaps the most important influence on research design is a firm's budget. A budget provides the constraints within which a research design must occur. The key driver of cost is the sample size. Normally, the greater the sample, the higher the cost. However, the length of the questionnaire, the frequency of administration, and the geographic dispersion of the customers all influence the costs in some way. Sophisticated, complex data analysis costs more than simple descriptive statistics.

Most firms have found it is easier to outsource much of the research design to research firms that specialize in data gathering and analysis. While outsourcing is faster, it still takes from 90 to 120 days to design and implement a CSM program and produce a research report. Complex projects can take longer.

Step 3: Identify the Attributes

Identifying the attributes is a critical portion of developing a CSM program. It is very unusual for a firm, or manager, to have a completely accurate picture of the customer's evaluative criteria. And, unfortunately, managers are even more inconsistent about estimating the relative importance among those criteria. To overcome this perceptual gap between managers and customers, the customer must first be carefully identified. Then qualitative research techniques must be used to identify the attributes that drive satisfaction for the customer.

Customer identification usually starts by defining market segments. Large corporate, small corporate, small business, home-based business, and consumers are five unique segments that would probably be quite distinct from one another. Within a segment, say large corporate, there could be healthcare, financial and banking, public utilities, and energy as distinct segments.

Within each of these segments, there are further choices. In a specific firm, who is the customer? It could be the "key decision maker," or it could be the actual user of the product or service. It could be an information systems manager or someone from purchasing. And each of these "customers" may have a different perception of customer satisfaction.

Once the customer or desired respondent has been clearly defined, the attributes that these customers use to evaluate products and services must be identified. For most organizations, this requires that three sources of information be carefully evaluated. These sources are secondary data, internal company records and/or databases, and customers themselves.

Secondary Sources.   Secondary data sources are those that are already published. By examining what other firms are doing, fresh new ideas are often generated. There are three major types of secondary sources of information that may reveal which issues, or attributes, are important to customers. First, there are business publications ranging from *Fortune, Business Week,* or the *Wall Street Journal* to industry-specific journals. For example, *Public Utilities Fortnightly* has published numerous articles about what utility customers want in a deregulated environment. These sources can be searched through the use of electronic databases available at most large public or university libraries.

In addition to the business press, most industries also have trade associations. These trade associations often conduct research or develop *white papers* that address the major issues facing the industry. Increasingly, one of the issues facing all industries is rapidly changing customer preferences and expectations. Closely related to trade associations are professional organizations such as those found in accounting, purchasing, sales, and most engineering disciplines. Often, the professional organizations have publications that address the key issues facing the profession. Since becoming customer driven is important strategically in organizations, the concept is also important to various functional areas. Another excellent source of information is from Malcolm Baldrige National Quality Award Winners, which can provide insight on world-class practices. Information concerning Baldrige winners is available by contacting the U.S. Department of Commerce[12] or the American Society for Quality (see note 7).

The third major source of secondary information is conferences. Most conferences include many presentations in which managers tell their "success stories." For example, each year the American Society for Quality and the American Marketing Association jointly sponsor the annual Customer Satisfaction Conference. Each presentation includes information about what is important to customers. Some managers attend conferences for the sole purpose of finding out what their competitors are doing.

There are many secondary sources of information about customers. While data is not always in the perfect form for a company, searching for secondary data adds a conceptual diversity that is often invaluable.

Internal Sources.   Just as with external, secondary data, there are also many sources of customer information internal to most organizations. But, as with external data, the internal data is often not comprehensive and detailed enough. For example, customer information could be captured as complaints, technical support issues, sales reports, or warranty documentation. Each of these provides a fairly narrow snapshot of what is concerning customers. Sales data may focus on price, technical support may be needed because of poor documentation, and complaints may be due to incorrect expectations. In total, internal sources are important, but, even when aggregated together, they provide only a partial view of what is critical to customers.

Customer Sources.   Even if good secondary and internal data about customers is available, it must be supplemented with input from the customers themselves. The secondary and internal data is very helpful in identifying what questions should be asked of customers. But, since customer expectations are constantly evolving, direct customer input is required to capture the current state of mind of customers.

The two techniques most commonly used to capture customer input are depth interviews and focus groups. Both approaches require direct interaction. *Depth interviews* are usually one-to-one interaction with customers, and *focus groups* usually involve 6 to 10 customers. To be successful, both techniques require careful planning and a structured agenda. Depth interviews are used increasingly because they are faster and cheaper than focus groups and produce very similar results. Depth interviews can be conducted by telephone, although richer, more detailed results can be obtained in face-to-face interviews.

A typical depth interview script would ask customers to identify the five key drivers of satisfaction. Customers might respond by saying, "Product quality, service, technical support, reputation, and price." The interviewer would then ask the customers what they mean by each term. Perhaps the interviewer would ask for specific examples of each or positive or negative experiences. The interviewer would keep *drilling down* until the appropriate level of detail is reached.

When a comprehensive effort is made to identify the attributes that are important to customers, a surprisingly large number are typically generated. In one recent study, over 80 attributes were identified through 12 depth interviews. In another, over 125 attributes were identified through the use of five focus groups. The implication is that the customers can express their *voice* in many different ways. The qualitative research may generate a list of 100 or more attributes, and a questionnaire may use only 60 of these. The challenge, then, becomes to sift out the important attributes from the less important. There are two ways to do this. One is qualitative and the other is quantitative.

The *qualitative* approach means that the evaluation of attributes is done based on judgment. The judgment can be that of managers or customers. Managers, preferably as a team, could sift through the attributes and use their experience to categorize the attributes. Unfortunately, this approach has a good deal of bias built in. A better qualitative approach is to have customers, as in a focus group, sort the attributes into two categories, those that are important and those that are unimportant.

If a *quantitative* approach is used, the reduction in the list of attributes is done with statistical analysis. This requires that a questionnaire be developed that includes all attributes. A sample of customers is then asked the questions. The results are statistically analyzed using some type of multivariate analysis.

A quantitative approach can be methodologically precise, but it is also costly. The bare minimum sample size must be 200, and a sample size of 300 or 400 is better. Therefore, this approach could cost at least $20,000 and possibly much more. This approach also requires a pretty good knowledge of advanced statistical analysis.

Recently, Southern California Gas conducted depth interviews and focus groups that identified 110 service attributes. A management team sorted through the 110 attributes and removed redundancies, reducing the list to 77. A questionnaire was developed that included all 77 and was administered to a large sample of customers. By using statistical analysis, 39 attributes emerged as most important. These 39 attributes were then included on subsequent global surveys.

The intent of the qualitative research is to identify those attributes that are important to customers. If a large number of attributes are identified, the list must be reduced to a manageable level so that a good questionnaire can be developed. If only 30 or 40 attributes are identified in the qualitative research, reducing the attribute list may not be necessary. Depth interviews are becoming more popular because they are faster and easier to administer and much less costly than focus groups. Regardless of which methodology is used, customers almost always identify attributes that have been overlooked by managers. The implication is that comprehensiveness at this step is important because these attributes will be converted into individual questions.

Step 4: Design the Questionnaire

A CSM questionnaire has at least four distinct types of questions. Each type of question has a specific purpose, but the whole questionnaire should be carefully crafted so that there is a good flow and continuity between different segments. All questionnaires used in a company should have consistency in terms of design, wording, and scaling.

As discussed earlier, one type of question is the global, overall measure. These may include overall satisfaction, willingness to recommend, repurchase intent, value for the money, and so forth. It is interesting that overall satisfaction is one of the more unstable overall measures. Specifically, overall satisfaction is more variable over time and more influenced by variation in service quality than some other global questions.

Value for the money is probably a better predictive variable when examining subsequent customer behavior. As discussed previously, this question can be linked to market share and financial performance. Customers' value perceptions also appear to drive their overall satisfaction, willingness to recommend, and repurchase intent when causal modeling is conducted.

These global questions should be exactly consistent in wording and location on the questionnaire across all business units, divisions, and questionnaires. For example, a global question placed at the first of a questionnaire will often have a different score than the same question placed at the end of the questionnaire. By maintaining consistency, customer satisfaction can be compared across business units or across different surveys. While the more specific attributes can vary from survey to survey, the global questions should not vary at all.

The second category of questions are attribute specific. An example might be, "Please rate the clarity of our billing invoice." These questions need to be very detailed and use the customer's terminology identified in the depth interviews or focus groups. The overall importance of these attributes is dynamic. If a firm is performing poorly in a specific area, that attribute becomes very important to customers. Customers appear to take high performance in some areas for granted.

For example, when you fly on an airline and you check baggage, you expect that baggage to arrive at your destination. Having your baggage arrive properly does not cause you to say, "WOW! What a great airline!" But if your baggage is lost along the way, you become very dissatisfied. If you were surveyed after having your luggage lost, the luggage issue would be quite important. So the relative importance is influenced by the extent to which the customer's expectations are being met or are not being met.

The third category of questions is open-ended questions. These questions are intended to give the respondents an opportunity to express themselves in some way. Some questionnaires simply have an "any comments?" question. Only a small portion of customers respond to this question. Instead, the customer might be asked, "What two thing should we do to improve?" This question will result in many more detailed comments by customers. These questions work well in telephone or face-to-face surveys but have low response levels on mail surveys. Customers normally do not want to take the time to write long responses, so answers are often short and truncated. Also, responses are not always representative of the whole customer base. For example, a mail survey to all customers may have a 25 percent response rate. Of those responding, perhaps 10 percent give a written response and half of those complain about billing. While billing may appear to be a problem, only 5 percent of respondents discuss the issue; and this represents only 1.25 percent of the total customer base. This is not representative of the customer base at all.

The fourth category of questions is demographic. These questions allow a researcher to partition and subdivide the data, and they allow a variety of questions to be answered. In customer firms, are key decision makers more satisfied with our products than the users of the products? Are old customers (those who have been with us several years) more satisfied than new customers? Are customers in the healthcare industry more satisfied than those in energy? Each demographic question that is asked should be able to answer a specific question of interest and allow a manager to better understand the customer in some way. One word of caution should be noted if the approach to demographic information is to ask the customer. Customers typically expect the caller to know something about them. That is why the call was made. Customers may become dissatisfied if the survey begins by asking questions the customers feel should be well known. For instance, a local newspaper calls several times asking if the customer is interested in subscribing. Since the customer is already a subscriber, he or she becomes dissatisfied that the local newspaper does not know this, nor acknowledges that person as a customer.

As already discussed, there are five major categories of attributes that are found in most value models. These five categories are product quality, service quality, price, image, and relationships. The global questionnaire should include all five of these areas. Each of the three categories of price, image, and relationship will typically consist of four to six more specific attributes. Product quality may be broken into several subcategories, each with four to seven attributes. Service quality often has six or more subcategories, each with four to seven attributes.

The single most common error is for managers to assume that the product issues are predominant and neglect other areas. Product quality is not just referring to a tangible product. Product quality also applies to the core service product if a firm is in a service business. In many industries, good product quality is taken for granted by customers; it is simply a basic expectation. As a result, product quality is often not the most important category to customers.

Service quality often includes many subareas such as billing, technical support, sales, training, customer service, installation, and maintenance and repair. The exact categories are dependent upon the specific product or industry. But service quality, collectively, is usually much more important to customers than product quality. As a result, it is not unusual for 60 percent to 70 percent of the attributes identified by customers to be dimensions of service.

If there is an area that tends to be underrepresented in the attribute identification process, it is image. Dimensions of image include broader, more conceptual attributes such as being reliable, innovative, or trustworthy. If a firm has a strong marketplace presence, the image category can be quite important to customers. IBM Rochester added image questions to its customer satisfaction survey in 1992 once it revalidated the importance of this attribute to overall customer satisfaction (see note 11).

The attributes identified earlier should be grouped into logically related clusters of some type such as image, sales, or billing. By grouping the attributes into the various categories, developing the questionnaire becomes easier. The grouping process also helps you to identify the differences between attributes.

Before getting into the technical structure of a questionnaire, there are a number of issues that must be considered. These issues may influence the design of the questionnaire or even aspects of the whole research program. Most of these issues flow from the fact that questionnaires are measuring customer perceptions and attitudes, and these are inherently fluid concepts that can be influenced in a variety of ways.

Customer attitudes may be volatile. That is, they may fluctuate over time. You need to give careful consideration to how customer attitudes change over a period of days, months, or years. Screening questions can be developed to capture the "best" situation. Or you may actually alter the timing of the survey. Does an electric utility want to survey after a severe ice storm? Does a manufacturer want to survey after a product recall? Does a firm want to survey after a merger? All of these could influence customer attitudes in some way.

Another issue is bias, and the goal is to minimize its impact. Bias occurs when the customers' responses do not represent their true attitudes. The most common cause of bias is the wording and sequencing of questions that lead a respondent. For example, saying, "Our employees are friendly," followed by an agree-disagree scale is a biased question because the customer is led to agree. Bias can also be introduced by sampling as well. Perhaps a sample frame only includes heavy users of a product who are more satisfied. The impact of bias can be very subtle. For example, image questions placed at the end of a questionnaire may have significantly different results than those at the beginning. This is because respondents are "educated" as they complete a questionnaire, and many new issues are raised to a top-of-mind awareness.

Validity is an issue that indicates whether a question really measures what it is supposed to measure. The most common problem here is ambiguous questions that are so general that customer can interpret the question in a way that was not intended. Validity is achieved by having specific, detailed questions in words that customers clearly understand. Terms such as *quality, service,* and *support* could be interpreted in many ways by customers. If the customer's interpretation is different than a firm intended, the results lack validity.

Another issue is the awareness level of the respondents. As a general rule, only customers who have a good awareness and knowledge level should be surveyed. The implication is that screening questions may be necessary. Asking very detailed questions of customers with little knowledge results in data that is of little value.

A questionnaire consists of a series of relatively distinct parts (Table 3.2). For the questionnaire to be most effective, all of these parts must be harmonized to mesh effectively. Therefore, a questionnaire should be customized to fit a particular organization and group of customers. However, all good questionnaires share some common characteristics.

- Introduction
- Directions and Transitions
- Global Questions
- Category Questions
- Attribute Questions
- Demographic Questions
- Open-Ended Questions

Table 3.2 Questionnaire Components.

A questionnaire should always have an introduction that explains the purpose of the survey, provides time estimates, and, if appropriate, identifies who is sponsoring the research. The introduction should also explain the benefits to the customer and ask for the respondent's cooperation and assistance. Since most refusals occur immediately after the introduction, a good introduction has a significant impact on cooperation rates.

After the introduction, there should be directions that tell the respondents exactly what is expected of them. Usually, this means explaining the scales to be used and the *don't know* option. If scales change throughout the questionnaire, there should also be new directions at the appropriate places. Related to directions are transition statements. These let the respondent know that you are finished with one topic and are moving to the next.

Global questions that capture the customers' overall perceptions should be placed at the beginning of the questionnaire. This is because these high-level questions can be influenced by asking more detailed questions. Common global questions are overall satisfaction, value for the money, willingness to recommend, and repurchase intent.

After the global questions, image questions should follow. The flow in a questionnaire should be from broad issues to specific details. After image questions, relationship questions commonly follow. This sequence is consistent with the broad-to-detailed sequence.

Once the global, image, and relationship questions have been asked, the next questions are groupings of product and service subcategories. The exact number of these categories and questions is a result of the qualitative research conducted previously and are unique to a specific product and/or service.

Following the product and service attribute questions, toward the end of the questionnaire, are demographic questions. These typically address characteristics of the individual, the organization, or the situation. For example, an individual's job title or functional area could be requested. The size of the organization or SIC code could be requested. The respondent's role in decision making could be requested. The results of these questions allow the partitioning of the results.

The last section of a questionnaire allows respondents to share their opinions in an unstructured way. This could take the form of "Do you have any other comments?" or "What could we do to improve?" In a telephone survey to business customers, it is not unusual to have about half of the respondents make some type of comment. For consumers, the proportion is much lower. One innovative application of asking open-ended questions at the conclusion of the survey is to ask, "May someone call you back?" With this approach, an engineer or someone else who is addressing a customer concern or issue has the opportunity to call the customer back to gain additional information or a better understanding about the concern.

By using this approach to the design of questionnaires, the problem of bias due to sequencing can be reduced. While the sequence can certainly be adjusted, the template described here is probably the one most commonly encountered.

Step 5: Design the Sampling Plan

An effective sampling plan requires that two issues be addressed. The first issue is defining the desired customer or respondent, which was briefly discussed previously. Deciding whom to survey is not as easy as it may seem. Most businesses have a variety of customers. There could be several market segments of end-users. There are channel intermediaries who are also customers. If these customer groups are quite distinct from one another, each may require a different questionnaire and sampling plan. If the customers are businesses, then defining the customer becomes even more complex. Is the customer someone from purchasing, production, engineering, or sales? Or, is the best sample a combination of these? Which level of the customer organization is best, senior management, middle level functional managers, or the actual users of the product? Determining whom in the organization to survey is very critical to the value of the data. Surveying the wrong person, such as only the decision maker and not the end-user, is a common fault. Both should be surveyed. This situation is often referred to as the *dog food scenario*. The person that is making the decision on which type and brand of dog food to purchase is not necessarily the one consuming it.

Once the customer has been defined, then a list of customer names, or sample frame, is necessary. In many companies, comprehensive lists of the right customers simply do not exist. As a rough rule of thumb, 25 percent of the names on any list are out-of-date and unusable. Getting information technology to extract a sample frame of customer names and phone numbers is usually far more difficult than one would expect.

Once the customer is clearly defined, then the second issue of sample size must be addressed. Sample size is almost always budget constrained. Large samples are always statistically more reliable, but they are also more expensive. Let us set the cost issue aside for a moment and look at the statistical justification of sample size.

A sample of customers does not exactly represent a total customer base. The sample results may be very close to the total customer base, but there is always some sample variation. The larger the sample, the less variation from the true population mean, in this case, the true customer satisfaction level. The primary considerations in determining sample size are how much variation we, as managers, are willing to tolerate, how confident we want to be about the results, and how much variety there is in customer attitudes.

This tolerable variation is referred to as *precision level*. A precision level is normally expressed as plus or minus so many percentage points, such as plus or minus 10, 5, 2, or 1 percentage points. If a manager used a small sample of 90, the conclusion might be that our customer satisfaction level is 82 percent, ± 10 percent. In other words, the true satisfaction level of the customer base would be between 72 percent and 92 percent. Obviously, that is not very good! With a sample of 360, the precision level is approximately plus or minus 5 percent. With a sample of 1440, the precision level is approximately plus or minus 2.5 percent. As precision is halved, say from ± 10 percent to ± 5 percent, the sample size will go up four times. Most customer satisfaction research has a precision of ± 5 percent. For this reason, the frequency of rolling up survey results should be considered. For instance, rolling survey results together quarterly instead of monthly may provide more precision and accuracy on which to base decisions.

Unfortunately, customer satisfaction results are seldom accompanied by precision levels. Normally, a senior manager will say, "Our scores are X percent," period. The

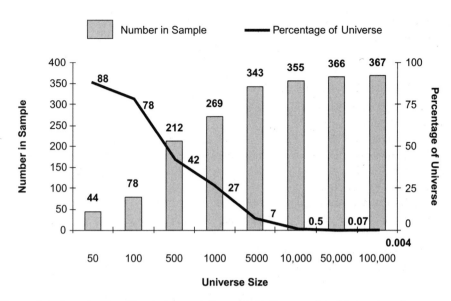

Figure 3.2 Sample Size Needed for ± 5 Percent, 90 Percent Confidence Level.

problem is that quarterly survey results could vary up or down several percentage points due purely to sample variation while the firm's actual performance may be constant.

The *confidence level* must also be specified to determine sample size. The confidence level indicates the statistical probability of making an error in our conclusions. The most common confidence level is 90 percent, and that was assumed in the previous example showing the relationship between sample size and precision. A 90 percent confidence level means that we are 90 percent confident that our results are accurate, ± X percent, but there is a 10 percent chance the results are in error. As confidence levels increase, sample size goes up. If a confidence level of 90 percent requires a sample size of 400, then a confidence level of 95 percent will require a sample of about 800.

The third element that influences sample size is the amount of variation in *customer attitudes*. If customers have a good deal of diversity, larger samples are required. If customers are very consistent in their attitudes, smaller samples are adequate.

There are many sample size formulas that will indicate the minimum necessary sample size given certain assumptions. But the conclusions from different formulas are approximately the same. If you are willing to settle for a precision level of plus or minus 5 percent, and a 90 percent confidence level, you need a minimum of about 360 respondents if respondents are homogeneous in their attitudes. But, if you have many subgroups or partitions within the data, you need a larger sample size. And if you want to be very precise, say a variation of 1 percent or 2 percent, you may need a sample size of over 1000. As a rough rule of thumb, sample size should be around 360 unless you have a very small customer base.

The required sample size is independent of the total size of the customer base, except when the customer base is small. The rough guidelines for the minimum sample sizes are presented in Figure 3.2. If a firm has a small customer base of 50, then completed responses must be obtained from 44 customers, or 88 percent of the customer base, to reach a precision of ± 5 percent at a 90 percent confidence level. If a firm has 1000 customers, 269 must complete a survey. However, the required minimum sample stabilizes in the 340 to 370 range as the customer base becomes large.

There is one additional factor that must be considered when determining the appropriate sample size and that is the nature of the data analysis. For descriptive statistics, the precision associated with a sample size is the primary consideration. But if a value model is desired, the absolute minimum sample size is 200 and 400 or more is much better. If a firm wanted to develop a value model of each of three market segments, there should be at least 200 respondents from each segment.

Step 6: Pretest the Program

Most firms operate under the mentality of "We are not sure what we want, but we want it tomorrow." As a result, there is a tendency to rush a questionnaire into the field. If there are flaws in the questionnaire, the errors will be replicated hundreds of times. Therefore, a pretest should always be conducted.

A pretest is a small trial run of the entire CSM program. The survey is normally administered to 30 to 50 respondents, and data is analyzed. All aspects of the research design are checked for problems. This includes the presentation of data to the internal customers. The most common changes tend to be in the wording of questions and in the presentation of the results. It is common to make improvements in a CSM program after a pretest, no matter how carefully it was initially designed.

In most cases, a pretest is undisclosed to the respondent. If a telephone survey is being used, the interviewer closely monitors the respondent's behavior. If a print survey is used, the responses are carefully evaluated. One of the key indicators of respondent difficulty is a large percentage of blank or *don't know* responses.

It is not unusual to revise a questionnaire four or five times during questionnaire design and then pretest and modify it once or twice more. Taking care during a pretest eliminates the *garbage in–garbage out* problem.

Step 7: Gather the Data

Few firms gather the data themselves. Most rely on a research firm to administer surveys, interview customers, and compile a database. This is due to the fact that most firms do not have the internal human resources to devote to field research. However, the act of surveying customers creates expectations among customers, regardless of who actually gathers the data.

When a survey is administered, customer expectations are elevated. The typical respondent feels that if a firm is going to solicit input, the firm must be serious about making changes. This creates higher performance expectations. If those elevated expectations are not met, then satisfaction levels will probably decrease. Therefore, if a firm is going to measure customer perceptions, there should be an equally strong commitment to continuous improvement and a plan to communicate the changes to the customers.

When the survey is to be administered, several decision rules must be addressed. For a telephone survey, the number of attempts must be specified. Most commonly, interviewers will attempt to reach a customer five or six times. But, if the customer base is small, that may be increased to seven or eight. And what should be done if the desired respondent is no longer there? Should a new respondent be substituted? These are pragmatic issues that can impact data quality.

Step 8: Analyze the Data

There are two types of data analysis; one is very complex, and the other is very simple. The complex analysis is used in modeling the data, developing the customer value

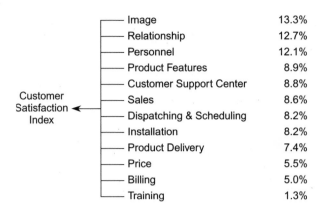

Image	13.3%
Relationship	12.7%
Personnel	12.1%
Product Features	8.9%
Customer Support Center	8.8%
Sales	8.6%
Dispatching & Scheduling	8.2%
Installation	8.2%
Product Delivery	7.4%
Price	5.5%
Billing	5.0%
Training	1.3%

Figure 3.3 Overall Value Model—Categories of Attributes.

models discussed earlier. There are a variety of statistical techniques that are commonly used for modeling, and these are referred to as *multivariate analysis*. Generally, multivariate methods examine the relationship between a dependent variable and a set of independent variables. The dependent variable is normally a single overall satisfaction measure or an index that is a combination of two or three measures. The independent variables are the individual attributes, and there may be over 50 of these. These techniques indicate the strength of the relationship between the dependent and the independent variables. The strength of the relationship is what indicates the relative importance of each attribute to the customer.

An example of an actual value model is presented in Figure 3.3. In this value model, the percentages indicate the relative importance of each category. The 11 categories include all aspects of product quality, service quality, price, image, and relationship that were identified by customers. The customer-identified attributes were grouped into categories that were consistent with the firm's value-creating processes.

To create this value model, a customer satisfaction index was created by adding the overall satisfaction, value for the money, and willingness to recommend questions. The index was then used as a dependent variable in a number of multiple regression analyses. It actually took about 20 regression analyses to create the value model, but, in each case, some combination of attributes was introduced as independent variables.

In multiple regression, the independent variables explain variation in the dependent variable. The more variation that is explained, the better an attribute is at predicting the dependent variable. In this model, if a customer had positive views of relationship, the customer was also very likely to be highly satisfied. Training was very unimportant because a customer could rate training as excellent, fair, or poor, and the rating on training had no impact on satisfaction.

The percentages simply reflect the predictive power of each category to explain variation in the customer satisfaction index. Each category consisted of between 3 and 6 more specific questions. For each question, the customer was asked to rate the performance of the company. For example, a question might be, "Please rate the accuracy of invoices. . . ." It should be emphasized that the relative importance was derived through complex, statistical analyses. There were no questions that asked customers to rate importance.

Asking a customer to rate importance is usually a statistically invalid approach. Customers usually indicate that most performance areas are highly important, and differences are usually much less than what would be expected from normal sample variation.

In addition to complex statistical analyses, every question should have complete descriptive statistics. These simple measures are often more easily understood by managers. The more common measures are frequency distributions, means, and mean differences. A frequency distribution is expressed as percentages of responses in a category. Examples would be a *52 percent top box* score or an *83 percent top two box* score. These are the figures that are tracked longitudinally and can also be used to develop competitive profiles.

Instead of frequency distributions, a manager could prefer means. For example, customers could be asked to rate performance on a 10-point scale. The firm's rating might be 8.7 compared to the competition's 8.0, which would give the firm almost a 10 percentage point competitive advantage.

If a firm uses response scales with 5 or fewer categories, only frequency distributions should be used because the data is categorical. If a firm uses response scales with seven or more choices, the data can be viewed as interval and either means or frequency distributions can be calculated. For most statistical purposes, interval data is somewhat more precise than categorical data.

Careful consideration should be given to the type of data analysis that will be used. Some statistical techniques require interval data, but most do not. It is essential to know which techniques will be used so the proper questions and scales can be used.

Step 9: Use the Data

The real value of customer satisfaction data occurs when the data drives organizational improvement. Therefore, the uses of the data should be considered when the objectives are determined. This ensures that the data is usable to the internal customers.

It is important to build upon successes. When using the data, it is helpful to identify what processes can be changed short-term versus those that will take more time. It is also helpful to identify those that can be changed with little or no resources and those that are controllable by one or a few people. So, identifying short-term, controllable changes that do not require financial investments is important. These are where the initial change efforts should begin. Pragmatically, it is always good to build upon these initial "wins" rather than trying to change the whole organization all at once.

There should also be strategic uses of customer satisfaction data. Senior managers are particularly interested in competitive profiles and financial performance measures. Some firms can link value perceptions to return on investment, economic value added, and stock price. Senior managers are also concerned with linking customer value perceptions to market share, customer loyalty, and share of spend. Regardless of whether the uses of the data are operational or strategic, they need to be carefully thought out well before the data is gathered.

Step 10: Improve the CSM Program

A CSM program should not be static; it should continue to evolve and improve. Virtually every program can improve in some way. The implication is that those responsible for administering a CSM program should strive for both technical improvements and improvements in the use of the data. In general, the uses of CSM programs have broadened so that data is integrated with behavioral indicators of employee attitudes, quality initiatives, and value chain alliances and partnerships. There is no reason to think that the concept of customer satisfaction has fully matured yet. Benchmarking can be used to continually improve the CSM program, as was suggested earlier in this chapter. One relevant reference is a book by Robert Camp entitled *Business Process Benchmarking: Finding and Implementing Best Practices.*[13] Chapter 15 of Camp's book provides an example of benchmarking the customer satisfaction management process employed by IBM Rochester. It is interesting to note that even those organizations that are considered world class continually strive for improvement.

SUMMARY

When designed and implemented properly, a global customer satisfaction measurement program is usually the central pillar of capturing the voice of the customer. Unfortunately, there are some very large organizations that make some basic, fundamental errors in methodology that severely constrain the ability to use the data.

By following the steps in this chapter, a firm can develop a reasonably good customer satisfaction program. However, designing a good program is more challenging and complex than most people realize.

CASE STUDY

GLOBAL CUSTOMER SATISFACTION SURVEYS

For a number of years, the approach at Johnson Controls, Inc., toward customer satisfaction measurement was sporadic and inconsistent. There are a number of business units within the Controls Business, each doing its own thing, more or less. Some units were surveying regularly, and others were not surveying customers at all. There were a few pockets of passion throughout the organization that were using the data to improve product or service delivery.

Some of the surveys were *one-time* studies that were conducted by different firms. For example, there were three different studies conducted by three different vendors. Each study used different questions, wording, and response scales and produced research reports that were each different. Making direct comparisons between survey results was impossible. So, in late 1996, changes were implemented.

The first step was to develop a consistent survey format. All of the global questions and research methodologies were moved to consistent wording, scaling, and reporting. This caused some problems initially because some of the quality managers had been tracking customer perceptions by using a 7-point response scale. Others were using a 5-point scale. All those who were surveying had their own databases and tracking approaches. Then, surveying was moved to a 5-point—Excellent, Very Good, Good, Fair, Poor—scale. As a result, the old and new approaches needed to be calibrated against one another.

A series of global questions were developed and put at the beginning of all questionnaires. This allowed for comparisons across all business units for the first time. Some of the global questions were subsequently used when an overall scorecard was developed.

Figure 3.4 Johnson Controls, Inc., Controls Business Customer Value Model.

When the transition was made to a new questionnaire, a series of depth interviews were conducted for each segment. It was desired that the questions being asked were the *correct* questions from the customer's viewpoint. This allowed for fine-tuning the questionnaire.

It took over a year before the pockets of resistance to the new approach began to subside. But, gradually, everyone bought into the new approach and accepted that the changes were made.

As focus was placed on external customers, more attention began to be paid to internal customers. One of the biggest *customers* for the equipment manufacturing business unit is the Controls Business's own Systems and Services (SS) unit. An internal customer satisfaction survey was developed that was consistent with the external surveys. However, the internal survey was administered through the Intranet, while the external surveys were administered using telephone interviews. It was the first time that internal customers had been surveyed, and it helped to reinforce the focus on customers of all types.

As is further explained in the case study at the end of chapter 9, the mission of Johnson Controls, Inc., is to "continually exceed customers' increasing expectations." Customer satisfaction is one of five core values and is the first of five overall company objectives. This focus emphasizes and aligns the importance of customer satisfaction to overall business performance and makes it a key driver for the activities of all company employees.

A value model (Figure 3.4) has been developed, based upon focus groups with customers, that defines customer satisfaction attributes. This value model, which is explored more in the case study at the end of chapter 11, has also been used to develop a Customer Satisfaction Index (CSI), which is used as a key measurement of performance across the Controls Business of Johnson Controls, Inc.

4

Transaction Surveys

transaction survey is an integral part of a comprehensive customer satisfaction program. Global customer satisfaction surveys are comprehensive, higher level surveys that are conducted every 3, 6, or 12 months in most firms. With transaction surveys, detailed customer input is sought soon after an event or transaction has occurred. Transaction surveys provide fast, timely feedback from customers to process owners. The questions are very specific, more detailed than those on a global survey, and tied to both the characteristics of the event or transaction and value-added processes. The timely and specific feedback from customers can be a valuable driver of process improvement.

Transaction surveys are often more actionable than the global customer satisfaction survey, because detailed customer input is sought soon after an event has occurred, normally between 7 and 30 days. The event is some type of direct contact between a firm and the customer, such as a training session, delivery and installation or repair of a system, or delivery of a proposal. The intent is to survey the actual user of a product or service while the experience is still fresh in the customer's mind. Therefore, in business-to-business situations, the *customer* is usually a middle- to lower-level manager in a distributor or an end-user in the customer organization.

To facilitate understanding the sequence of decisions that must be addressed when implementing transaction surveys, a flowchart has been developed (Figure 4.1). While some decisions could be made simultaneously with others, the flowchart includes the major issues and the order in which they typically occur. This chapter provides discussions that address the key factors that must be considered when making each decision.

ORGANIZATIONAL COMMITMENT

There must be a commitment by the process owners to actually use the data once it is captured. Customers who have just had an interaction with a company are usually very willing to share their perceptions. However, surveying customers also creates an expectation that performance will improve. Thus, customer expectations actually increase. If performance does not improve, satisfaction scores usually go down. The implication is that surveys should not be done just for the sake of surveying. If the organization or process owners are not committed to continuous improvement, do not survey.

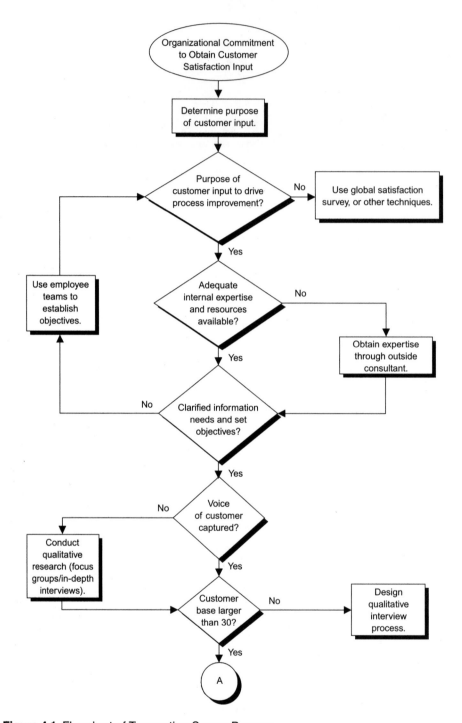

Figure 4.1 Flowchart of Transaction Survey Process.

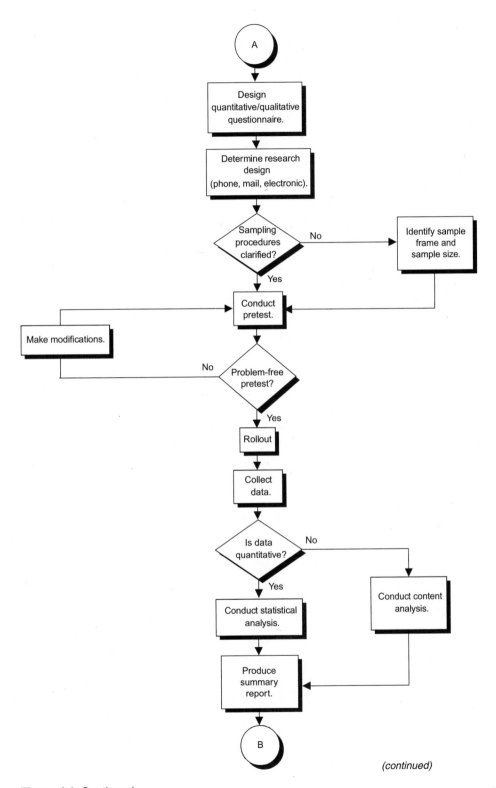

(continued)

Figure 4.1 Continued.

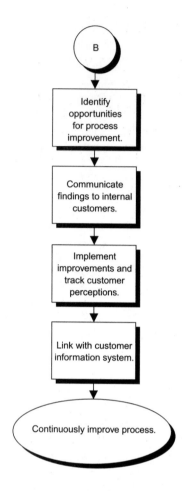

Figure 4.1 Continued.

CONTINUOUS IMPROVEMENT

Transaction surveys typically occur continuously and provide a continual flow of information back into the organization. But, because sample sizes are usually small, the data usually has a low level of precision. Transaction surveys are excellent for providing feedback to Six Sigma teams about process changes and improvements. Transaction surveys are *not* good for performance evaluation and incentive compensation because they lack the necessary precision. So, if the goal of the survey is to provide feedback to process improvement teams, transaction surveys are excellent. If the goal is anything else, there are probably better techniques, such as global surveys.

EXPERTISE AVAILABLE

An early task is to determine if there is sufficient expertise internal to the organization to design surveys, gather data, and analyze the results. If the expertise is available, the transaction survey program can be conducted internally. If the expertise is not available internally, the logical alternative is to use the services of an external consultant or research firm.

Since transaction surveys are relatively simple, they do not require an extremely high skill level. But, unfortunately, many firms are under "head count" pressure, so getting a skilled person's time is often difficult.

DEFINING THE RESEARCH OBJECTIVES

An important early step in a transaction survey process is to define the research objectives. This is normally done by clarifying the general goals, identifying who will actually use the data, and determining the desired format of the data. From these three issues, research objectives emerge. Clearly defining research objectives is a process.

If the individuals who are to use the transaction data are actively involved in defining the objectives and designing the transaction survey process, obtaining ownership and use of the data is much more likely. Since getting people to actively use the transaction data is every bit as important as actually gathering good data, obtaining individual support should not be overlooked. Therefore, it is recommended that a team of individuals from specific process areas be involved in defining the objectives and in designing other aspects of the transaction survey program. This could be the Six Sigma process improvement team, for example.

Given the considerations of the goals, who will use the data, and in what form the data should be, specific research objectives can be developed. The following two objectives are those that commonly emerge:

1. To measure and track customer satisfaction with the event

2. To solicit ideas from the customer to improve the event

Transaction surveys normally examine only those product and service attributes that relate to a specific event or value-added process. In most cases, this means that 10 to 20 attributes are measured in a transaction survey. The challenge for a manager is to make sure that the 10 to 20 attributes measured are those that are important to the customer. IBM Rochester employed a very simple transaction-based survey (see note 11). Ninety days after a computer system was installed, engineers or programmers would call the customer, thank him or her for the purchase, and simply ask the customer how things were going. This simplified approach provided immediate feedback to those responsible for designing the system. It was relatively easy to assess the satisfaction level of the customer based upon the response. The intent was not to gather statistically valid survey data, but rather to capture feedback about the product.

Capturing the voice of the customer means that, at some point, qualitative research should have been conducted to ensure that the *correct* questions are being asked. As discussed in the previous chapter, this is normally accomplished through depth interviews. But, instead of addressing key drivers of satisfaction, in general, the qualitative research should focus only on those issues related to the specific event. The issues, or attributes, identified by customers would be converted into questions on subsequent steps.

SIZE OF THE CUSTOMER BASE

If the size of the customer base is small, less than 30 customers, conducting quantitative research is inappropriate. There simply are too few respondents to conduct meaningful statistical analysis. In these situations, the research should be more qualitative, consisting of open-ended questions.

If the customer base is sufficiently large, a quantitative research approach can be used. Quantitative research means that the questions are scaled (that is, 1 to 5, 1 to 7, 1 to 10) and that the results are analyzed statistically. Since most firms have more than 30 customers, transaction surveys are most often quantitative in nature.

QUESTIONNAIRE DESIGN

Designing a questionnaire is both an art and a science. Typically, when designing any type of customer satisfaction measurement (CSM) questionnaire, everything must be done from the perspective of the customer. In the case of transaction surveys, however, both internal and external customer audiences must be considered for the questionnaire to be both meaningful and actionable.

There are a few general guidelines that are beneficial to follow when designing a questionnaire. These guidelines deal with the structure and flow of questions and topics.

A Questionnaire Is a Funnel

A questionnaire should be thought of as a funnel. There should be a logical transition from the opening introduction all the way through to the last question. The broader, easier-to-respond-to questions should come first with the more detailed, specific, and sensitive questions coming later.

There may be a series of filters in the questionnaire. Those filters screen and route the respondents to the next appropriate question. For a written questionnaire, the routing may be done with arrows to graphically lead the reader. For verbal questionnaires, the respondents may not even be aware that they are being screened. These screening questions avoid asking irrelevant questions and losing the customer's interest.

Wherever possible, related questions should be clustered together in distinct segments of the questionnaire with a specific transition statement about the topic. An example of a transition would be, "Now I'd like to ask some questions about the service that you experienced in your last visit." This would be followed by three or four service-related questions. Then another transition to another topic would appear, followed by another cluster of questions.

This allows the respondents to feel that they are progressing through the questionnaire. Also, a long list of 20 to 25 similarly scaled questions is visually unattractive in a mail survey. Respondents may scan the questionnaire and file it in the garbage because it does not look good.

The process of completing a questionnaire educates the respondent about many issues. The questionnaire may raise some issues to a top-of-mind awareness. Therefore, the sequential relationship among specific questions or separate segments should be considered in this educational context. If the questions do a lot of educating, they should appear late in the questionnaire. Since general questions often do little educating, they are usually located at the beginning of the questionnaire.

Keep It Simple

Strive for simplicity in all aspects of the questionnaire—the introduction, directions, question wording, and scaling. The more complex and difficult the task is for the respondent, the greater the likelihood of misinterpretation and confusion. When the respondent is uncertain, reliability usually declines rapidly.

The directions and questions should be short. Respondents often do not read or listen to long introductions, directions, or questions completely. Many respondents read or listen enough so that they *think* they know what is being asked and then skip the rest. Therefore, all aspects of the questionnaire should be as short and concise as possible and still achieve the research objectives.

For mail surveys, questions should not exceed 20 words. Long words, technical jargon, and words with multiple meanings should be avoided. Some questions may be grammatically incorrect but still be very good questions. Questions should be worded for a person with an eighth grade education. That is the average level of everyday spoken English. The need for simple wording also applies to response categories and scaling.

Be Specific

Except for a few general, lead-in questions to start a questionnaire, each question should be as specific as possible. Normally, the common rule of one concept per question is good advice. This question appeared on a CSM survey, "Please rate our product and service quality." Such *double-barreled* questions are confusing. How should the customer answer if product quality is good and service quality is terrible? It would be far better to break this into two questions and aggregate the responses or weight them differentially for an overall score.

Terms like *you, regularly,* and *recently* are vague in many cases. For business customers, does *you* refer to the respondent personally, to the respondent's department or functional area such as engineering, or purchasing? Or, does *you* refer to the company in general? It would be far better to say *you personally* or *your department* or *your company.*

Instead of *regularly* or *recently,* a question should refer to *in the last week, in the last 30 days,* or *the last time you used . . . .* This type of wording provides the respondent with a specific frame of reference, making it easier to respond, and is particularly important in transaction surveys.

No Opinion/Don't Know

While awareness questions indicate something about the respondent's overall knowledge of a subject, these measures do not suggest that a respondent knows something about every attribute of interest to the researcher. Yet, most respondents will offer a response to most reasonable questions, even though they may know very little about the topic.

However, if accurate, precise data is desired, then inclusion of the *no opinion/don't know* category is also desirable. It has been shown that up to one third of respondents who would give a response would select the *no opinion* were it offered. Inherently, these uninformed responses are less reliable and could skew the overall results if a consistent response pattern were shared by these respondents. Therefore, *no opinion/don't know* should be included as a response option for most quantitative questions.

When using open-ended questions, it is not necessary to repeat the option with every question. The use of *no opinion/don't know* is usually built into the initial directions and, occasionally, into the transition statements between sections for reinforcement. By building the *no opinion* category into the initial directions, the respondent is implicitly being sent the message that thoughtful, knowledgeable answers are important.

Introductions

Questionnaires that are mailed to respondents are usually accompanied by a cover letter that explains the rationale for the study. These questionnaires typically have little, or nothing, in the way of an introduction. The questionnaire simply begins with a set of directions. Telephone transaction questionnaires typically have an introduction. The introduction is normally a condensed version of a cover letter, typically three or four sentences long, that tries to elicit customer cooperation in completing a questionnaire. A short, succinct introduction informs the customers why the survey is being done and how the data will be used, asks for cooperation, tells what is to be done with the questionnaire, and thanks them for their patronage and assistance.

Directions

The directions can range from nothing to complex. If complex directions must be provided for a section, that section should not appear at the beginning of the questionnaire. Move the complex section toward the end of the questionnaire. The first set of directions should be as short and simple as possible to quickly get the respondent into the flow of answering questions. The logical extension of this discussion is that the first question should also be easy.

The First Questions

The first few questions should be general, easy to answer, and directly related to the research purpose that was stated in the cover letter and/or introduction. If an unrelated question is quickly introduced, the continuity of the transition into the questionnaire may be destroyed.

These first questions should be general questions related somehow to CSM. The most common first question is about overall satisfaction. For the transaction survey, exactly the same global questions should be asked as on other surveys and in the same position. For example, a firm might use the question "How satisfied are you in doing business with _____?" using the 5-point scale (very satisfied, satisfied, neither satisfied nor dissatisfied, dissatisfied, very dissatisfied) on all surveys. One or two of these global questions should appear on all surveys. If the respondent is still with you after these easy warm-up questions, the probability of completing the entire questionnaire is quite high.

Before moving on, you should notice that none of the overall measures include a *no opinion/don't know* category. The assumption is that all customers have at least a very general opinion that the researcher is trying to obtain. Absence of the *no opinion* category forces respondents to make some type of rating. For the more specific evaluations, a *no opinion* option should be included for each question.

Expectations Measures

Over the past few years, there has been an increasing use of *expectations measures* in CSM questionnaires. There are two primary reasons for this. The first is that most managers now realize that customers' expectations are constantly moving upward as competition intensifies. A firm's actual performance can remain constant, and satisfaction ratings will go down. Or, a firm can actually improve, but at a slower rate than customer expectations increase, and satisfaction ratings will go down.

The second reason is somewhat related to the first. More firms are embracing the idea that the customer is the ultimate judge of quality. Thus, meeting the customer's expectations is critical for a firm that is trying to deliver high quality. Meeting customer expectations is central to being a *customer-driven* firm. And, some of the more innovative firms are realizing that to create *customer delight,* the customer's expectations must be *exceeded.*

In order to get the most accurate information, the respondent should be asked two questions. The first question determines how much of an attribute *should* be present in an ideal firm; in other words, what is the expectation? The second questions basically asks "How do we compare to that standard?" In a fairly simple format, it might appear as follows:

When a customer phones an excellent firm, the phone should be answered within how many rings?

[1   2   3   4   5   6   7 or more]

When you phone (company name), the phone is answered within how many rings?

[1   2   3   4   5   6   7 or more]

This approach is more actionable for several reasons. First, the respondent gets to pick the ideal from a concrete set of alternatives. Then the ideal can be used as a standard. Probably as important, however, is the ability to determine the accuracy of the customer's perceptions of your performance.

Let us say the *ideal* answer time is within three rings. Then the customer responds that it takes four to reach your firm. The performance standard could easily be monitored to determine if it takes two, three, or four rings. If the customer's perceptions of performance are incorrect, then the implication is that the firm needs to educate the customer about actual performance levels.

If the possible response alternatives are not as easily identified as rings on a phone, and most are not, then the question can be reworded so that it is a completion format. With a completion format, the customer is asked to fill in a blank or describe ideal performance. In this way, the respondent freely decides the response criteria. All of these more sophisticated types of expectations questions allow three things to be done. First, the customer's expectations can be tracked over time to determine the rate of change. Second, the customer's perceptions of the firm's performance can be tracked over time and, in some cases, be compared to actual data to measure accuracy of perceptions. And third, the size of the gap between *ideal* and actual performance can be precisely calculated suggesting the magnitude of change necessary to change the firm's competitive position. By knowing the magnitude of change necessary, more accurate assessments of the financial costs can be made as well. This information is usually very actionable.

Performance Ratings

Questions on a transaction survey should ask the customer to rate the specific dimensions of performance in a very specific detailed manner. One of the best and most commonly used question formats follows:

Please rate the performance of technical support for following up on your requests?

[Excellent   Very Good   Good   Fair   Poor   Don't Know]

This type of wording is objective and unbiased because the respondent is not led to a more favorable response in any way. The response scale is simple and clearly understood, and a *don't know* option is provided. This question format is probably the most widely used on customer satisfaction questionnaires.

Open-Ended Questions

Transaction surveys usually include a mix of both closed, quantitatively scaled questions and open-ended probes. If the research design and preliminary work were comprehensive, the quantitative questions should be relevant and valuable. One does not, however, ever want to discourage a customer with a comment or idea. When a request is made for *additional comments* in some fashion, usually only a small portion of respondents bother to respond and many of these responses are short, terse comments of just a few words.

There are a few things that can be done to improve the quality of open-ended responses. Instead of asking simply for comments, ask for a specific or numeric response. Examples of open-ended questions that will have a better response rate are:

- Please list the three things we need to improve the most.

- What was your most positive experience?

- What was your most negative experience?

These questions make very clear what is requested of the respondent. Thus, respondent difficulty is reduced and responses are more frequent. Also, a *why* probe following an important question may elicit a response, particularly for important issues. Phone or personal interviews are the best medium to probe issues. Open-ended questions allow for more detail on what is causing the customer's perception. A good example is an IBM Rochester transaction survey. At the end of the survey, they ask customers if someone may call them back to better understand their concerns or issues.[14] Then the person who has been assigned responsibility for resolving the issue—for instance, an engineer that needs to make a design change—can call the customer back to better understand all the implications of the issue and to verify that the solution addresses all the issues.

RESEARCH DESIGN

A *research design* is an overall description of the transaction survey program. There are a variety of different research designs that can be developed depending upon a manager's preferences and the specific objectives. There is really no one best approach to a research design. Some organizations use a telephone survey methodology, while others prefer mail or fax. Some organizations use only closed-ended questions; others use open-ended questions. Some organizations use sophisticated data analysis; others use simple analysis.

All good research designs, however, share some common characteristics. All are based on clearly defined objectives. All are reliable, valid, and unbiased. Most recognize the issues of precision in some way. These concepts determine the quality of the data. Understanding and addressing each of these characteristics is important.

Reliability

Reliability is the ability to get approximately the same results time after time. Reliability is influenced by many aspects of the research design. Having very small sample sizes or samples that are very different in composition can reduce reliability. Questionnaire design can reduce reliability due to poor introductions, directions, transitions, or sequencing of questions. The actual wording of questions can reduce reliability due to ambiguity, complexity, or inappropriate response scales. Reliability can also be reduced due to data-gathering issues such as interviewer characteristics and behavior, inaccurate mailing lists, or inaccurate data analysis. Reliability is one of the most important considerations in evaluating a research design. To ensure reliability, attention to detail at the design phase is critical.

Validity

Validity is the ability to measure what the transaction survey program is supposed to measure. A survey lacks validity if the respondent interprets a different meaning than the researcher intended. As with reliability, validity can be influenced by a variety of issues such as sampling procedures, questionnaire design, and question wording. However, the most common validity problems flow from problems with the specific wording of questions. An example may illustrate this point. Suppose a researcher wanted to measure the degree to which products were free of defects at installation. The researcher may use the wording, "Please rate the quality of _____ products." The key word is *quality,* which is intended to mean *free of defects.* A customer may interpret *quality* to mean *durability* (it will not break if dropped), *reliability* (we never have any problems), or *upgradability* (we can improve the existing system). None of these interpretations quite match the intended *free of defects,* so the question could have a validity problem. The way to reduce validity problems is through initial qualitative work that allows customers to verbally describe their interpretations. Additionally, customers could be asked to state the reasons *why* they rate certain questions lower than others. This input could be used to assess whether the survey questions need to be changed or whether the organization needs to redefine its definitions to match the customer's more closely.

Bias

Bias occurs when responses do not match a customer's true feelings or attitudes. Bias can be introduced by sampling only those with favorable attitudes, through introductions and questions that lead respondents in a certain way, and by question wording and scaling. Bias can be very subtle. Bias can occur by sampling only brand loyal customers who tend to have more favorable attitudes. Bias can occur by only asking questions about issues where favorable responses are expected. Bias can occur by not providing respondents with a scale that reflects their true opinions. Bias is generally overcome by ensuring two actions: that samples are randomly drawn to the extent possible and that the questionnaire is objective in its approach.

Research Design Methodologies

There are four research design methodologies: personal interviews, telephone interviews, mail surveys (including fax machines and computer diskettes), and electronic surveys such as those deployed by E-mail and on the Internet. Each of these alternatives has advantages and disadvantages that involve cost, time, staffing support, and data-quality. While telephone interviews are most commonly used for transaction surveys, all design alternatives have been used.

Personal Interviews

Personal interviews, face-to-face interaction between a manager and a customer, are a very effective way to develop relationships with customers. Some organizations conduct monthly site visits with key customers to gather a variety of data. Personal interviews are particularly valuable in gathering qualitative customer input regarding where and how improvements can be made.

The disadvantages of personal interviews are that they are costly and time-consuming. Costs are high due to salary of the interviewer and travel expenses. Personal interviews are time-consuming due to scheduling appointments, often weeks in advance, and interview length, which can be an hour. Because of these limitations, personal interviews are normally used for very small samples where in-depth qualitative customer responses are desired. The sale of a very large system would be an example of such a situation. To minimize the imposition on the customer, one interviewer or a team would normally gather the customer input in a very coordinated effort.

Telephone Interviews

Telephone interviews are the most popular research design alternative for transaction surveys because they represent a compromise between personal and impersonal methods. Transaction surveys administered by phone are normally less than 10 minutes in length. It is normal to make 20 to 30 telephone calls to get one usable response. If callbacks are scheduled, however, a higher participation rate can be obtained.

Telephone interviews require that questions be short and concise and have relatively simple response scales. A survey that would be fine for a mail survey may be far too complex for a telephone survey. Telephone interviews have the ability to gather qualitative data from respondents, although the detail is not as great as with personal interviews.

A primary advantage of telephone interviews is the speed of gathering data, normally only a few days. The cost is moderate due to interviewer time, and response rates are usually high (40 percent to 70 percent). Because transaction surveys are normally fairly short and some qualitative data is desired, the need for simplicity is not a big constraint.

Mail Surveys

Mail surveys, or those sent and received by fax or computer diskette, are the lowest-cost research alternative, particularly for large samples. The greatest cost is often in the initial questionnaire design. The mail questionnaire is best suited for quantitative, closed-ended questions, which can be longer and more complex than telephone surveys. Printing and mailing are simple, and data analysis is straightforward as well. Optical scan questionnaires make the data input even easier.

There are two limitations with mail surveys. First, response rates are often low, 25 percent or less. A higher response rate occurs when the respondent's cooperation is obtained at the time of the transaction event. Somewhat related to the response rate issue is the fact that the researcher is never certain who actually completed the survey. Some target respondents have been known to have a secretary or subordinate complete the survey, a problem that seldom occurs in personal or telephone interviews. The responses from those who agree to complete a survey may be quite different from those who refuse, a problem that increases as response rates decline.

The second limitation is that mail surveys are good for quantitative data but poor for qualitative data. Making detailed written responses to open-ended questions is too great an imposition on respondents. If the transaction survey objectives are to track customer perceptions over time, mail surveys could be very appropriate, especially for large samples. But, if qualitative data is necessary to achieve the research objectives, mail surveys are probably not the best choice. Mail surveys have a tendency to provide the extreme, or tail, responses—those customers that are very satisfied and those customers that are very dissatisfied. In many cases, the statistical validity of mail surveys is questionable and caution should be taken with how the information is used.

Electronic Surveys

Electronic surveys, normally using electronic mail or the Internet, have become more popular recently. In many respects, an electronic survey is much like a mail survey in appearance. Currently, some respondents find electronic surveys novel and may participate when a paper survey would be discarded. Since the length of the questionnaire is not apparent initially, customers usually complete the survey entirely once they begin. Interactive voice response questionnaires are a cross between telephone interviews and electronic surveys. Respondents can use a phone pad or voice response to input data, depending upon the system. Unfortunately, there is not currently enough knowledge of interactive voice response surveys to estimate their acceptance by customers. Since customers must initiate the contact, there must be some incentive to gain their participation.

The current difficulties in using electronic surveys deal with accessibility, technology, and acceptability. Accessibility is facilitated through growing Internet usage. To use electronic surveys, a manager would need customer databases with Internet addresses for individual managers in customer organizations. Electronic surveys, like mail surveys, also appear to provide the extreme, or tail, responses—those customers that are very satisfied or very dissatisfied. So, although these types of surveys may be easy to implement, caution should be exercised on how the data is used by the organization.

A technological concern is the incompatibility of different systems and/or software across customers. Related to this are differing levels of computer literacy and comfort. Acceptability is influenced by the fact that some customers view electronic surveys as inherently impersonal, thus reducing response rates and cooperation.

Although electronic surveys are certain to increase in the future, currently their application is inconsistent. The use of electronic surveys of all types requires that customers be asked their preferences at the time of the transaction.

SAMPLING PROCEDURES

Developing and implementing a sampling procedure is a challenge to most managers. It is a more subjective process than some might think. A sample size discussion includes considerations of cost, precision, and reliability and is linked to the objectives. The discussion here includes some simple sample size guidelines, but the more complex sample size computations are available in most survey research books. The pragmatic sampling issues of frequency, time considerations, and identifying the right respondent are discussed. A decision must be made about whether the sampling procedure will be open or closed loop. An open-loop CSM program provides no feedback to customers when negative comments or complaints are voiced. A closed-loop system means that every negative comment gets a direct response from the company. This has obvious implications for sampling procedures.

Using a Sample

Sampling should be thought of as a sequential process that consists of several interrelated steps. The quality of each step is dependent upon and limited by the quality of the previous step. Therefore, errors made in one step directly influence and reduce quality in each of the subsequent steps.

Develop a Customer List

From company records, a comprehensive list of specific customers, by name, should be developed. The comprehensive customer list constitutes what is often referred to as the *sample frame.* The sample frame is a pool of customers from which a sample will be drawn. If all customers in the sample frame are contacted, the research is a census. If only a portion of the customers are contacted, regardless of how large a portion, then the research is a sample. There are many specific ways that a sample can be drawn, and this step is commonly referred to as selecting the sampling procedure.

Select the Sample Procedure

There is a wide variety of sample procedures, or ways to draw a sample from the pool of customers in the sample frame. The major distinctions are sequential versus fixed samples. And each of these categories could be further divided into several more types of sampling procedures. Every type of sampling procedure carries with it a unique set of advantages and disadvantages. The final choice of a sampling procedure should flow, as do most other research decisions, directly from the objectives of the research program.

Sequential Samples

Sequential samples are commonly used in transaction survey programs. Many firms are trying to stay close to their customers and to use timely customer data to drive continuous process improvement. Since most of these firms are familiar with and widely use statistical process control (SPC) for internal operations, a continuous flow of external, customer-driven data is a logical extension of internal improvement practices. These firms are culturally and managerially able to use the continuous flow data.

The most common form of sequential sampling is after some type of customer contact. It could be after a purchase transaction, a service call, an inquiry, or a complaint, for example. The problem is that each type of contact may influence the customer's responses. Therefore, a manager must decide which type of contact is most appropriate, given the research objectives. Then a manager must decide how soon after a contact to administer the questionnaire. Surveying a customer at the time of complaint is likely to elicit a different response than surveying a customer one week later, after a cooling off period. Generally, a customer should be surveyed within one week of contact so that the issues being addressed are fresh, recent, and, hopefully, more accurate.

Determine the Desired Sample Size

Determining the appropriate sample size is a complex decision involving many trade-offs. While the formulas found in most statistics books would lead you to believe that sample sizes are calculated based on a few criteria, in practice, a wide variety of factors influence the decision. The following sections discuss some of the key factors that influence the sample size.

A significant consideration is the amount of time available. The larger and more complicated the sample, the more time it takes to gather the data. Many managers may want the data *yesterday,* and intense time pressure tends to depress sample sizes. Also, large data sets take more time to enter and analyze; thus, smaller sample sizes lead to a faster turnaround of the whole project, not just the data gathering. With intense time pressure, there is also a tendency to compress or streamline some of the up-front steps of identifying the customer groups and developing a sampling frame for customers.

Variation in Customer Base

The more consistent customers are in their views, the smaller the necessary sample size. The greater the variability, the larger the necessary sample size. In statistical terms, this variation in a population is referred to as the *variance*. Since the exact variance of a population is seldom, if ever, known, an estimate for the population can be calculated from a sample. This calculated estimate is known as the *standard error* of a sample and is usually denoted by the *Sx*. This statistic is standard output on virtually all software programs and most handheld calculators. This calculated element is one of the key components of sample size formulas.

While the size of the customer base is not used directly in formulas for sample sizes, the size of the customer base does exert an indirect influence. As the customer base increases, there is more potential variability; hence, the variance increases. As the variance increases, sample sizes always go up, as well. So, potentially, an increase in the customer base can lead to an increase in sample size but does not always do so.

Precision

Precision is the width of an estimate. Political polls are often stated as being *within plus or minus x percentage points,* a statement of precision. The mean percentage of voters in favor of a candidate may be 60 percent, plus or minus 4 percent, with the width of the interval from 56 percent to 64 percent. The narrower the interval, the more precise the statement about a characteristic.

In a customer satisfaction context, the proportion of customers who are *satisfied* may be calculated in a variety of ways. If a researcher states that *90 percent of customers are satisfied,* without providing an accompanying statement of precision, a very crude indicator of satisfaction is being determined. A satisfaction level of 90 percent, with a ±10 percentage point interval, is far less useful than a satisfaction level of 90 percent, with a ±2.5 percentage point interval. In the first instance, the researcher is fairly certain that the *true satisfaction level of the customer base* is between 80 percent and 100 percent. In the second situation, the researcher is fairly certain that the true satisfaction level is between 87.5 percent and 92.5 percent.

The desired precision can be specified in sample size formulas. As the precision goes up, narrowing the precision interval, sample size also goes up. However, the relationship between precision and sample size is multiplicative. If the width of the precision interval is reduced by a factor of 2 (halving the interval) the sample size increases by a factor of 4. In our example, reducing the precision interval from ±10 percentage points to ±5 percentage points would require a sample 4 times as large. Reducing the interval from ±10 percentage points to ±2.5 percentage points requires a sample 16 times as large as the original, if everything else remains unchanged.

If a population is very homogeneous, having a small variance, then the exponential relationship between precision and sample size may not be a big problem. If a ±10 percentage point precision interval is desired, a sample size formula may indicate a minimum sample size of 90. Reducing the precision interval to ±2.5 percentage points would require a sample of 1440.

But, if a customer base is very heterogeneous, having a large variance, the initial required sample size may have been 200, for a precision of ±10 percent. To reduce the precision interval for this study to ±2.5 percentage points would require a sample of 3200, an increase of 3000 respondents.

The point of all this is that a high degree of precision can be costly in some situations, most notably when there is a very diverse customer base. The desired precision level is, again, one of those managerial decisions that should flow from the objectives of the research. If a primary goal is the improvement of value-added processes, the level of precision should not be a big issue, within reason.

Confidence Level

The third major component in sample size formulas, in addition to variance and precision, is the *confidence level.* The confidence level indicates how certain we are about our conclusions. The most commonly used confidence levels are 90 percent, 95 percent, 97.5 percent, and 99 percent.

A researcher might use a 90 percent confidence level in a research project. Using our earlier figures, that researcher would be *90 percent confident that the mean customer satisfaction level is 90 percent, ±2.5 percentage points.* However, to be more confident, and maybe to impress the users of the data a bit more, a researcher may decide to use a 95 percent or 97.5 percent confidence level. As the confidence level increases, sample size also increases.

The same type of relationship exists between sample size and confidence level as with precision. A 90 percent confidence level implies that a 10 percent chance of being wrong exists. If the chance of error is reduced by half, the sample size goes up by a factor of 2. Increasing the confidence level from 90 percent to 95 percent increases the sample size 2 times. Increasing the confidence level from 90 percent to 97.5 percent increases the sample size 4 times.

Presented in Figure 4.2 are some rough guidelines that describe appropriate sample size. Please keep in mind that this figure addresses only a confidence level of 90 percent and precision ±5 percent. It does not take into consideration variance. Populations with a small variance may require a smaller sample size, while a population with a large variance would require a larger sample size than those indicated.

If a researcher desires to be very confident, say 99 percent, and very precise, say ±2 percentage points, very large sample sizes will result. The more conclusive and detailed the results, the larger the sample size and the greater the costs. This is particularly true when a customer base displays a good deal of heterogeneity, resulting in a large variance. The frequency of rolling up the survey results may be lengthened as an alternative to using data that has a lower error rate. For instance, it may be more advantageous for the organization to roll up and use survey data quarterly because the confidence level is better than to act on monthly data, which may be less accurate. But there are a few other issues that must be considered.

Multiple Segments and Measures

The discussion to this point has assumed that the variance, precision, and confidence level are easily determined. These factors are easily calculated or determined for a *single* question. Unfortunately, a one-question customer satisfaction questionnaire is pretty rare. *Each question* has its own accompanying variance. The same question, used on six different customer groups, may have a different variance in each group.

The impact of multiple questions and multiple segments is that, when sample size is held constant, both the precision and confidence level vary somewhat from question to question. For questions with a large variance, precision and confidence are lower (wider

90% Confidence
Error = ± 5%

Population Size	Required # of Respondents
100	80
200	132
300	169
400	197
500	218
1000	278
1500	306
2000	323
2500	334
3000	341
5000	357
10,000	370
20,000	377

The "Required # of Respondents" identifies the
number of usable surveys that you must *get back*.

Figure 4.2 Sample Size Requirements.

precision intervals and lower confidence level). For questions with a small variance, precision and confidence are relatively higher.

The conservative approach would be to determine the variance for all questions and use the largest variance in sample size calculations. This would result in the largest possible sample size. A more realistic approach would be to examine the variance for the key, most important questions and use that variance in calculations.

Another problem in deciding which variance to use is the use of multiple measurement scales. A variance of 1.7 is greater on a 5-point scale than on a 7-point scale. Since most CSM questionnaires utilize a variety of response categories, the same absolute variance may be relatively more, or less, from question to question.

Sample Size Guidelines

Sample size formulas suggest that an exact figure can be calculated for each study. In reality, this is not the case. Constraints of time and resources, the nature of the sample and subgroups, the length and type of questionnaire, and the consistency in the variance can all influence the sample size. Additionally, the desired precision and confidence levels are important considerations. Collectively, these factors all work together to "muddy the waters," making the final decision rather subjective.

PRETESTING

Pretesting is an absolutely essential step in the design of a transaction survey. While no respectable researcher would ever argue against pretesting, few guidelines exist that indicate exactly what should be pretested and how the pretest should be conducted. Therefore, the goal of this section is to provide some guidance on how to effectively conduct a pretest.

A pretest is simply a test of a miniature transaction survey program. Everything is evaluated, from sample composition to introductions, to questionnaire issues, to data analysis, to use of the data. A pretest is *not* just a test of the questionnaire. If you examine only the questionnaire, you may be asking great questions but using the wrong respondents. Or, you may be analyzing the data in a way that the internal customers, the users of the data, cannot use. Essentially, then, what you are trying to do is to critically evaluate every aspect of the program.

Once again, the point should be made that a pretest is not just a pretest of specific questions or of an entire questionnaire. A pretest is a critical evaluation of a complete transaction survey program. One of the first issues that typically arises is the appropriate sample size for a pretest. There are no set rules or formulas that can tell you how large the pretest should be. A normal size range for a pretest is between 25 and 75, with 50 being fairly common. If several pretests are anticipated, the initial pretest may be smaller, relatively, with subsequent pretests getting progressively larger. There is also a general relationship between the targeted sample size for the full transaction survey program and the pretest sample size.

If you plan to use a monthly sample of 200 customers to provide tracking feedback, a pretest of 50 is very adequate. However, if your program calls for a monthly sample of 2000 or more, then a pretest of 100 to 200 is more appropriate. The larger the sample, the larger the pretest sample should be. For some companies, the total population of customers is very small. In these cases, a pretest of only 10 customers may be completely adequate.

A pretest sample should *not* consist of colleagues, managers, or employees. Using these individuals for revisions is fine, but a pretest sample should approximate the desired customer group as closely as possible.

There are several issues related to the questionnaire that need to be examined in the pretest. The first is the reaction of the respondent to the overall questionnaire. A second issue is the respondent's perceptions of the questions. A third issue consists of scaling, measurement, and response categories.

DATA ANALYSIS

Once the data has been gathered, it must be analyzed in an objective, consistent manner. Since some of the data will be qualitative, generated by open-ended questions, and some will be quantitative, several techniques must be used. Qualitative analysis is discussed first.

Qualitative Analysis

A common objective of transaction surveys is to solicit customer input on how products, services, and processes can be improved. This usually requires open-ended questions that result in unstructured, verbal responses from the customer.

The process for evaluating qualitative data is referred to as content analysis. Content analysis was discussed previously for depth interviews—multiple evaluators, using some uniform criteria, group comments made by respondents into categories. The categories are usually predetermined after reviewing a portion of the responses. Each evaluator reviews all responses and develops a frequency distribution for the entire survey. Then the two or more evaluators compare the results.

If a high degree of similarity exists, or inter-rater reliability, then Pareto charts can be developed. If a low degree of similarity exists, the implication is that the evaluators interpreted the responses differently. The evaluators must then jointly evaluate the responses and reach a consensus interpretation.

Pareto charts are simply bar charts that visually indicate the topical categories used on one axis and the frequency of mention on the other axis. Managers normally find the verbatim transcripts that support the Pareto charts to be quite interesting.

This type of analysis indicates very clearly what issues the customers are thinking about. However, content analysis does not give an indication of the relative importance among the issues. For example, product reliability may be mentioned 4 times as frequently as technical support. That does not mean that reliability is 4 times as important. Reliability is probably more important than technical support, but qualitative data does not allow a researcher to determine the magnitude of difference.

This is due, in part, to the fact that open-ended responses tend to be influenced by critical incidents. A critical incident is a specific situation that the customer recalls when responding. Characteristics of that situation may strongly influence a respondent's overall perception. For example, a customer whose phone call was not returned may view a company as unresponsive and say that company does not listen to its customers. Or, a customer may find a single employee to be friendly and very technically competent and generalize that all employees are great.

It is easier for customers to recall negative incidents than positive incidents. Positive experiences are often taken for granted, assuming that it is just the way it is supposed to be. But negative incidents stand out. They are not what was expected, so they are more memorable.

The implication is that open-ended responses need to be interpreted carefully. Making significant organizational changes based on only a few comments may not be justified. However, in some cases, a few very innovative customers may have excellent ideas for improvement.

Quantitative Analysis

There are two types of quantitative analysis that are done with transaction data. The most common is tracking analysis. Less frequently done is modeling to determine the relative importance of the attributes.

Tracking Analysis.   The primary purpose of tracking analysis is to identify the sequential changes in customer responses from one time period to the next. In most cases, this means tracking and posting the key metrics so the results can be used to drive process improvement. As a result, much of the tracking analysis is quite similar to statistical process control (SPC) techniques used in production situations. Tracking analysis involves the use of techniques that describe patterns in the data. Thus, these techniques are referred to as descriptive statistics. Descriptive statistics include means, standard deviations, frequency distributions, and cross tabulations.

Means and Standard Deviations.   Calculating means for tracking analysis is pretty straightforward, and numerous examples of this have been provided previously. Unfortunately, the analysis of means is often abused. The most common error is to not consider the standard deviation and sample size when comparing means. The result is that erroneous conclusions are drawn from the data. This is particularly true when making comparisons between mean scores for different attributes in one study or between mean scores from two different time periods.

When several samples are drawn from a population of customers, sampling theory suggests that there will be variations in mean scores across the various samples. It is very unlikely that all the mean scores would be exactly the same. It is also very unlikely that any of the samples will exactly represent the entire population of customers. This variation in sample means is referred to as *sampling error.* Sampling error exists in every survey. The key issue is to make an estimate of sampling error through the use of the standard deviation and sample size. The size of the sampling error allows conclusions to be made about the difference between mean scores.

Let us say that a firm is trying to evaluate the relative importance of 15 attributes by using a 10-point scale with *1* being *very unimportant* and *10* being *very important.* It would not be at all unusual to have 10 of the 15 attributes have a mean rating of greater than 9.0 on this scale. Very often, a firm will simply rank order the means from highest to lowest and conclude that this is the order of importance to the customer. Doing this is fundamentally incorrect!

There is a statistical procedure that should be used to determine if the means are significantly different from one another. The test is relatively simple and considers the mean, standard deviation, and sample size. In our example, if the means of the attributes are in the range of 9.05 to 9.48, hypothetically, then the means are probably not statistically different from one another. The differences could be due simply to sampling error and not real differences in customers' perceptions. Hence, the proper conclusion would be that *these 10 attributes are all equally important to our customers.*

The implication is that, when calculating means, the researcher should not attempt to "split hairs" and try to infer that the data is more refined and precise than it really is. Often this implies that the researcher must educate the users of the data regarding how to interpret the data. This requires that means, standard deviations, and significant differences be calculated and explained fully to the users of the data.

Having said all of this, mean responses to interval data can be presented as numerical means, bar charts, line graphs, or process charts. The decision on how to present the data is based on the preferences of the user groups.

Frequency Distribution.   If the questions have been scaled using categories, normally from three to five, then the responses are categorical, not interval. Therefore, data analysis must use frequency distributions, not means and standard deviations, as is sometimes done. Frequency distributions indicate the frequency of responses in each category. The results of frequency distributions are usually presented as percentages of respondents falling into various categories. These percentages then become the key metric that is tracked from one period to the next. Top box and top two scores are an example of this.

Xerox used a 5-category scale to measure overall customer satisfaction. Any respondent indicating a 4 or 5 is considered to be satisfied. AT&T, on the other hand, also used a 5-category scale but feels that only a score of 5, which represents excellent, is enough to retain a customer. AT&T considers a customer who selects a 4 or lower to be vulnerable to competitive alternatives. The decision to select one or two or even three categories as satisfied is purely a managerial decision.

Some firms will use cross-tabs between independent and/or dependent variables to support other statements. For example, a firm may say that *a customer who is very satisfied (a 5 on a 5-point scale) is 4 times as likely to remain a loyal customer.* This type of statement is made by comparing response patterns of those selecting a 5 versus those who select a 4 or lower. Again, aggregating all categories of 4 or lower is a subjective, managerial judgment.

Using five or fewer response alternatives certainly results in categorical data. Technically, a scale with six or seven response alternatives is also categorical. However, studies have shown that a 7-category response structure closely resembles true interval data. Thus, when using six or seven response categories, the data can be analyzed using both categorical and interval techniques. The results will generally be about the same. The use of categorical data requires that different formulas be used.

COMMUNICATING YOUR CSM RESULTS

One of the most important components of all types of customer satisfaction measurement is to communicate the findings of the study. With transaction surveys, it is most important to communicate results to middle management and frontline employees. The data can also be used in conjunction with the other survey data to communicate with customers, which has a potentially powerful marketing effect. Communicating results within and outside of the company requires a concerted effort but is well worth the time. The more that the employees know about the customers, the better they can serve them.

Survey results need to be explained in a consistent but simple manner. The purpose of communicating results is both to give recognition for jobs well done and to help identify areas for process improvement efforts. When employees, be they senior managers or frontline workers, start seeing the same presentation for customer input, understanding and focus is much faster.

CRITICAL PROCESSES ULTIMATELY DRIVE CUSTOMER SATISFACTION

Once the attributes that impact customer satisfaction are identified, employees need to identify the internal processes or activities that create or affect that attribute. The company culture must encourage cross-functional teams to provide input to the improvement process.

The real benefits of transaction surveys are realized when the results are spread widely. Both individuals and Six Sigma teams should have the opportunity to suggest how processes can be improved. This also implies that authority to make process improvements needs to be decentralized. The greater the number of employees who use the data, the more successful the transaction survey program is likely to be.

An example of process improvement can be found in Marriott Corporation. Marriott International's Lodging Group is composed of their four hotel and suite divisions as well as a service group that provides food and facilities management, distribution, and retirement center management. As a part of Marriott's total quality efforts, Marriott embarked on a comprehensive customer satisfaction process to determine what attributes impact a guest's satisfaction most. The research identified the five key attributes for customer satisfaction for guests: check-in speed, friendliness, cleanliness, value, and breakfast.

With the exception of breakfast, the other attributes all occur or are evaluated during the guest's first 10 minutes at the hotel. Marriott initiated a *first 10* program, which focuses on the Marriott processes that impact those first 10 minutes of a stay. By making all necessary arrangements when the reservation is made for the room (i.e., room preference, credit card, etc.), guests can go almost immediately to their room and essentially bypass the traditional check-in process. Phones are being removed from the front desk so that front desk Marriott employees can concentrate uninterrupted on guest needs. These employees can create and maintain a more friendly attitude as well. (The phones, incidentally, will be placed in a customer service center.) Value is also an area where Marriott has some differentiating advantage, as Marriott has a separate target market for each of their hotel groupings: Marriott Resorts, Hotels, and Suites (full-service hotels); Courtyard (moderate price); Residence Inn (extended stay or relocation); and Fairfield Inn (economy lodging).

SUMMARY

Transaction surveys are another method for gathering data about customer satisfaction with a small set of attributes about products or services. They serve as a mechanism for providing immediate feedback so improvements can be made to products, services, or processes, thus preventing higher levels of dissatisfaction among the entire customer population. Transaction surveys should be constructed and conducted with the same level of diligence as global surveys. Users of transaction survey data need to understand the limitations surrounding transaction survey data.

Data analysis should be conducted with the intent of making the results as *user-friendly* as possible. Overly complex and technical analysis tends to intimidate many users who are unfamiliar with statistical analysis. Intimidation is a large part of the reluctance to accept survey results. A building products regional manager, when waiting for the results of a rather expensive customer satisfaction measurement process, said, "We're not interested in the numbers, just give us the verbatims." This same person had a negative experience with a market researcher in the past and never trusted the results of surveys. This lack of trust was simply due to a lack of understanding of very basic statistical concepts, as well as to the market researcher not educating the regional manager through simple graphs and charts.

It is also important to have credibility within the organization for the integrity of the data and data analysis. Data must be kept confidential and anonymous unless the customer allows identification. Although data should be widely dispersed throughout the organization, the database should be "locked" to prevent the accidental alteration of the data by a user.

Credibility issues can also arise with both a consultant-assisted and in-house process. It is important for the individuals conducting the research to understand all specific details of each type of analysis, and, most importantly, the researcher must be able to articulate the statistical analysis in layperson terms and metaphors that are user-friendly. The inability to do this will result in the data being filed on the shelf and forgotten.

CASE STUDY

TRANSACTION SURVEYS

The Controls Business of Johnson Controls, Inc., among other activities, installs heating and ventilation equipment that maintains a building's environment. Each installation, whether a complete system installation or a modification and upgrade, generates an event-driven survey.

When a job is completed, the project manager turns the associated paperwork in to one of 24 Area offices in North America. The Area offices then transfer the data to Controls Business headquarters in Milwaukee, Wisconsin, by the end of each month. There is a single person in the Milwaukee office who extracts the data and transfers a sample frame to the research firm, Naumann & Associates. This occurs by the fifth day, approximately, of each month.

Naumann & Associates first checks the database for duplicate names. Many large clients could have several projects at different locations, and the decision rule is that an individual respondent can be surveyed no more frequently than once every 6 months. This check has been put in place to prevent *oversurveying* customers. Once the database is *cleaned,* surveying begins.

Telephone surveying of installation customers is usually conducted during the second and third weeks of the month. It is normal to reach about 70 percent to 80 percent of the sample frame. Some phone numbers are wrong, disconnected, or are dedicated to fax machines, but the largest portion of nonresponse is for voice mails that are never answered. Each number in the sample frame is attempted a minimum of 5 times. When bad numbers are encountered, appropriate information is transferred to a person in Controls Business headquarters who then searches for the correct information and updates the database.

Surveying is always spread over 2 weeks so that respondents on vacation or out of town during a given week will be attempted the following week. Surveying is conducted in both French and English, as well as Spanish when necessary. Surveying is stopped by the fourth week of the month.

The complete sample frame is developed for each month. This again requires *cleaning* to locate any data input errors. Once the database is cleaned, it is transferred to the contact person at the Controls Business headquarters in Milwaukee. It is then integrated into the comprehensive customer database.

The database is maintained using *Access* software. As a result, both Johnson Controls, Inc., and Naumann & Associates had to be working off the same version of Access. Also, the individuals using Access had to be well trained.

Initially, hardcopy reports were prepared each month and distributed to each Area General Manager as well as headquarters executives. Monthly reports were time-consuming to prepare and resulted in a bit of data overload. As a result, reporting was shifted to an electronic format so that results were posted on the Controls Business Internet. Finally, the reporting format was switched to a quarterly basis. The primary reason for moving to quarterly reports was statistical reliability. The monthly sample sizes varied widely, with each month having a different precision level. Due to sampling variation, the scores would fluctuate up or down somewhat. By aggregating 3 months of data, the scores were much more stable and reliable due to the much larger sample size. The quarterly data also had a much better precision level. This was important since the customer satisfaction scores were used as part of an overall scorecard.

It is important that the survey data be used to improve the way business is conducted, especially from the customer's perspective. Customer satisfaction results, including issues and actions, are reviewed with each Area General Manager quarterly. The case study at the end of chapter 11 illustrates the linkage of customer satisfaction results to Johnson Controls, Inc., processes. This alignment between processes and customer satisfaction results helps individuals within the organization more easily relate their activities and actions to changes in customer satisfaction. In today's environment, employee turnover has had a major impact on customer satisfaction. The processes used to select and train employees and retain and reward employees, as well as the processes that are used to establish relationships and communications between the customer and the Area account teams, have all been analyzed and modified recently.

5

Customer Loyalty Analysis

Customer loyalty is an outcome of delivering good customer value. If all five drivers of value meet or exceed customer expectations, good value is created. If one or more drivers of value fail to meet customer expectations, the customer's perceptions of value are lower. When value perceptions are higher, customers tend to be very loyal. When value perceptions are lower, customers search for alternatives. Some of these customers defect.

Since loyalty is based on customer perceptions, there will probably always be some level of defection. A firm may exceed all of its own internal quality standards and still lose customers. Some customers may simply have a quite different expectation of service quality, for example. If a firm wants to keep these customers, service quality performance would have to be improved. But an equally valid alternative may be to let the demanding customers leave since improving service quality, in this example, may completely erode profit margins.

The purpose of this chapter is to present a methodology that identifies why a firm's valued or desired customers defect. The first part of the chapter briefly discusses the concept of loyalty and presents a model that provides a framework for understanding the cause-and-effect relationships. The second part of the chapter discusses the differences between attributes that create delight and those that cause dissatisfaction. The final part of the chapter discusses the methodological issues that must be addressed to conduct lost customer analysis.

THE VALUE PAYOFF MODEL

The impact of customer loyalty on profitability is well known. There is a strong, positive correlation between retaining customers and profitability. Perhaps the best single reference on this subject is Frank Reichold's excellent book, *The Loyalty Effect.* Unfortunately, achieving high levels of loyalty is rather complex. Many things must happen well before loyalty is achieved. In other words, loyalty is simply the outcome of a complex process. The major steps in this process are captured in the Value Payoff Model (Figure 5.1).

This model provides a framework for the major cause-and-effect relationships that are related to customer loyalty. The model is a mix of perceptual and behavioral concepts.

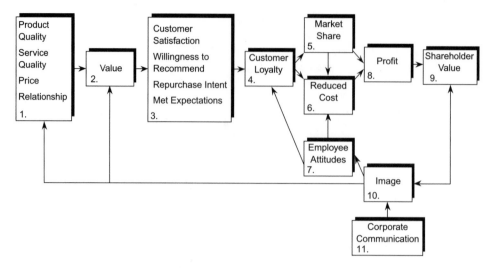

Figure 5.1 The Value Payoff Model.

Boxes 1, 2, 3, 7, and 10 consist of customer perceptions. The remaining boxes contain behavioral issues. The importance of this distinction will become more apparent shortly.

Box 1: Customer Perception

The customer has expectations for each of the four categories of product quality, service quality, price, and relationships. The expectations may be based on the customer's own experiences, on competitive alternatives, or on implicit and explicit advertising claims. Of course, product quality, service quality, price, and relationship are not equally important. Certain attributes within each category emerge as key drivers of satisfaction. For example, *follow-up* may be a key driver of *relationship*. Being *customer driven* may be a key driver of *image*. Or, *providing proactive solutions* to the customer may be a key driver of *service quality.*

For a firm to create good value, it must meet or exceed the customer's expectations in the various performance areas. Obviously, it is much easier to meet customer expectations if a firm actually knows what the expectations are. Identifying customer expectations is the primary reason for the rapid growth in customer satisfaction research. As discussed in the two previous chapters, customer satisfaction research can indicate both the relative importance of each attribute to the customer and the customer's perceptions of a firm's performance.

It may be difficult for a customer to form precise expectations of each performance area. This is particularly the case when the product is highly technical. For example, an information technology (IT) manager in a customer firm may not know all of the technical aspects of computers and printers. But the IT manager knows that buying an IBM or Compaq personal computer or a Hewlett-Packard printer is a safe decision, even if the price is higher than other roughly equivalent products. The implication is that a firm's image influences the customer's expectations.

The influence of image is also a bit of a dilemma. A firm's image can elevate a customer's expectations. The image of Lexus as a high-quality luxury car leads to extremely high expectations by Lexus owners. Customer expectations are far higher at the Ritz Carlton than at many other hotels. The image of Oakley, Ray Ban, or Gargoyle sunglasses influences the customer's expectations, as does the name Harley-Davidson for motorcycle enthusiasts. Image can be particularly challenging for firms with a broad product line. IBM Rochester added *image* to its customer satisfaction surveys in 1993 after it discovered the importance of this attribute in influencing and driving overall satisfaction.[15]

Hewlett-Packard produces DeskJet printers that sell for around $200 at retail. They also sell LaserJet printers for thousands of dollars, depending on the model. There is a very small profit margin on the DeskJet compared to a LaserJet. But customer expectations of technical support are probably very similar for both products since both are Hewlett-Packard printers. Unfortunately, the cost structure of a DeskJet does not allow for extensive technical support. Any firm with a broad product line faces this challenge.

Box 2: Value

Customers integrate their perceptions of product quality, service quality, price, relationship, and image into a perception of customer value. Customers essentially make a cost-benefit trade-off. Costs include price paid and life cycle cost. Benefits include the whole bundle of benefits created through product quality, service quality, relationships, and image. Therefore, value is also very much of a perceptual issue. But, the concept of value, in most sophisticated multivariate statistical analysis, emerges as the single best predictor of subsequent customer behaviors. The implication is that virtually all customer research should measure value perceptions in some way. There are both perceptual and behavioral outcomes of value perceptions.

Box 3: Perceptual Outcomes

There are many concepts that are a direct outcome of a customer's value perceptions. These concepts are usually measured by a set of broad, global questions on a customer satisfaction survey. The most common concepts are overall customer satisfaction, willingness to recommend, repurchase intent, and met expectations. All of these are perceptual issues that are closely related to one another. Delivering good value makes a customer satisfied, makes a customer willing to recommend the firm to others, and meets a customer's expectations. Delivering good value also leads to the formulation of a repurchase intent. The likelihood of repurchase is a perceptual measure of future loyalty, but it is not an exact predictor of loyalty behavior. It may not even be a better predictor of loyalty than the other global questions. Individuals do not always do what they say they are going to do. However, IBM Rochester (see note 15) was able to determine that customers repurchase in a manner in which they say they will on customer satisfaction surveys, which is shown in Figure 2.5. But this is not always the norm and should be tested by first asking customers on a survey whether they intend to repurchase and then measuring whether or not they do at some future date.

A number of consumer confidence surveys have been conducted for years. Consumers are asked if they plan to buy an item in the next year such as a car, television set, or major appliance. It is not unusual for only half of the consumers to actually do what they said they were going to do. However, business customers have a much higher fulfillment of repurchase intent.

Some authors have stated or implied that customer satisfaction is not a good predictor of loyalty behavior. It is true that satisfaction is not as good a predictor of consumer loyalty as it is of business-to-business loyalty. Many consumer purchases are less frequent and are typified as separate, distinct transactions. Business-to-business purchases are more often part of an ongoing relationship. So the whole nature of the customer-supplier relationship is different for consumers than for business customers.

The other issue that is ignored by those who say that satisfaction is unimportant is the concept of consumer motivation. Some customers do not want to buy the same product again. To illustrate, I have a weakness for sports cars. My last sports car was a Corvette. The new Corvettes are excellent cars with good acceleration and great handling characteristics. I was very satisfied with the car. After owning the Corvette for several years, I decided to get another sports car. Even though I was very satisfied with the Corvette, I wanted to try a different sports car. So I bought a Porsche 911 Carrera. It is a great car; I am very satisfied with it. I am not dissatisfied with my Porsche in any way, except, perhaps, that it leaks when it rains. That is a problem common to all Porsches with a Targa top. But my next car will be something different, probably one of the old Cobras or perhaps a Dodge Viper. One of my primary motivations is the desire to experience different types of sports cars.

The travel tourism industry constantly faces this dilemma. Consumers want to experience different destinations. A skier may be very satisfied with Vail but may want to try Steamboat or Sun Valley or Park City or Whistler-Blackcomb the next time. Going back to the same mountain each time could get a bit boring.

The implication of this is that the customer's motivation must be understood to develop loyalty metrics. To say that satisfaction is not linked to loyalty is quite simplistic. This is where it is important to include questions on the customer satisfaction survey that ask about a customer's repurchase intentions and then to compare the results against overall satisfaction scores to test for correlation between the two questions.

Box 4: Customer Loyalty

Customer loyalty is a behavioral concept. The customer's behavior can and should be measured. One of the primary behaviors that can be measured is the defection rate. The defection rate is the percentage of customer accounts that go dormant in a year. If the customer-supplier relationship is continuous and the customer abruptly switches to another supplier, the defection may be obvious. If the customer-supplier relationship is sporadic or intermittent, the customer may switch to another supplier and the previous supplier would not be aware of the defection.

Defection is not the only measure of loyalty. A customer could remain an open account but drastically reduce the purchase level. For example, if a customer switches 80 percent of his or her purchases to a different supplier, would that be a defection? The answer is probably *yes* since most of the customer's revenue has gone elsewhere. But this would not show up as an actual defection or closed account on most customer databases.

The implication is that loyalty is not always a clear distinction. When a firm is tracking defection, significant changes in revenue should also be considered.

Box 5: Market Share

Firms that have high customer loyalty usually have high market share in their defined markets. The higher loyalty makes marketing and promotional expenditures more effective. For example, having a defection rate of 15 percent of the customer base is pretty common for an average firm. To hold revenues constant, at least an equivalent number of new customers must be acquired to replace those who depart. Realistically, a somewhat larger number of new customers will need to be added since new customers often have lower per capita revenues than the average customer.

If a firm has a defection rate of only 5 percent instead of 15 percent, an equivalent marketing campaign will result in a 10 percent growth rate. Of the 15 percent of new customers acquired, only 5 percent are needed to replace lost customers. The remaining 10 percent contribute directly to growth. In the simplest form, high loyalty leads to higher market share because more of the customers acquired through marketing efforts are retained.

Also, if the customer base is highly satisfied and loyal, the current customers are more likely to generate word-of-mouth referrals. These new customers have a very low acquisition cost since they were not attracted through traditional marketing and promotional efforts.

Box 6: Reduced Costs

New customers are more costly to a supplier than the more established customers. IBM Rochester (see note 15) determined that a company must expend 5 times the amount of money to gain a new customer than that needed to keep a current customer satisfied, and must expend 12 times more expense to win a customer back that it lost. Initially, there are all of the acquisition costs of advertising, sales calls, credit applications, and processing. After the customer is acquired, there are still other costs. New customers have much higher technical support costs as they are learning how to use the products or services. To illustrate, Hewlett-Packard's Printer Division gets well over a million calls annually at its Customer Support Center. About 70 percent of the calls are from individuals who have owned their printers for 2 months or less. After a customer has used the printer for 6 months, the customer has learned everything that he or she needs to know.

Higher market share contributes to lower per unit costs by allocating a marketing campaign over a larger number of units. Since the marketing effort is essentially an overhead charge, there is an economy of scale. The same could be said of research and development and administrative charges, as well.

Costs are also reduced through positive employee attitudes. As employee attitudes improve, there is less absenteeism and turnover. Also, more satisfied employees are more apt to be involved in their work and to make more suggestions for improvement.

Box 7: Employee Attitudes

There are many factors that influence employee attitudes. This model addresses only those that are relevant to the other concepts in the model. Developing a comprehensive employee satisfaction model is beyond the scope of this chapter.

There is a positive correlation between employee attitudes and customer attitudes. The employee-customer interaction is most apparent in dimensions of service quality and relationship that directly touch the customer. Employees who have more positive attitudes make their views apparent at the points of customer contact. Nortel has found a direct correlation between employee attitudes in a department or function and the customer's satisfaction with that department. IBM Rochester found a direct correlation between employee satisfaction, productivity, cost of quality, customer satisfaction, and market share (Appendix A) (see note 3).

As mentioned previously, positive employee attitudes contribute to reduced costs. This could occur for many reasons such as better superior-subordinate relationships, a more participatory work environment, and better training and development.

One of the factors that contributes to positive employee attitudes is the image and reputation of the firm. The better the firm's image, the more positive the employee's attitudes tend to be.

Involvement in Six Sigma teams is often rewarding to employees despite the hard work. Employees feel they have real input into the decision-making process and can directly affect how work gets done. This higher involvement in participatory decision making is one of the key drivers of employee satisfaction in any business.

Box 8: Profit

The relationship between market share and profitability has been well documented in the PIMS (Profit Impact of Market Strategies) studies. As a firm becomes an industry leader in market share, that firm tends to have higher profitability.

Also, as a firm reduces its cost structures, particularly with a high market share position, profitability improves. Being a market leader often results in a price premium. Customers are willing to pay slightly more for the well-known products because they convey a certain quality. The result of reduced costs and a price premium is a gross margin significantly above average for the industry.

Box 9: Shareholder Value

Profits, or the expectation of profits, are the key drivers of shareholder value. While many activities drive profits, customer satisfaction is one of the most important drivers, as was discussed earlier. There is a strong correlation between top box scores and shareholder value at the individual firm level. There is also a strong correlation between the American Customer Satisfaction Index and the change in stock price for a very large group of firms. (These issues were discussed previously in chapter 2.) (See note 6.)

The implication is that shareholder value is an indicator of the confidence that investors have in the managerial ability of a firm. Focusing on satisfying customer needs and being committed to continuous improvement are apparently strongly linked to shareholder value. And, a firm's image is one of the more important issues.

Box 10: Image

The image of a firm also influences shareholder value. There are many dimensions of image, and the various stakeholders are concerned with somewhat different issues. Customers may be concerned that a firm is customer driven and innovative. Employees may be concerned that a firm is most admired or a good place to work or that it has management ability. Investors may be concerned that a firm is a good corporate citizen, has good revenue growth, or is an industry leader.

A strong corporate image may directly influence shareholder value by causing investors to pay a slight premium for stock due to historic performance. A strong corporate image can influence shareholder value indirectly through customers and employees as well.

Customers often use a firm's image as a surrogate cue for product quality and service quality. A good image implies higher product and service quality and justifies a price premium. A strong corporate image helps attract the best and brightest employees and fosters more positive employee attitudes.

There are two primary influences on image. One is the performance and decision making of the firm. Over time, the actions of the firm cause stakeholders to formulate opinions. Changing those opinions is a very slow, challenging process. The second major influence on image is corporate communications.

Box 11: Corporate Communications

Corporate communications have a direct impact on a firm's image. There are four major stakeholder groups for most firms: customers, employees, investors, and the community in which the firm operates. Since each of these groups is concerned about different aspects of image, the corporate communications should be tailored to fit each constituency.

The communication with customers should stress the key drivers found in the value model. This reinforces the most important aspects of customer value. The internal communication strategy with employees should focus on the key aspects of the work environment, and the communications strategy with shareholders should focus on the aspects of investments most important to them. While each should be customized, they should also be harmonized so that there are common messages being sent out.

Model Summary

Customer loyalty and retention have emerged as important strategic topics in business. Unfortunately, loyalty is often viewed as a goal by itself without an understanding of what causes customers to stay or leave. The purpose of the model was to identify the linkages among the concepts related to customer loyalty.

The antecedents of customer loyalty are the five drivers of value: product quality, service quality, price, relationships, and image. These five areas are integrated by the customer into an overall perception of value. This value perception drives global perceptions of performance and loyalty. The implication is that, to improve loyalty, a firm must deliver good customer value.

Conversely, if a firm wants to find out why customers are defecting, the firm must find out where performance is not up to a customer's expectations. While many managers will say, "The customer switched to get a lower price," the role of price is usually overstated. Customers will use price as a reason to leave if some other aspect of value is sub par. For example, if technical support personnel are not helpful, if sales people are unresponsive, if there is no follow-up to a customer's request, the customer may say that the price is too high. In fact, the message that the customer is sending is that the service quality does not justify the price. The manager may attribute the customer defection to pricing strategy when the real problem is inadequate service delivery.

The causes of customer defection are almost always found among the drivers of customer value. However, the factors that drive customer satisfaction are seldom the factors that drive customer dissatisfaction.

TWO-FACTOR MODEL OF CUSTOMER SATISFACTION

Research conducted by Naumann & Associates indicates that customer satisfaction and customer dissatisfaction are caused by different factors. Most of the factors that cause customer dissatisfaction, whether product, service, price, or relationship characteristics, tend not to cause customer satisfaction. The absence of, or low performance on, some attributes will quickly cause customer dissatisfaction. High performance on those same attributes contributes very little to high levels of customer satisfaction. Low performance on these attributes will prevent a firm from ever reaching high levels of customer satisfaction, however.

Conversely, the factors that cause extreme customer satisfaction are usually not identified as factors that cause customer dissatisfaction. These are often the *above-and-beyond* things that a firm does for its customers. These are often activities that the customer likes but does not really expect. Thus, low performance on those attributes causing high satisfaction does not usually cause customer dissatisfaction.

Therefore, there appear to be two general categories of factors. One category consists of the hygiene factors that contribute to customer dissatisfaction. The other category consists of the delighters that contribute to extreme customer satisfaction. This relationship is depicted in Figure 5.2. IBM Rochester (see note 15) determined that there is a different set of actions to move a customer from dissatisfied to satisfied than for moving a customer from satisfied to very satisfied or delighted.

If a firm performs at a very high level in delivering the hygiene attributes, customers perceive the product as being acceptable but not spectacular. Even if a firm is delivering hygiene attributes at a Six Sigma quality level, high levels of customer satisfaction are never achieved. But, a firm must deliver hygiene attributes with a reasonable level of proficiency before the delighters become important.

Hygiene attributes collectively constitute some threshold level of performance to customers. These are sometimes referred to as *table stakes* or *minimum expectations*. Failure to meet that threshold level causes customers to become dissatisfied. Performing at a very high level on hygiene attributes might yield the customer response, "So what? You're expected to do that."

The satisfiers are those performance areas in which a firm has the opportunity to create real customer delight. If a value model contains 70 to 80 attributes, there are probably less than 10 attributes that could be viewed as satisfiers. These are usually the areas of personal contact between an employee and customer.

Figure 5.3 presents such a broadened concept. On the vertical axis are the hygiene attributes that customers expect to be delivered. These attributes could be product characteristics or service elements. They could be the delivery of a product on time, accuracy on a billing statement, or getting some expected use from a product. On the horizontal axis are the delighters. These factors are often the above-and-beyond things that employees provide for customers. They could be exceptional product quality but more often are outstanding follow-up, customer care, or presale consulting and advice.

The four corners of the matrix represent radically different situations. Regardless of the industry or type of business, a firm in the lower left corner will be in a crisis. Customer satisfaction will be low, and customer turnover will be high. Although the firm may muddle along here for a short while, the long-term outlook is bleak. Unless a firm in this corner becomes strongly committed to radical changes to get closer to the customer, it will soon be out of business.

The firm in the upper left corner has a much greater chance for survival. This firm is performing very well on the basic attributes demanded by customers. Unfortunately, however, it has neglected other attributes. The firm may be, for example, a restaurant that serves good food but has a poor atmosphere and poorly trained waiters or waitresses. The degree of competitive intensity will largely determine the survival of this firm. If the restaurant's competitors also have not achieved high customer satisfaction levels, then this firm has a chance to maintain its status quo. However, as its competitors begin to perform at a high level and deliver better value to customers, this firm's market position will quickly erode. The areas that hold potential for customer delight could be the focus of a Six Sigma team to improve the value-creating processes. The goal would be to deliver the *delighters* at a consistent, high quality level.

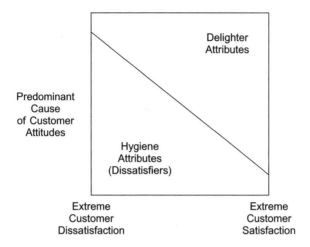

Figure 5.2 Cause of Customer Dissatisfaction and Satisfaction.

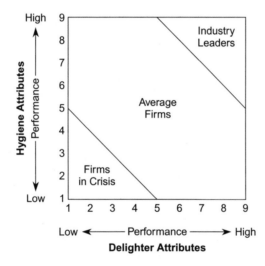

Figure 5.3 Customer Satisfaction Grid.

Firms in the bottom right corner of the matrix are in a puzzling situation. Their performance is high on some or all delighters, but hygiene factors remain deficient. Firms that have been disappointed with the market results of their total quality management efforts are probably in this condition. Tangible products may have considerably higher quality levels, but low performance on hygiene service factors may be a constraint to improving market position. The firm may complain that it has a great product, if only the customer would realize it. The customer may want higher service support. These firms are simply not delivering good value across all product or services attributes. Since firms in this corner are performing well on delighters, they have a good deal of potential. These firms simply need to be more thorough and comprehensive in their identification and delivery of hygiene attributes.

The top right corner is where the innovative, industry leaders are located. These firms have a good grasp of all customer expectations and have developed and implemented

• Creating a Good Relationship
• Product Delivery for Completeness
• Installation by Completion Date
• Establishing Two-Way Communication
• Follow-Up by Personnel
• Maintenance & Repair Professionalism
• Becoming a Customer-Driven Company
• Ordering Responsiveness
• Quality of Engineering Solutions
• Knowledge of Technical Support Personnel

Table 5.1 Ten Drivers of Satisfaction.

effective value-added delivery systems. These firms have goals of 100 percent customer satisfaction, creating customer delight, and Six Sigma quality. Firms in the top right corner that compete with firms elsewhere in the matrix leave little doubt about who the winners will be. Such innovative firms have developed a sustainable, competitive advantage.

Implicit in this model is the idea that the causes of a customer's firing a firm are found in the lower left portion of the customer satisfaction grid. Generally, the cause is low performance on attributes deemed important by the customer. To determine which attributes contribute to customer turnover, root cause analysis must be conducted. This simply means that firms must track the root causes of customer turnover, primarily through exit interviews with lost customers. The pattern of causes will quickly become evident in most cases.

The causes of customer turnover are not always uniform across market segments. What may be extremely important to one customer group may be unimportant to another customer group. Therefore, root cause studies should also be segmented by market segments or customer groupings

An actual example of the delighters and hygiene factors illustrates the distinction between the two categories of factors. The company in this example is in a high-technology business, and the customers are other businesses that are dependent upon reliable equipment.

The key drivers of satisfaction, or delighters, are presented in Table 5.1. These are the factors associated with extreme satisfaction. These factors were statistically extracted from a very comprehensive value model that included over 70 attributes.

The drivers of dissatisfaction were determined in a roughly similar manner. Multivariate statistical analysis was used to determine the factors associated with extreme dissatisfaction. The top 10 drivers of dissatisfaction are presented in Table 5.2. The only attribute that is associated with both satisfaction and dissatisfaction is *product delivery for completeness*. Most of these other hygiene factors are simply table stakes; the customers assume that they should happen. For example, having on-time product delivery may keep a customer from getting upset, but being on time does not make the customer get delighted.

The issues discussed to this point can be determined through fairly sophisticated analysis of an aggregated customer database. Specifically, customer responses to survey questions can be analyzed to identify why customers become dissatisfied. There is another approach that can be quite valuable. That approach is lost customer analysis.

- Product Delivery for Completeness
- Pricing Flexibility
- Engineering Performance for Meeting Customer Requirements
- Installation Performance for Completeness
- Personnel for Keeping Commitments
- Training Effectiveness
- Product Delivery for Being On Time
- Dispatch Personnel for Professionalism
- Installation Personnel for Technical Competence
- Personnel for Knowledge of Your Company

Table 5.2 The Top 10 Drivers of Customer Dissatisfaction.

LOST CUSTOMER ANALYSIS

Lost customer analysis requires conducting a follow-up, exit interview shortly after a customer defects. The purpose of the interview is to identify why a customer left. Normally, the interviews are conducted in person or by telephone. If the lost customers are quite important, personal interviews are most appropriate. If the customers are less important or more widely dispersed geographically, telephone interviews are probably adequate. But, before discussing interview guidelines, there are a number of other questions that must be answered.

Which Products?

Few firms produce a single product. Most produce a variety of products and services, some more important than others. Should lost customer analysis be conducted for customers of all products? It may not be worth the research costs to interview customers of relatively minor products. So, a firm must address which products are worthy of lost customer analysis.

In some cases, the analysis may not even address a specific product. Many firms with business customers use proposals to secure business. Any *lost proposals* are excellent opportunities for lost customer analysis. Finding out why proposals were lost is probably as important as finding out why customers leave.

Which Customers?

As with products, there are many customer issues that must be addressed. Customers could be end-users of a product or service or a channel intermediary, such as a distributor or retailer. Loss of a retailer could preclude ever reaching an end-user. So, a firm must decide which type of customer is most critical to long-term success.

For each type of customer, there may be some market segments that are more important than others. Also, within each segment, some customers may be far more important than others. Using the traditional ABC customer analysis, A customers, those who are quite important, may leave for totally different reasons than less important C customers.

In the retail banking industry, the three main causes of losing C customers are inconvenient hours, long lines, and minimum balance requirements. These three issues cause 60 percent of the defections of C customers. Conversely, the A customers, who generate most of a bank's profits, leave for different reasons. The three most common reasons for the defection of *A* customers are low rates of interest, rude or inattentive employees, and mistakes. These account for 63 percent of *A* defections.

While *C* customers constitute about 70 percent of the customer base, a strategy to retain *C* customers has little impact on *A* customers. Since *A* customers contribute most to profits, profitability may be only marginally affected. Conversely, a strategy to retain *A* customers has little impact on *C* customers.

In addition to the types of customers, segments, and ABC analysis, a lost customer analysis in business-to-business relationships requires that specific individuals be identified. The *best* individual in the customer organization must be interviewed. Normally, this would be a key decision maker who actually made the decision to switch suppliers. However, in some cases, a team may have made the decision, so the team may be the appropriate unit of analysis.

For lost customer analysis, the term *customer* must be clearly identified. This often requires some background research to get the names, phone numbers, and addresses.

When Does Defection Occur?

As mentioned previously, if a firm has a continuous relationship with a customer, identifying a defection is relatively easy. If a firm has service contracts with customers, failure to renew a contract may mean a defection has occurred, but not always. Some contracts are simply renewed a month or so after a contract has expired, but the expiration of the contract may trigger a lost customer interview. Likewise, a firm may fail to renew a service contract and move to a time and materials relationship. The customer is still a customer but is probably now a different type.

For products with an extended life, identifying when a defection occurs is more challenging. For example, a personal computer may have a product life of three years. Let us say that a small business has several IBM PCs. It would be very difficult for IBM to know that the next purchase was a Compaq and the next two were Micron PCs. For IBM to determine defection rates, IBM would probably conduct a survey of users from previous years to determine repurchase patterns.

In addition to the total defection of a customer, a customer may drastically reduce its purchases. A business traveler may reduce his or her flight mileage on Delta from 50,000 miles to 1000 miles and still be considered a valid customer. But something probably caused the drastic reduction in miles. If a firm has a sophisticated customer database, identifying large decreases in revenue may be possible. But, if this is only done on an annual basis, there may be a significant lag in time before the defection is detected. Therefore, continuous monitoring of large accounts is probably worthwhile, whether done through database analysis or sales force reporting.

Interview Alternatives

There are really only two research choices when conducting lost customer analysis. These are personal interviews or telephone interviews. In many respects, the exit interviews are much like a depth interview, very qualitative. Personal interviews are even more qualitative than a phone interview because a more open dialogue evolves. This usually occurs because the interviews are conducted by one or more managers from the vendor firm. Conversely, the telephone interview is often conducted by a third party, such as a research firm.

- Sales and Service
- Technical Support
- Price Competitiveness
- New Product Communication
- Relationships
- Customer Service
- Proactive Offering of Solutions
- Cost Efficiency

Table 5.3 Key Value Drivers.

The personal interviews normally last 30 to 60 minutes, while 15 to minutes 20 are more common for telephone interviews. Because the interviews are highly qualitative, they should be tape recorded if possible. If they are not taped, there should be a designated note taker. It is often difficult for the interviewer to conduct a probing interview while simultaneously taking detailed notes. Regardless of which approach is used, a detailed agenda or script should be prepared.

Personal Interview Agenda

Since the causes of customer defection are found among the drivers of customer value, the agenda should draw upon value models if possible. The customer would be asked a variety of questions that would identify the relative importance and competitive performance of each key driver. For example, a firm might have the eight key value drivers found in Table 5.3.

The customer would be asked to rate the importance of each category. This could be done by ranking the categories from 1 to 8. Or, it could be done by having the customer allocate 100 points across the categories based on the relative importance of each. The customer should also be allowed to add any categories as appropriate.

After identifying the importance of each category, the customer should be asked which are basic table stakes or hygiene factors and which are differentiators or delighters. Most customers tend to identify most of the categories as table stakes (hygiene factors). There are relatively few areas where a firm can create real customer delight.

The customer should then be asked to rate the performance of the former vendor as well as one or two *toughest competitors*. This could be done using almost any scaling technique such as 1 to 5, 1 to 10, or 0 to 100. First, the customer should identify the performance of the former vendor in each area. Then the toughest competitor, identified by name, should be evaluated, followed by a second competitor.

The latter part of the interview should include some open-ended questions. These should address more specifically why the customer left and should probe for detail. It is common for customers to identify very specific incidents that caused them to leave. In a recent study, almost exactly half of defecting customers left because of a specific negative experience while the others left because of a perception of overall low general performance.

The agenda interview may conclude by asking what it would take to win the customer back and when that might occur. Since this is often a sensitive question, it should come at the end of the interview. Face-to-face interview of a large, strategic customer that is lost is best done by the senior executive, or even the CEO level.

Telephone Interviews

A telephone interview is more structured than a personal interview, but the approach is roughly the same. The customer should be asked to identify the firm's toughest competitor, and a list of six to nine competitors is usually on the questionnaire.

The customer is then asked to rate the performance of the current supplier and the former supplier on specific attributes. The questions would address three to five global questions and 10 to 15 more specific performance areas. These specific questions would be followed by three or four open-ended questions like those at the end of the personal interview. Since these will be asked by phone, permission to tape record the discussions will be needed.

Data Analysis

The data analysis should be done on two levels. The individual customer data should be fed to the appropriate salesperson for future follow-up. This is particularly important when the customer indicates there is a good chance of returning.

Descriptive statistics should be compiled for all quantitative questions. This allows the tracking of competitive profiles. Since the data was gathered from customers that were frustrated enough to defect, there is often a rather substantial gap between the former vendor's performance and the current vendor's performance. This gap is quite an eye opener for many managers.

The open-ended comments should be evaluated through the use of content analysis. Content analysis requires that two or more people read all the verbatim comments made by customers and allocate the comments into various categories or *buckets*. The categories are most often presented in the form of bar charts in Pareto analysis.

For maximum benefit, the lost customer reports should be distributed widely in a company. The more that managers read and use the data, the more valuable the lost customer analysis.

SUMMARY

Analysis of lost customers identifies which value-creating processes are operating poorly. The performance is so bad that process outcomes cause the customers to defect and take their business elsewhere. Since about half of lost customers will identify a specific, critical incident as the cause, the Six Sigma team must link the incidents to processes and conduct root cause analysis. Then the team must redesign the process to prevent the low performance from occurring. It is very difficult for process managers to argue that process performance is fine when customers are defecting.

CASE STUDY

CUSTOMER LOYALTY ANALYSIS

With the Controls Business of Johnson Controls, Inc., transaction surveys are used to assess customer satisfaction immediately following an equipment installation of some type. Unfortunately, identifying when an installation customer is lost is difficult. If a proposal is submitted to a current customer and Johnson Controls does not get the business, the defection is apparent. But, if Johnson Controls was not asked to submit a proposal, the customer could switch without Johnson Controls being aware of the defection. There is a portion of the business in which defections are quite apparent, however.

In addition to installations, the Controls Business also provides comprehensive maintenance services for buildings. These result in professional services agreements (PSAs) or maintenance contracts. The normal duration of a PSA contract is one or two years. Unfortunately, the renewal rate is not 100 percent. So, the failure to renew a PSA contract is a good indication of a defection. However, this is not quite as clean as it may appear.

Some customers who fail to renew a contract do so one or two months later. They may have just been slow in getting the necessary authorizations and new contract signed. It may take a month or two for the renewal to finally show up on the customer database. Therefore, surveying of these lost customers can be a bit embarrassing. It is not a pleasant task to phone customers and ask why they defected and have the customers say, "We didn't. Don't you know your own customers?"

In these situations, the research firm shoulders the responsibility. They immediately apologize and say the error was theirs, not Johnson Controls, and that a simple database error was made. The interviewers are trained in how to handle this situation.

Some lost customers may not have switched to a competitor. They may have simply switched from a maintenance contract to a time and materials basis. Technically, they are still a customer but of a different type. In essence, they are maintaining their own facilities. Still, it is important for us to know *why* the customer made this type of decision.

The majority of expired contracts switch to a competitor. It is particularly important to know who they switched to and why. This data may be broken down by each Area office. Some competitors are more formidable and aggressive in some areas than in others. Therefore, the questionnaire in Appendix C is administered as soon after a defection as possible. This is normally within 30 to 60 days. The data is gathered and reported in aggregate and by area office.

The Controls Business of Johnson Controls, Inc., analyzes customer satisfaction survey data and determines "vulnerable" customers who may defect or may have already defected. The response to the question of overall satisfaction is monitored for low scores. Open-ended questions are asked to determine causes for dissatisfaction or low scores. A Customer Satisfaction Index (CSI), which is explained in the case study at the end of chapter 3, has been created and monitored as a predictor of current and future behavior. Finally, one question that is asked and closely monitored is the one that asks the customer to rate the best, second best, and third best supplier of the equipment they just purchased and installed. If a Johnson Controls customer does not rate the Controls Business as best, this is an indication of a customer that is ripe for defection.

6

Complaint Management Systems

The flight from Sydney, Australia, to Bangkok, Thailand, on the Lauda Airline's new 747 had been smooth and uneventful, with the exception of a few toilets becoming inoperable. For some reason, the new vacuum toilet system, which saved space and weight, had been prone to occasional failures, so having a few toilets out of service was not particularly alarming. However, about an hour after reaching a cruising altitude of 43,000 feet on the 14-hour flight from Bangkok to Vienna, things got worse. The flight attendant, in a cheerful voice, announced to the 300 or so passengers who had just finished the first round of beverages, "We regret to inform you that all of the toilets have become inoperable. However, for your flying convenience, we have buckets at the rear of the aircraft if mother nature calls. Please feel free to ring your flight attendant button if we can be of assistance. Have an enjoyable flight!" The passengers squirmed nervously in their seats, wondering if they were going to need to use the buckets or if they could hold out until the landing.

Imagine the reaction of Lauda Airlines CEO Nikki Lauda, the former Formula 1 world champion driver. Whether negotiating the hairpin turns of Monaco or roaring down the straightaway in Brazil at over 200 miles per hour, Nikki Lauda expected precision engineering and meticulous maintenance, an expectation that carried over to his airline. To have something as mundane as a toilet system fail was almost unthinkable.

Assume that you are the customer service manager for Lauda Airlines. What would you do to satisfy these customers? If you were the customer service manager for Boeing or the customer service manager for Boeing's supplier that designed and manufactured the toilet system, what would you do? If the response to this situation is too straightforward, let us try a few more typical customer complaints.

A customer just had his jet boat serviced at Wards Marina in Anchorage, Alaska, and was looking forward to a day of salmon fishing in the Alaskan wilderness. After a few hours' drive north of Anchorage, the boat was launched in the Susitna River, known locally as the "Big Su." The Big Su is a large glacial river with many channels, islands, and log-jams, and all parts of the river are fast and icy cold.

After going only a few miles downstream from the launch site, a bearing in the jet unit froze up. Apparently, a careless service technician forgot to grease the new bearing after installation. When a bearing seizes, the boat is basically powerless, just an awkward raft. The boat drifted sideways down the river and into a logjam, almost capsizing as it became entangled in the logs, with the water within inches of overflowing the upstream side. If the boat capsized, the current would have pulled the man and his family under the logs where drowning was highly probable. After a few harrowing minutes and some frantic chopping with an ax, the boat was freed from the logs.

The customer had to flag down a passing boat and hitch a ride back to the landing site. Then he had to drive 100 miles to Anchorage, get the necessary parts, drive the 100 miles back, and hitch another boat ride. Then he had to disassemble his jet unit and make the repairs on a sandbar. What would have been the appropriate response by Wards to mollify this customer?

As the Christmas buying season began, a western regional bank decided to increase automatically the credit limit of all its credit card holders by 15 percent. Surely, this would increase customers' ability to purchase and would create higher levels of customer satisfaction (as well as interest income). Unfortunately, a computer programmer for the bank made an error that resulted in all credit limits being automatically *lowered* to 15 percent of the credit limit.

Customers, including some of the bank's own executives, were stranded around the world. Nearly all customers suffered the embarrassment of having their credit card purchases declined. This was all accomplished by a few strokes on the keyboard. How should this situation have been handled?

Situations such as these are commonplace. Millions probably occur every day, though possibly not as memorable or severe as these. With no formal systems or guidelines for responding to customer complaints, organizational responses to these types of situations tend to be ad hoc and inconsistent. In this highly competitive business environment, customers experiencing ad hoc and inconsistent complaint handling are very much at risk.

A complaint does not have to be generated by an actual product failure or an error as in the previous examples. If a product fails to meet the customer's expectations in any way, a complaint may be caused. To a customer, an unmet expectation may be just as critical as an actual product failure. Unfortunately, some firms only offer atonement if a product is defective. This is a rather narrow, shortsighted view that may have very negative consequences.

At the other end of the continuum is the Nordstrom policy of accepting any return, no questions asked. A Nordstrom customer once returned a set of tires that the customer said had been purchased in another state. The store manager accepted the return although he knew full well that no Nordstrom store ever sold any automotive products.

ENCOURAGE COMPLAINTS!

Many firms dread hearing complaints from customers, trying to avoid any type of negative feedback. Many firms track customer complaints as a quality metric. The more complaints, the worse the performance quality. These firms are operating on the assumption that if there are no customer complaints, everything must be great. This is sometimes referred to as the *Ostrich theory*. If you bury your head in the sand, the problem will go away. Unfortunately, such an assumption can be a fatal mistake.

Depending on the industry, studies show that between 10 percent and 50 percent of consumers report that they have experienced problems recently, as illustrated in Figure 6.1. Thus, in virtually every industry, customers experience problems of some type. Customers who experience problems are 2 to 3 times as likely to quit doing business with that firm as customers who experience no problems, as shown in Figure 6.2. These studies do

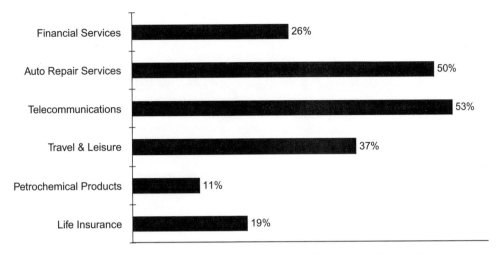

Percent of Respondents Experiencing Problem(s)

Figure 6.1 Why It Pays to Do the Job Right the First Time—Customer Problem Experience in Preceding Six Months.

Repurchase Intention

Industry	Problem	No Problem
Financial Services	40%	73%
Auto Repair Service	44%	87%
Telecommunications	60%	93%
Travel & Leisure	70%	93%
Petrochemical Productions	70%	91%
Life Insurance	69%	89%

Figure 6.2 Intent to Repurchase Is Strongly Influenced by Problems.

not differentiate between whether the customer perceives that the problems were major or minor; nor do they indicate the number of times that a problem had been experienced. The implication is that problems of any type lead to a dramatically higher probability that customers will leave.

Reinforcing these research findings are the well-known Technical Assistance Research Program (TARP) studies.[16] These were broad-based studies that examined a variety of consumer goods. The major findings of the TARP studies are presented in Figure 6.3. The major findings of the TARP studies are that most dissatisfied customers do not complain; they take their business elsewhere and tell others of their woes. If customers are satisfied with the way a complaint was handled, they remain loyal.

Another study expanded on the TARP findings. This study, done by the Service Impact Group, found that there were significant differences in customers' propensity to

- **30%** of customers with problems complain to the direct provider of the product or service
- **2–5%** of customer complaints get voiced to the headquarters level
- A satisfied customer tells **4–5** people about her or his experience
- A dissatisfied customer tells **8–10** people about her or his problem
- **70–90%** of complaining customers will do business with you again if they are *satisfied* with the way the complaint was handled;
- **20–50%** if they are *dissatisfied* with the way their complaint was handled
- Only **10–30%** of customers with problems who do **not** complain or request assistance will do business with you again
- The average business spends 5 times more, on average, to attract new customers than it does to keep old ones
- Why do customers quit?
  - **3%** move away
  - **5%** develop other friendships
  - **9%** leave
  - **14%** are dissatisfied with the product
  - **68%** quit because of an attitude of indifference toward them by the owner, manager, or some employee

Figure 6.3 Why Have Satisfied Customers?

complain across industries. These results are presented in Figure 6.4. This study reinforced the fact that most customers who are dissatisfied do not complain. IBM Rochester discovered that 12 percent of customers who were dissatisfied did not complain, even though they had spent several hundred thousand dollars on a computer system.[17]

An example may illustrate the severity of this situation. Let us assume that 40 percent of a firm's customers have experienced some type of problem over the past 6 months. Let us further assume that 50 percent of customers experiencing problems formulate an intention to switch suppliers (and this is a conservative figure). This means that 20 percent of a firm's customers are ready to switch suppliers and may be actively searching for an alternative.

However, if 10 percent of customers with problems actually complain, this is only 4 percent ($.10 \times .40 = .04$) of the total customer base. Most firms would make the assumption that the remaining 96 percent must be satisfied. Unfortunately, nothing could be farther from the truth.

So, the sad fact is that actual customer complaints are really only the tip of a very large iceberg. For most firms, the size and shape of the iceberg of customer discontent lies hidden beneath a sea of relative tranquility. The magnitude of customer discontent will only be exposed after the firm's ship strikes the iceberg and begins to hemorrhage—not blood, but revenue. Trying to make repairs after the collision with the iceberg is like trying to repair a sinking ship. Efforts are often too little and far too late.

The way in which complaints are handled has a direct impact on the loyalty of customers. To again refer to the Service Impact Group research (Figure 6.5), customers who have either major or minor problems and do not complain have a very low repurchase intent, 9 percent and 37 percent, respectively. If customers complain but the complaints go unresolved, the repurchase intent improves somewhat. But, if complaints are resolved, especially if the resolution is fast, the customer indicates a high repurchase intent, up to 95 percent.

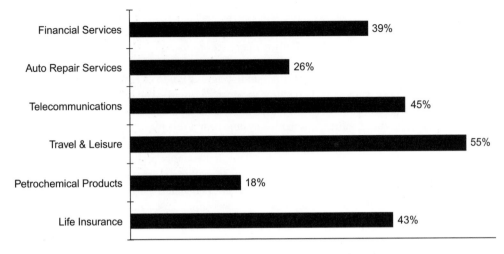

Percent of Unarticulated Complaints

Figure 6.4 Many Customers Do Not Complain.

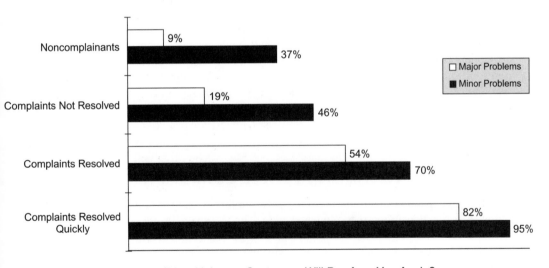

Figure 6.5 How Many of Your Unhappy Customers Will Buy from You Again?

Another study had similar results. In this study, 69 percent of customers had experienced no problems. These customers had a repurchase intent of 87 percent. The remaining 31 percent of customers had experienced a problem. The customers who had experienced a problem and who did not complain had a repurchase intent of 47 percent. If the customer complained and the complaint was handled poorly, only 23 percent of customers would repurchase. If the customer complained and the customer was satisfied, the repurchase intent was 96 percent.

The message from these studies is worth repeating. Customers who have problems and do not complain have low levels of loyalty. Customers who do complain and have their complaints handled poorly can become even less loyal. Customers who complain and have their complaints handled well are even more loyal than a customer who experiences no problems. Unfortunately, in one study, only 11 percent of customers were satisfied with the way their complaints were handled. Fully 89 percent of customers who complained were dissatisfied with the response.

So, the overall goal of a customer complaint system *is not* to effectively respond to the vocal minority of 5 percent to 10 percent of the customer base. The overall goal of a customer complaint system is to determine the shape, size, and cause of the complaint iceberg. Quite simply, this requires a proactive system, not a reactive system.

In order to be proactive, a firm must understand *who* does or does not complain and *why* those customers do or do not complain. The first issue is probably a little easier to address than the second. Customers who complain are seldom representative of a total customer base. Consumers who complain tend to be better educated, have higher incomes, are younger, and are part of larger households than noncomplainers. With regard to personality, complainers tend to be independent, assertive, imaginative, self-sufficient, politically committed, and self-confident.

Very little data exists about complaint behavior in a business-to-business context. However, it appears that business customers that are more innovative, creative, and demanding tend to complain more frequently.

Whether the complainer is a consumer or a business customer, both groups share a common characteristic. Complainers have an expectation that the supplier firm will actually *do* something as a result of the complaint. This expectation often has two parts. First, the customer has an expectation regarding *what* should be done to correct the immediate problem. This also includes an expectation of *how* the complaint should be handled. Second, customers often have ideas about what should be done to prevent similar problems in the future. Customers may expect to see a change in processes or procedures as a result of their efforts. In effect, these customers are saying, "Look, here is something you can do to improve your business!" They are, in many cases, giving you one last chance to correct the situation before defecting.

WHY DON'T PEOPLE COMPLAIN?

The reason customers with problems *do not* complain is another story. The most common reason is that it is just too much trouble. This is especially the case for firms that require customers to put the complaint in writing. For many firms, the requirement to put complaints in writing is just a way to discourage customers from voicing any complaint at all.

Another reason for not complaining is that the customer does not know where to complain. After trying several phone calls, a customer usually gives up. As an example, a consumer attempted to complain about an arcane business practice at one of the leading grocery chains in the United States. When the consumer called the corporate office to complain after normal business hours because of time zone differences, the phone call was routed to the front security console. The company did not have a complaint function of any type.

Another reason for customers to remain silent is the expectation that complaining would not do any good. The customer may feel that the firm just does not care and would not make any changes. Or, the customer may fear that complaints would cause worse service in the future.

The Chevrolet Division of General Motors provides a good example of a customer complaint system that integrates many of the preceding issues. There are over 36 million Chevrolet vehicles on the road, sold by a dealer network of over 5000 dealers. In the past, when a customer had a complaint, it was handled by the local dealer. With over 5000 dealers, there was a good deal of inconsistency in the way that complaints were handled. If the local dealer was unable to resolve the complaint, the customer was referred to one of Chevrolet's 44 branch offices. Each branch office maintained a small customer service staff that handled complaints as they saw fit. This decentralized approach resulted in a fragmented, inconsistent response to customer complaints. Chevrolet had no systematic way to collect and analyze the customer feedback. Chevrolet simply did not know the frequency of complaints. They had no way of identifying the persistent causes of problems.

As a result, Chevrolet centralized its customer service into a single Customer Assistance Center. Chevrolet found that about 40 percent of customers with problems would actually complain. But, 80 percent of those customers expressed an intent to repurchase if the complaint was handled in a professional, efficient, concerned manner. Interestingly, the complaint did not have to be fully resolved for a repurchase intent to occur. Essentially, the customer simply wanted people to listen and do what they could to help.

Of the 60 percent of customers with problems who did not complain, only 10 percent of those would repurchase. So, for every 100 customers experiencing problems, 60 remained silent. Of those, 6 would repurchase, the other 54 would buy a competitor's product. Thirty-two of the 40 customers that actually complained were willing to repurchase. The message to Chevrolet was clear: They needed to get all customers with problems to complain!

To provide easy customer access, Chevrolet installed a toll free 800 phone line to the Customer Assistance Center. The number is printed in owners' manuals, sales literature, posters in the sales area, and most phone books in the United States. The number is available through 800 information and has been publicized in newspapers and magazines.

The Chevrolet Assistance Center now gets over 5000 calls daily, handled by a staff of over 200 service representatives. The normal waiting time for customers is only 5 seconds, and 80 percent of the calls are answered on the first ring.

Chevrolet's predominant goal was to get *all* customers with problems to break the silence and open a dialogue with the company. The second goal was to then handle the customer complaints in a professional, efficient manner.

The experience of Chevrolet is not unique. In the first two years of Mazda Motor Company's toll free 800 customer service phone line, over 437,000 customers contacted the company. While not all of these were complaints, this represents 14 percent of the 3.2 million Mazda owners in the United States. The majority of these calls were from owners of cars less than two years old. So Mazda was able to open a dialogue with a significant portion of its recent buyers.

The implication from all of this is that a firm must develop a system of easy access for customers and publicize it extensively. A company must not sit back and wait for customers to complain. A firm must proactively *encourage* complaints. And, once a customer does complain, the firm should dazzle the customer with the response and close the loop and say, "Thank-you for letting us know where we need improvement!" As expressed earlier, a measurement system that focuses on the number of complaints received, with a goal of zero, is not a good strategy. Although a measurement system should be established to assess the effectiveness of the complaint management system, it should consider some improvement in the complaint rate such as an improvement of the number of complaints received normalized by the number of products shipped or services performed, for example. It should also include measurements for complaint resolution time as well as customer's satisfaction with the complaint resolution. Further examples of what components and measurements ought to be included, or at least considered, are discussed in the following section about characteristics of world-class complaint systems.

CHARACTERISTICS OF A WORLD-CLASS COMPLAINT SYSTEM

Regardless of the industry, the nature of the complaints, or volume of complaints handled, all good customer complaint systems share some common characteristics. However, since customer complaint systems must be adapted to fit the corporate culture and the customer base, there is no one best approach for each characteristic. The following discussions illustrate the findings of several best-in-class benchmarking studies.

AT&T found four major characteristics of excellent complaint-handling systems. These common characteristics are presented in Table 6.1. While these characteristics are stated rather generally, they are consistent with other benchmarking studies. The International Benchmarking Clearinghouse study identified eight common characteristics of complaint-handling systems (Table 6.2). By combining these benchmarking studies, eight common characteristics emerge (Table 6.3).

Easy Access: How Customers Want to Complain

Customers should have easy access to a complaint-handling system. But, in order to have easy access, a firm must know how customers prefer to complain. At Mazda Motor Co., 64 percent of complaints were through phone calls to a toll free 800 number or an executive, 29 percent were on a mailed customer satisfaction survey, 6 percent were made in response to a delivery phone survey, and 1 percent were in the form of letters. Conversely, Hertz has 80 percent of the complaints made in person at the rental counter, 10 percent on comment cards, 7 percent in complaint letters, and 3 percent by phone calls. For a firm to provide easy access, these types of preferences must be understood.

Customer complaints can be made to customer contact personnel, through channel members, through the mail, by phone, over E-mail, by fax, or directly to executives. In extreme situations, complaints could come through Better Business Bureaus or government agencies. Or, the complaints could be expressed on a customer satisfaction survey or a payment invoice. A good customer complaint system allows customer input to quickly enter the system, regardless of where it originates.

British Airways has video booths in Heathrow Airport so that passengers can express their attitudes immediately after completing their flight. Marriott has a 24-hour customer service hotline designed to solicit immediate feedback from customers while they are still in the hotel. Many firms have installed suggestion boxes to solicit ideas for improvement from customers. In all of these examples of easy access, customers generally identify areas where they have experienced problems of some type.

To this point, we have seen that businesses need to actively *encourage* customers to complain if they experience problems. Businesses must make it easy for customers to lodge a complaint through whatever means is convenient. The remainder of this discussion focuses on what should be done *after* the complaint is received.

- The champion must participate in and dedicate financial support to the complaint group.
- The company vision for the future, company culture, company attitude, and policy toward its customers must be understood by all complaint representatives.
- The complaint-handling job requires full-time, dedicated employees whose sole responsibility is to process customer complaints, manage the day-to-day operation, and report customer information to the rest of the company.
- Each complaint representative must be connected to the computerized complaint-tracking system for easy access to past and present customer data.

Table 6.1 AT&T Benchmarking Study: Characteristics of Excellent Complaint-handling Systems.

- Executive Champion/Management Commitment
- Team-Based Structure That Includes Various Departments
- Solicits Complaints by Providing Incentives to the Customer and Accessibility
- Database That Identifies Trends & Allows Root Cause Analysis
- Trains Employees in Interpersonal & Technical Skills
- Empowers Employees by Giving Authority for Immediate Response
- Provides Psychological/Physical Atonement
- Follow-Up

Table 6.2 International Benchmarking Clearinghouse: Complaint-handling System Characteristics.

- **Easy Access.** Customers should have many ways to express complaints.
- **Fast Response.** Customers should receive fast, personalized acknowledgment and resolution.
- **No Hassle.** The complaint system should not require excessive documentation and effort.
- **Empowered Employees.** Employees must be empowered to resolve customer problems.
- **Employee Staffing and Training.** Employees, particularly customer service employees, must receive both technical product training and interpersonal skills training.
- **Customer Database.** The firm should have a computerized, accessible database on all customers.
- **Follow-Up.** Follow-up with the customer should occur to ensure that problems have been resolved.
- **Organization Commitment.** Top management must commit resources and attention to complaint resolution, and an executive champion should be evident.

Table 6.3 Key Characteristics of a Customer Complaint System.

Fast Responses

A good complaint system provides fast, personalized response. When Solectron, a Baldrige Award winner, receives complaints, the customers are contacted within 24 hours. The contacts are normally made by phone, or fax if that fails. Solectron acknowledges the complaints, thanks the customers for expressing themselves, and seeks any necessary clarification. Within one week, Solectron gets back to the customers and says, "Here is what caused the problem, and here is how we changed our processes to prevent the same problem from happening again." Solectron also has a no-hassle return policy so customers can easily return any defective merchandise.

Solectron's system illustrates the two components of fast response. The first issue is simply acknowledging that the complaint was received and that the business is investigating the problem. The acknowledgment should be personalized to the customer if at all possible. But even the dreaded form letter to the generic "Dear Customer" is better than nothing. And doing nothing is the option many firms choose when handling complaints.

In a recent study of large consumer products firms, nearly 25 percent of customers received no response to their complaints. The perceptions of corporate image held by those customers plummeted across all six dimensions measured (fairness, satisfaction, reputation, interest, courtesy, and quality). About 25 percent of customers received only a letter responding to their complaints. These customers perceived the corporate image to be far better, 20 to 30 percentage points higher, than customers receiving no response. About half of the customers received a letter and a free item such as a product replacement, some type of coupon, or a refund check. These customers held a corporate image that was better than customers receiving only a letter, by a margin of about 10 percentage points.

For customers receiving a response of any type, a quick response resulted in a better image than a slow response by a margin of 2 to 10 percentage points. The implication of all this is that a firm should quickly respond to *all* complaints, if only to acknowledge the receipt of the complaint.

This brings us to the second aspect of fast response. A firm must resolve the complaint quickly in some way. The complaint resolution could take many forms, from psychological to material atonement. *Psychological atonement* occurs when the customer service employee admits there is a problem, that a mistake was made, and/or that something happened that was not right. The employee might say to the customer, "You're right, there was a problem, I am sorry. What can I do to help?" Psychological atonement is calming to the customers because the customers often feel they will have to have a battle to get resolution of the problem. For effective psychological atonement, the employee must actively listen to the customer and personally apologize for the problem. The employee should create a sense of urgency to quickly solve the problem by empathizing with the customer's situation. If possible, the employee should take immediate action by offering physical or material atonement. The *physical or material atonement* is saying, "Now let me do something to correct the problem." That could be a complimentary night stay in a hotel, a free meal, or whatever it may be in the situation. For example, if an airline loses your baggage temporarily, some will give the customer $25 certificates.

When deciding the appropriate resolution, a firm should weigh the cost of satisfying the customer versus the cost of losing the customer. Normally, the lifetime value of a customer is far greater than the resolution cost. But, whatever option a firm chooses, the choice should be made quickly.

IBM Rochester has implemented a complaint measurement system that does not assign an arbitrary date to complaint resolution time (see note 17). When complaints are received and assigned to an owner, such as an engineer or programmer, the customers are asked for their expectation of the complaint resolution time. Usually, this is negotiated between the customer and the engineer/programmer, once the problem is better understood. For instance, if a design change is required, the problem may not be resolved for several months—until the new design is released. This process helps set customers' expectations and prevents the organization from becoming internally focused. The Malcolm Baldrige National Quality Award criteria suggest that a good complaint management system includes an assessment of its effectiveness and closes the loop with the customer to ensure customer satisfaction with complaint resolution, including complaint resolution time.

No Hassles

The complaint system should not be an endurance course, rewarding only those customers who persevere. One of the larger U.S.-based airlines advertised that it had partnership arrangements with several foreign airlines so flyers could get credit for mileage flown on those foreign airlines. The customer planned a trip from the United States to New Zealand and Australia. At ticketing, he gave the frequent flyer card to the ticket agent at the U.S. airline who said she could give credit only for the U.S. miles. She said he should give his mileage number to the foreign airline. At the ticket counter in Los Angeles, he attempted to give the frequent flyer card to the ticket agent for the foreign airline. She had no idea what to do, so she called a supervisor. The supervisor provided a form that needed to be completed for each leg of the flight. The form was to be given to the person who takes the tickets at the gate. When the customer tried to give the form to the person at the gate, the agent said he had never seen the form before and told the passenger to hang onto it. No one at any of the foreign cities would take the form.

After returning to the United States, the customer complained to the original ticketing personnel, who said that he was welcome to complain to the company if he wanted. The customer complained that he had just spent the last 10 minutes explaining the situation to them; after all, they are the airline. The employees simply said, "We don't handle complaints, that's home office." So the customer asked for the tollfree customer service number. The person at the desk said, "We don't have one. We want complaints in writing." The customer was instructed to write a letter explaining everything, include all boarding pass stubs for documentation, and then send it to the home office. The customer growled, "You've already got my itinerary on your computer." The person at the desk responded that it was the airline's policy.

After complying with the request for documentation, the customer sent everything to the customer service department. The customer never heard back from the airline. When the customer made his next trip a month later to the South Pacific, he flew on a different airline.

Unfortunately, situations such as these are not terribly unusual. These types of situations are what makes Wal-Mart's "no hassle return policy" or Quill Corporation's "100 percent satisfaction guarantee" so effective with customers. When customers have bad experiences with one firm, those customers are more appreciative of good service at another firm.

For firms utilizing a channel of distribution with several intermediaries, a *reverse channel* should be designed. Most channels are designed for the outbound flow of products to the ultimate customer or consumer. The channel should also be designed for the return flow of defective or returned merchandise. For most consumers, it is easier to simply return merchandise to the retailer where the item was purchased rather than ship the item to a customer service center. But for such a no hassle system to work, the entire channel must be coordinated.

Research shows that unconditional, no hassle return policies are seldom abused by customers. Many firms have found that by advertising such policies, their corporate images have been significantly enhanced.

Empowered Employees

In order for fast, no hassle response to occur, employees must be empowered to make decisions on the spot. Installing bureaucratic hurdles and approval processes slows responses and typically increases the burden of proof on customers.

Empowering employees is more of a corporate attitude than a set of actions. Empowerment requires that *managers* have faith in the ability of *employees* to make the right decisions. At one end of the continuum is McDonald's empowering employees to make sure customers are satisfied, providing a free meal if necessary. At the other end of continuum is Lexus empowering dealers to do "whatever it takes" to satisfy a Lexus owner. In both cases, no approval from higher-ups is necessary. Ritz-Carlton employees can spend up to $2500 to resolve a customer complaint.

One aspect of empowerment is behavioral. It is a firm recognizing that it has good employees capable of making good decisions. The firm not only *allows* employees to make decisions but *encourages* employees to proactively respond to customers, and the firm then *recognizes* outstanding customer care.

In addition to empowering employees to act, employees must be given guidelines and parameters to assist their decision making. For some firms, this may mean a certain dollar limit for authority, giving employees flexibility within that range. For other firms like Marriott, employees are told that their job is "to ensure that guests experience excellent service and hospitality." Marriott employees are given wide latitude in achieving that goal.

The issue of empowerment is not restricted to customer service employees. Certainly, empowering customer service employees is important. But all employees that have customer contact need to be aware of the customer complaint system, guidelines, and procedures. All of these employees must be empowered to make decisions quickly to resolve customer complaints.

Employee Staffing and Training

Employee staffing and training are critical aspects of any corporate activity, and customer complaint handling is no exception. A customer service department requires good, well-trained employees, not low-skilled, part-time workers. Many companies make customer service an initial career track starting point.

Hewlett-Packard (H-P), like many other firms, staffs customer service departments with college graduates. Within H-P, customer service positions lead to careers in marketing, product development, sales, quality, and human resources. After two years in customer service, employees have a thorough understanding of how important satisfying the customer is. By making customer service a career starting point, H-P also sends the message to the entire organization that customer service is important.

Training in customer complaint handling should not be restricted to just customer service employees. All customer-contact employees need to understand the company policies and procedures. Therefore, the complaint system needs to be well marketed within the firm to all employees. For most firms, this means a formal training effort that explains the how, what, and why of the customer complaint handling system.

The more difficult training challenge lies with comprehensive training of the customer service staff. The first challenge is deciding how much training is appropriate. General Motors requires 4 weeks, Federal Express requires 5 weeks, and H-P requires 4 weeks. For these firms, this is just the initial training for new hires. These firms also have an extensive array of ongoing group and individual training.

The group training addresses issues common to all customer service personnel such as product characteristics, system changes, and so forth. The individualized training is based on each employee's strengths, weaknesses, and career aspirations. Firms like Dow Chemical and H-P develop catalogs of courses from which customer service and other employees can choose. While most of these courses are delivered internally, external courses and seminars are also available. But the training is not restricted to just courses.

Customer service personnel can be included on site visit teams so they gain a firsthand understanding of the problems facing the customers. They can also be involved in cross-training such as production, new product development, and quality improvement so they can see how customer input can be used in these areas. Intuit, the creators of the popular Quicken financial software, has a *Follow Me Home* project in which customers allow product engineers into their homes as the customer loads the software and begins to use the product. It has been a great way to see the issues from the customers' perspectives, as they deal with something seemingly simple from an engineers viewpoint!

A strong argument could be made that customer service personnel need more extensive training than most employees, since their job is inherently more diverse, requiring a broader range of skills. For good recovery to customer problems, an organization must develop a strong, well-trained customer service function. The question that logically emerges is, *What type of training is best?*

Most customer service training falls into one of two broad categories: behavioral and technical. The behavioral training deals with communication and interpersonal skills. The behavioral training for General Motors includes topics such as defusing angry customers, stress management, time management, negotiation, and interpersonal communication. This training is delivered through a combination of classroom instruction, role playing, and experiential exercises. The goal of the behavioral training is to improve the service representative's interpersonal skills so that the interaction with the customer moves toward a *win-win* situation instead of the initial adversarial position where most complaints begin.

Many of the phone calls to customer service centers are not complaints. At General Motors, about 40 percent of calls are complaints; the rest are inquiries about company products or policies. The implication is that customer service personnel need to know much more than how to resolve a customer complaint. This leads to the need for service reps to be well versed in technical areas.

At the Hewlett-Packard Network Printer Customer Support Center, over 600 employees receive extensive technical training in the installation and operation of new products before the new products are released. Each new introduction brings a flood of customer inquiries. H-P employees also receive extensive training in various software packages such as word processing, graphics, and spreadsheets since each program has unique peculiarities with its interaction with printers. Knowing a great deal about only printers would be woefully inadequate. Therefore, an employee must be well trained in technical product features, in addition to being trained about other types of products as well.

Since many customer contacts to service centers are not complaints, Monsanto found that sales training was very beneficial. Customer service personnel receive training in competitive strengths and weaknesses, sales promotion, pricing structures, and delivery schedules. The customer service people have been very successful at sales efforts and now work closely with marketing and distribution.

Technical training can include company policies, procedures, computer system training, and product knowledge. Customer service personnel need to know much more than just product features to be effective.

Extensive training of many types must be provided for employees handling customer complaints. And, all employees must be trained in the handling of customer complaints. Computer applications, the next characteristic to be discussed, are closely related to the training issue.

Customer Databases

The trend in organizational handling of customer complaints is to centralize the operation to one location. This has occurred primarily through technological advances in computer hardware, software, and communication systems.

Virtually every firm should have a computerized customer database accessible to customer service personnel. Such a database should have all of the traditional demographic and sales histories, but the account should also have a section for all customer service contacts. For example, at Cellular One, all customer service contacts are recorded. The service rep knows when the last contact was, what the problem was, and when and how the problem was resolved. Each new contact is added to the customer's database.

An important aspect of a complaint database is the bucketing of individual complaints into various categories. By having predetermined categories, the data analysis is much easier. For example, the Hertz database has over 20 categories such as mechanical/safety, vehicle cleanliness, wait time for a vehicle, incorrect reservation, rate misquote, and so on. Diamond Shamrock also uses over 20 categories such as rude employees, employee attire, fuel problems, dirty restrooms, and so on. Some companies have well over 50 categories. For example, AlliedSignal uses seven broad categories with over 50 more specific buckets. This complaint data is a key input to Six Sigma teams that are trying to define process performance parameters.

The complaints should not go only to the customer database, however. The complaint data should go to engineering and new product development. The engineers can get daily and weekly reports on the problems being experienced by customers. This type of feedback clearly identifies areas of needed product or service improvements. H-P has a similar system called Spirit that feeds current customer data into new product development teams.

A key feature of many complaint systems is an exception report. The computer automatically identifies which complaints have not been resolved in a certain time period such as 24 hours or seven days. For example, Texas Instruments has a standard that 95 percent of inquiries get response within 2 hours. Related to the computerized database is the call management system. At Quill Corporation, with a volume of over 7000 calls daily, the goal is to have a delay period of less than 15 seconds. At General Motors, the normal delay is

5 seconds with 80 percent of calls answered in the first ring. At H-P, the employees know how many calls are in the queue, the average hold time, and the longest hold time.

Some companies design their phone systems so that calls are routed directly to line managers. In other companies, customers on hold for 30 or 45 seconds will leave their name and number and be phoned back within 30 minutes or an hour. The technological capability exists for firms to design their direct-dial systems any way they wish.

Polaroid has implemented a toll free line for the hearing impaired. Many firms have hired bilingual or multilingual service staff to respond to minorities such as people of Hispanic, Chinese, or Korean descent. This is a particular concern for multinational corporations, since many countries have a high degree of linguistic diversity. Customer service centers in Europe often have over a dozen languages available on a menu.

Technological advances in hardware, software, and telecommunications have enabled firms to develop integrated customer databases that facilitate high levels of personalized service. Any firm that does not have such a database will soon be at a competitive disadvantage.

Follow-Up

Another characteristic of a world-class complaint system is follow-up to close the communication loop. This means that someone contacts the customer to determine if the problem has been resolved to the customer's satisfaction. In many cases, the company may think the problem has been resolved but the customer has a quite different view.

A well-known Fortune 500 firm conducted a transaction survey each month for its larger business customers. During the course of normal telephone surveying, dissatisfied and/or angry customers were easily identified. Per company policy, dissatisfied customers were subject to a *hot sheet* escalation to an appropriate person in a field office. The field office employee was supposed to contact the customer and resolve the problem. During one of the telephone interviews, one of the customers cynically commented that the supplier had never followed up before and he did not expect them to start now.

To determine if the cynical customer was accurate, the research firm, without client approval or funding, conducted a follow-up with hot sheet customers after a 30-day period. After tracking the follow-up for 3 months, the research firm compiled a brief research report that indicated which customers should have been contacted, which field service employees had been notified, and which employees had or had not contacted the customer. Fully 80 percent of hot sheet customers had not been contacted by the field service employees to resolve the problem.

The senior management in the company initially wanted to fire some employees. Cooler heads prevailed, and the brief report was sent to all employees. When the employees saw their names in the report, they were furious. However, the company made it clear that a follow-up contact would be made after all hot sheet escalations. Within a few months, the resolution of problems went from 20 percent to almost 100 percent.

The implications of this example are relevant for almost any organization. Following up to ensure resolution sends a strong message to both employees and customers that quickly resolving problems is important. Solectron follows up with customers after 7 days. Johnson Controls follows up after 2 weeks. H-P wants 90 percent of the customer's concerns to be answered on the first call. If the follow-up results are linked to the customer complaint database, it will become very easy to evaluate the effectiveness of the complaint-handling system.

Organization Commitment

As is evident from the preceding discussions, high-quality customer complaint handling will not result from superficial, ad hoc support. An organization must be strongly committed to allocate enough resources for staffing, training, and support systems. The more innovative firms approach complaint handling as an investment rather than an expense.

L. L. Bean, as with many other companies, has found that customers who complain are more loyal after the complaint is resolved than the average customer. As a result, employees are told to do whatever the customer asks. Only higher levels of management have the authority to say *no* to a customer. L. L. Bean has made a significant investment in and commitment to its system of encouraging and resolving customer complaints.

One of the primary indicators of organizational commitment is the presence of an *executive champion.* This was evident in the AT&T benchmarking study presented earlier. The champion could have a title of *Customer Care* or *Customer Advocate* or *V.P. of Customer Relations.* Whatever the title, the individual should be highly visible in the company. Lew Platt, the former CEO of H-P, had a staff of senior managers that dealt directly with him to resolve customer complaints.

SUMMARY

An organization's complaint management system is one of the key processes that needs to work effectively. All the actions in the world cannot make up for a poor, or nonexistent complaint management system.

Customer complaints do more damage to a firm's reputation and image if the complaint is not registered with the firm. Bad news spreads fast, and disgruntled customers are usually eager to tell others about their misfortune and bad experiences. Therefore, a firm should approach customer complaints proactively, putting out the spark of customer discontent before it becomes a raging inferno that eats market share.

Customer complaints are opportunities, opportunities to identify overlooked problems, opportunities to drive continuous improvement, opportunities to retain dissatisfied customers. Customer complaints are not something to be dreaded and avoided at all costs! That is a 1970s and 1980s way of looking at the problem—bury your head in the sand, and maybe the problem will go away.

Companies must proactively seek out, solicit, and *encourage* customers to complain. Thus, complaint-handling systems must be inherently proactive in nature, not reactive. The complaint system must be easily accessible, designed for no hassle, fast response. Employees must be fully empowered to resolve problems, supported by comprehensive training and computerized support systems. The whole organization must be committed to customer satisfaction and customer retention. Such a commitment means a significant allocation of resources to effectively handling complaints and enhancing customer loyalty. But the alternative, ignoring customer complaints, carries an even greater cost. That cost is called survival.

A company needs to measure the effectiveness of its complaint management system. The goal should not be *zero* complaints, but the measurement system should allow for some determination of improvement over time. For instance, the volume of complaints could be normalized by the number of products shipped or services performed. The measurement system should also assess the time it takes to resolve complaints, as this is a critical customer satisfier. Finally, an organization should look at how its complaint management system can be made to be more effective by soliciting direct feedback from customers on parameters such as their satisfaction with complaint resolution, including complaint resolution time.

| **CASE STUDY** |  |

COMPLAINT HANDLING

Complaints from customers can come in various ways. A customer can complain to an employee, a customer can phone or write in, or a customer can complain during the customer satisfaction survey process.

The Controls Business of Johnson Controls, Inc., attempts to capture all complaints and bring them to resolution within 2 weeks. The resolution time has changed from 30 days to 14 days based upon customer input. In many cases, an immediate action is performed to rectify a customer situation such as ordering a part or scheduling a service call. But a final resolution is to be communicated to the customer through a formal Failure Analysis Report (FAR) within 14 days.

All complaints are supposed to be entered into a database so that frequency and magnitude of various problems can be tracked. The difficulty in assuring that all complaints are captured and recorded usually occurs when a customer complains outside a formal system such as through a survey or when a service call is placed. When a customer complains directly to an employee, the employee usually takes ownership of the problem and tries to bring it to resolution. If the problem can be handled locally, the complaint data often does not get entered into the system. Certainly, taking ownership and resolving complaints is good, but it is still necessary to determine what caused the issue in the first place so processes can be improved. Additionally, Pareto analysis of complaint data is used to prioritize process improvements and to select Six Sigma projects.

If a customer complains by phone or writing, the customer is immediately contacted to let him or her know that Johnson Controls is aware of the problem and to apologize. The customer is also informed of the status of the complaint. The complaint information is transferred to the local Area office since most problem resolution must be done locally. The local office has responsibility for reaching resolution with the customer. Two weeks from the original complaint, the customer will get a follow-up call to ensure that the complaint has been brought to resolution. If it has not, which is rare, it is then escalated for priority handling.

The Customer Dissatisfaction Alert (CDA) process is used to handle customer dissatisfaction data from surveys conducted by the research consultant, Naumann & Associates. A CDA can be generated by low scores on surveys or by a request for contact during the interview. Naumann & Associates transfers the complete survey results and any customer comments within minutes of the interview with the customer electronically to a contact person in the Controls Business headquarters office in Milwaukee, Wisconsin. The CDA information is then transferred to the Area offices for follow-up. Normally, the CDA is in the Area office within one or two hours of the customer interview. The local office then immediately contacts the customer to resolve the issue.

This has resulted in a few interesting situations. The customer satisfaction survey process is not *blind* or anonymous. The Controls Business wants to know what each customer feels about Johnson Controls, Inc. However, some customers assume that the survey is anonymous and occasionally give low satisfaction ratings. A few customers have been a bit embarrassed to receive a follow-up from Johnson Controls, Inc., within hours of the interview. On a person-to-person basis, these customers were much less willing to share their negative perceptions. But, at the very least, the customer knows that Johnson Controls, Inc., cares about their attitudes and takes the survey process very seriously.

All complaints that are formally received are categorized and logged in the *ProbTrak database.* This is a homegrown tool that uses Access software as its base. The database allows analysis of problems based upon a number of factors including Area office, customer name, problem type, and severity. Analysis of the data allows for determination of pervasive issues. Problems are categorized based upon severity, and some of the problems in the ProbTrak database are actually customer requirements that will not be addressed until future designs or product releases. An overdue report is generated and published weekly. This report identifies any problems that have gone beyond the resolution date, usually 14 days. The owner is automatically notified before a problem goes on the overdue report, usually in no less than 24 hours. Management is also identified and notified of overdue problems. There is a built-in escalation system used for problems that are not addressed, and the next layer of management is copied when resolution dates are further missed.

7

Building Relationships with Key Accounts

M ost organizations have a well-defined customer base. Within the customer base, there are usually some very valuable, important, key accounts. These customers often generate the majority of the firms' profits and/or revenues. Although they may constitute only 10 percent, 20 percent, or even 30 percent of the customer base, they may produce 70 percent, 80 percent, or 90 percent of total revenues. They often buy in larger quantities, and, in many cases, these are more innovative, larger customers. These customers have expectations of better product quality, better service quality, and more competitive pricing. While these customers are critical to a firm's success, they are typically much more demanding.

Since these customers are extremely important to a firm's success and since they have higher expectations, administering a normal customer satisfaction survey is insufficient to represent them adequately. Even when the survey results for key accounts are segmented out from the average customer base, survey statistics often do not capture their voice completely. Therefore, the key accounts need a different, more customized approach. This is further accentuated by another trend among many firms.

Many of the larger firms are moving toward supply chain management. Firms are attempting to integrate the whole value-creating chain more fully. An initial step in supply chain management is the elimination of lower quality suppliers. For example, Xerox and Motorola have reduced their supply base by 80 percent to 90 percent, keeping only those that are world-class suppliers. The more innovative firms then foster deeper, closer relationships with the remaining suppliers. In fact, the quality of relationship has emerged as an important criteria in supplier evaluations in the past few years.

In order to have a good relationship with customers, a firm must deliver all aspects of customer value. The five major drivers of customer value are product quality, service quality, price, image, and the quality of relationships. Product quality has been a universal concern for quite a while. Regardless of the explicit strategies used to maintain it, product quality has become an area of sophistication for most firms. Good product quality is now a basic expectation of customers. Delivering high product quality, in most industries, does not differentiate a firm from its competitors. Many companies are paying more attention to service quality as well—response time, technical support, and those types of issues. Service quality remains an area in which firms can effectively differentiate themselves from the competition.

Most companies are also increasingly concerned with pricing strategies, making sure to develop competitive prices, logical price breaks, and more flexible price structures. Likewise, image is often the result of a well-developed program using advertising and promotional messages. These messages are usually concept tested for their effectiveness before media campaigns are rolled out.

The fifth element of customer value is the quality of relationships. Relationships are those personal, organizational linkages between people in the customer organization and people in the supplier organization. While there are explicit strategies to develop the other four aspects of value, there are seldom any specific plans to develop better customer relationships. Developing good relationships is often viewed as the responsibility of sales or marketing; or, even worse, relationships with customers are just supposed to naturally evolve. But, to deliver good customer value, all five of these elements must be harmonized into an effective delivery system. Letting one element evolve ad hoc will undermine the total value proposition.

This chapter presents a systematic, structured approach to capture the voice of the key accounts. This approach is the *Relationship Builder Process*. The Relationship Builder Process integrates relationships into the other elements of customer value in a way that explicitly recognizes the importance of key accounts. The 15 steps in the process are presented in Figure 7.1.

RELATIONSHIP BUILDER PROCESS

The Relationship Builder Process has 15 steps, but the steps are not discreet, completely independent activities. Instead, there are interactions and feedback that cause changes and modifications of the various steps. As a firm customizes the process to fit a particular customer, there are learnings that lead to refinements and improvements. Firms that use the Relationship Builder Process should modify the process to fit their culture as closely as possible.

Define Objectives

Clearly defined program objectives guide many of the other activities in the Relationship Builder Process. While firms should develop their own objectives, there are four that are most common.

Objective One: Create More Personal Contact.   In many, if not most, organizations, the salesperson is the primary point of contact with all customers, including key accounts. The salesperson has predominant responsibility for developing and maintaining the supplier-customer relationship. Unfortunately, most salespeople are evaluated and rewarded based on sales revenue or acquiring new accounts. Most salespeople are not evaluated and rewarded for simply improving relationships with existing customers.

By utilizing teams of individuals in both the supplier and customer organizations, the responsibility for managing the linkage with the customers is broadened considerably. Specifically, the four, five, or six team members have direct contact and communication with their counterparts in the customer organization. Each team member may have responsibility for improving different processes or resolving problems that the customer has experienced. In total, the personal contact between the teams in both the supplier and customer organizations facilitate better relationships.

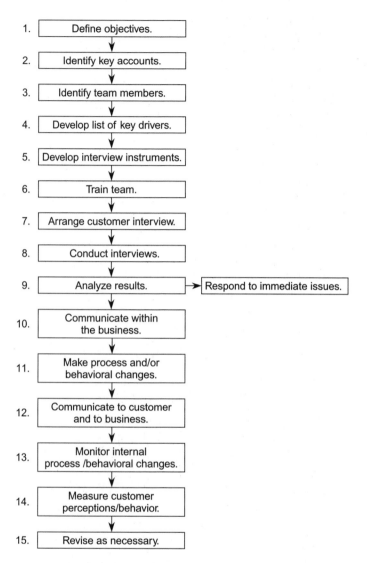

Figure 7.1 The Relationship Builder Process.

Objective Two: Better Understanding of the Customer.   If a supplier knows precisely how the individual customer uses a product or service, the customer's needs can be met more effectively. This type of information would never appear on a customer satisfaction survey. For example, a supplier could evaluate a customer's equipment, production processes, quality control systems, training programs, and workforce skills. Each of these could influence the way that a product or service is used. By gaining an understanding of these issues, a supplier could proactively recommend improvements.

When the Stone Container Corporation (SCC) acquires a new, large customer, SCC requests that a site visit be made before an order is placed. SCC essentially provides a free consulting service that evaluates a customer's packaging needs and suggests creative solutions. The solutions can range from customer-designed shipping cartons to changes in equipment, material flow, or plant layout. The cost of savings to customers is often several hundred thousand dollars. Without a thorough understanding of the customer's operation, Stone could not be proactive.

Increasingly, key accounts are expecting suppliers to be proactive partners. By developing a thorough understanding of the customer's needs, a firm's value-creating processes can be harmonized with those of the customer. Without an understanding of the key accounts, Six Sigma process improvement would focus on only one portion of the value chain.

Objective Three: Identify Future Plans.   This objective looks beyond the customer's current situation and examines the customer's future goals, directions, and plans. Survey efforts, such as a customer satisfaction program, seldom, if ever, provide insights into a customer's future needs. A future change in the customer's strategies could cause a supplier to invest in new production equipment, training of workers in new skills, or adjusting the workforce size. Identifying future needs is particularly critical in dynamic, rapidly changing industries.

Zytec, a Malcolm Baldrige National Quality Award winner in the manufacturing category, conducts a comprehensive, annual planning review. The strategic planning process is not a highly guarded, secret process conducted by top management as in some companies. Over 20 percent of all employees are directly involved, representing every organization level and every department. The draft strategic plans are circulated to employees to critique and offer comments. Then a final draft is developed. At this point, Zytec invites its major customers and suppliers to review and critique the strategic plan in an all-day retreat. In this way, Zytec aligns the strategic plan with its customers and suppliers.

Similarly, Solectron, a two-time Baldrige Award winner, has developed a comprehensive process to foster enduring relationships with customers. While there are daily and weekly interactions between Solectron and its customers, there are also monthly management reviews. A Solectron team visits each customer to discuss and improve tactical issues. On a quarterly basis, executive reviews are conducted at the customer's site to align long-term strategic goals. If a customer anticipates using a new technology or process, Solectron harmonizes its processes as needed. In some cases, this means that Solectron buys new equipment. In other cases, Solectron employees might need to learn new skills.

The primary drivers of training needs in Solectron are the future needs of the customers. As an indication of this commitment to continually improving the knowledge and skills of employees, Solectron employees average over 150 hours of formal training annually. This is two to three times the average amount of training in U.S. firms.

Objective Four: Calculate Financial Impact.   All major processes and activities in an organization should contribute to profitability, and the Relationship Builder Process is no exception. Therefore, a firm should track the financial impact of improved relationships by customer. There are several potential financial metrics. One is the share of spend discussed in an earlier chapter. If a customer is highly satisfied with a supplier, that supplier captures an increasingly large share of the customer's expenditures for the relevant product or service. For example, Nortel has found that there is a strong correlation between a customer's satisfaction score and the probability of using multiple suppliers. When satisfaction scores are low, customers use numerous suppliers. The customers are probably diversifying their supply dependency risk and are also searching for the more capable suppliers.

Related to the share of spend issue is revenue growth. Highly satisfied customers, particularly those who are industry leaders, have higher revenue growth than the average customer. Nortel found that customers who give a top box satisfaction score (very satisfied rating or 5 on a 5-point scale) have revenue growth twice that of the average customer. If the average revenue growth was 5 percent, the highly satisfied customers would have a revenue growth of 10 percent, for example. Solectron's results are very similar. Solectron has experienced phenomenal growth by delighting its rapidly growing customers. Johnson Controls also found that customers who gave a *very satisfied* rating on the overall satisfaction question had revenue growth that was twice that of *satisfied* customers (see Figure 2.14).

Whatever financial metrics are used, a firm should plan their use well in advance. This allows a baseline level of performance to be determined. Changes away from this baseline can then be attributed to improvements in customer satisfaction resulting from the Relationship Builder Process.

Clarifying and prioritizing the objectives is essential to identify the effectiveness of the Relationship Builder Process. The success of the program is measured against these objectives, and the objectives are the guide for other decisions in subsequent steps.

Identify Key Accounts

The key accounts should be clearly identified by developing explicit selection criteria. The most common criteria are *total revenue* and *profitability*. Total revenue for individual customers is usually available in most organizations. IBM Rochester identifies its *millionaire* customers—those who continually repurchase IBM products about every calendar year.[18] However, total revenue may not be the best, sole criteria. Some large customers put a good deal of price pressure on suppliers. The result is that, although total revenue may be high, profitability may be low. Therefore, profitability should also be a selection criteria for key accounts. Unfortunately, unless a firm has a good activity-based cost accounting system in place, identifying the profitability of individual customers may be difficult. In addition to total revenue and profitability, there may be other selection criteria.

Some smaller customers may be highly innovative, emerging firms that have high growth rates. These may be identified as key accounts due to their growth potential. Other firms may be identified as key accounts because they are opinion leaders. For example, doing business with the Singapore government is viewed as highly prestigious in Southeast Asia. The same situation applies in many countries. Likewise, many industries have clearly identified opinion leaders.

Once the key accounts have been identified, the Relationship Builder Process should be phased in. Normally, two or three customers are selected for a pilot program. The Relationship Builder Process is implemented with the cooperation of these firms. The program should be jointly critiqued by the customers and the supplier. After the pilot program and subsequent refinements, the program should be gradually rolled out to other key accounts.

Identify Team Members

The team should be composed of individuals that represent the most important value-creating processes. Certainly, this includes the account representative or salesperson responsible for that customer. The other team members could be from engineering, production, billing, technical support, or order fulfillment. A good starting point in team development is to identify all those processes that directly touch the customer. From these potential areas, a team of 4 to 6 people should be selected.

Since the team has the ultimate responsibility for changing processes to harmonize with the customer, the individuals should be the process owners. As we shall subsequently discuss, one of the outcomes of the customer meetings is a mutually agreed upon action plan. It would be difficult to develop an action plan without the input and support of the key decision makers.

Another important consideration is the organizational level of team members. The composition of the team is largely mirrored in the customer organization. For example, if a firm wishes to identify the customer's long-term strategic plans, senior executives in the customer firm need to be involved. For that to happen, there typically needs to be an equivalent level executive from the supplier firm involved. Having senior executives involved also signals strong commitment to the customer and that the customer is quite important.

An important reason for team involvement is to move away from individual, one-to-one relationships that can be lost if an individual in either organization leaves. For example, one of the frustrations that some of the Japanese firms have had with U.S. firms is that, in the Japanese firms, teams may stay in place for five to ten years. In a U.S. firm, it is unusual for a person to stay in the same position for five to ten years. The result is that the Japanese see many U.S. firms as having a revolving door for employees, and this causes problems of continuity in the relationship. If there is a team in place, then it is unlikely that all of the members of the team will turn over quickly. Some will remain longer than others, so there will be an organizational memory created.

One of the key aspects of relationship development is identifying the right people. This includes the right people in the customer organization as well as in the supplier organization. In the customer organization, the right people could be individuals from headquarters or from various divisions or departments. It could be people at different levels of the organization. There needs to be a clear understanding of who the current points of contact are in the different businesses in both the supplier and customer organizations.

In addition to the current points of contact, the desired points of contact must also be defined. When developing a good relationship with key accounts, usually there are more points of contact than the one-to-one relationships. There is a wider array of individuals in the customer organization involved and a wider array of individuals in supplier organization. Usually there are higher levels of managers involved, because one of the goals is to identify the long-term directions and strategies. Another goal is to identify how strategies will change over the next year or two and the impact on the supplier. To the extent possible, the level, the functional areas, and, possibly, the names of the individuals who are desired on the team should be specified. This should include individuals that have authority to make decisions and are able to change the processes. This applies to both the customer and supplier organizations. The more important the supplier's products and services are to the customer, the more willing they will be to be involved.

Develop a List of Key Drivers

Once a team has been formed, the team should identify the key drivers of satisfaction and value for the customers. The list that is developed will eventually be used as a menu by the customers. Since each customer firm will probably have a somewhat different set of key drivers, the list of key drivers should encompass 15 to 20 potentially important areas. The key drivers are often referred to as *performance attributes*. Essentially, these are the broad performance areas that a customer uses to evaluate a supplier. At this point, the attributes should be stated at the fairly broad, conceptual level.

- Responsiveness
- Follow-Up
- Innovativeness
- Product Quality
- Service Quality
- Two-Way Communication
- Information Technology Systems
- Delivery
- Ordering
- Billing
- Technical Support
- Customer Service
- Maintenance & Repair
- Value for the Money
- Proactive Suggestions
- Knowledge of Customer's Business
- Employee Attitudes
- Employee Knowledge
- Employee Accessibility/Contact

Table 7.1 Common Attributes Important to Many Customers.

Research has indicated that the two most important attributes are often trust and communication. The customer must trust the supplier firm. There must also be good, open, accurate two-way communication. These two attributes are characteristics that flow through almost any relationship in any organization, whether it is internal to the organization or whether it is external. In fact, you can make the argument that these are fundamental to any kind of personal relationship. If trust is lacking in a marriage, then there are problems. The same thing applies to organizations as well.

In addition to these attributes, there is a wider array of other attributes that may be important to customers (Table 7.1). These are not intended to be an exhaustive list, but these are things that often pop to the top when asking the customers what is important to them. Please note that they are not in order of importance. The attributes simply illustrate the different things that might be important to customers.

Each customer and each industry are different from one another. This implies that the same attributes are not important to all customers. Therefore, a list of attributes should be developed that can be a menu so that the customer can select the attributes that are important to them. But, since the list may not include all of the issues important to the customer, the customer should be able to add attributes. This allows the interview instrument to be customized to the needs of a specific customer.

Identifying these attributes is the first step in moving toward the development for the actual interview instrument. Subsequent steps show how these attributes are used in the design of the instrument.

Develop the Interview Instrument

Assuming that the list of attributes is complete at this point, they are now converted into questions. The wording and scaling of the questions should be consistent with any other

Name(Supplier team leader) _____   Title/Function _____
Name _____   Title/Function _____
Name _____   Title/Function _____
Customer organization: _____
Name(team leader) _____   Title/Function _____
Name _____   Title/Function _____
Name _____   Title/Function _____
Division/department/business unit _____
Telephone number (____) _____   Date _____

Figure 7.2 Sample Team Information Form.

surveys that may have been completed in the organization. Therefore, the team should evaluate any earlier surveys that may have been used. This consistency and harmonization of surveys permit the comparison of the results of the Relationship Builder Process with other customer surveys. If exactly the same wording and scaling of questions are used on all surveys, comparisons are pretty straightforward. If there is a change in the wording of questions, then making comparisons is pretty difficult.

There are five parts of the Relationship Builder Process interview instrument. The first part deals with specification of the team members and their roles, titles, and responsibilities. The second segment deals with background information and demographic data about the company so that comparisons can be made to other organizations. The third part focuses on the key attributes. These are the 10 to 20 attributes that were identified earlier. In the fourth section, there should be open-ended questions that solicit qualitative responses. In the fifth section, there should be global questions that are linked to any other surveys. One or two of these overall questions come at the beginning or at the end of the interview.

The team member portion of the questionnaire is intended to clarify the roles of the individuals from both organizations that are present at the team meeting. It is important to identify the people, their titles, and the points of contact such as phone numbers or E-mails. In this way, the responsibilities of each team member is clarified. This should be done not only for the customer's organization but for the supplier's team as well. This allows the customer to determine the different areas of responsibility. Typically, the teams have four to six people, so there should be enough space to capture the necessary information. An example is provided in Figure 7.2.

The background information consists of demographic information about the customer. This could be a functional area within the company, such as accounting or production or engineering. It could be job level. It could be total sales that the customer buys from the supplier organization. It could be SIC codes. It could be geographic regions of the country. Any number of factors could go into the background data. All of this information should be consistent across the different surveys that are conducted for different key accounts. This allows the segmentation or aggregation of the data in different ways.

For each of the 10 to 20 key attributes identified, the team should drill down a bit deeper and add some additional dimensions. The team could ask if the supplier's performance has met the customers' expectations. The team might ask if performance is getting better or worse on that attribute. The team might ask about competitive performance. Or, the team could ask the relative importance of the attribute. The team could also ask some open-ended questions about the attribute. Each of these *drill down,* follow-up questions probes for a deeper understanding.

RESPONSIVENESS

Do we respond to you in a timely manner?

- Accessible
- Provide Proactive Suggestions
- Responds Quickly to Requests for Information
- Fast Resolution of Complaints
- Frequency of Contact
- Has Good Follow-Up

A. MET EXPECTATIONS

How would you describe ACME's performance on responsiveness?

Significantly Above Expectations	Somewhat Above Expectations	Met Expectations	Somewhat Below Expectations	Significantly Below Expectations
❏	❏	❏	❏	❏

B. PERFORMANCE IMPROVEMENT RATING DURING PAST YEAR

Would you say the ACME's performance has:

Significantly Improved	Improved	Stayed the Same	Declined	Significantly Declined
❏	❏	❏	❏	❏

C. OUR PERFORMANCE

How Does ACME's performance on responsiveness compare to the competition?

Significantly Above Competitors	Somewhat Above Competitors	Same As Competitors	Somewhat Below Competitors	Significantly Below Competitors
❏	❏	❏	❏	❏

D. IMPORTANCE

How important is "responsiveness" to you?

Very Important	Moderately Important	Somewhat Important	Unimportant	Very Unimportant
❏	❏	❏	❏	❏

E. WHAT DO WE DO WELL Regarding Responsiveness?
- Who? What area? Functional area?
F. WHAT SHOULD WE DO TO IMPROVE RESPONSIVENESS?
G. WHAT COMPANY IS MORE RESPONSIVE?
- How? Why?

Figure 7.3 Responsiveness.

A *responsiveness* example (Figure 7.3) illustrates these points. There are sample questions for met expectations, performance improvement, competitive position, and so forth. The team may not use all of these drill downs or may use some in addition to these. These are simply different ways of drilling down and identifying which issues are most critical to key customers. If questions like these are asked, the team will find out how responsiveness stacks up to the competition and how it has changed over the past year or so.

- What trends do you see in your industry that may affect the products/services you will need from us in the future?
- What, if anything, stands in the way of you doing more business with us?
- What could our organization do to help you achieve your business objectives?
- Based upon this interview, what three immediate actions should we implement?
- How and when will the actions be monitored and measured?
- What do we do well?
- What areas warrant our immediate attention?
- What actions can we take to make you more successful or help you achieve current challenges and objectives?

Table 7.2 Open-Ended Questions.

In addition to those structured questions, there should also be some open-ended questions that indicate what should be done to improve. Other open-ended questions might ask for a description of what companies were more responsive. Very often this is a good place to start benchmarking efforts because customers may identify another firm that does a great job in this area. There are many different open-ended questions that could be asked. The team should use this combination of the structured questions and open-ended questions for each of the key attributes. The interview instrument will probably include a page for each one of the key attributes. Therefore, the interview instrument may have over 20 pages.

Toward the end of the questionnaire, there should be some additional open-ended questions. These are important questions. These open-ended questions allow the capture of information that does not show up on the structured portion of the questionnaire. Examples of these questions would be to "identify the trends in the industry" or "what stands in the way of doing more business" or "what actions should we take" (Table 7.2). In fact, the most critical open-ended questions are numbers four and five.

Those questions are based on the entire interview and identify three immediate actions that should be implemented. This also clarifies how and when the actions will be monitored and measured. These questions link very clearly to an action plan, so that the data goes from what the customer is saying directly into process improvements. The actions for improvement are discussed in the presence of the customer so that, when the team walks away, the customer knows what is going to be done. In some cases, the team may not have adequate information. The team may have to do some more research or get some more information and have a follow-up meeting. But, ultimately, the goal is to have the customer and the team leader sign off on the changes that are going to be made. This provides a clear starting point for process improvement. A Six Sigma process improvement would be responsible for developing the specific process improvements.

Train the Team

The team needs to be trained in depth interview techniques. The real value of the interview is in the drill down discussions. Therefore, a planned interview strategy should be developed. This requires identifying a team leader and the roles of each team member. The team leader should assume the role of moderator or coordinator. The individual team members should all be actively involved in the interview. This is best accomplished by assigning specific questions to different team members.

Out of respect for the customer's time, the interview should have a detailed agenda with approximate time allocations for each question. The team leader is responsible for adhering to the agenda.

One of the team members should be assigned the role of *scribe*. In this manner, the quantitative responses can be captured, as well as the qualitative comments. An alternative strategy is to tape-srecord this meeting and develop a verbatim transcript. This technique is more costly and time-consuming but does result in more detail.

It is very important for the team to keep in mind that the interview is not a sales effort. The goal is to get the customer's input as a driver of process changes. Therefore, all team members should actively listen and probe for details. The discussions should not be dominated by just a few individuals. Team training for customer meetings should show members how to act and behave during face-to-face customer meetings. Topics or areas of training should include teaching on behaviors such as not making false promises, not acknowledging or committing resources for which you have no authority, active listening, and dealing effectively with customer data and complaints.

Arrange the Interview

Since the relationship builder is based upon an in-depth interview with key customers, there is obviously a good deal of planning that is going to have to take place. The date, time, and location of the meeting is going to have to be arranged. For the interviewers to go over a questionnaire with 15 or so attributes and get good detail, the team should plan on a meeting of at least two to four hours. Therefore, the team should allow for a half-day meeting in most cases. The meeting should be at the customer's location or nearby to minimize the disturbance to the customer's workday. After the meeting, the team should plan for some social interaction so the individuals can meet informally. For example, a morning meeting could be followed by lunch. Keep in mind that the goal is to develop relationships with the customers. Part of the relationship development comes as discussion of issues in the interview instrument and the related business issues. Some of the relationship development is personal, such as individuals talking about trips they are taking or places they are going to and so forth.

Because of the planning necessary in terms of arranging dates, meetings, and the busy schedules of people, a month in advance is about the minimum that the team can arrange an interview with key customers. Sometimes the meetings are planned two or three months in advance. When the meeting is requested, the customer should be sent an agenda and a copy of the interview instrument to provide clear expectations.

If possible, the supplier should request the specific team members from the customer organization that are to be involved. If the individuals are not apparent, then the primary contact in the customer organization should assist in involving the appropriate people. By introducing the supplier team, titles, agenda, and interview instrument, the customer should be able to solicit the correct people.

Conduct the Interview

If the previous seven steps have been performed thoroughly, the actual interview is pretty simple. There are only a few general guidelines. The tone of the meeting should be positive and proactive, not defensive. The intent is to identify what can realistically be done to improve. Everyone should be treated with respect and individual opinions and comments encouraged. The meeting should not exceed the specified time. If the customer team has expectations of being done at one o'clock, then those expectations must be honored. It is better to plan for four hours and use three than to plan for three and use four.

At the end of the first meeting, the team should set a date for the next follow-up meeting. For example, if a Quarter 1 interview is conducted in January, sometime in March or April there should be a follow-up meeting to see how performance has actually changed. There should be enough time between the meetings to allow for corrective actions to be made and identified.

Immediately after the meeting occurs, there should be a debriefing period. The debriefing normally takes the team one to two hours. Often, there is necessary follow-up information that has to be gathered, as well. The team should specify the additional information required and identify which individuals are going to perform the follow-up. There should be a summary report of the interview that summarizes the questionnaire results. In addition, there should be a summary that draws all the findings together and provides some insight and direction. The summary should be shared with the customer as well as distributed in the supplier organization. This allows the customer to see exactly what the supplier is going to do as a result of the meeting. It removes the imposition to the customer of compiling a lot of redundant notes. The immediate debriefing, the questionnaire, and any follow-up assignments should all be kept in a file for that customer so that there is a central collection of information.

Analyze Results

If only one or two firms are piloted, the analysis is substantially complete at the end of the meeting for individual customers. But, if there are a large number of customers involved, the data analysis becomes more complex. If this occurs, a relationship coordinator may be necessary to manage the program.

For the program to be most effective, there should be consistent data analysis. There are two types of analysis. One is the longitudinal analysis for each customer. This type of analysis examines the changes over time for that customer. There also needs to be aggregate analysis to identify those areas that are common themes across all of the key customers. For example, communication, responsiveness, and follow-up are all issues that are important to many customer groups, and it may be that the supplier organization strategically needs an initiative that focuses on those three dimensions.

For the aggregate analysis, if there are a large number of customers, a database has to be set up. This allows the data to be analyzed by different segments and different partitions to the data. The partitions are usually created by the responses to the demographic questions that were asked. Most organizations can handle this kind of analysis internally, particularly for the individual accounts. In some cases, the database can be outsourced. An outside vendor would compile all of the summary results and then circulate a summary report to all of the key players.

Communicate within the Business

There should be a clearly delineated strategy to share the customer feedback throughout the company. Normally, this takes the form of a condensed executive summary. The purpose of this communication is to let employees, particularly those without direct customer contact, to hear the voice of the customer. This builds support for any behavioral and process changes that need to be made. This also enhances the formulation of the process improvement teams if necessary.

Make Process and/or Behavioral Changes

One of the primary outcomes of the relationship builder interview is the development of action plans that address the customer's needs. If you recall, this was the focus of several open-ended questions that identified specific changes that needed to be made. The open-ended questions also identified how those changes were going to be measured. The action plan is simply an extension of those issues. While the second half of this book focuses on improvement techniques, the relationship team and the Six Sigma process improvement team should be closely coordinated. The relationship team should identify the changes in general that need to be made to processes, both on the long- and short-term basis. For each of the changes, it is necessary to identify who has responsibility over that change. The areas of responsibility should be communicated to the customers so they know who is responsible in the supplier organization.

It is important to identify what resources are needed to make the changes and secure those from senior management. Because these are important accounts, it is typically not too difficult to get top management to approve resource allocation as needed to improve processes for these customers. Previously, it was pointed out that the team needs to identify how to measure the performance changes. But now the team needs to link those performance measurements to actual process metrics in the organization. This allows the team to measure the impact of the changes internally. The team should be able to track performance before meeting with the customer again. This provides documentation for the next follow-up interview. These issues are discussed in much more detail in subsequent chapters.

The team should also identify a detailed project time line that indicates when each of the changes will be implemented. Some changes can be implemented on a weekly, monthly, or quarterly basis. In some cases, the time line may take much longer than that. But many changes can be made within a month or so that will have an immediate impact on the customer. For every one of the changes, a detailed time line for implementation must be developed.

Communicate to Customer and to Business

Once an action plan, time line for implementation, and areas of responsibility have been determined, a summary report should be sent to the customer. In essence, the Relationship Builder interview identified what needed to be improved and roughly what would be done. This report provides more detail and specifics that show exactly when certain actions will be taken. This report is important behaviorally because it shows the customer that specific actions were taken as a direct result of the meeting. This makes the customers much more willing to cooperate in the future. Many firms implement customer-driven changes, but many customers are unaware of the firm's efforts. The act of communicating directly with customers about action plans typically improves customer satisfaction scores significantly.

Monitor Process/Behavioral Changes

Based upon the activities in previous steps, internal process metrics should have been identified as part of the action plan. The team should periodically reconvene and review the process changes. By doing so, internal changes can be made prior to meeting with the customer. Subsequent chapters of this book address this issue in detail.

The whole purpose of gathering customer data is to improve products, services, and processes. The organization should be able to align internal process metrics with customer satisfaction results. Six Sigma teams should be using customer satisfaction data to determine opportunities and identify projects on which to improve. Customers should be able to see the benefits of the changes and notice a difference.

Measure Customer Perceptions/Behaviors

The meetings with the key accounts are ongoing, normally on a quarterly basis, but occasionally on a semiannual basis. By using exactly the same interview instrument and the same team, the changes in customer perceptions can be tracked. While scores for all the quantitative questions can be tracked, it is most common to track the global, overall questions that appear at the beginning or end of the interview instrument.

Monitoring changes in customer behavior takes a longer time horizon. The primary behavioral changes are share of spend, total revenue, and repeat business. If a supplier is capturing 30 percent of the customer's expenditures for a type of product or service and total annual revenues for that customer are $100,000, then capturing 40 percent of the customer's budget would yield $133,000. Capturing 50 percent of the customer's budget would yield $166,000, and capturing 60 percent would yield $200,000. There is normally a good deal of potential revenue growth among the existing customers. Managers in most firms overestimate the share of their customer's budget that they are currently capturing.

In addition to share of spend, tracking annual revenue growth is valuable. Since there is often a good deal of variation in short-term revenue for an individual company, an annual time frame is most appropriate. By using annual data, it takes several years to develop a solid picture of revenue changes. Some firms, such as AT&T, have been tracking the linkage between customer perceptions and behavior and financial metrics for well over 10 years. These firms have consistently found a strong, positive correlation between customer perceptions and revenue. The more satisfied customers spend more with that supplier. IBM Rochester research demonstrates that very satisfied customers not only contributed more revenue but also repurchased sooner than satisfied customers (see note 18). The more satisfied the customers, the more they spend with you, in a more frequent time frame.

Revise as Necessary

The Relationship Builder Process should be customized to fit a firm and its customers. Therefore, program characteristics should gradually change and evolve over time. It is quite common for the team membership in both the supplier firm and customer organization to evolve to get the *right* people involved. Meeting frequency and locations are also commonly adjusted. In many cases, the performance metrics become more refined.

One aspect of the process that should not change is the interview instrument. If data is going to be tracked over time, the questions and scaling should remain constant. If the questions are changed, making direct longitudinal comparisons is inappropriate.

Relationship Builder Summary

The Relationship Builder Process is a rigorous, very systematic approach that yields excellent results. However, it is relatively time-consuming and, therefore, is only appropriate for key customers. Many organizations may want to develop better relationships with important customers in a less labor-intensive manner. The remainder of this chapter provides other approaches to develop better relationships with customers.

OTHER TYPES OF PROACTIVE CONTACT

A *proactive approach* means that the organization initiates contact with the customer for the purpose of getting advice and input that may not show up on customer satisfaction surveys. A proactive approach means that a firm contacts some of the 90 percent to 95 percent of customers that will never voice complaints or initiate contact.

The term *customer* is used broadly here and means much more than just consumers or end-users of a product. The term *customer* also includes channel intermediaries such as wholesalers, distributors, and retailers. In many cases, facilitating organizations such as marketing research firms or shipping companies or advertising organizations need to be integrated into the firm's decision-making processes. The philosophy that underlies every aspect of customer integration is that all types of customers are valuable assets or portions of the value-added chain, and they need to be treated accordingly. Customers are not targets; they are assets that must be nurtured and developed.

Executive Contact

The president of Pepsi-Cola North America takes time to talk to several customers each day. Executives at Proctor and Gamble conduct consumer intercepts in grocery stores to interview customers and get their opinions about Proctor and Gamble products. Proctor and Gamble executives also answer customer service phone lines periodically. At Hewlett-Packard, executives are assigned to key clients to maintain regular, open, high-level contact. IBM Rochester assigns executives and key technical personnel to all key customer accounts.

The message that cascades through these organizations is that the customer is vitally important. If the top management is concerned enough to contact customers, it is probably in the best interest of other managers as well.

Customer Visits

At Motorola and 3M, managers from the CEO on down make visits to customers' facilities. These visits are often conducted by a team of managers that meets with the actual users of their company's products, not just executives of the customer firm. These visits often result in written reports that are broadly shared throughout Motorola or 3M. The primary reason for such visits is to get direct feedback about products and ideas for improvement from customers who would never see a customer satisfaction survey or initiate direct contact.

Other companies have pioneered the customer visit concept at the senior levels of the company. The CEO of Porsche spends 25 percent of his work time with customers, both end-users and dealers. You can probably bet that much of the time is spent driving around! The CEO at Harley-Davidson pursues the same strategy and credits the resulting customer feedback as the source for most technological advances. At Xerox, senior executives are assigned one or two major account customers and they serve as champions of their accounts. Former Motorola CEO Bob Galvin rediscovered customers during the Baldrige

Award application process. Galvin visited one customer a month, spending the day on its production floor and in the customer service and accounting departments and talking with all levels of employees. He then wrote extensive trip reports that were communicated throughout the company.

Staff managers and vice presidents can often get left out of the customer visit process because such personnel do not usually have direct contact with customers. In fact, having the vice president or general counsel of the firm visiting a customer could be perceived as intimidating. What innovative firms are doing in order to include staff officers in customer contact is to have the managers meet with their peers at customer firms. In this way, discussions about practices and issues that concern those managers form the common ground. The vice president of human resources meets with the customer's vice president of human resources, and they can discuss employee or labor relations; the general counsels from both firms can discuss upcoming legislation and how it will affect their relationship; and the directors of corporate communications can discuss upcoming communication campaigns and get firsthand feedback from each other on positioning. Staff manager visits to customers can therefore provide an unexpected source of both information and organizational strengthening of the customer relationship.

New Product Development Teams

When Boeing was considering the development of a more fuel efficient aircraft, representatives of eight major customer airlines were involved in the initial concept discussions. Areas of common concern and unique differences were identified early in the design process. Major suppliers also were involved in the initial concept discussions to provide ideas and suggestions as well as to learn about the ultimate customer's evolving needs.

As Hewlett-Packard begins development of a new laser printer, key customers are involved from the start. Hewlett-Packard views early customer integration as an important part of cycle time reduction and improving speed to market. By obtaining customer feedback early in the product design stage, the firm needs less time for test marketing. Design changes are made early in the development process, not after the production begins.

The entire AS/400 commercial midrange computer system launched by IBM Rochester in 1988 was developed jointly by IBM engineers working hand in hand with customers.[19] This concept led to immediate success of the product and is a cornerstone for its success even today.

The line between customers and suppliers often becomes very hazy in new product development. General Motors and General Electric often have researchers working at each other's facilities in a joint commitment to continuous improvement.

Beta Sites

For some firms, prototypes are furnished to key customers for trial and feedback. Those beta sites constitute a type of user lab that allows early customer input. Xerox uses this technique to test new products and identify necessary changes before full production begins.

A beta site does not have to be highly technical. Some computer firms have customers simply go through the process of uncrating and installing a computer just to find out if the directions are actually read. On the other hand, IBM Rochester chooses the most critical, demanding customers—those that use the product to its extremes—to serve as its beta sites. Also, beta sites should reflect the environment that the product or service is being developed to meet. For example, if a product is being developed to meet specific needs in a market such as Asia, it should be beta tested in that market and not just in a geographic market that is more convenient to the development organization such as the United States.

Customer Panels

Both Bank of America and Weyerhaeuser have panels of key customers that meet regularly at corporate headquarters to advise the company how to improve. At Bank of America, the customer group sits on stage in an auditorium, and the managers in the audience ask the customers questions. After these lengthy sessions, the managers develop action plans based on customer preferences.

At Weyerhaeuser, customers and executives meet for four days. The results of the discussions help identify customer needs as well as facilitate the formation of partnerships by identifying common opportunities.

Some firms have found that data from customer satisfaction measurement programs provide an excellent starting point for these discussions. The empirical data often identify issues that need more detailed analysis and discussion. Both Humana Corporation and Marriott Hotels-Resorts use survey data as a starting point for more detailed root cause analysis discussions with key customers.

IBM Rochester meets with customer user groups twice a year at a formal conference called *COMMON*. At these conferences, customers and IBM executives and technical personnel discuss strategies, future requirements, and problems and issues. At the Controls Business of Johnson Controls, Inc., executives and engineers chair or attend industry panels to better understand industry and customer trends and future requirements.

Customer Representatives on Internal Teams

IBM invited key customers from around the world to join in a top-level strategic-planning conference. The customers were asked to tell what IBM was doing right, wrong, or not at all. Such top-level, face-to-face contact with customers was designed to ensure that the voice of the customer made it to the top level of IBM. With the launch of the AS/400 commercial midrange computer system by IBM Rochester in 1988, customers were directly involved with the design of the product, a practice that has made the product and the AS/400 business successful even today (see note 19).

Adopt-a-Customer Programs

Customers should not be restricted to only executive-level contact. Customers could be involved in a variety of cross-functional teams at all organizational levels. Boise Cascade Corp. has a program that was initiated at one of its paper mills. Cross-functional teams have adopted specific customers. The teams include individuals from the manufacturing floor, customer service, technical support, sales, and accounting. The team personally addresses any problems or complaints that arise with their adoptee. The customer visits by the team are powerful for both Boise Cascade and the customer.

Setting the Agenda

The agenda for proactive customer contact should be a reflection of your program objectives. Your customer contact should not be just an informal discussion of how your products are perceived. A list of possible agenda items are included in Table 7.3. The details depend on the particular situation, however.

- Goals of the customer's company in terms of growth, market changes, product modifications, new product introductions
- Plans for quality improvement, quality goals, supplier alliances
- Manufacturing process, anticipated process improvement, product and process control systems
- Cost control systems and goals, use of activity-based costing
- Purchasing processes, materials storage and flows, inventory control procedures
- Education, training, and development programs
- Finished product quality control, consumers' expectations, trends
- Current downstream channels, anticipated changes, distributors, wholesalers, retailers
- Role of your company's products in the customer's value-added processes
- The most acute problems and challenges facing your customer due to industry, technology, workforce, or competitive changes
- What do you see as the major changes taking place in your industry?
- How will your company's strategies change in response to those industry changes?

Table 7.3 Possible Agenda Items for Customer Contact.

The specific agenda should reflect a genuine desire to develop a more thorough understanding of your key customers and their individual situations. Everyone who makes customer contact, particularly in the case of a team site visit, should be working from the same agenda and share a common understanding of the goals. A customer contact should not be an attempt to sell products. In fact, a sales effort is likely to destroy the credibility of the customer visit.

SUMMARY

Building customer relationships often have the biggest impact on improving customer satisfaction and financial performance of the organization. This chapter has presented a variety of techniques that build better relationships with key customers. The Relationship Builder Process has 15 distinct steps that provide a rigorous, systematic approach to relationships development. This approach captures customer feedback that can serve as a driver of Six Sigma improvement efforts.

There are other, less rigorous approaches that can also capture feedback from key customers. These are executive contact, customer visits, new product development teams, beta sites, customer panels, and adopt-a-customer programs. Each of these provides a somewhat different type of customer input.

Regardless of the type of industry, key customers are expecting that their critical suppliers foster and maintain close relationships. The topics discussed in this chapter provide a menu of choices from which to choose.

<table>
<tr><td>**CASE STUDY**</td><td></td></tr>
</table>

BUILDING RELATIONSHIPS WITH KEY ACCOUNTS

As with most companies, building better relationships with customers at the Controls Business of Johnson Controls, Inc., was viewed as the responsibility of the account managers or the technicians on the customer's site. However, there are some very large customers who are critical to the success of Johnson Controls, Inc. Therefore, a more formalized approach to customer relationship management was designed and implemented.

The first thing that was found was that there was no clear definition of who the key accounts were. There was a rather substantial difference of opinion about how many of the customers were actually key accounts. This was caused by not having clearly stated criteria. As a result, all of the customers were treated the same, more or less. Because key accounts were consistently more demanding, uniform performance and treatment could be dangerous.

A team of senior managers developed a set of criteria to delineate key accounts. The customer database was filtered using this criteria, and a list of key accounts was developed and distributed. From this list, several key accounts were selected for a pilot project. The criteria that the Controls Business of Johnson Controls, Inc., has developed for determination of key accounts include revenue spent (absolute), repeat business, and share of spend.

The customer relationship development program described in this chapter was implemented with the pilot customers. First, the appropriate Johnson Controls, Inc., personnel attended a half-day workshop on how to design and implement the program. The program owner was account management, but the quality organization also provided strong support.

The first thing that was discovered was that the organization did not know nearly as much about its customers as was thought. For example, in one organization, it was requested that a certain individual (customer) be included on the customer team, only to find out that the individual had died two years previously.

The results of the pilot program significantly exceeded expectations. Customers were delighted that this amount of effort would be exerted to implement such a program. The Johnson Controls, Inc., team was excited to learn more about its customers. The benefits showed up very quickly in revenue changes. Because of the success, the program was gradually rolled out throughout all Areas in North America.

For key OEM accounts, such as major furnace companies that purchase Johnson Controls, Inc., components including thermostats for use in their own products, special customer relationships are established. All key positions within the customer's organization are matched with a counterpart within the Controls Business of Johnson Controls, Inc. The teams interact formally at least once a month, and executive face-to-face meetings are held quarterly. These OEM meetings are used to discuss industry trends and strategies of both Johnson Controls, Inc., and the OEM customer.

Since implementing a more robust customer relationship program at the Controls Business of Johnson Controls, Inc., more information about customers is made available to all employees. Employees are part of customer teams, which work in defining solutions or resolving issues. Voice of the customer data, as well as customer satisfaction survey results and customer comments, are available to all employees through the Intranet. In addition, a new tool has been implemented that allows for easy access and manipulation of customer data by Area offices, geography, customer teams, and other demographics. What is important about this is the availability and accessibility of customer data to employees at all levels in the organization.

Part III

Preparing the Organization for Six Sigma

The preceding chapters have addressed why the concept of Six Sigma is important and how the voice of the customer can be captured. Part 3 of this book assumes that some of the previous techniques have been used so that customer needs and expectations are clearly understood. If the Six Sigma initiative is begun prior to capturing the voice of the customer, the focus is primarily on cost and cycle time reduction with little consideration of the customer.

Part 3 consists of three chapters that deal with getting ready for a Six Sigma initiative. In previous chapters, the importance of senior leadership has been stressed. Chapter 8 presents a much more detailed discussion of how Six Sigma can and should be linked explicitly to vision and mission statements and corporate strategies. The chapter discusses how to cascade the concept throughout a company and also stresses the importance of developing a balanced scorecard that reinforces customer-centered Six Sigma.

Selecting the right processes is discussed in chapter 9. When beginning a Six Sigma initiative, it is important to select processes that are well suited for initial efforts. Starting with a negative experience can undermine the credibility of the concept.

Once the target processes are selected, a Six Sigma team must be formed. This is the focus of chapter 10. There are many considerations when forming a team, and perhaps none is more important than team leadership. Both the leader and the team must be well trained in both behavioral issues and technical Six Sigma tools and techniques. If an organization carefully prepares for the Six Sigma initiative, chances for success are far greater.

8

Corporate
Strategy/Leadership

Developing a Six Sigma corporate philosophy and culture is an arduous, long-term challenge. Significant resources are required for training and development of employees during this time period. The organization needs to realize that Six Sigma is not another fad of the year, nor should it be viewed as a *program* that is the responsibility of a few people or a functional area. In most organizations, fully implementing a Six Sigma culture takes four or five years, once senior leadership has made the initial commitment. The senior team must be fully and visibly committed to Six Sigma. In the book *Jack Welch and the GE Way*,[20] Jack Welch stated that it took General Electric (GE) more than five years to fully implement Six Sigma and to see significant, tangible results. Other firms that have undertaken a Six Sigma initiative have created a culture in which management is discouraged from positioning Six Sigma as a *program*. Some firms have even implemented a system of fining anyone who refers to Six Sigma as a *program*.

At Motorola, Bob Galvin and George Fisher were strong proponents of Six Sigma. At GE, Jack Welch lead the charge but described Six Sigma as the most challenging and potentially rewarding initiative he had undertaken at GE. When Larry Bossidy left GE to become CEO at Allied Signal, Six Sigma was the initiative he used to transform the corporate vision and mission statements into action. In all three of these organizations, the speed of decision making, innovation, and rate of change accelerated as a result of implementing a Six Sigma culture.

VISION/MISSION STATEMENTS

As part of an organization's vision or mission, achieving quality and customer satisfaction goals is an important part of creating a culture that is supportive of Six Sigma. This is because the customer is the ultimate judge of all aspects of a firm's performance. In addition to visible senior leadership support and commitment to a Six Sigma initiative, inclusion of quality and customer satisfaction as part of an organization's vision or mission visibly reinforces the importance of the customer to employees and all other company stakeholders, including suppliers. This book does not discuss how to develop vision and mission statements. However, there are many examples from firms that can be used to demonstrate a linkage between vision statements and the importance of quality and customer satisfaction. For instance, the vision at IBM Rochester[21] in the early 1990s was "to

- Six Sigma Quality
- Total Cycle Time Reduction
- Product and Manufacturing Leadership
- Profit Improvement
- Participative Management

Table 8.1 Motorola's Operational Initiatives.

be the undisputed leader in customer satisfaction." The mission to support this simply read, "IBM Rochester excellence . . . customer satisfaction." There were a number of objectives and goals put in place to support the vision and mission including specific customer satisfaction measurement targets. Part of the deployment of this was through a Hoshin Planning concept that included a statement in everyone's performance plan that read, "In order to assist IBM Rochester achieve its customer satisfaction objective, I will . . . ." After IBM Rochester achieved customer satisfaction leadership, the vision and mission were changed (see note 21).

Also in the early 1990s, Motorola's fundamental objective was "total customer satisfaction." Satisfying the customer was the responsibility of everyone in the company and the focus of all efforts. To achieve this objective, Motorola developed three strategic goals. These three goals were:

1. Increased global market share

2. Best in class in terms of people, technology, marketing, products, manufacturing, and service

3. Superior financial results

Since these three goals were a bit general and would have been difficult to cascade throughout the organization, Motorola derived five operational initiatives from these goals that are illustrated in Table 8.1. These five operational initiatives provided strategic alignment for the entire organization and were reflected in the goals for all levels of the company. Two of the five key elements, Six Sigma quality and total cycle time reduction, go hand in hand with one another. These two initiatives were managed and achieved through participative management, which involved all parts of Motorola. As quality improved and cycle time was reduced, product and, particularly, manufacturing leadership were achieved. Collectively, these five initiatives lead to profit improvement.

Senior Leadership, Visible Commitment, and Involvement

Within Motorola, the CEO chaired the Operating and Policy Committee that reviewed progress toward the five operational initiatives twice each quarter. By visibly supporting Six Sigma efforts and monitoring progress toward the five initiatives, CEO Bob Galvin made the importance of the initiatives clear to everyone. He demonstrated visible leadership and personal involvement and commitment. He walked the talk. Bob Galvin's successors, George Fisher and now Chris Galvin, have continued the emphasis on Six Sigma. Having management commitment to Six Sigma efforts is the first and most important step in ensuring its success.

At GE, Jack Welch was an insider with over 20 years with the company and was appalled by GE's bureaucracy. When he became CEO in 1981, he began a radical transformation of the company. His first strategic initiative was called "Number 1, Number 2." He told managers to "fix, close, or sell" every business unit that was not first or second in global market share. GE sold 400 business units or product lines that could not be fixed. By 1988, GE was organized into 14 major business units that had high growth potential.

Welch's focus then shifted toward internal operations. His goal was to get everyone to operate as though they were entrepreneurs. His philosophy was "one room, one coffee pot, one team, one shared mission." The greatest resistance to change came from middle managers. To overcome this resistance, Welch implemented a *Work Out* program, which called for groups of managers to meet for several days, led by a trained facilitator, to develop ways their business units could be improved. The Work Out program became the framework for the Six Sigma initiative, an extension of GE's continuous improvement philosophy.

The 1998 GE Annual Report[22] indicated that Six Sigma had saved GE over $750 million in 1998. Savings from Six Sigma efforts in 1999 were projected to be $1.5 billion. The magnitude of savings is why Jack Welch refers to Six Sigma as potentially the most rewarding initiative ever at GE.

Many of Larry Bossidy's actions at Allied Signal were patterned after the successes he witnessed during his tenure at GE. Bureaucracy was reduced and speed was emphasized. Six Sigma was instituted as a team-based approach to improve the organization. Consultants were brought in to train the facilitators, who then became the trainers. Six Sigma became a cultural platform at Allied Signal, not just a program.

Like Motorola and GE, Allied Signal began an extensive supply chain process improvement effort. The goal was to reduce the number of suppliers and keep only those who were committed to significant quality improvement. Allied Signal informed suppliers that prices would have to be reduced 10 percent to 15 percent and cycle time reduced by 30 percent. Allied Signal required suppliers to develop action plans to move toward Six Sigma quality.

The common theme running through all of these organizations is that Six Sigma quality is more of a cultural imperative that changes the way decisions are made, rather than a traditional quality effort or program. Everyone in the organization should know how they each contribute to the organization's strategy. Hoshin Planning is a specific technique that can also be used to permeate and align a company's Six Sigma goals and strategies throughout the organization.

HOSHIN PLANNING

Hoshin Planning is a method of aligning the goals and performance of all employees around a company's strategic goals. The term *Hoshin* is Japanese for *policy*. In practice in U.S. firms, the term *goal* is perhaps a better translation. The underlying assumptions are that company policy should be the guide for individual performance and that everyone in the organization should be able to clearly see how their work efforts and outputs contribute to achievement of company strategies, goals, and objectives. The application of Hoshin Planning in an organization does not require a one-to-one match for every strategy and goal at all levels. However, all major goals for lower levels should relate to some of the strategic goals. The implication is that each unit or function contributes to some of the strategic goals in a unique way.

Hewlett-Packard (HP) has been using Hoshin Planning for a number of years to coordinate the efforts of over 50 relatively autonomous business divisions. Hewlett-Packard develops an overall, annual strategic plan. Each business division and level of the organization derive their Hoshins from the overall strategic plan. To illustrate, each of HP's divisions develop divisional goals that support the overall strategic plan. Each business unit within the business division develops goals that support the division's strategy. Each functional area or department develops their goals from the business unit Hoshins. And, each employee derives his or her personal performance goals from the functional area or department Hoshins. The performance of everyone, from the individual employee on up, is measured against the Hoshin goals.

By using Hoshin Planning, everyone in the organization knows how their jobs contribute to the organization. They know how they fit in. Everyone in the organization knows their performance objectives, how they will be evaluated against these, and how their objectives contribute to achievement of overall company strategies, goals, and objectives. Because the use of Hoshin Planning is such a successful method for use in institutionalizing changes in an organization, its technique is discussed in various forms throughout this book. The case study at the end of chapter 9 illustrates a Hoshin Planning approach used by the quality organization at Johnson Controls, Inc., Controls Group. A more detailed example, and one that illustrates achievement of Six Sigma and total quality initiatives more clearly, is included in Appendix D.

The example, which is detailed in Appendix D, is from a company that must remain anonymous. This company began its pursuit of Six Sigma performance in 1995. To stress the importance of the initiative, the CEO wrote the forward to a program document that described exactly how and when the steps to achieving Six Sigma would be taken. The document has been edited to show only key concepts in each category. A specific schedule was developed for each category. Since this company consists of numerous business divisions, the document was intended to provide a consistent approach for strategy deployment. The company referred to the document as "Vision 2000—Total Customer Satisfaction." Everyone in the company knew what the various aspects of Six Sigma were, the expected time line, and the implications for their jobs.

BALANCED SCORECARD

Once senior leaders have committed to a Six Sigma culture and developed a plan for strategic deployment, progress toward the plan should be measured through some type of performance evaluation. As suggested earlier, Hoshin Planning aligns strategic goals with business unit, departmental, and individual performance. Performance is measured against the contributions to the corporate strategic goals. This usually requires the use of some sort of report or scorecard for use by the upper levels of management. The use of a balanced scorecard as a performance evaluation tool is discussed here.

The philosophy behind a balanced scorecard is quite simple. Since mission and vision statements usually have various dimensions and implications across a variety of stakeholders (for example, employees, shareholders, suppliers, communities, etc.), performance management should also have various dimensions. An organization should not have to, nor be expected to, review hundreds or thousands of measurements on a regular basis to assess performance of the organization. Likewise, there are not just one or two measurements that can provide this same assessment. However, there are typically a handful of measurements that are true reflections of a company's overall performance and are aligned with the company's vision, mission, and strategies.

Robert Kaplan and David P. Norton developed a *Balanced Scorecard* approach, which is described in a number of *Harvard Business Review* articles.[23] The concept of a Balanced

Scorecard suggests that there are four major categories of performance that should be addressed when a company assesses its overall performance. The four major categories are:

1. Financial

2. Customer

3. Internal business processes

4. Learning and growth

The *financial* category could include performance metrics such as return on investment, economic value added, revenue growth, profitability, or cash flow. Some firms may want to include market indicators such as market share as a financial metric, while others may include these under the *customer* category, or even create a separate category for market-oriented dimensions. This *market* category might also include metrics for the rate of new product introduction and innovation. Some firms may include cost reduction and productivity improvements as financial metrics while other firms might include those measures as internal, operating indicators along with cycle time reduction. One lesson learned here is that classifying performance metrics into one of four major categories may be difficult for an organization. However, the selected performance metrics should be aligned with its vision, mission, and strategies. Another lesson learned here is that it is important for a company's Six Sigma initiative to align with the company's performance management system. In the case of financial performance, Six Sigma gains in the areas of cycle time reduction, waste elimination, improved quality, and improved productivity all clearly fall into a financial-type category. Measuring and managing the financial impact of Six Sigma is critically important.

Customer measures could include customer satisfaction, loyalty or retention rates, customer acquisition, customer profitability, and complaint rates. In practice, the satisfaction level could be derived from an individual customer satisfaction survey question such as overall satisfaction or value for the money. Or, the customer satisfaction level could be measured by the use of a satisfaction index consisting of three to six questions that are strong predictors of customer satisfaction. Loyalty and retention rates are somewhat more difficult to determine for some products with long life cycles but easy to evaluate for ongoing service contracts. Customer acquisition could be indicated by the number of new accounts opened or the percentage of projects awarded compared to proposals submitted to prospective customers. Customer profitability is a very admirable metric but almost impossible to determine unless a firm has an activity-based-cost (ABC) accounting system in place.

All of the customer category metrics could be further segmented by key accounts versus average customers, customer size, geography, market segments, and so forth. Customer metrics could also include measurements such as warranty expenses or warranty claims, since these directly impact what a customer experiences with a company's products. With a Six Sigma initiative, customer measurements need to be determined and tracked. Most commonly, customer metrics include key measurements such as improvements in customer satisfaction scores, volume or percentage of additional customer business, and reduction in customer complaint rates and warranty expenses.

The *internal business process* category could include measures of innovation in products, services, and processes. But, in practice, the two most common metrics for inclusion here are cycle time reduction and productivity improvement. Waste, scrap, defect rates, rework, and quality levels could also be included as internal metrics in this category. In some organizations, supply chain metrics are also viewed as internal operational metrics. The supply issues could include a whole range of material, cycle time, and service issues.

Linkage to Six Sigma initiatives are clearly in this category of performance metrics, especially as the metrics relate to waste elimination and productivity improvements.

The fourth category in a balanced scorecard is *learning and growth* of employees. Performance metrics in this category could include employee satisfaction, average hours of training per employee, overall education expenses, employee suggestion program participation rates, percentage/amount of employee involvement in teams such as Six Sigma teams, or percentage/number of employee certifications by professional organizations. The logic of this category is that all organizations compete based on the knowledge level of employees in the long term. In essence, all organizations are now knowledge organizations. Many companies expand the use of this category to include a larger array of employee-related metrics such as absenteeism, injury, and retention rates. These are all indirectly related to a company's acquisition or retention of employee knowledge and skills. Or, a company may choose to add an additional category that covers other employee-related issues beyond growth and learning. Again, the lesson here is that a company's human performance metrics need to align and support its strategic objectives. From a Six Sigma perspective, this category could include metrics such as the number of Six Sigma teams in existence, the number of Six Sigma team leaders and/or champions, the level of Six Sigma leader training (how many, how much), and the level of buy-in by employees on the company's Six Sigma efforts as measured by some type of employee survey.

The challenge for an organization is to design a balanced scorecard that reinforces the strategic direction and initiatives. To ensure that the scorecard is taken seriously, executive performance evaluation could also be tied to the scorecard, along with incentive compensation. There then are three additional issues that must be addressed in the creation of a balanced scorecard. These are identification of the correct metrics, the relative importance weight given to each metric, and the desired performance level.

The *correct metrics* to use are dependent upon the organization's vision, mission, strategies, and culture. For example, a large telecommunications firm used a comprehensive customer satisfaction survey to measure customer attitudes. The survey included a single overall satisfaction question, and the company used this one measurement in the *customer* category of the balanced scorecard. Of the broad global questions, the question of overall satisfaction is the least stable and more apt to fluctuate up or down somewhat from survey to survey. But, since this was the question that executives were used to seeing and reflected the culture that had been created at the company, it was included on the balanced scorecard. Not every executive or everyone in the organization will agree with each component and metric, but they will probably agree with the concept. Most everyone in an organization would be satisfied to regularly review a handful of key metrics that represent various areas of the business and that are displayed on one sheet of paper.

If done correctly, the company's key stakeholders will have some say in what metrics are included on the balanced scorecard. After all, the balanced scorecard is meant to reflect a company's true overall performance, support the interests of all key stakeholders, and align metrics to support the company's vision, mission, and strategies. Many companies validate their set of balanced scorecard metrics with their employees and customers or at least apply a great deal of diligence to ensure the metrics support the *customer's view* as opposed to an internal view of performance.

Once the metrics have been identified and agreed upon, the *relative weights,* or importance, of each on the scorecard must be determined. The easiest way to weight the scorecard is to make all categories equal. If there are four major categories as suggested by Kaplan and Norton's Balanced Scorecard model, each would comprise 25 percent of the overall evaluation. If there are five categories, each would represent 20 percent, and so forth. But, if a dimension of the strategy was of particular importance, perhaps cost reduction, it could be rated relatively higher due to its strategic importance. A company can adjust these weights to emphasize the importance of a particular strategy or initiative. For example, a firm may want to weight balanced scorecard categories or metrics that have a greater impact on achievement of Six Sigma goals to help kick start its Six Sigma deployment efforts. The implication is that the weights among the components should reflect importance of each strategic initiative.

A company could actually determine the importance of each dimension statistically and use these actual weights as part of its balanced scorecard. IBM Rochester used multivariate, statistical analysis to determine that there were only five performance metrics that demonstrated strong correlation to each other and also supported overall financial performance. Using 10 years' worth of data, IBM Rochester determined strong statistical correlation among the factors of employee satisfaction, productivity, cost of quality, customer satisfaction, and market share (Appendix A) (see note 3).

The third issue relating to the balanced scorecard is determining and measuring the *desired performance level*. Performance levels for each metric can be set using a number of methods. For example, a company might have a goal of 15 percent revenue growth per year. Each business unit would then set a goal of 15 percent or greater revenue growth. Or, a company could have a goal of a 55 percent top box score on overall satisfaction. The company could then compare actual and planned performance levels on the same metric for different divisions with the company. Benchmarking performance levels against competition, industry leaders, and other world-class organizations is another method that can be used to set specific performance objectives. Finally, the organization could ask its key stakeholders about their expectations on the balanced scorecard performance metrics by using a team to develop the appropriate performance metrics.

Once performance levels for the various metrics have been determined, the company needs to assess performance against these levels. Executive performance evaluations could be based on an integration of all components. In this situation, a single score could be developed from the weights and performance levels for each component. High performance in one area could offset a somewhat lower score in another area. Another way to assess overall performance of the complete balanced scorecard is to describe some threshold and stretch level of achievement of all the metrics. In other words, an organization may state that it has established threshold targets for each performance objective, which trigger a minimal payout. There could also be stretch goals that trigger a higher level of payout. The exception to this may be financial performance, where the goal is to achieve 100 percent of the target. Another approach is to set threshold and stretch performance levels for each component that *must* be met. In some organizations, executives must meet the threshold levels in each area or there is no incentive compensation, regardless of performance in other areas. For example, a company may set a threshold level of 80 percent satisfied (as indicated by top two scores) on the customer satisfaction survey score. If the results are 78 percent satisfied, the executive would receive no incentive compensation despite the fact that they may have met the threshold levels on all the other performance metrics. Above the threshold performance levels, some organizations set stretch goals and increase the incentive compensation based upon achieving significantly higher levels of performance above the threshold levels.

From this discussion, it should be obvious that a balanced scorecard has some very real advantages for reinforcing the desired behavior necessary to achieve strategic initiatives such as Six Sigma. But it should be equally obvious that a balanced scorecard must be carefully designed and implemented. Most often the design of the scorecard is done by a team of executives intimately familiar with the company's strategy, culture, and overall objectives. Figure 8.1 shows the balanced scorecard employed by IBM Rochester (see note 3). It

Vision: *TO BRING THE INTEGRATED VALUE OF AS/400 TO e-BUSINESS*

Mission: *Provide high quality systems which enable fast deployment of e-business solutions through superior integration of mainstream technologies and industry leading service and support.*

	Financial/Market Share	Customer/Satisfaction/Loyalty	Product/Channel (Priorities)	Core Processes	People/Skills
GOALS	• Revenue growth that drives improved market share • Industry leading profit margins • Significant growth in new business	• Undisputed leader in customer satisfaction in our industry • Industry leading quality, reliability, and availability • Sustained improvement in customer retention and loyalty • Differentiation through Service and Support	• Rapid deployment of e-business solutions through superior integration of industry leading technologies • Provide product scalability that meets market needs at a competitive price • Improve overall channel productivity and increase number of key Solution Providers and Business Partners • Leadership in Java, collaborative computing, and data warehousing • Competitive e-Commerce, Web serving, and BMS offerings	• Excel as a reliable supplier to our customer, providing products on time and as expected • Improve cost competitiveness and return on investments	• Strengthen our competitive edge in network computing through a high performance culture, characterized by highly skilled, diverse, and motivated people committed to winning in the market place
OBJECTIVES	• Revenue = $X Billion in (year) • Worldwide market share = X% by (year) • Balanced growth of PTI with revenue	• Yearly improvement in customer satisfaction gap to competition • Release-to-release product availability and quality improvement	• Best in industry time-to-deploy e-business • Price-to-competition gap of X% by (year) • High-end performance within X% of competition	• On-time delivery greater than X% • Responsiveness better than X%	• Identify and close key skill gaps • Less than X% attrition in key skills

OBJECTIVES	• Greater than X% revenue from new customers	• Continued improvement in key customer satisfaction areas	• Increased channel productivity • Recruit X number of Business Partners by (year) • Competitive Java cost performance and leadership in Java deployment • Cost performance within X% of Industry leader • Leadership in data warehouse installations	• Cost Competitive Index (CCI) better than X by (year) • Improve inventory turns to X by (year) • Improve hardware warranty expense to revenue (E/R) to X by (year) • Best-in-Industry Time-to-Profit	• Improve unit and individual team work scores to X% by (year) • Improve and maintain employee morale by X% • Increase diversity of workforce —% new hires that are woman and/or minorities

MEASURES	• Revenue
	• Volumes
	• Market Share by key segments
	• Pre-tax Income
	• Gross Profit
	• Development Expense
	• Brand SG&A
	• New Customer Revenue
		• Worldwide customer Satisfaction score
		• % customer loyalty
		• % customer retention
		• System availability
		• Field hardware quality
		• Software defects
			• Application deployment speed
			• Number of NC and Java applications
			• Price gap to competition
			• High-end performance gap
			• Channel productivity
			• Number of Business Partners recruited
			• Number of data warehouse installs
				• On-time delivery
				• On-time ships
				• Responsiveness
				• Warranty E/R
				• CCI Index
				• Inventory Turns
				• Hardware warranty E/R
				• Time-to-profit
					• Percent completed skill gaps
					• Percent attrition in key skills
					• Employee survey scores for:
					  —Team work
					  —Morale
					• Percent new hires
					  —Women/ Minorities

Figure 8.1 IBM Rochester's Balanced Scorecard.

was developed with direct assistance by David P. Norton. You will notice that the balance scorecard metrics support key objectives and strategies, as well as the vision and mission statements. Because of the strategic alignment, IBM Rochester developed five categories instead of four. You will also notice that the IBM Rochester balanced scorecard metrics support the study shown in Appendix A that demonstrates correlation among the factors of employee satisfaction, productivity, cost of quality, customer satisfaction, and market share (see note 3).

SUMMARY

Clearly visible senior management support for Six Sigma initiatives is absolutely critical. There are many reasons for this. Most notable is the fact that Six Sigma must be a cultural imperative, not an incremental program. Significant training and development expenses will be incurred over the three- to five-year implementation period. Six Sigma cannot be implemented quickly with no expense.

The Six Sigma initiative must be formally cascaded to all employees at all levels of an organization. Hoshin Planning can be a useful tool in achieving this. The goal is to ensure that every employee knows how their jobs contribute to all strategic goals, including Six Sigma.

The performance of individuals and business units must be measured against the performance goals. This can be done through a balanced scorecard for upper levels of management. A balanced scorecard combines performance measurement in a variety of areas such as financial, customer, processes, and human resources. Even at the individual level, performance should be measured against strategic goals, including the Six Sigma initiative.

CASE STUDY

CORPORATE STRATEGIES

The vision, mission, and strategic objectives of Johnson Controls, Inc., are shown in Figure 8.2. These describe and support a culture that is focused on quality, customer service, and continuous improvement.

The Controls Business implemented a Six Sigma initiative in 1999 as part of its overall continuous improvement journey and total quality management initiative. The overall quality strategies for the Controls Business are shown in Figure 8.3. Clear alignment and clear definition of goals are demonstrated between the Johnson Controls, Inc., strategy and the Controls Business Quality Strategy. Hoshin Planning described at the end of chapter 9 shows further alignment of organizational and individual goals and objectives to both the corporate and Controls Business strategies.

Johnson Controls, Inc.

OUR CREED

We believe in the free enterprise system. We shall consistently treat our customers, employees, shareholders, and the community with honesty, dignity, fairness, and respect. We will conduct our business with the highest ethical standards.

OUR MISSION

Continually exceed our customer's increasing expectations

WHAT WE VALUE

Integrity: Honesty and fairness are essential to the way we do business and how we interact with people. We are a company that keeps its promises. We do what we say we will do, and we will conduct ourselves in accordance with our code of ethics.

Customer Satisfaction: Customers satisfaction is the source of employee, shareholder, supplier, and community benefits. We will exceed customer expectations through continuous improvement in quality, service, productivity, and time compression.

Our Employees: The diversity and involvement of our people is the foundation of our strength. We are committed to their fair and effective selection, development, motivation, and recognition. We will provide employees with the tools, training, and support to achieve excellence in customer satisfaction.

Improvement and Innovation: We seek improvement and innovation in every element of our business.

Safety and the Environment: Our products, services, and workplaces reflect our belief that what is good for the environment and the safety and health of all people is good for Johnson Controls.

OBJECTIVES

Customer Satisfaction: We will exceed customer expectations through continuous improvement in quality, service, productivity, and time compression.

Technology: We will apply world-class technology to our products, processes, and services.

Growth: We will seek growth by building our existing businesses.

Market Leadership: We will only operate in markets where we are, or have the opportunity to become, the recognized leader.

Shareholder Value: We will exceed the after-tax, median return on shareholders' equity of the Standard and Poor's Industrials.

Figure 8.2 Johnson Controls, Inc., Vision, Mission, Values, and Objectives.

JOHNSON CONTROLS, INC, CONTROLS BUSINESS—QUALITY STRATEGY

QUALITY POLICY
We, individually and as a team, will deliver products and services that consistently conform to our customers' requirements and exceed their increasing expectations.

QUALITY STRATEGY
We will achieve a "step change" in quality performance. A fundamental change in our quality culture and a strengthening of discipline will be achieved to realize a sustained improvement in quality performance.

INITIATIVES
Three major initiatives will drive our change:
- Six Sigma Performance
- Software Process Improvement (SPI) to achieve SEI CMM Level 5
- Process and Systems Globalization

OBJECTIVES
1. Excellence in customer satisfaction
   - Achieve "top box" survey ratings for the three most important customer satisfaction attributes.
2. Consistent conformance to customer requirements
   - Minimize variation to prevent defect occurrence.
   - Achieve six sigma performance levels for key characteristics of core products and processes.
3. Achieve SEI CMM level 5 performance capability in software engineering and development.
4. Eliminate "special cause" failures (field recalls, updates).

STRATEGIES
1. Rigorously apply accepted best practices that are defined by our ISO 9000-certified Quality System.
2. Globalize core processes (best practices) and systems; continuously improve.
3. Employ common metrics to direct performance improvement efforts.
4. New Product Development:
   - Accurate, complete market requirements will drive hardware, software, and system specifications.
   - Apply advanced Project/Program Management methods.
   - Develop robust designs and capable processes; demonstrate their sigma performance levels.
5. Manufacturing and Delivery of Products:
   - Prioritize and improve existing core products and processes, demonstrating sigma performance.
   - Apply advanced order management, advanced material planning, and demand-flow technology.
   - Complete global PDM system for component, part, and product data management and change control.
6. Post-Sales Support
   - Measure and improve product field performance and application.
   - Ensure timely, thorough handling of product problems and complaints.
7. Supplier Management
   - Rigorously select, develop, and manage key suppliers; require and validate their sigma performance.

PERFORMANCE GOALS
Specific performance goals have been developed, but are not shown here due to the confidentiality of their nature.

Figure 8.3 Controls Business, Johnson Controls, Inc., Quality Strategy.

9

Selecting the Right Processes

When an organization is initially starting a Six Sigma improvement effort, selecting the *right* processes to work on is critical. Initial projects are often viewed as pilots, trial balloons, or experiments. If the project goes well, the improvement effort is rolled out more broadly throughout the organization. The initial improvement effort is usually closely scrutinized while in progress. The results of the effort are even more closely evaluated. Therefore, starting with a successful project is important to achieve more widespread organizational buy-in and acceptance. What is critically important, however, is that an organization's Six Sigma efforts be tied to process improvements as opposed to improving just some performance metric that the organization has not tied to either a process parameter or customer requirement. This chapter introduces the use of value models, competitive profiles, and the use of cost/benefit analysis as methods for selecting the right process to attack with your Six Sigma efforts.

In an organization that has an ongoing continuous improvement effort, the selection of a process is less critical. The organization has probably accepted and supported the continuous improvement concept. There is less of a need to prove that the concept is viable in general. However, a need to educate managers who are less familiar with improvement techniques may still exist. An organization's Six Sigma efforts should complement and support an organization's overall continuous improvement efforts. After all, it would not be advantageous to apply the same level of rigor demanded of a true Six Sigma effort to every process in the organization, especially those that are performing as expected.

Regardless of whether the selection of a process to be improved is for the first time or for the fiftieth time, some issues must still be considered by the organization. The four primary issues to consider when selecting a process are the relevance of the processes to an organization's strategic goals, the costs associated with a particular process, the importance of the process outputs to the customer, and the competitive strengths and weaknesses of the organization. Before discussing these four issues in detail, discussing which processes *not* to select is equally important.

WHICH PROCESSES *NOT* TO SELECT

Several situations undermine or constrain the effectiveness of continuous improvement efforts. These red flags should be avoided or corrected before starting a project. If these issues are ignored, a Six Sigma or other improvement team may devote a good deal of time and effort to a project and be met with frustration and disillusionment. The following are the five situations that can cause an improvement effort to be ineffective.

No Senior Management Support

If there is not clear support from senior management for the improvement effort, Six Sigma initiatives should not be started. The reason for this is that a majority of an organization's key processes cut across organizational and functional boundaries. In most organizations, senior management involvement and support is necessary to gain participation from all of the relevant parties. In essence, senior management becomes a coordinating mechanism that breaks down barriers associated with cross-organization, cross-functional process improvement efforts.

The Six Sigma team requires resources. The team needs to allocate 10 to 20 working days for an average project. This results in a significant labor charge. For some areas, particularly if they are understaffed, this may cause resistance. If the team members are widely dispersed geographically, there are also travel expenses. Since senior management usually has budgetary control, resource allocation requires its approval and support.

Senior management support usually results in an executive-level champion being appointed for the Six Sigma initiative. This person provides a visible focal point for Six Sigma efforts. They typically oversee several projects at once and are ultimately responsible for the results and success or failure of the project. The champion should have some budgetary control to support the direct costs as well as the influence to resolve conflict and encourage support. For example, each major business unit within Allied Signal has a vice president for Six Sigma. If support for the Six Sigma effort comes only from an enlightened middle manager, that manager can probably influence actions in his or her own area. But, unfortunately, the manager will be unable to implement broader, organization-wide changes where the largest benefits usually reside.

No Support from Process Owners

Somewhat related to the issue of no senior management support is the issue of no support from process owners. For instance, a human resources vice president may not be particularly excited about a Six Sigma effort devoted to employee training and development. Without the vice president's support, implementing changes would be difficult.

Since most organizations are structured around departments or functional areas, the department head may play a role similar to that of the process owner. A process may depend heavily on the Information Technology (IT) department. If an IT manager is unwilling to change procedures or modify databases, significant process changes are unlikely. Thus, functional area managers that are centrally involved in a specific process should be in support of the Six Sigma effort, preferably on a voluntary basis.

Finally, a process owner, regardless of functional responsibility or reporting structure, may take offense at a Six Sigma team wanting to improve his or her process. After all, this may imply a level of incompetence on the part of the process owner, whose job it has been to ensure the efficient performance of the process. The Six Sigma team leader must work with the process owner to gain his or her commitment or buy-in, even involving the process owner directly on the improvement team. The absence of the process owner from the team could be a detriment.

Ambiguous Processes

Some processes in organizations are ambiguous and ill-defined. Ambiguity may include no clearly defined starting or ending point, no identification of specific customer inputs or process outputs, or no clearly defined process steps. Process ambiguity results in no clear definition of process performance or control metrics and measurements. Without understanding process performance parameters, including costs and cycle times, a Six Sigma team's efforts would be wasted on trying to improve the process.

Communication is an important process in most organizations, but there are many starting and ending points associated with this process. The direction of communications can be top down, bottom up, or lateral. Communication can be viewed as being one way, two way, or multiple ways. Communication can involve internal and/or external customers. A Six Sigma effort to improve communication can undoubtedly have positive benefits to an organization, but the organization would need to define the scope of the effort in terms of what communication subprocess warrants the most attention and then clearly define process parameters and metrics as a starting point for improvement. Therefore, communication or similar processes are typically not a good starting point for Six Sigma efforts.

No Trivial Processes

When processes are selected, particularly for the initial project, the processes should be significant and important, not minor or trivial. Since initial projects are evaluated very critically, there should be some potentially significant benefits that can be documented. The more significant processes have higher costs, more employees, longer cycle times, and more direct impact on the customers. When benefits are achieved in these processes, other employees in the organization are quick to recognize the value. Benefits can also be tied to significant financial performance improvements. However, if a process is not significant, others in the organization may be skeptical of the value from the proposed improvement efforts.

Another way of looking at this situation is to divide processes in macro and micro levels. Focusing a Six Sigma improvement effort on a macro process such as *communications* may be too large of a project for a Six Sigma team. But, focusing on the executive-to-employee communication subprocess may be more manageable for a Six Sigma team. However, focusing lower into the subprocess may be of little benefit or value to the organization. It is important for senior leaders, champions, and Six Sigma team leaders to separate the many trivial process improvement proposals from the vital few that warrant the biggest impact on the organization. The trivial many can be left for the organization's overall continuous improvement efforts as opposed to being assigned to a Six Sigma team.

No Processes in Transition

If a process is undergoing a major change for some reason, that process should be avoided until the changes have been fully implemented for a period of time. Processes that are in a state of flux make it difficult to develop an *"As-Is"* process. Employees are often not sure of procedures and activities. Therefore, it is also difficult to identify disconnects or activities that are in need of improvement. After major changes have settled in, opportunities or problems with the process will once again become apparent.

As an example, an organization decided to improve its billing process, an area that was important to customers. A Six Sigma team was assembled, involving all the appropriate players to improve the process. After four or five days of meetings, the IT manager mentioned that the CEO had made a decision to switch the billing system to a new software package that was designed specifically for the company's industry. At that point, no one knew the specifics of the software package. Since most Six Sigma efforts require extensive database interaction, primarily to retrieve or analyze performance data, the team did not know what information would be available, when, and how it could be accessed. As a result, the billing team was severely constrained and had to focus on everything about the process except the software issues. The team should probably have postponed its efforts until after the new billing software was implemented.

The previous five issues are proven constraints to Six Sigma efforts, as well as to other process improvement efforts that the organization may decide to undertake. If any of these issues are present, the Six Sigma team experiences frustration and meaningful results are difficult to achieve. However, if these issues are not evident, or if the Six Sigma team leader recognizes and resolves these issues, the effort has a good probability of being successful. Success is obviously enhanced by selecting the right process in the first place.

SELECTING THE RIGHT PROCESSES

There are four characteristics of good processes that should be considered. The process should be strategically important to an organization's overall goals. The process should have significant costs, either labor or material, associated with it. Often, processes with high cycle times also have significant costs. The process should also be important to customers. And, the process should build upon competitive strengths or correct weaknesses. Each of these four characteristics is further explained here.

Strategic Importance

Virtually all organizations develop annual strategic goals and plans that address areas such as revenue growth, cost reduction, customer satisfaction, and/or new product development initiatives. Some organizations have strategic goals that address the development and retention of employees. Others have strategic goals that address alliances or partnerships with other firms in the value chain. Some organizations, like GE, even have Six Sigma strategic goals. If Six Sigma efforts can be linked directly to an organization's strategic goals, several benefits can result.

First, senior management is likely to be supportive of any initiatives that directly support strategic goals. This often results in resource allocation to support Six Sigma efforts. Second, others in the organization are more often willing to support or be involved in Six Sigma efforts because of its linkage to strategic goals and the high visibility it will ultimately receive.

A technique of rolling strategic goals down through the organization is Hoshin Planning, which was discussed in the previous chapter. Each department and manager incorporates strategic goals into annual plans. This usually cascades down between three to five organizational levels. Every strategic goal is reflected in the annual action plans for each unit, department, or manager. If the Six Sigma team addresses important goals that are common to many functional areas, the teams generate benefits to various functional areas. This enhances overall support.

Another, less-structured approach than Hoshin Planning is to simply identify the critical business issues that support the organization's strategic goals. Rather than linking strategic goals to each process, a few critical business issues could be identified. For example, an overall critical business issue could be to reduce operating costs by 20 percent. The critical issue for a process could be to reduce cycle time by 30 percent, to reduce labor costs by 20 percent, or to reduce material costs by 30 percent, for example. Conceptually, this is much the same as Hoshin Planning but less comprehensive. However, the critical business issue becomes the clear objective for the Six Sigma improvement team.

The strategic goals are usually established by a team of senior executives. Deriving subgoals or critical business issues for a process is typically done by middle management. Implementing the process improvement recommendations is done by frontline employees, those actually performing process activities.

While all Six Sigma initiatives should have explicit goals, deriving these goals from the strategic goals is very useful. This linkage makes obtaining support and buy-in from others in the organization much easier. For most organizations, the strategic goals are also related to the other issues of cost, importance to the customer, and competitive position.

Costs

High-cost processes are good candidates for Six Sigma improvement. The logic behind this is simple. If a 30 percent cost reduction is achieved in a process that consumes $500,000 in resources, the savings to the company are $150,000. If a 30 percent cost reduction is achieved in a process that consumes $200,000, the savings are only $60,000. For most Six Sigma projects, the time and effort required of an improvement team are the same for a $150,000 savings project as they are for a $60,000 savings project.

Unfortunately, few organizations actually know what their process costs truly are. In most organizations, traditional accounting systems provide only very aggregate, departmental data that reinforces functional silos. Since most processes are cross-functional, cutting across department boundaries, processes typically consume portions of many different department budgets. Overhead and selling, general expenses, and administrative costs (SGA) are often allocated very crudely to finished products or services, regardless of how resource intensive the product or service may have been. The only current solution to identify true process costs is activity-based-cost (ABC) accounting. An ABC approach does just what the name implies, examines the costs associated with activities. Since activities are the building blocks of processes, all of the activities are individually evaluated and then aggregated for labor, material, and support costs as well as cycle times. But, since most organizations do not have an ABC accounting system, there are some other less-refined approaches in use by many organizations.

One approach is to simply examine staffing in an organization. If 40 percent of the workforce is devoted to a particular type of work, that work is probably a good candidate for improvement. In most organizations, labor costs, including associated benefits, are the largest or one of the largest controllable expenses. Since cycle time reduction is a common result of Six Sigma efforts, a shorter process cycle translates directly to labor savings. An extension of this approach is to have every person account for every minute of his or her time against a particular project or account. In this way, all labor and expenses associated with individuals in an organization can be aggregated and assigned directly to a company's products or services.

Another approach is to examine material costs. Processes that consume large amounts of materials are often good candidates for Six Sigma efforts. A reduction of waste and scrap is a common result of process improvement. This may also take the form of better inventory control and turnover, lower shrinkage rates, less acquisition costs, and lower rates of obsolescence of old inventory.

A third approach is to examine processes that provide customized products and services. Processes that provide standardized products and services typically evolve over time into more efficient activities. However, those processes that provide customized products to fit a specific customer's needs are more variable and adaptive. Often, these processes "reinvent the wheel" each time. The result is a more inefficient use of both labor and materials, as well as other costs. The concept of *mass customization* provides a partial solution to this situation. Mass customization requires that a core, standardized product or service be identified, upon which certain modular units are added to provide a customized or unique product for the customer.

The processes that are strategically important and consume high costs are usually also important to the customer. Rather than the internal focus within an organization, the next issues to consider in selecting processes are external. These are customers and competitors.

Importance to Customers

Processes that are important to customers are prime candidates for improvement. An organization needs to examine processes that constitute the key drivers on customer satisfaction or dissatisfaction. One of the predominant lessons to be learned from this book is the importance of listening and learning from customers and applying this to the company's Six Sigma improvement efforts. That is, an organization should focus improvement efforts on processes that have the highest impact on customer satisfaction or dissatisfaction as opposed to only using costs or cycle time.

It is also important to view processes through a customer's eyes. IBM Rochester focused on a number of processes that were felt to be important, including the manufacturing process. Customers stated, however, that they did not view the manufacturing process as all that important but only cared that the product was easy to order and delivered as they expected. This caused IBM Rochester to focus on the larger fulfillment process, which included the ordering subprocess, the subprocess of handing the order off to manufacturing, and the delivery and installation subprocesses. Customers stated that they were only concerned with the fact that they could order a product, IBM delivered it, and it worked.[24]

In order to find out what is important to customers, their opinions and expectations must be captured in some way. The chapters in Part 2 of this book present the major alternatives to capturing the voice of the customer. In general, the data is either qualitative or quantitative. Qualitative data results from sample sizes that are too small for rigorous statistical analysis. For small samples, the survey approach is more general and open-ended. A common qualitative survey question is, "What two things could we do to improve?" An example of the results from this question are presented in Table 9.1. In this case, the customers made a total of 340 comments on a survey. Of the 340 comments, 137 dealt with technicians and 73 dealt with sales. While neither technicians nor sales are actually processes, the data certainly identifies areas in need of improvement such as training on product offerings or on customer relationship management.

The most frequent comment within the technician category was to "improve response time." Therefore, a process would deliver as an output an emergency repair service. Having their system quickly become operational again was important to customers. A Six Sigma team could improve the process that began with a request for emergency service and ended with a restored system. The sales organization is closer to a process than the technicians. Within sales, the most critical issues were increased contact and better customer follow-up. The sales approach could be modified to call on certain customers at exact intervals desired by the customer, for example.

Customer-Identified Areas for Improvement	Number of Times Mentioned
Technicians	*137*
Improve response time	53
Follow-up after service call	31
More extensive training of technicians	17
More professionalism of technicians	13
Larger technicians staff	12
Assign technicians to businesses	6
Concerned with the subcontractors	5
Sales	*73*
Increased contact from sales personnel to customers/including returning calls	24
Better follow-up after the sale	17
More knowledge about products and services	10
Information on upgrades and improvements sent	9
Need for more planning of customers' long-term needs	9
General improvement of sales personnel	4
Company Policies	*45*
Become more customer focused	17
Have better internal communication	14
Have better supply of replacement equipment available	11
Better retention of employees	3
Customer Support Center	*41*
Increase professionalism of staff	13
Return phone calls faster	9
Have a local person for customers to contact	6
Increase level of training	5
Have a special phone number to answer technical questions	4
Have customer information system available at time of call	4

Table 9.1 Customer-Identified Areas for Improvement.   *(continued)*

Customer-Identified Areas for Improvement	Number of Times Mentioned
Billing	*17*
Improve billing practices including accuracy	17
Pricing	*16*
More competitive pricing	16
Customer Training	*5*
Give customers more training	5
Delivery	*5*
Faster delivery of parts	5
Engineering	*1*
Overall improvement of engineering	1
Total	340

Table 9.1 Continued.

If the data is quantitative, value models can be developed that indicate the relative importance of processes to customers. The topic of value models was discussed previously in chapter 3 and is explored in additional detail in chapter 11. An actual model is presented in Figure 9.1. The percentages in the value model indicate the relative importance to the customer of each performance area, based on multivariate statistical analysis. Since the attributes were identified by the customer and grouped into related categories, all of the categories do not directly correspond to processes. For example, image and personnel are not clearly defined processes, although it may be argued that image is an outcome of a process. However, product delivery is clearly a process. The customer support center, dispatching and scheduling, and repair are all different phases or subprocesses of a service call process. Installation, training, and billing are clearly all processes.

In the value model, relationship is the most important category that could be identified as a process. Chapter 7 presented a structured approach for developing better relationships with key accounts that could be used in any organization. The next most important area is product delivery, a well-defined process. If the customer support center, dispatching and scheduling, and repair are grouped into a *service call* process, that process, collectively, becomes most important to customers. This is very consistent with the qualitative results presented in Table 9.1 for the same business.

The use of the value model identifies three process areas—relationship, product delivery, and service calls—that are good candidates for Six Sigma improvement. Process areas such as installation, sales, training, and billing are of lesser importance to customers and should not be priorities for Six Sigma improvements until the more important areas are addressed.

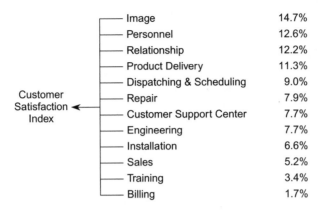

Image	14.7%
Personnel	12.6%
Relationship	12.2%
Product Delivery	11.3%
Dispatching & Scheduling	9.0%
Repair	7.9%
Customer Support Center	7.7%
Engineering	7.7%
Installation	6.6%
Sales	5.2%
Training	3.4%
Billing	1.7%

Figure 9.1 Overall Value Model–Categories of Attributes.

It should be noted that each of the categories in the value model consists of a variety of more specific attributes that would assist in identifying what should be improved. For example, the product delivery category includes the more specific attributes of on time, lead time, and order completeness. Being on time and lead time were of very high importance to customers. Each of the categories consisted of between three and six more specific attributes.

The value model indicates the relative importance of each category. By combining importance with actual performance data, an *importance performance grid* (Figure 9.2) can be developed. Again, this data was collected and analyzed as part of a customer satisfaction survey effort. The performance data could be calculated in several different ways, but, in this example, the percentage of satisfied customers (top box scores) was used in each category as the specific measurement of satisfaction.

Personnel (Number 1) and relationship (Number 2) are most important to customers, as indicated by the value model. But these two areas, along with installation (Number 8), are areas of relatively high current performance. Product delivery is the third most important area. The customer's view of product delivery performance is low, based upon the customer satisfaction scores, so this should be a priority for a Six Sigma improvement project. There are three areas—sales (Number 9), training (Number 10), and billing (Number 11)—that are lower in performance, but these areas are also of relative low importance to customers. The three aspects of a service call (customer support, dispatching and scheduling, and repair) are next in importance, but are of only moderate performance.

The implication of combining both importance and performance is that priorities can change somewhat. These changes can be caused by a number of factors, including time, customer size, customer experience, and so forth. Based purely on importance, the category of *relationship* was a candidate for Six Sigma improvement. But, since performance is already good in this area, product delivery and service calls would become priority areas for improvement.

Value models that identify the relative importance of processes to customers are quite useful when selecting processes for improvement efforts. The models are particularly useful when used with actual performance data that identifies a firm's strengths and weaknesses. The issues of importance and performance can be enhanced even further by developing an objective competitive profile.

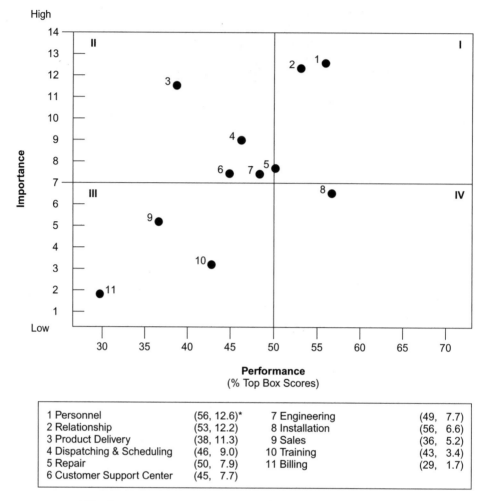

Figure 9.2 Importance Performance Grid.

1 Personnel	(56, 12.6)*	7 Engineering	(49, 7.7)
2 Relationship	(53, 12.2)	8 Installation	(56, 6.6)
3 Product Delivery	(38, 11.3)	9 Sales	(36, 5.2)
4 Dispatching & Scheduling	(46, 9.0)	10 Training	(43, 3.4)
5 Repair	(50, 7.9)	11 Billing	(29, 1.7)
6 Customer Support Center	(45, 7.7)		

* The first number in parentheses is the top box score. The second number is the importance rating from the value model.

Competitive Profile

There are several ways of conducting a competitive profile, but the objective is to identify the company's strengths and weaknesses. This is done by making performance comparisons against the competitors. In this way, a competitive strength could be exploited or a weakness improved. Competitive profiling could be gathered through the company's own customers, especially if customers deal with several competing companies for the same products and services. Customers are continually making competitive comparisons when selecting suppliers. However, there are usually some biases associated with a firm identifying itself and asking customers for competitive performance comparisons. Customers tend to give more favorable responses to the company that is surveying, thus creating a response bias.

A better approach to conducting a competitive profile is to conduct a *blind survey*. In a blind survey, the customer does not know who is conducting the research. Customers are asked to identify their primary suppliers of a product or service and then to rate the

Performance Area	Sponsor's Top Box Score (% of Respondents)	Competitor's Average Top Box Score (% of Respondents)	Competitive Performance Gap
Personnel	56	70	−14
Relationship	53	51	+2
Product Delivery	38	44	−6
Dispatching & Scheduling	46	52	−6
Repair	50	54	−4
Customer Support Center	45	56	−11
Engineering	49	46	+3
Installation	56	48	+8
Sales	36	44	−8
Training	43	40	+3
Billing	29	32	−3

Table 9.2 Performance Comparison.

suppliers' performance. From a research standpoint, it is more difficult to obtain customer cooperation using this approach, but the results are more accurate and meaningful. An actual example illustrates the value of this approach.

A firm conducted a blind competitive survey using the same questionnaire that it used for its own customers. The sample size was 200, about the minimum for reliable results. A 5-point rating scale was used, with categories of excellent, very good, good, fair, and poor being used to describe the customer's rating. The first comparison—performance comparison—is shown in Table 9.2. The firm that conducted the research is referred to as the *sponsor.* The competitor's customer satisfaction score is based on the average of responses from the competitor's customers. The right-hand column of Table 9.2 indicates the competitive performance gap. A positive number (+) means that the sponsor firm is performing above the competitor average, whereas a negative number (−) means that the sponsoring firm is performing below the average. The sponsoring firm has a positive performance gap in the areas of installation, engineering, training, and relationship. However, only installation has a significant gap, while the three areas are only slightly above (2 to 3 percentage points) the competitor average. Unfortunately, all four of these areas are of lower importance to the customer. In other words, the sponsoring firm is performing well in areas that are less important to the customer.

The largest negative performance gaps against industry averages are for personnel (−14), customer support center (−8), product delivery (−6), dispatching and scheduling (−6), repair (−4), and billing (−3). These are well below the competitor's average. When the sponsoring firm examined only its own results, the area of *personnel* was viewed as a strength as this area had the highest top box performance score (56 percent). But, when this score was compared to the industry average, the sponsor's personnel were rated much

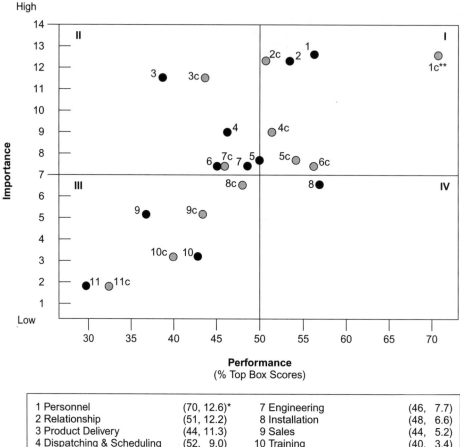

1 Personnel   (70, 12.6)*   7 Engineering   (46, 7.7)
2 Relationship   (51, 12.2)   8 Installation   (48, 6.6)
3 Product Delivery   (44, 11.3)   9 Sales   (44, 5.2)
4 Dispatching & Scheduling (52, 9.0) 10 Training   (40, 3.4)
5 Repair   (54, 7.9)   11 Billing   (32, 1.7)
6 Customer Support Center (56, 7.7)

* The first number in parentheses is the top box score. The second number is
   the importance rating from the value model.

** c denotes competitor's score

Figure 9.3 Competitor Importance Performance Grid.

lower than the competitors' personnel by a relatively large amount. Since customers base
their actions on competitive comparisons, the firm made improvements in the area of *personnel* a high-priority initiative.

Product delivery has a large performance gap (–6) and is relatively important to customers. This area should also be a priority for improvement. While sales has a slightly
larger performance gap (–8), the sales area is of less importance to the customer. The service call area (consisting of customer support center, dispatching and scheduling, and
repair) has large performance gaps and would remain a priority for improvement.

A fairly straightforward method of presenting the competitive scores is to plot them on
the same importance performance grid as the sponsor's scores. This is illustrated in Figure 9.3.
The small *c* denotes the competitors' scores. Comparing the scores on an importance performance grid is an excellent way to identify improvement priorities for a Six Sigma team.

There is a danger in comparing a firm's performance to the industry average. While
an average is an easy reference point, it is just what the name implies, an average. Some

Overall, how would you rate *(competitor's name)* personnel performance?				
	Top Box	**Don't Know**	**N**	**Total**
Competitor Average	70.1	4	197	201
Individual Competitors				
A	69.6	2	69	71
B	83.4	0	12	12
C	60.0	0	5	5
D	75.0	0	12	12
E	73.3	1	15	16
F	82.4	0	17	17
Other	64.2	1	67	68

Table 9.3 Individual Competitor Performance.

firms are above the average, and some firms are below. It is rare for a firm's strategic goal to become an industry average. Most firms have goals to gain market share and revenue, which is accomplished by trying to be the best, or one of the best, in their respective industry. Therefore, it is often helpful to identify scores by individual competitor. When a customer leaves a company, the customer usually goes to the industry leader, not an industry laggard or the industry average. Comparing a firm's performance to the individual competitors can be more enlightening. This is illustrated in Table 9.3.

The industry has six or seven major competitors and an array of other, smaller competitors that are grouped into an *other* category. Competitor A has a market share of about 35 percent as reflected in the sample size. But Competitor A's personnel are viewed as about average by the customers. Competitors B and F have substantially higher scores for the area of personnel, but have smaller sample sizes, so making firm conclusions is difficult. The *other* category has a lower performance score (64.2 percent) than any of the major competitors. This type of direct comparison is much more helpful in identifying areas for performance improvement and is most beneficial for a Six Sigma team that is interested in optimizing its efforts and overall performance results.

SUMMARY

There are many issues that must be considered when selecting processes for Six Sigma improvement efforts. The processes should be strategically important, have significant associated costs, be important to customers, and consider competitive performance. Unfortunately, most process improvements in the past have focused almost exclusively on cost and cycle time reduction. The use of value models that indicate the key drivers of customer satisfaction can ensure that selected processes are important to customers. The use of competitive profiles can build on competitive strengths and/or correct weaknesses. By using a combination of these considerations, a firm can develop a balanced approach to selecting the *right* processes.

CASE STUDY

SELECTING THE RIGHT PROCESSES

High-level processes are determined through business needs and ability to meet customer requirements. For instance, the hardware and software development processes are designed based upon their ability to produce a new design on time. A whole host of internally and externally driven parameters are monitored for process performance, including the ability to release a new product on time, to the functional specifications, and within budget. Cycle time, defect levels, test times, test results, beta customer feedback, and budget are just a few of the parameters that are monitored. Process improvement efforts focus on these parameters as well as the alignment and importance of the process to customers.

Chapter 9 cited examples of the use of qualitative customer satisfaction survey data (Table 9.1), value models (Figure 9.2), and the importance performance grid (Figure 9.3) for use in selecting processes in which to improve. These techniques are also used by the Controls Business of Johnson Controls, Inc., for use in selecting the right processes and projects to apply continuous improvement efforts. Similar case study data and examples for Johnson Controls, Inc.'s, use of value models and qualitative use of customer satisfaction data for identifying process improvement opportunities are described at the end of chapter 11, so they are not repeated here. Without revealing specific company strategies, a generic model depicting key quality and customer satisfaction strategies that are aligned with overall company strategies for growth and expense reduction are shown in Figure 9.4.

Deployment of Six Sigma efforts and results are an active part of Johnson Controls, Inc., Controls Business's overall business strategy, with specific measurable results identified. An example of Hoshin Planning, that is, deploying the high-level strategic objectives of growth through customer satisfaction improvement and expense reduction (or cost reduction or waste elimination) through the Six Sigma deployment are shown in Figure 9.5, Figure 9.6, and Figure 9.7 for the quality organization.

JOHNSON CONTROLS	Controls Business Quality Strategy	
Company Strategies	Reduce Expenses ↓	Growth ↑
Quality Strategies	Waste Elimination and Improved Product Quality through Six Sigma	Increased Sales and Customer Satisfaction through Six Sigma
		Increased Revenue and Sales through Customer Satisfaction Management
	Market Quality and Customer Satisfaction Results Internally with Our Employees and Sales Personnel	Market Quality and Customer Satisfaction Externally with Our Customers and Partners
Goals	$XX in Waste Elimination through Six Sigma By End of (Year)	XX % Improvement in Overall Customer Satisfaction Score By (Year)

Figure 9.4 Overall Quality Strategy of Controls Business, Johnson Controls, Inc.

Controls Business Quality Organization

VISION/MISSION:

The **Vision** for the Controls Group Quality organization is: "Undisputed image of world-class quality leadership of our products and services with our employees, customers, shareholders, and the public as a whole."

This will be accomplished by the following **Mission:** "Ensuring quality and customer satisfaction are key factors influencing tactical business and product/service decisions, and by positively impacting and influencing strategic business and product decisions that affect future quality and customer satisfaction results."

The Controls Group Quality organization supports SP and SS locations worldwide.

Strategies and Goals for Accomplishing the Vision/Mission:

1. Ensure key measurements, reports, and reviews are in place which are customer or business-based, that allow Controls Group personnel to predict or react to issues, and that drive quality improvement behavior.
2. Maintain or gain, and efficiently manage certification to any required customer/industry standard (e.g. agency registration, ISO 9000, UL, CSA in North America, and provide expertise and guidance on worldwide agency certification requirements).
3. Provide or manage audits, assessments, and/or reviews of compliance and readiness initiatives, products/services, processes, or procedures as required or requested.
4. Influence behavior of customers, executives, and employees through communication of Controls Group quality/customer satisfaction posture and improvement activities.
5. Provide expertise and guidance in current and emerging quality practices by sharing knowledge and assisting organizational improvement and learning.
6. Develop and broadly deploy initiatives and activities that allows Controls Group to achieve Six Sigma commitments to our shareholders and the Corporation.
7. Influence business process definition and management, procedures and documentation, and measurements that drive commonality, completeness, and integration across Controls Group operations worldwide.
8. Develop and broadly deploy initiatives and activities that assess our customer satisfaction performance posture, including our position within the industry and against competition, and that lead to improved customer satisfaction, market share, and revenue results.
9. Manage escalated customer problems and issues to resolution, ensuring all problems are resolved to our customers expectations and that Controls Group executives and employees are aware of current customer issues and our complaint posture.
10. Efficiently and effectively manage all resources, maintaining a highly motivated workforce.

Figure 9.5 Example of Hoshin Planning Deployment of the Quality Strategy of Controls Business, Johnson Controls, Inc., to the Quality Organization (Part 1).

Controls Business Quality Organization

Mission: Ensure quality and customer satisfaction are key factors influencing tactical business and product/service decisions, and positively impact and influence strategic business and product decisions that affect future quality and customer satisfaction results.

Goal 6: Develop and broadly deploy initiatives and activities that allows Controls Group to achieve Six Sigma commitments to our shareholders and the Corporation.

Measurements:
♦ Work with organizational deployment leaders on identifying Six Sigma improvement opportunities that allow Controls Group to meet its Corporate commitments
  • Allocate, and gain commitment on waste elimination targets by Controls Group organization by 03/01/XX
  • $XXM in committed identified improvement opportunities, fully achieved by 09/30/XX
♦ Identify and deploy Six Sigma training needs for all organizations that allow them to achieve commitments
  • XX trained champions by 01/15/XX
  • XX trained black belts by 06/30/XX
  • Employee six sigma awareness training developed and deployed to all employees by 03/01/XX
♦ Establish and deploy measurements of progress and success
  • Publish results to Controls Group executives as part of the Controls Business quality report
♦ Establish progress reviews with organizational executives (individually) and with Controls Group executives (collectively)

Figure 9.6 Example of Hoshin Planning Deployment of the Quality Strategy of Controls Business, Johnson Controls, Inc., to the Quality Organization (Part 2).

Controls Business Quality Organization

Mission: Ensure quality and customer satisfaction are key factors influencing tactical business and product/service decisions, and positively impact and influence strategic business and product decisions that affect future quality and customer satisfaction results.

Goal 8: Develop and broadly deploy initiatives and activities that assess our customer satisfaction posture, including our position within the industry and against competition, and that lead to improved customer satisfaction, market share, and revenue.

Measurements:

- ♦ Develop and conduct customer satisfaction surveys worldwide
  - Create a forum for sharing customer satisfaction results with Controls Group executives and employees on a regular basis
  - Quarterly customer satisfaction report
  - Quarterly Area issues/action reviews
- ♦ Be the champion for Control Business customer satisfaction
- ♦ Devise, propose, and sell an updated SSNA Scorecard that reflects desired behaviors on Customer Satisfaction improvement and aligns Area customer satisfaction results with Area Scorecard results by 04/01/XX
- ♦ Develop a methodology that allows Areas easy access to customer satisfaction data and allows for easy manipulation of data for maximum usage
  - Create and deploy tool by 03/01/XX
  - Success based upon user input on usability
- ♦ Advocate changes that will improve customer satisfaction and loyalty worldwide
  - Create methods to "sell" the importance of customer satisfaction to employees and executives
  - Include Customer Satisfaction targets as part of the overall strategy by 03/01/XX
- ♦ Ensure complete communication of customer satisfaction issues, results, and actions
  - Develop a customer satisfaction newsletter by 04/01/XX that sells customer satisfaction improvement and results for SSNA and customers
- ♦ Improve customer satisfaction results
  - XX% improvement year-to-year

Figure 9.7 Example of Hoshin Planning Deployment of the Quality Strategy of Controls Business, Johnson Controls, Inc., to the Quality Organization (Part 3).

10

Forming the Six Sigma Teams

Virtually all Six Sigma projects require the use of teams. The projects require more work and knowledge of activities than one person possesses. Most Six Sigma projects are process oriented, cutting across departments, and consisting of diverse activities. To be effective, the team must have familiarity with all the activities and their interrelationships.

Since teams are so critical to successful Six Sigma projects, the design of the team is extremely important. The primary design issue is the composition of the team. The second most important issue is the leadership of the team. These two issues are discussed first, followed by other characteristics of successful Six Sigma teams.

DESIGNING THE TEAM

The design of the team initially must address who should be involved, or team composition. Inherently, this occurs after a problem has been identified by a Six Sigma steering team or Six Sigma sponsor or champion. Since the selection of the process was addressed in a previous chapter, the issue is not addressed further here other than to say that the initial selection of a process for Six Sigma improvement is usually made by upper management. The challenge at the process level is to effectively implement the Six Sigma initiative.

Team Composition

In its simplest form, a team should consist of those individuals who have the technical knowledge necessary to improve a process. The initial composition of the team is usually determined by the executive champion or process owner based on managerial judgment. In most cases, once the initial team has been selected, the team must evaluate who else should be involved. This is often done by developing a relationship map.

A *relationship map* is a flowchart that begins with an input and ends with an output. Between the beginning and ending points, all of the functional areas that touch a process are identified. Each of the functional areas that touch a process should be represented on the Six Sigma team at some point. The core team may consist of individuals from areas most centrally involved in a process. Those less involved may be ad hoc members, appearing when needed. A very simple relationship map for order fulfillment might look like Figure 10.1. This relationship map indicates who should be part of the Six Sigma team.

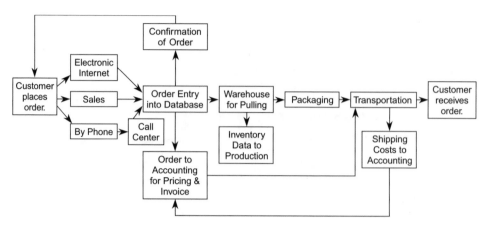

Figure 10.1 Order Fulfillment Relationship Map.

On this map, customers could place an order in three ways. They could enter the order electronically over the Internet, they could place an order with a salesperson, or they could place the order by telephone. If an order is sent electronically, the order is reviewed for completeness and accuracy by someone and then entered into a database. If the order is placed with a salesperson, the salesperson manually completes an order form and faxes it to an order entry location. If the order is placed by telephone, the call goes to the customer service center. Regardless of how the order is initiated, the order is entered into a database, which is maintained and designed by the information technology department.

The database automatically sends the information to the warehouse for order pulling. The database also notifies accounting that an order is placed so that an invoice can be developed. In the warehouse, the pulled order is transferred to the packaging department where it is prepared for shipment. Packaging delivers the packaged order to the transportation department in order to determine the proper shipping mode and cost. Transportation then notifies accounting of the shipping cost that is to be added to the invoice. Accounting prepares the invoice and sends it to transportation so the invoice accompanies the package to the customer.

Based on this relationship map, the Six Sigma process improvement team should consist of individuals from each of the following departments: sales, the call center, order entry, accounting, warehousing, packaging, transportation, and information technology. If the product was custom built for the customer, the team may also include the production, engineering, or purchasing functions. In total, the team would consist of 8 to 12 individuals. The individuals should have the necessary expertise to understand how each functional area performs the necessary activities. This may mean that two or more individuals from a functional area are necessary on the team.

For example, within an IT department, there may be one person who is responsible for production scheduling, warehousing, and inventory databases. Another individual may be responsible for accounting systems, order entry, and costing. Both of these individuals would need to be included on the team.

Therefore, the composition of the team is determined by the nature of the Six Sigma project. A simple project may have only four or five team members, while a complex project may have over 15 members. Most commonly, the average team size is 8 to 12 members.

The composition of a team does not remain static. It may be necessary to bring in a technical specialist for several meetings to provide advice. It may be useful to include internal or external suppliers or customers. As a team explores an issue, it may be necessary to add permanent members from other functional areas.

For example, accounting touches the order fulfillment process in several places. Accounting could probably be viewed as a subprocess that involves a variety of activities and individuals. It may be necessary for the team to bring in three or four people from accounting for a few meetings to understand their needs.

While the composition of the team may change somewhat over time, the majority of the core members should remain constant for the entire project. This ensures that there is continuity in problem solving. If new core members are added, the new team members must be brought up to speed without the benefit of the initial training. This slows the progress of the team and can frustrate other team members.

Since continuity is so important, some facilitators impose a rule that if anyone misses two consecutive meetings, that person is removed from the team. Attendance at the meetings is viewed as an indication of commitment. The Six Sigma project must be a priority activity for all team members.

Behavioral Considerations

In addition to the technical knowledge that is indicated on the relationship map, there are a variety of behavioral considerations that should be considered when forming a team. There should be a high level of commitment to the project by team members as just discussed. The commitment is often more easily achieved if participation on the improvement team is voluntary, particularly when an organization is just starting with Six Sigma. The cynics who doubt the concept seldom volunteer.

The team members should be well respected by their peers in the functional areas and more broadly across the organization. This makes the implementation of changes more easily accepted. Very often, the team's recommendations must be *sold* to others in the organization, especially those who need to change behaviors.

On a personal basis, the individuals selected for team membership should be innovative, creative, enthusiastic, and good communicators (both talking and listening). They should be individuals who are willing to try new ideas and who are not bound to the status quo. The team members should be opinion leaders so they can more easily sell the team's recommendations to the functional areas. Usually, these individuals are well experienced and have a thorough understanding of the job and related activities.

Team composition should avoid any direct superior-subordinate relationships, if possible. Subordinates are often hesitant to challenge the views of their manager in a group situation. This reduces the creativity and the contribution of the subordinate.

TEAM LEADERSHIP

Six Sigma teams require effective leadership. At leading Six Sigma companies such as General Electric and Motorola, the teams are lead by *blackbelts*. Blackbelts have gone through extensive training on both the Six Sigma tools and behavioral aspects of group dynamics. Essentially, the blackbelts are internal consultants that spread the concept of Six Sigma. The term *blackbelt* is copyrighted by the Six Sigma Academy.[25] Other organizations use titles such as *grandmaster* or *champion* to signify similar training certification.

When a team is first starting on the road to Six Sigma, the technical expertise necessary for team leadership is often lacking. Hiring a trained consultant or facilitator for the first several projects can be valuable until the skills are developed internally. There are a variety of consulting firms that provide facilitation services in Six Sigma. But, the external consultant should not be the team leader. While the external facilitator has the technical knowledge, they lack the cultural understanding of the organization. They also lack the personal credibility necessary to manage the team.

The team leader must perform a variety of roles. The leader must monitor the behavioral dynamics of the group. This could require keeping discussions on track when tangential issues emerge. The leader must summarize and integrate the discussion and get consensus. The leader must manage the activities of the group so that all team members are actively engaged.

The team leader must also manage all of the support activities. The team develops numerous graphics such as process maps and lists of assumptions, benefits, and recommendations. The handwritten flip chart notes need to be captured. The team leader is responsible for managing this process and getting copies to the team before the next meeting.

The team leader is responsible for developing summaries of each team meeting and developing a written agenda. The team leader usually plays the primary role in gathering the cost or productivity data necessary for detailed analysis by the team.

The team leader must also manage the communication process. This means that the progress of the team must be communicated to others in the organization. Periodic presentations to senior management are very helpful to both the team and management. The team leader is the coordinator and liaison in setting up these presentations.

The implication is that the role of team leader is demanding in terms of technical knowledge, behavioral skills, and support activities. If a person is lacking in any of these areas, that person should not be the team leader. It can be argued that the technical skills can be hired. But, at the least, a person must possess good behavioral skills and be able to obtain good support.

CHARACTERISTICS OF SUCCESSFUL SIX SIGMA TEAMS

In addition to the composition and leadership of the teams, there are 15 additional characteristics of successful Six Sigma projects. Many of these characteristics relate directly to the team activities while some are broader organizational issues. It may be possible to be successful without one or two of these characteristics being present. But, if a significant number are absent, the team will probably be unsuccessful. The 15 characteristics are presented in Table 10.1.

Clear Team Goals and Mission Statement That Are Linked to Corporate Strategy

It would be nice to be able to say that all employees in an organization know the corporate strategy and work toward achieving that strategy. Unfortunately, most employees in most organizations are unaware of the corporate strategy. As a result, employees often do not know how their jobs relate to what top management wants to do. Employees often have only a crude understanding of how their jobs relate to others in the organization. To overcome these constraints, the team should be familiarized with the corporate strategy and how Six Sigma projects support that strategy.

- Clear project goals and mission statement are linked to corporate strategy.
- Team goals are visibly supported by senior management.
- There is an executive steering team or individual that is the sponsor/champion.
- The organization has adopted a process orientation, and process owners are identified.
- Customer expectations are known, measured, and tracked.
- Supplier capability is known for all key inputs.
- The team has received both behavioral and technical training.
- The individual team members have clearly defined expectations, roles, and responsibilities.
- There is open communication based on respect and trust within the team and within the organization.
- The team is fully empowered with authority and autonomy to act.
- Team decisions are based on data and facts.
- The team has adequate time and resources to perform thoroughly.
- The contributions of individuals and teams are recognized and rewarded.
- The team uses common performance metrics that are linked to the customer and other performance areas within the organization.
- The team produces identifiable financial and performance results.

Table 10.1 Characteristics of Successful Six Sigma Teams.

For some companies, Six Sigma is an explicit pillar of corporate strategy. In these situations, linking the team's goals to corporate strategy is easy and obvious. More commonly, however, Six Sigma is not a major part of corporate strategy. In these firms, other linkages must be found. The linkages are usually through efficiency or productivity improvements, cost reductions, cycle time reductions, or improvements in customer satisfaction.

When corporate goals such as these are stated, the team goals must be derived from them. The more specific the goals, the easier it is to measure team success. As discussed in a previous chapter, explicit goals might be to reduce cost or cycle time by 30 percent. Or, a team's goals might be to reduce cost by 30 percent, cycle time by 50 percent, and improve top box customer satisfaction scores for the process by 10 percentage points simultaneously. To attain these goals, the team must be able to identify before and after measurements. But the standard for success will be the initial team goals.

Team Goals Are Visibly Supported by Senior Management

In most organizations, few employees interact with senior management. Therefore, there is often uncertainty and skepticism among employees about what management really wants to do. Visible support by senior management clarifies the commitment to the Six Sigma philosophy. This is particularly important since Six Sigma requires a company-wide shift in corporate philosophy. Without strong executive leadership, Six Sigma success will be piecemeal.

Visible support can be demonstrated in a number of ways. Statements in company newsletters are read by some employees. Statements in employee meetings are heard by most employees. However, visible support is most apparent when senior management actually attends some of the team meetings. Having a CEO or other senior executive at the initial goal-setting meeting sends a clear message that the Six Sigma project is important. Subsequently, periodic presentations to senior managers will reinforce the importance of the effort.

Visible support is also demonstrated by senior managers letting middle managers know that attendance at the team meetings is a priority. The middle managers must approve the time away from normal jobs to attend team meetings. Also, visible support is demonstrated by providing support services and budgets to the team as needed.

There Is an Executive Steering Committee or Individual That Is the Sponsor/Champion

A Six Sigma initiative is most effective when the philosophy and efforts are owned by someone at a high level. In some organizations, this role can be filled by an executive steering committee. Committee members can represent different functional areas, business units, or geographic areas depending upon the organization's structure. The role of the committee is to track the progress of the team and to coordinate activities. However, executive steering committees are usually found only in organizations with well-developed Six Sigma efforts. More common is an individual sponsor or champion.

The individual might be a vice president of quality, for example. At some organizations, the individual might be the vice president of Six Sigma and productivity. Regardless of who the champion is, someone must own the effort, at least initially. This individual communicates to the teams and across the organization. The individual coordinates the Six Sigma efforts and resolves any conflicts that emerge. The individual must be high enough in the organization to have resource and budget control to support the team. And, the executive should be evaluated on the results of the Six Sigma teams.

The Organization Has Adopted a Process Orientation and Process Owners Are Identified

Processes are the mechanisms that create value for customers. Each functional area should add value to a process in some way. Or, the functional area should directly support the value-creating process. If a functional area does not create value or support value creation, the function should be considered for elimination. Despite the fact that processes are the essential value-creating elements, few organizations are organized around processes.

Perhaps the reason goes back to Frederick Taylor and his call for job specialization. Perhaps the cause lies with early organizations that lacked our current technological capability to manage information. Certainly, business education in universities has contributed to the problem for the past 60 years by producing functional specialists who know little about other parts of the organization. There are marketing majors who know little about finance or information technology. There are accounting majors who dread dealing with customers or selling. There are finance majors who want to reduce the world to formulas and models but know nothing of motivation and human behavior. Whatever the reason, the fact remains that most organizations are organized around functions such as engineering, production, marketing, customer service, finance, human resources, and accounting.

These functional areas are typically led by a functional manager that represents and defends their particular functional silo. The functional managers are often the primary constraint to major improvements since the managers have responsibility and accountability for their area, not the value-creating processes. Maximizing the performance of a functional area may constrain process performance. Perhaps information technology (IT) is attempting to reduce costs by reducing staffing. Reduced IT support may severely constrain a Six Sigma initiative that requires better databases and information access. Only when functional managers view their area as a link in the value-creating chain will the functional silos be pierced.

Achieving a process orientation requires that functional managers closely coordinate their activities. Initially, this often requires the guidance of senior managers. In a very real sense, the power of a functional manager must be subordinated to that of the process. Releasing power is difficult for many managers unless mandated by executives.

Much business literature is rife with references to the *process owners.* Unfortunately, since few organizations are organized around processes, there are seldom any true process owners. Typically, the manager of the functional area with the largest role in the process becomes the process owner. In lieu of this, some organizations select a senior manager to be the process owner. But, in either case, the process owner must support the Six Sigma team. The process owner also plays an important role in the implementation of changes recommended by the team, as is seen in subsequent chapters.

Customer Expectations Are Known, Measured, and Tracked

Capturing the voice of the customer was discussed extensively in Part 2 of this book. The focus of the earlier discussion was on external customers. The logic behind this was that every major process produces an output that is of value to the customer. So, in essence, the customer is the ultimate judge of value, fitness for use, and quality of the output. Therefore, it is only logical that customer expectations are well understood throughout the organization and by the Six Sigma teams. However, instead of the external customers, some processes may have only internal customers.

Knowing what is important to internal customers is critical. For example, training and development is an internal process that seldom directly touches external customers. Yet, virtually all employees benefit by the output of training and development. To maximize the benefit of training, the needs and expectations of both internal and external customers must be known. The owners of internal processes have just as much need to clarify the expectations of internal customers as other processes have to capture the voice of external customers. For example, the primary drivers of training for Solectron are the plans of external customers. Solectron employees are trained based on the anticipated future expectations of customers so that the organization is ready when the customer demands new products or services. A major complaint of customers, and one that caused General Electric to relaunch its efforts, is that a company's focus on Six Sigma often misses the issue of customer benefits. Customers did not see the benefits of Six Sigma initially, and, in fact, stated that it was harder to do business with the company than before Six Sigma was launched. Therefore, more customer-centered measures were used to evaluate Six Sigma results.

Supplier Capability Is Known for All Key Inputs

Few firms have a fully integrated value-creating chain. Most firms rely on an array of suppliers. This applies to both manufacturing and service firms. The value-creating chain is only as strong as the weakest link, and the weak link may be an external supplier.

For a tangible product, suppliers may provide components or subassemblies. For services, suppliers may provide information management or service support. For example, a consulting firm may subcontract out a large-scale customer survey to a survey research firm. The data quality from the survey is only as good as the performance of the research firm. So, the consulting firm's outputs, consulting recommendations, are directly affected by service quality inputs.

The implication is that any process that relies on inputs to create value must also assess the quality of the inputs and supplier capability. If the suppliers provide important inputs, having suppliers on the Six Sigma team as permanent members could be valuable. At the least, critical suppliers could be ad hoc team members as needed. Regardless of whether suppliers are team members or not, the quality of process inputs should be evaluated for contribution to the team's goals. It may be that suppliers can suggest major innovations based on their knowledge and experience with other organizations.

The Team Has Received Both Technical and Team Behavior Training

The Six Sigma team needs an initial one day of training to begin. The training can be provided by the team leader or a facilitator and should cover both technical and behavioral issues. The technical training should address the Six Sigma tools presented in Part 4 of this book. The behavioral training should address group dynamics, ground rules, and operating procedures.

The goal of the training is not to make each team member a blackbelt; that could take a month or more. The goal of the training is to provide the team members with a basic understanding of both technical and behavioral issues that will be used during the project.

The behavioral training should address the desired team environment, one that emphasizes respect and trust for all individuals. Individuals should be encouraged to talk openly and be encouraged to take risks and challenge assumptions. Individuals should actively listen to others and encourage full participation.

The team needs to be aware of resource and time constraints. The resource issue should address time away from the normal job as well as any direct expenses, such as travel, that are allowable. The team needs to estimate the duration of the project so meetings can be scheduled well in advance.

At the end of the day of training, the team should develop two things. The first is a clear *goal statement* that provides guidance and is measurable. The goal statement is the standard against which the team's performance is measured. A goal of "improving the order fulfillment process" is too general. The goal should be "to reduce cycle time by 30 percent" or "to reduce costs by 20 percent." Or, the goal could be "to design the process capability to reach Six Sigma standards." If management has a mandate, such as cost reduction, that should be made clear by the team leader at the start of the process.

The second output of the first day is a set *agenda of meetings* for the entire project. This allows all team members to plan for the meetings and to make attendance a priority. Since the duration of the project is often 3 to 5 months, developing the agenda early reduces subsequent conflicts. A simple project may only require 4 or 5 days to complete, while a complex project may require 30 days of meetings.

If meetings are held infrequently, such as every 3 or 4 weeks, the meetings should be for 2 days. If the meetings are held more frequently, one-day meetings will work. The problem with all-day meetings held only once a month is that there is an hour or so of review and relearning each time. This relearning, however, is not necessary with frequent meetings. Also, infrequent meetings cause teams to lose some of their initial enthusiasm. There is less of a feeling of progress with infrequent meetings.

A good structure for the training is to spend half an hour introducing the purpose of the team. This is followed by 2 hours discussing the Six Sigma tools and 2 hours on behavioral issues. In the afternoon, a hypothetical case can be used that provides the team members an opportunity to develop a relationship map, an "As Is" process map, a list of disconnects or problems, a "Should Be" process map, and an implementation plan. This gives the team an overview of the entire project so that everyone understands why each step is so important. Without adequate training, a good deal of subsequent meeting time will be wasted on unproductive activities.

The Individual Team Members Have Clearly Defined Expectations, Roles, and Responsibilities

After the training session, all team members should know what is expected of them. Specifically, individuals should know why they are on the team and how their participation contributes to the team's success. This is enhanced by having the team establish or refine the team's goals.

Throughout the project, individual team members may be responsible for homework between meetings. Individuals may have to gather data from their area and develop summaries for the rest of the team. If information resides outside of areas represented on the team, the team leader should be responsible for gathering the necessary data.

The purpose of the behavioral training and establishing operating procedures is to ensure that all team members know how the team will function. Role clarity of team members reduces ambiguity and conflict and enhances individual involvement.

There Is Open Communication Based on Respect and Trust within the Team and within the Organization

The behavioral training should address intrateam communication. This should be monitored by the team leader so that everyone has the opportunity to participate.

The more difficult communication is with the rest of the organization. The senior management and champion should be kept abreast of the team's progress. This may take the form of meeting summaries or monthly reports. At key progress points, the team should make presentations to the senior management and champion. The purpose of the meeting is for two-way communication. The team should develop a plan for what is to be communicated, when the communication is to take place, and who is responsible for writing the report. A summary of the total project should also be made at completion of the project. By communicating the successes, broader organizational support is enhanced.

The Team Is Fully Empowered with Autonomy and Authority to Act

The team must have the ability to act and to try new ideas. It is to be expected that not every recommendation will prove successful. However, the organization, and senior management in particular, should allow the team to implement the majority of its recommendations.

The recommendations may either be fully implemented immediately or phased in over a period of time, or a designed experiment could be developed to test the recommendations before full rollout. The details of implementation are discussed in a subsequent chapter. But, the team should be allowed to try its recommendations, subject to reasonable resource constraints. If team recommendations are vetoed by senior management with little or no explanation, obtaining subsequent involvement on teams may be very difficult.

Team Decisions Are Based on Data and Facts

Whenever possible, the team should base decisions on data and facts rather than opinion. An important type of data is the calculation of cycle times. A process is composed of a series of activities. There may be from 10 to 50 or more discreet, identifiable activities in a process. Each activity consumes time and resources in some way. At the very least, labor is involved for each activity. The sum of the activities' costs is the total of the direct variable costs for a process.

If a firm uses activity-based-cost (ABC) accounting, the activity costs are often known. However, since most firms do not use ABC yet, the team is often responsible for developing cost estimates for each activity. To illustrate, the order fulfillment flowchart (Figure 10.1) includes an order-pulling activity. If the cycle time for order pulling was not known, the team would be responsible for calculating how long it took an employee to pull an order. This would likely require work sampling. Perhaps 100 orders would be tracked. The minimum, maximum, and average activity times could be calculated. The times could then be multiplied by the hourly labor charge (including fringe benefits). This would yield the activity costs for the labor component of order pulling. This approach would address only the productive time that a person is actually working. This does not include time for getting started in the morning, breaks, and getting ready to go home. If the team wanted to aggregate all of the nonproductive time and productive time, the total number of orders pulled per day could be divided by the total labor hours to determine the average time per order.

This type of data should be calculated for all activities in a process. Other costs, such as materials and support costs, could also be calculated. The team should gather all relevant data so that decisions and recommendations can be justified with detailed cost data.

The Team Has Adequate Time and Resources to Perform Thoroughly

The team should have adequate time to thoroughly analyze and investigate all activities and explore alternatives. If a team is rushed, decisions may be based on incomplete data and beneficial options may be overlooked. The implication is that the team meetings should be allowed to run their course naturally.

During a Six Sigma project, subprocesses often become apparent. Some of these processes may be in need of improvement. It is not unusual for a project to give birth to another project. However, the initial project should be brought to closure, if possible, before starting the second project so that energy is not diverted. If there is an ample number of employees in the organization, it may be possible to start a new team while the initial team is still operating.

Some Six Sigma projects may require external benchmarking to identify the best practices utilized at other companies. This may require budgetary support for travel. Resource support should be available to the team to develop the best possible recommendations.

The Contributions of Individuals and Teams Are Recognized and Rewarded

The team leader and/or champion should identify the contributions of individuals on the team. On most teams, a few individuals go above and beyond and make exemplary efforts. The functional managers should be informed of the outstanding efforts of team members from their areas.

More broadly, the performance of the team should be recognized and rewarded. This recognition should be part of the communication plan that was discussed earlier. The project results should be made known throughout the organization in order to build support for the effort.

The most common reward is simply the recognition itself. The use of financial rewards is somewhat more controversial. If financial rewards are given, they should go to all employees in the form of a gainsharing program, not just to team members. Nonetheless, if participation on a team is important, then a reward and recognition system based upon team performance, rather than individual performance, needs to be put in place in order to change the behavior and culture of the organization. A performance management system also needs to support a teaming environment.

The Teams Use Common Performance Metrics That Are Linked to the Customer and Other Performance Areas in the Organization

The various Six Sigma teams should use some common metrics. For example, failure rates could be calculated in many different ways. If each team uses a different methodology, comparing results is much more difficult. As part of the initial training, the team should be informed of the performance metrics that have been valuable to other teams. Standardized metrics enhance the documentation of project results.

Some organizations have developed a pool of questions for use on internal and external customers surveys. Standardized wording and scaling facilitate the development of consistent, comprehensive customer databases. Nortel has certain mandatory questions that must appear on every questionnaire. In this way, Nortel can make direct comparisons with other research results. Likewise, the Controls Business of Johnson Controls, Inc., has also implemented a common set of questions to be asked on all surveys.

Each of the performance metrics used by a team should be linked directly to the customers' needs and expectations. Therefore, the internal process performance metrics must be harmonized with related questions on customer surveys. This may require modifying either the way performance is measured or the wording of survey questions.

The Team Produces Identifiable Financial and Performance Results

Successful teams must be able to document the results of their recommendations. This requires a *before* and *after* comparison of key performance indicators. Therefore, the current performance level must be documented initially and cost estimates developed. Since many organizations do not have this type of data, the team often must conduct work-sampling studies and make estimates.

After process changes and recommendations have been made, the team must make estimates of the new performance level. New cost estimates are then made for the revised process. These estimates are presented to management at the final presentation.

The team must also develop a system for measuring actual performance improvements after the process has been changed. The actual performance is then compared to the estimated performance for accuracy.

POTENTIAL PROBLEMS WITH TEAMS

There are a number of potential problems with teams that must be monitored by the team leader or the team as a whole. The presence of these problems can severely limit the effectiveness of the team. These potential problems are presented in Table 10.2.

- Interpersonal versus Task Orientation
- Premature Solutions
- Groupthink
- Unequal Airtime
- Personalized Disagreement

Table 10.2 Potential Problems with Teams.

Interpersonal versus Task Orientation

If an individual works alone, that person typically focuses on task-related activities. When working as part of a team, the task-related activities are supplemented by a whole set of social, interpersonal challenges. For individuals to be an effective part of a team, they must build interpersonal relationships with other team members to achieve acceptance of their ideas.

When teams do not have a set of clearly identified operating procedures, social activities can consume a disproportionate amount of time. In these cases, the team discussions evolve toward areas of agreement to develop group cohesion and avoid areas of controversy and disagreement. For individuals with Type A, achievement-oriented personalities, time spent on developing social cohesion can be viewed as unproductive and therefore cause frustration. These are typified as meetings where there is a good deal of discussion, but little progress is actually achieved.

The challenge for the team and team leader is to strike a balance between the development of social cohesion and progress on task-related issues. Since the optimum balance between social and task activities is largely a reflection of an individual's personality, this issue can become a real problem, particularly as the team size becomes large.

Premature Solutions

If a team uses an unstructured, free-flowing discussion, problems in a process tend to be discussed individually, and the team has a tendency to shift the discussion to how that specific problem should be solved. In this way, some team members feel they are finally making progress. A team is much more effective if all of the problems are listed and then grouped by areas of commonality. A team should then, as a separate discussion, focus on the causes of the problems. Then a team should focus on the solutions. By distinguishing clearly between problems, causes, and solutions, team creativity is greatly enhanced in both the number of ideas and the diversity of ideas generated.

Groupthink

In unstructured team meetings, social pressures for group conformity typically emerge. An individual with a strong, forceful personality might present an idea. Other team members may support and expand on the idea. Individuals who have a different view may feel constrained to express their ideas and simply withdraw from the discussion. This problem can be particularly acute if the team includes some individuals who are high-status, highly knowledgeable people who tend to lead discussions. The expression of opposing ideas could be viewed as criticism of the respected individual, something that some people may be hesitant to do.

Unequal Airtime

The quality of team decisions is typically reduced when one or two individuals dominate a discussion. If there are 12 people on a team and a meeting lasts for 2 hours, there is an average of only 10 minutes of talking for each individual. Thus, in a completely balanced situation, an individual would listen for 110 minutes and speak for 10 minutes. If a few people dominate the discussions, airtime for the remaining individuals drops dramatically. The implication is that each team member should be involved in each discussion. Team leaders should monitor the situation and pull all team members into the discussions.

Personalized Disagreement

When a disagreement or conflict occurs within a team, the results can be either dysfunctional or productive. If disagreement occurs and is personalized, hard feelings often result, which undermines group effectiveness. If the conflict is smoothed over by humor or withdrawal, the hard feelings remain. The solution is to separate the individual from the process problem and then focus resolution on the problem.

Any of the preceding potential problems can undermine the effectiveness of teams. Fortunately, there are some well-developed techniques that can be used to provide structure and guidance for teams. By creating a clear operating structure, most of the problems never materialize. A particularly appropriate approach to create a structured team environment is the use of *nominal group technique*.

NOMINAL GROUP TECHNIQUE

Nominal group technique (NGT) is a structured process for soliciting ideas and solving problems. The term *nominal* is used because individual team members write their ideas down, independent of other team members. After all ideas are written, the ideas are shared, one at a time, in a round-robin format. The team leader captures all the ideas on a flip chart, and discussion does not occur until all ideas have been presented.

The application of NGT is most appropriate for Six Sigma teams after an "As Is" process map has been developed. Once a process map identifies all the activities and their interrelationships, the problems, or disconnects, in either an activity or its interrelationships must be identified. The following example illustrates how NGT could be used effectively at this point.

The team leader begins at the start of the "As Is" map. Each team member is asked to write down the problems that actually do occur or could occur with a specific activity. In some cases, if the map is broken into phases, the whole phase can be evaluated. Once all team members are finished writing, the team leader asks that individual team members present one idea from their lists. The leader proceeds in a round-robin format, capturing the ideas on a flip chart, until all ideas have been presented. In this way, individual team members are assured that all of their ideas are shared with the team.

Once all of the problems are presented, each is clarified for meaning so that the whole team understands what each person meant. This process proceeds for each activity, or phase, in the "As Is" map. It is not at all unusual to develop a list of 50 to 60 problems, or disconnects, in the process.

At this point, it is often helpful to group the problems into related categories. For example, a team may group the problems by information technology, employee training and skills, and materials. Or, the problems might be grouped by engineering design, manufacturing, installation, and technical support. Once the grouping is done, another round of NGT occurs.

The team leader asks each team member to identify what caused each problem in a particular category. These are written down and shared in a round-robin format. The causes are then captured by the team leader as discussed earlier. This process is repeated for each of the groups of problems. Once the causes for all the problems have been identified, each is discussed for clarification. Then all of the causal factors are discussed collectively and grouped into related categories.

Throughout this process, the team leader should probe for the true root causes. This is very similar to the Japanese *five why* strategy. Each problem is analyzed by asking "Why?" at least 5 times. Once the causes have been thoroughly discussed and grouped, the NGT approach is applied once again.

The team leader asks everyone on the team to write down a solution or recommendation for each cause and/or group of causal factors. The solutions are individually captured. Once all of the solutions or recommendations are captured, they are then discussed fully. In particular, the assumptions necessary to support the solutions are identified.

For each of the discussions of problems, causes, and solutions, it is sometimes helpful to prioritize the issues. Once the problems, causes, or solutions have been grouped into categories, the team members can be asked to rank order the categories or items within a category. This is again done in writing, independent of other team members. The rankings can be shared by having team members indicate their most important item, working down through the list in a round-robin format until all of the rankings have been presented. Once the rankings have been presented and captured, an open discussion of the relative importance can occur.

There are some very real benefits to using NGT for Six Sigma teams. The overall creativity and effectiveness of the team is greatly enhanced. The structured discussion tends to result in much higher levels of team member satisfaction and feelings of accomplishment. And, virtually all of the potential problems of teams are overcome. However, NGT is effective only when the team meets in a face-to-face situation. There is another technique that is useful when some of the team meetings are conducted electronically or through audio- or videoconferencing.

DELPHI TECHNIQUE

A Delphi Technique (DT) is similar to NGT in several respects. Individual team members share all of their ideas in writing. The team leader compiles all of the input from team members. But, unlike NGT, the team leader sends out a copy of all the input for further review and feedback.

A DT makes use of a questionnaire that asks individuals to respond to several, specific questions. The individuals E-mail their responses to the team leader. The leader compiles all responses, interprets, summarizes, and develops new questions. This can be done for problem identification, causal identification, or solutions.

While a DT is effective for soliciting ideas, the synergy of face-to-face interaction is lost. Therefore, its use for Six Sigma teams should be limited to occasional, clearly defined activities.

SUMMARY

The effective design of Six Sigma teams is critical for project success. Also, the team must have effective leadership. Because of technical and behavioral issues, the team leader must be chosen carefully and be very well trained. While the whole team does not need as much training as the leader, the team should receive some training as well.

This chapter has discussed 15 characteristics of successful Six Sigma teams. An organization may achieve success without having all characteristics in place, but, the fewer characteristics that an organization has, the less likely the project is to be successful.

CASE STUDY

FORMING THE TEAMS

The Controls Business of Johnson Controls, Inc., has been focused on process management and continuous process improvement as part of its value and heritage. A focus on employee well-being and satisfaction is a core value. Work is performed by teams, and the Controls Business of Johnson Controls, Inc., has implemented a series of actions to promote a healthy team environment. A teamwork assessment is part of performance reviews. The Merit Award program recognizes teams that have worked well together in the accomplishment of significant results that support the mission of "continually exceeding customers' increasing expectations." The support structure is in place to promote a teaming environment, and an extensive use of teams has been used to improve processes.

The Controls Business of Johnson Controls, Inc., implemented Six Sigma as part of its overall improvement methodology in 1999. This initiative involved teams of employees that identified and selected processes in the greatest need for improvement, focusing on parameters such as total cycle time, impact on customers, process cost, number of people involved with the process, number of process steps, and customer satisfaction. Over 40 Six Sigma teams selected more than 52 major processes for improvement. These were major, mega processes and those whose performance, breadth, and depth warranted improvement to the degree advocated by a true Six Sigma team.

The responsibilities, duties, and attributes of Six Sigma champions and sigma specialists are shown in Figure 10.2. The term *sigma specialists* is used to designate the team leaders because the use of the term *blackbelt* is copyrighted by the Six Sigma Academy (see note 25).

Sigma Champions

RESPONSIBILITIES, DUTIES:
- *Responsible for achieving Sigma project results*
- *Identify, select, and scope projects based on $, business impact*
- *Review, track, and report Sigma project progress and results*
- *Eliminate project barriers, assure proper project resourcing*
- *Identify, recruit, develop Sigma Specialists*
- *Manage 4–8 Sigma Specialists (part time champions), 10–12 (full time champions)*
- *Reward, recognize Sigma Specialists and Sigma project team achievements*
- *Communicate Six Sigma, Drive Six Sigma culture change*

REQUIREMENTS:
- *Strong leader*
- *Collaboration skills*
- *Influence in organization*
- *Strong mentoring skills*
- *"Out of box" thinker*
- *Change agent*
- *Project Management Skills*
- *Excellent Communications Skills*
- *Computer Proficient*
- *Demonstrated leadership/ management*
- *Respected by the organization*

Sigma Specialists

RESPONSIBILITIES, DUTIES:
- *Organize, plan, and lead Sigma projects; confirm results with data*
- *Project barrier escalation to champions; project tracking, reporting*
- *Collaborate in waste, defect, time reduction opportunity identification*
- *Apply Six Sigma skills and expertise to project execution*
- *Goal: target 2 projects per year*
- *Responsible for leading teams and for Results*
- *Train, mentor project team members on Six Sigma methods, tools*
- *Collaborate in Sigma Specialist community, shares best practices*
- *Full-time position, average 2 years*

REQUIREMENTS:
- *High achiever*
- *Excellent people skills*
- *Project management skills*
- *"Out of box" thinker*
- *Statistics comfort, aptitude*
- *High organizational respect*
- *Company experience and knowledge*
- *English reading skills*
- *Good analytical skills*
- *Motivator, Delegation skills*
- *Computer Proficient*
- *Self motivator, Drive*

Figure 10.2 Champion and Sigma Specialist Responsibilities, Duties, and Attributes at the Controls Business of Johnson Controls, Inc.

Part IV

Six Sigma Tools, Techniques, and Implementation

Part 2 of this book addressed how to capture the voice of the customer and how to develop a clear understanding of customer needs and expectations. Part 3 of this book addressed what must be done to get the organization ready for a Six Sigma initiative. The fourth, and final, portion of this book focuses on the tools and techniques more commonly used by Six Sigma teams. The sequence of the chapters follows the normal progression of a Six Sigma project.

Aligning the needs of the customer with internal processes is the focus of chapter 11. The assumption is made that an organization has already captured the voice of the customer in some way. It is critically important to make sure that customer needs are explicitly linked to the value-creating processes.

Once the process's outcomes and customer needs are aligned, the process must be mapped and analyzed. This is the focus of chapter 12. A team normally identifies a substantial number of disconnects or problems in a process.

A variety of problem-solving tools can be used by Six Sigma teams. These are addressed in chapter 13. After the team has developed recommendations to solve the problems, a new, "*Should Be*" process map must be developed to show how the process should perform.

An overview of the entire Six Sigma project, including recommendations, should be presented to senior management for approval. The characteristics of effective team presentations are presented in chapter 14. Assuming management approval, chapter 15 addresses the development of detailed implementation plans.

The more technical, statistical calculations associated with Six Sigma are presented in chapter 16. Chapter 17, the last chapter, addresses changes and evolution that are affecting not only Six Sigma but overall organization performance.

11

Alignment of Customer Needs and Process Performance

U p to this point, the discussions in this book have centered on how to capture the voice of the customer and how to get the organization ready for a Six Sigma project. This chapter and those that follow focus on more detailed implementation issues. The first step, and perhaps the most often neglected, is to align the needs and expectations of the customer with the internal processes that fulfill those needs. A true Six Sigma strategy begins by emphasizing the importance of the customer in identifying improvement opportunities. The customer can usually identify exactly where performance needs to be improved. The Six Sigma Academy states that an organization's approach to Six Sigma should begin and end with the customer (see note 25). The unfortunate reality of most implementation approaches is that customer expectations and needs quickly become lost in the attempt to improve processes.

Six Sigma projects are usually selected based upon potential cost savings, an admirable goal. General Electric is a leader in implementing Six Sigma, and Jack Welch, in his book *Jack Welch and the GE Way,* cites numerous examples of how GE improved its bottom-line financial results as a consequence of Six Sigma improvement projects.[26] However, the discussions of improvements in customer satisfaction are much less common. The book also points out the fact that, soon into its improvement efforts, customers were asking GE how Six Sigma improvement benefited the customer as well. Customers were not necessarily asking for cost savings to be passed directly on to them, although this was probably one unarticulated motivating factor. The customers were asking why process improvements saved GE money but did little to simplify the way customers did business with GE. Many of the Six Sigma changes were completely invisible to the customer. The lesson here is that a company's approach to Six Sigma should consider and show benefit to customers and shareholders alike.

ALIGNMENT OF CUSTOMER NEEDS WITH PROCESSES

Since Six Sigma focuses heavily on process performance, it is only natural to first understand the linkage between a company's processes and customer satisfaction. Figure 11.1 depicts a customer view model developed by IBM Rochester. Based upon customer input, 44 specific attributes were identified and grouped into six major categories: technical

Customer View of IBM AS/400 Product

Customer Satisfaction Measurements
Overall Satisfaction, Loyalty, Recommend

Common Attributes
Ease-of-Doing-Business-With
Partnership
Responsiveness
Knowledge of Customer's Business
Customer Driven

Major Categories → Customer Attributes ↓	Technical Solutions		Maintenance and Service Support		Marketing/Sales Offerings		Administration	Delivery	Image
	Hardware	Software	Hardware Service	Software Service	Channel	Salesperson			
	Quality/Reliability		Single Contact Point		Central Contact Point		Purchasing Procedure	On Time	Corporate Citizen
	Availability		Flexible		Information		Billing Procedure	Without Defects	Community Interests
	Ease-of-Use		Available		Solution Provider		Terms and Conditions	To Specification	Social Concerns
	Disaster Recovery Process		Product Knowledge		Product Knowledge		Warranty Expiration Notification	Post-Delivery Process	Environment Consciousness
	Documentation		Accessible		Education		Financial Alternatives	Accurate	Technology Leader
	Openness		Empowered		Empowered				Financial Stability
	Growth				Competent				Executives' Image
	Price/Pricing				Ethical				Empathy
	Warranty								
	New Technology								
	Installation/Upgradeability								

Figure 11.1 IBM Rochester View Model (6 Major Categories, 43 Customer Attributes).

solutions (hardware and software quality), maintenance and service support (hardware and software service), marketing/sales offerings, administration, delivery, and image. Recognizing that these six major categories and 44 attributes are the principal drivers of overall customer satisfaction, IBM Rochester then determined the processes that impacted these attributes (see note 24).

The alignment of the customer view model, processes, and internal measurements of IBM Rochester is shown in Figure 11.2. Discussion of development and use of value models (customer view model) appears later in this chapter, but it is important to understand the alignment of customer needs and expectations with internal processes. For instance, IBM Rochester previously focused quite heavily on the *manufacturing* process, but customers stated that they viewed IBM Rochester as not having a *manufacturing* process but rather a *fulfillment* process. Customers stated that they placed an order for a product and that the product was delivered. What happened in between was irrelevant to the customer unless it caused the product to be shipped defective or late. Therefore, IBM Rochester expanded its overall fulfillment process to include the ordering subprocess, the subprocess used to hand off the order to the manufacturing process, and the delivery subprocess. When the organization can link customer needs, expectations, and requirements to its processes, the process can be redesigned to improve not only the financial performance of the company but also customer satisfaction.

Since the customer is the ultimate judge of performance, the Six Sigma team must clearly understand customer expectations. Chapter 3 through chapter 7 discussed capturing the voice of the customer and understanding requirements, needs, and expectations of customers that drive overall satisfaction and purchase/repurchase behavior. It is against the customer's expectations that process performance will eventually be evaluated. Therefore, the team must align internal processes around the customer's needs and expectations. The remaining part of this chapter presents three tools that are particularly helpful in accomplishing this alignment. These tools are value models, customer expectations/process matrices, and quality function deployment.

VALUE MODELS

Value models have been discussed in several previous chapters. Value models take on several forms, and companies have given them a variety of names including voice of the customer model, customer view model, and so on. As value models provide a good framework for linking customer needs and processes, they are discussed from that perspective here.

Value models typically include five major categories of attributes that drive the customer's perceptions of value and customer satisfaction. These five categories are product quality, service quality, image, price, and relationship. If an organization lacks the resources to conduct a detailed analysis of customer satisfaction attributes, these five categories provide a conceptual framework. While all five areas are the outcome of some types of processes in an organization, the following discussion focuses on only dimensions of product quality and service quality. Six Sigma teams most often focus initially on product and service dimensions.

A partial value model containing only product and service quality is presented in Figure 11.3. This is an AT&T value model for business telephone equipment. By conducting qualitative research (depth interviews and focus groups) with customers, a comprehensive list of customer needs or attributes was developed. These customer needs were then

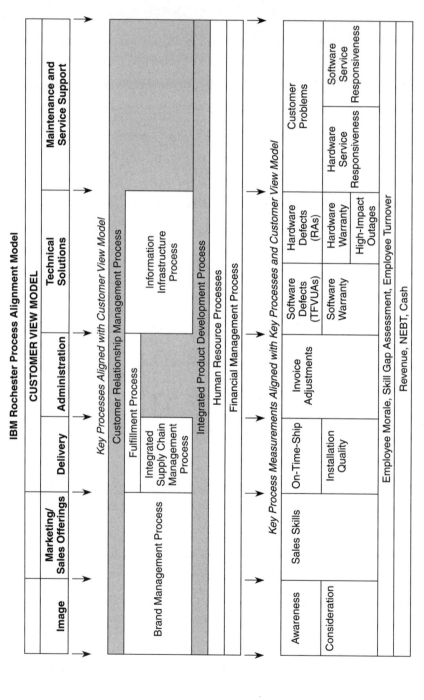

Figure 11.2 Alignment of IBM Rochester Customer View Model Attributes with Key Processes and Key Process Measurements.

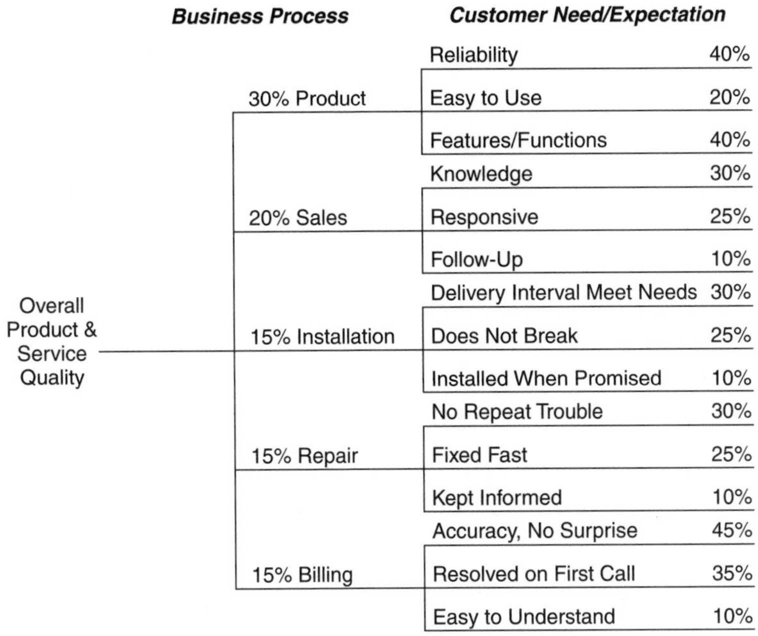

Business Process	Customer Need/Expectation	
	Reliability	40%
30% Product	Easy to Use	20%
	Features/Functions	40%
	Knowledge	30%
20% Sales	Responsive	25%
	Follow-Up	10%
	Delivery Interval Meet Needs	30%
15% Installation	Does Not Break	25%
	Installed When Promised	10%
	No Repeat Trouble	30%
15% Repair	Fixed Fast	25%
	Kept Informed	10%
	Accuracy, No Surprise	45%
15% Billing	Resolved on First Call	35%
	Easy to Understand	10%

Overall Product & Service Quality

Figure 11.3 AT&T Value Model.

grouped into categories that were generally aligned with internal processes. A questionnaire was designed to fit these groupings. It should be noted that this value model is not complete, therefore categories do not add up to 100%. For simplicity and illustrative purposes, only the three most important customer needs are presented in each category. Some of the categories had over six specific attributes. Therefore, the percentages within a category do not always sum to 100. Also, there were several categories that were deleted, such as training and customer service, due to low importance ratings.

AT&T surveyed a sample of business customers, asking them to rate AT&T's performance on each attribute. The data was analyzed using multivariate statistics. For ease of presentation, the statistical results were converted into percentages associated with each process and each attribute within the process. The larger the percentage, the more important the process or attribute was to the customer.

First, at the process level, product attributes as a set were clearly most important to customers. Of the service categories, the sales process was most important with installation, repair, and billing processes sharing equal importance. To have the biggest impact on customer satisfaction, the product and sales processes should be the focus of the improvement efforts.

Each group of customer needs must be coordinated with the process that produces that attribute. This can be accomplished by developing an internal performance metric for each customer need. The addition of the internal performance metric is presented in Figure 11.4. While an organization may gather customer perceptions on a periodic basis, quarterly for example, the internal performance metric could be measured continuously. An organization should be able to predict customer satisfaction results by monitoring internal process performance and measurements. Additionally, by developing a performance metric for each customer need, employees are able to see how they contribute directly to customer

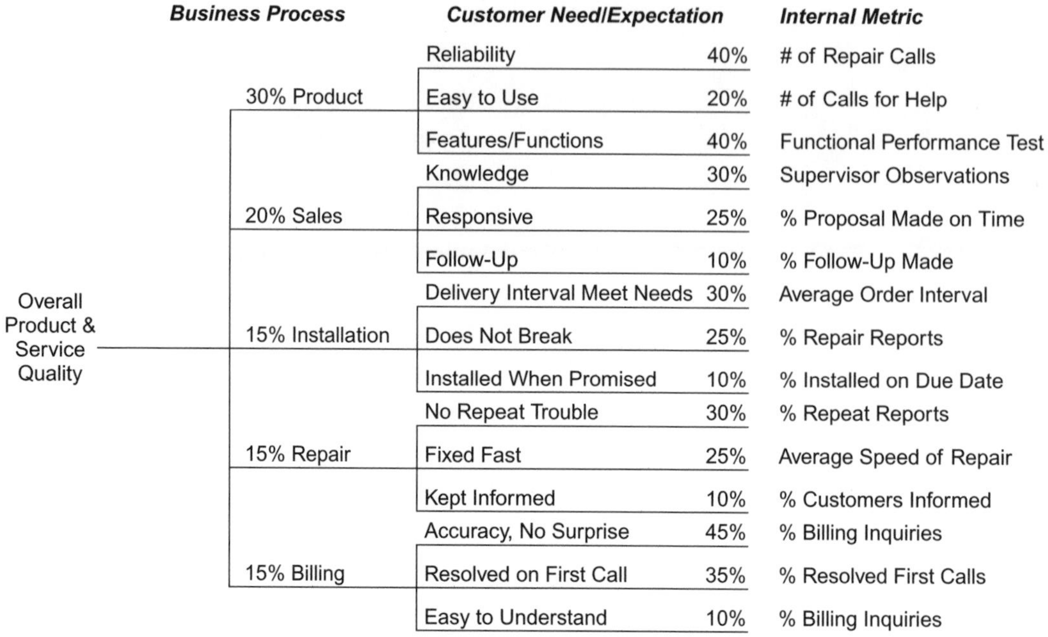

Business Process	Customer Need/Expectation		Internal Metric
	Reliability	40%	# of Repair Calls
30% Product	Easy to Use	20%	# of Calls for Help
	Features/Functions	40%	Functional Performance Test
	Knowledge	30%	Supervisor Observations
20% Sales	Responsive	25%	% Proposal Made on Time
	Follow-Up	10%	% Follow-Up Made
	Delivery Interval Meet Needs	30%	Average Order Interval
15% Installation	Does Not Break	25%	% Repair Reports
	Installed When Promised	10%	% Installed on Due Date
	No Repeat Trouble	30%	% Repeat Reports
15% Repair	Fixed Fast	25%	Average Speed of Repair
	Kept Informed	10%	% Customers Informed
	Accuracy, No Surprise	45%	% Billing Inquiries
15% Billing	Resolved on First Call	35%	% Resolved First Calls
	Easy to Understand	10%	% Billing Inquiries

Overall Product & Service Quality

Figure 11.4 AT&T Value Model with Internal Metrics.

satisfaction. Employees can more easily relate to an internal performance metric or process as opposed to a customer satisfaction value.

The development of performance metrics that link to each key driver of satisfaction is often a difficult task. A team can develop and suggest specific performance metrics, but it is usually the process owner that decides on the *best* metric to track.

Developing a single performance metric works well when there is a dominant performance issue creating the attribute. In the AT&T model, getting proposals to the customer on time influenced the customer's perceptions of sales responsiveness. However, some attributes may not be so easily linked to a single performance metric.

A product's features/functions comprise a highly important attribute to customers. But, there may be numerous dimensions of features and functions. In a business situation, call forwarding, messaging, conferencing, speaker phone, programming, and upgradability could be important features for customers. There are several options that could be used to determine the relative importance of each feature. One is to make the *feature/functions* attribute a separate category containing the six or more specific attributes (from the AT&T model). In this way, a single performance metric could be developed for each of the more specific attributes.

Unfortunately, there are some situations where several processes combine to create or contribute to a single attribute. The AT&T model does not work as well in these situations. Instead, a *customer expectations–process matrix* could be developed.

CUSTOMER EXPECTATIONS–PROCESS MATRIX

A customer expectations–process matrix uses a row and column format to match customer expectations and processes. All customer expectations are listed on one axis, and the value-creating processes are listed on the other axis. A sample matrix is presented in Figure 11.5.

Product or Service Performance Metric

Value-Creating Customer Expectations \ Processes	PS 1	PS 2	PS 3	PS 4	PS 5	PS 6	PS 7	PS 8
A-1	○	☆						
A-2		○				△		
A-3		△	○			△		
A-4			○				☆	
A-5		○			○			
A-6		☆			○	☆		
A-7								
A-8	☆					△		☆

☆ Strong Relationship
○ Medium Relationship
△ Weak Relationship

Figure 11.5 Customer Expectations–Process Matrix.

Because the use of this model would get extremely complicated if 50 or 60 attributes were evaluated at one time, normally each major grouping, such as products, sales, or installation from the AT&T value model, would be the focus of a separate matrix.

On the vertical axis of the matrix are the customer expectations. Each attribute would be listed, one for each row. On the horizontal axis, the processes that create value are listed. There may be one or more for each process. Each performance metric would have its own column. The strength of the relationship between each attribute and each product or service requirement is indicated by the use of a symbol. In this example, strong, medium, and weak relationships are depicted.

If a row, such as *A-7,* has no product or service requirement associated with it, the implication is that the organization is not paying attention to how this attribute is created. If A-7 were very important to the customer, this could have serious negative consequences.

If a column, such as *PS-4,* has no impact on any attribute, the need for the product or service requirement must be questioned. Perhaps there is a valid reason for the requirement, but it is unrelated to customer expectations.

By using a matrix, the relationships between customer expectations and the internal product or service requirements necessary to meet the customer's expectations can be examined. Accordingly, the matrix can be a very good planning tool. However, the matrix can be expanded substantially through the use of Quality Function Deployment.

QUALITY FUNCTION DEPLOYMENT

Quality function deployment (QFD) is a planning tool that translates customer needs and expectations into product and service requirements, performance metrics, areas of responsibility, and priorities for action. QFD is sometimes referred to as *the house of quality.* The use of QFD typically enhances customer satisfaction and reduces cycle time for product and service deployment and delivery. In essence, the use of QFD forces an organization to become customer centered. For Six Sigma teams, the use of QFD identifies areas of responsibility and performance metrics quite clearly.

In the simplest form, QFD is a technique that translates customer expectations into product and service requirements or features. The customer expectations–process matrix, discussed earlier, can be used as a starting point for matching customer requirements with processes, identifying performance metrics, and expanding these inputs into a house of quality (HOQ) format. The goal is to harmonize product and service features with customer expectations.

Figure 11.6 depicts a QFD model, which illustrates the HOQ format. In an HOQ format, the original labels for the two axes are *what is expected* and *how to achieve it*. Often, these are simply truncated to *what* and *how*. Perhaps more accurately, the *what* can be described as *customer expectations* on the left side of the HOQ. There would be a row for each customer expectation. The *how* can be described as *product and/or service requirements* on the top of the HOQ. There would be a column for each dimension of process performance, so a single process might have three or four related columns.

To this basic HOQ, there are usually several additions. First, an organization develops a performance metric or standard for each product or service requirement at the bottom of the HOQ. For example, a standard could be to answer 90 percent of the phone calls on the first ring or to resolve all customer complaints within 24 hours. These are usually added to the bottom or the basement/foundation of the HOQ so that each performance requirement at the top of a column has a corresponding performance metric or standard at the bottom of the same column. Obviously, the performance metric should correspond to what the customer expects.

Some firms conduct their own competitive assessment on each of the performance requirements for key competitors. In this way, the firm identifies what it perceives to be its own strengths and weaknesses. This internal self-assessment would appear at the bottom (foundation) of the HOQ. As an example, for most high-technology products, the first products produced are often purchased by competitors, who then disassemble the product using reverse engineering to identify strengths and weaknesses of the product, design, and processes. The competitor then builds the strength of the new innovation into their own products and avoids and/or exploits the weaknesses of the competing product. For personal computers and printers, a firm may spend a year of research and development to produce a new model. Within 60 days of introduction, all the new innovations have been copied by competitors. Motorola's experience in introducing a new pager found it took a Taiwanese company only weeks to have an equivalent product in the market.

The second addition to the HOQ is actual *customer perceptions*. This addition is usually placed on the right-hand side of the matrix so that each customer expectation row can be matched to a customer's perception of actual performance. This is where the feedback from customer satisfaction surveys, complaint data, focus groups, and customer interviews are fed back into the QFD matrix. The *customer perception* column could consist of top box scores, top two scores, or mean values for each corresponding question on a survey, for example.

At this point, there are several considerations that are critical. The description of the customer expectations and customer perceptions should be in the customer's words, and the description of the customer perceptions should be harmonized with the relevant performance metric. That is, the wording of the customer expectation and the corresponding performance standard should be closely aligned with one another. This makes the customer perceptions, often gathered from customer satisfaction survey data, more actionable.

The feedback from customers can also be supplemented with a competitive assessment. This data could be gathered through a blind, competitive survey, discussed in

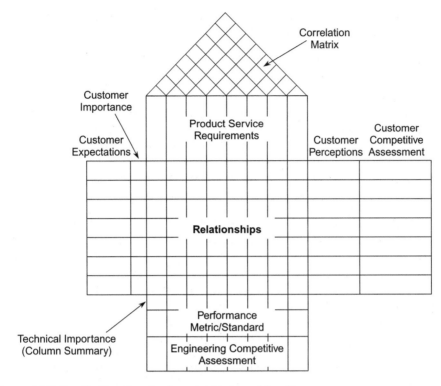

Figure 11.6 Quality Function Deployment-House of Quality.

chapter 3. By gathering competitive data, a firm can develop a profile that identifies strengths and weaknesses from the customer's perspective. By administering the same customer satisfaction survey questionnaire to competitors' customers, the competitive profile would be consistent with other information in the row. The competitive assessment should be compared to the results of the self-assessment (at the bottom of the HOQ) described earlier. This allows the validation of strengths and weaknesses, providing both an internal view as well as a customer's view. If there are major discrepancies between customer perceptions and actual performance, there could be important implications for marketing and communication strategies.

Another addition to the HOQ is the *roof*. The roof is simply a correlation matrix among the product and service requirements. The purpose of the correlation matrix is to show how the performance areas interact with one another. These are qualitative correlations assigned by experienced individuals. The correlations could be strongly positive, positive, negative, strongly negative, or none at all. For example, the horsepower of a motorcycle engine may be strongly, positively correlated with acceleration (as measured by 0 to 60 miles per hour elapsed time) but strongly, negatively correlated with fuel economy (miles per gallon) and negatively correlated with vehicle weight. The design specification involves a series of trade-offs among performance requirements that optimize value to the customer. For example, a customer may want a powerful motorcycle but also want it to be light and easy to handle.

The HOQ is nearly complete. As discussed in previous chapters, primary attention should be given to those areas that are important to customers. Therefore, there should be some type of importance rating determined for each customer expectation. In Figure 11.6, this is represented by an importance column on the left side of the HOQ. Ideally, this would be provided by a value model that derived the importance of each customer expectation through statistical analysis. The most important customer expectations should receive priority attention, particularly if performance is low on these.

The importance of each product or service requirement should also be rated. This is done by multiplying the customer importance for each expectation by the strength of relationship. A strong relationship might be assigned a value of 5, a moderate relationship a value of 3, and a weak relationship a value of 1. The importance weights could be calculated for each column to obtain an aggregate importance rating for each product and service requirement. This is indicated by the technical importance row at the bottom of the HOQ. Requirements that have a large impact on the customer by influencing several expectations would be of high interest to the Six Sigma team.

There are some pragmatic limitations to the use of QFD. It is not at all unusual for customers to identify over 100 attributes that may be used to evaluate a product or service. Of these, perhaps 30 to 40 may be relatively important to the customer. Developing an HOQ with 30 to 100 customer expectations with one row for each expectation would be a daunting task since there may be an equal number of performance requirements with one column for each of these. Needless to say, a 50 by 50 matrix for the basic HOQ would be quite cumbersome. The solution is to decompose the total project into smaller segments. If the decomposition is done based on processes, a Six Sigma team finds the unit of analysis quite useful. For example, a sales process might be under review. Customer expectations of sales might be expressed as salesperson's knowledge, developing a consultative relationship, frequency of contact, follow-up, and friendliness, among others. A list of 10 customer expectations/attributes is quite workable in an HOQ.

Another approach to decomposing a larger set of customer requirements may occur when there are multiple types of customers, each with different expectations, requirements, and importance ratings. For instance, a new, inexperienced customer may have a different set of requirements and expectations than a long-term customer that is very experienced in the use of the product. An example might be the quality of product documentation, which is very important to the new customer but less important to the experienced customer.

An HOQ model could be developed at the process level, such as sales, billing, or customer service, so that the interrelationships among processes could be identified. For instance, if an organization has seven key processes (from the AT&T value model), seven more specific HOQs could be developed. Six Sigma teams would find an HOQ model that was based upon processes to be of most benefit for identifying and prioritizing improvement opportunities.

SUMMARY

One of the most difficult steps in becoming customer centered is the alignment of the customer's needs and expectations with the value-creating processes that fulfill those needs. This alignment needs to first identify which processes fulfill which needs. Then, the performance of the process needs to be monitored to determine the degree to which customer needs are being met. This alignment greatly benefits from the use of several tools. Value models, customer expectations–process matrices, and quality function deployment each provide a structured framework to achieve the alignment. Failure to make this explicit linkage between customer perceptions and processes is probably the most common flaw in Six Sigma initiatives. Although Six Sigma is touted as being customer focused, often the results do not benefit or favor the customer and, in some cases, make it more difficult for the customer to do business with the organization.

CASE STUDY

ALIGNING CUSTOMER NEEDS AND INTERNAL PROCESSES

Research has been conducted with Controls Business customers of Johnson Controls, Inc., to determine the factors that influence customer satisfaction and purchase/repurchase behavior. The value model associated with this information is shown in Figure 11.7.

The Johnson Controls, Inc., value model is similar to that developed by AT&T. Statistical analysis was used to determine the relative weight of each attribute on overall satisfaction. The use of customer satisfaction data at Johnson Controls, Inc., has resulted in the creation of a customer satisfaction index (CSI), which is a compilation of the scores from each major customer satisfaction attribute. An overall CSI score is compiled each month and used for comparison purposes to assess improvements in customer satisfaction across the entire customer base and by geographic area.

The use of customer satisfaction data at Johnson Controls, Inc., has resulted in targets and goals being established and monitored for customer satisfaction improvement. Each marketing Area reviews the results of customer satisfaction in its respective area each quarter with executive management. CSI scores are used for consistency in measurements across all marketing areas. In addition to reviewing CSI scores, actions to improve customer satisfaction are also reviewed. Improvements in CSI scores become part of the scorecard used to assess an Areas' performance, which ultimately impacts variable compensation of Area personnel.

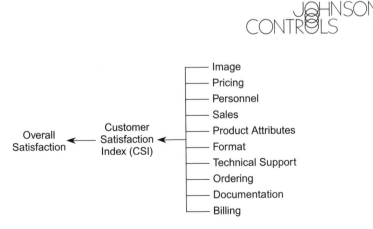

Figure 11.7 Customer Value Model for the Controls Business of Johnson Controls, Inc.

Quality of Relationship	
Survey Question	**Business Process**
Q12 Being Customer Driven	• Account Management • Customer Needs Assessment • Customer Relationship Teams • Key Accounts
Q6 Quality of Relationship	• Account Management • Customer Needs Assessment • Customer Relationship Teams • Key Accounts
IQ44 Guaranteeing Quality of Work	• Proper Checklist • Project Sign-Off • Estimating • Turnover • People Development
IQ47 Willingness to Resolve Problems	• Complaint Resolution • Employee Empowerment • Coaching • Recognition • Kickoff Meeting
SQ50 Handling Customer's Problems	• Complaint-Handling Process

Figure 11.8 Linkage of Customer Satisfaction Attributes to Key Business Processes for Controls Business of Johnson Controls, Inc.

The linkage of customer satisfaction attributes to key business processes for some questions is presented in Figure 11.8. Each question on a questionnaire is aligned with the internal processes or activities that influence the customer's perceptions. For example, the *quality of relationship* category consists of five questions. A variety of factors influence customer perceptions on each question. Since processes across Areas are pretty consistent, the linkage of customer satisfaction actions and results to key processes allows the sharing of best practices across all Areas to foster overall customer satisfaction improvement.

12

Analyzing Processes and Identifying Problems

In the previous chapter, the needs and expectations of the customers were aligned around internal product or service requirements. This alignment could be achieved through the use of value models, customer needs/process matrices, or quality function deployment. Regardless of the technique used, the customer expectations must be matched, to the extent possible, with processes that actually produce the product or service requirement in an organization.

Most often, this analysis requires a horizontal view of the organization, not the traditional vertical view depicted in an organization chart. Command or control is accomplished through vertical relationships. Most work is accomplished through horizontal relationships. This dichotomy between command or control and accomplishing work is, perhaps, the greatest challenge to overcome with any continuous improvement effort, including Six Sigma.

The traditional organization is managed as a pyramid with many functional silos (Figure 12.1). At the top are the chairman, the CEO, and the chief operating officer. The next layer down consists of the vice president level. There are typically functional vice presidents of finance, marketing, human resources, manufacturing, and, in some organizations, quality or customer satisfaction. Sometimes the chief information officer is at this level. These individuals each lead their functional area, often with very little experience in areas other than their own. In a flat organization, there may be three or four additional layers of functional managers below the vice presidents. In a more bureaucratic organization, there could be five or more.

The functional managers at any level are each primarily evaluated on the management of their functional area. The performance measures usually emphasize productivity issues such as staffing and behavioral issues such as employee satisfaction. Some managers may have additional performance evaluation components in addition to these, which presents a very major challenge. Functional managers are usually evaluated based on making their individual area look good, not making a process look good, or get better. This is why functional area, middle managers are viewed in many organizations as the biggest impediment to major process changes. This is clearly illustrated later in this chapter.

Since most customer value is created through horizontal processes, improvement efforts must focus on processes. Process improvement consists of four major steps, each of which contains several subareas. First, processes must be mapped to indicate exactly

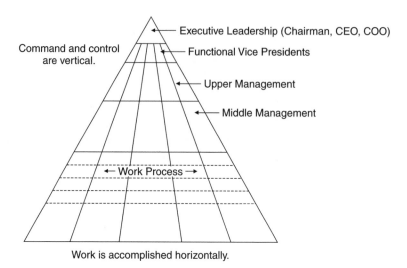

Figure 12.1 The Traditional Organization.

how work gets done. Second, all of the problems or disconnects within the process that can or do occur must be identified. Third, the causes of the problems must be isolated. Fourth, recommendations for improvement are incorporated into a map that shows how the process should work.

The remainder of this chapter focuses on Steps 1 and 2. First, process mapping is discussed in detail, followed by problem identification. The third and fourth steps are covered in subsequent chapters.

PROCESS MAPPING

Process mapping is graphical representation of a process from beginning to end, with all intermediate steps, activities, and relationships included. A detailed process map allows the critical analysis of how work actually gets done in an organization, and a process map identifies where attention must be focused to achieve the project goals. For example, a project goal of major cycle time reduction requires that the team focus on the activities with the longest cycle time and on the sequencing of activities. A cost reduction goal requires that the team scrutinize the high-cost activities and components. A zero defects goal requires that a team focus on activities that have the highest failure rates or causes of productivity inefficiencies.

Relationship Map

The first step in process mapping, after the selection of a process, is identifying the functions and individuals that are involved with a process in some way. The identification of the appropriate functions and individuals is often done through the development of a relationship map. In chapter 10, the use of a relationship map to identify team membership was discussed.

To briefly review, a relationship map is a flowchart that begins with an input and ends with an output. Between the beginning and ending points, all of the functional areas that touch a process are identified. At this point, identifying all the various activities is not

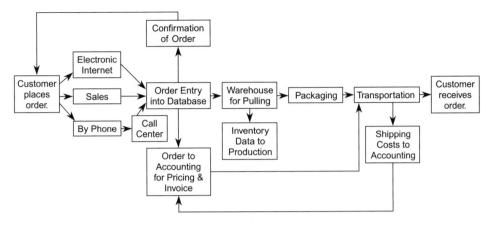

Figure 12.2 Order Fulfillment Relationship Map.

important, but identifying all of the individuals or departments involved with a process is very important. The very simple relationship map for order fulfillment discussed previously is presented in Figure 12.2. All of the departments or functional areas are represented as "swim lanes" in the "As-Is" map.

Preparing for Process Mapping

The team leader should ensure that the team is well prepared. The mapping should take place in a large room since an "As-Is" map of how a process currently works may take 30 feet of wall space. The team leader should have an ample supply of large, rectangular sticky pads (that is, Post-it® notes) and smaller, square pads. There should be a roll of blank paper 3 to 4 feet wide and plenty of masking tape. There should be an ample supply of markers in various colors, pencils, and erasers.

The team leader should tape 20 to 30 feet of the blank paper to the wall and then vertically list all of the departments or functional areas identified in the relationship map. Generally, it works best to have the customer and the department starting the process at the top and list other functional areas sequentially downward, with support areas such as accounting or information technology farther down the list. At the bottom is usually a database row.

Each of the functional areas involved in a process should have its own "swim lane." A swim lane is created by drawing horizontal, dotted lines that separate each department or functional area from one another. The combination of functional areas and swim lanes provides the framework on which all process activities are arranged.

The "As-Is" Map

The team identifies the beginning and ending points of the process and all intermediate activities and relationships in more detail. To continue with the order fulfillment example, a team might define the beginning point as the customer placing an order. The ending point might be the customer receiving the order and accompanying invoice. The map that describes all activities, or how things are actually done, is referred to as an "As-Is" map. An "As-Is" map for the order fulfillment example is presented in Figure 12.3, Parts 1 and 2.

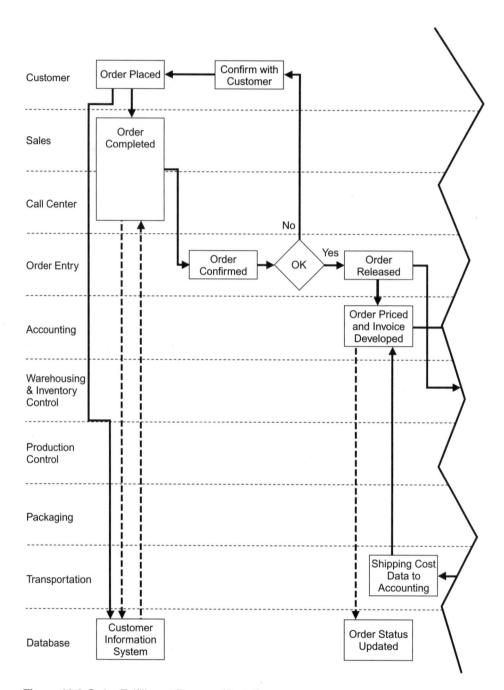

Figure 12.3 Order Fulfillment Process (Part 1).

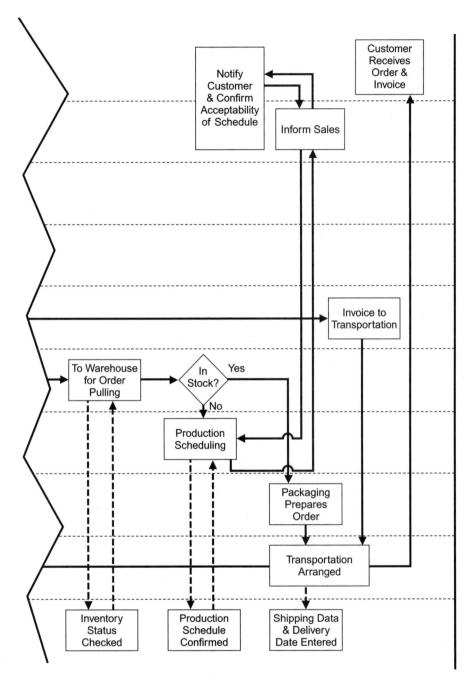

Figure 12.3 Order Fulfillment Process (Part 2).

This map was developed by having the team walk an order through the entire process, from beginning to end. Initially, the various activities were written on the large sticky pads and positioned in the appropriate swim lanes, indicating which area was responsible for performing a specific activity. The direction of workflow was indicated by drawing in pencil the relationships among activities. As the team develops a map, there are usually different perceptions about who is responsible for which activities. As a result, the boxes and lines are often rearranged until consensus is reached. Key decisions or alternatives are represented by the diamond boxes.

While this order fulfillment map is relatively simple and easy to follow, most process maps are much more detailed and complex. The following discussion provides an example of this complexity. This is an actual process map for a maintenance/repair process (Figure 12.4).

The firm in this example sold appliances and performed maintenance and repair on home appliances. The firm repaired virtually any type of appliance, including furnaces, air conditioners, washers, dryers, refrigerators, and even spas and barbecues. Their goal was to provide the customer with complete support service, a one-stop shop for all of the customer's needs.

The company had been successful over the years and had grown steadily. It had offices in about 10 cities in a western state, and this created a problem. It seemed that each area office had its own way of doing things. The maintenance and repair portion of the business was significant, generating about 30 percent of total revenues and employing about the same proportion of the workforce. Because of the importance of the repair process, the senior management of the company decided to embark on a process improvement initiative, the first ever undertaken.

The relationship map that was initially developed by two managers identified the functional areas or jobs that were involved in the repair process. These were the call center, area office associates, service technicians, the service foreman, inventory control/warehouse, suppliers, and computer information systems. In addition to representatives from the six internal areas, other individuals were ad hoc team members from time to time. These individuals were from areas such as accounting, purchasing, and outside suppliers. Since there were 10 area offices, some functional areas were represented by individuals from several offices. The intent was to identify the points of variance and commonality from office to office. The team consisted of about 10 core members.

The repair process began with the customer identifying a need and requesting service. The service request could be made through the call center since the firm had a centralized customer service center that was staffed 24 hours a day, seven days a week. Or, the customer could walk into one of the 10 stores and request service from one of the office associates (employees). In some cases, long-time customers would request work directly with the service technician or with the service foreman.

If the work request came into the call center, the necessary information was captured and entered into a customer information system database. The dotted line in the figure indicates an information flow. The work request was then sent over the computer network to the appropriate area office. If the work request was a normal nonemergency situation, the work was scheduled by the service foreman. If the work request was viewed as an emergency, such as a faulty furnace on a cold winter night or a gas leak from an oven, the call center personnel would contact the service foreman or service technician directly.

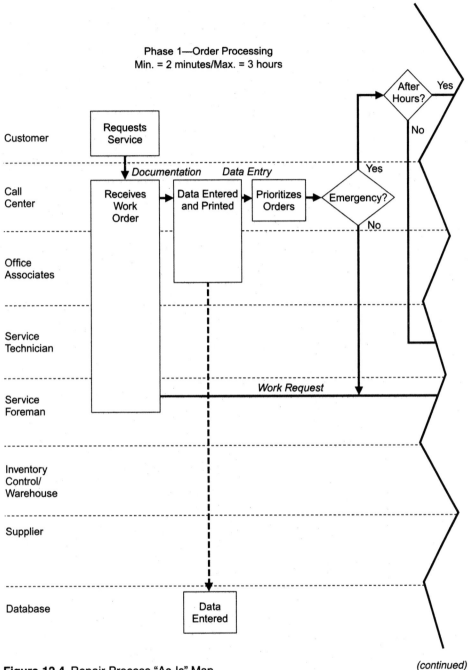

Figure 12.4 Repair Process "As-Is" Map.

(continued)

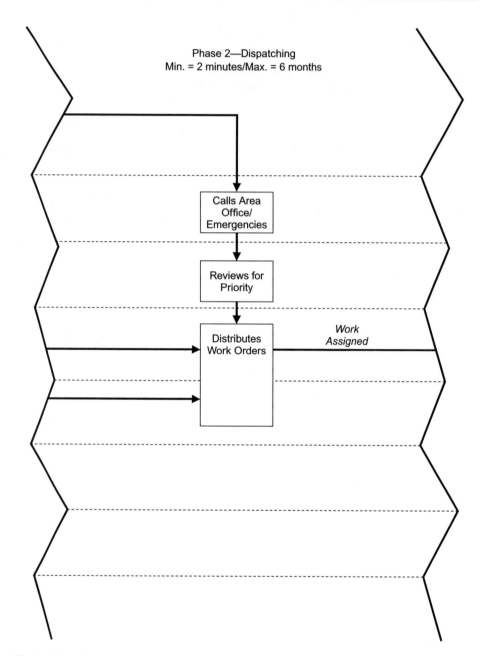

Figure 12.4 Continued.

If the work request came into the area office, to the service technician, or to the service foreman, the same information was supposed to be captured and entered into the database. In this situation, the scheduling and dispatching were handled locally.

Thus far, the process map consists of two phases. The first is order processing, and the second is dispatching. It is often helpful to break a process into phases. This makes identifying problems and developing solutions easier.

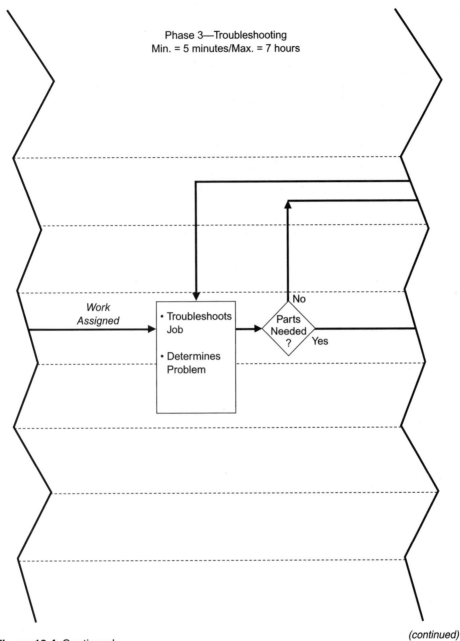

Figure 12.4 Continued.

(continued)

The third phase is troubleshooting. This occurs when the technician arrives at the customer's house and determines what is wrong with the product. However, the map has a major flaw between the dispatching and troubleshooting phases. The Six Sigma team initially forgot to allow for travel time. Each work request required 10 to 15 minutes to get to the customer's house. Since each technician made about 4 to 6 service

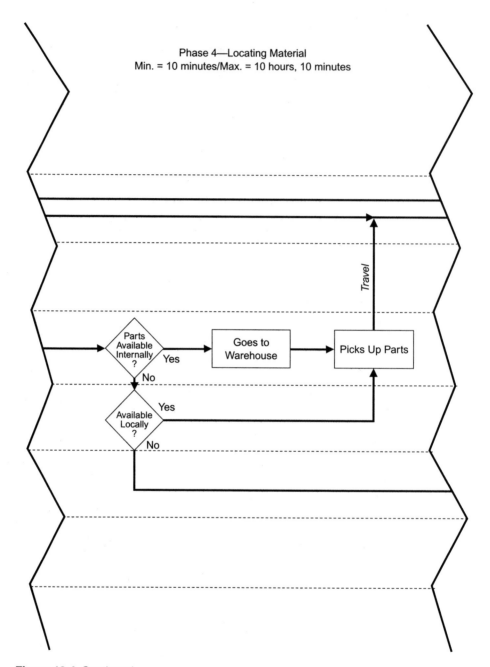

Phase 4—Locating Material
Min. = 10 minutes/Max. = 10 hours, 10 minutes

Figure 12.4 Continued.

calls a day, travel time getting to the customer's house consumed 40 to 90 minutes each day, a significant portion of the technician's time.

Based on a study of work requests, the team found that about 10 percent could be fixed with no parts needed. In these situations, the technician completed the work and completed the *service delivery* phase of the map. The more common situation was for parts to be needed to fix the problem.

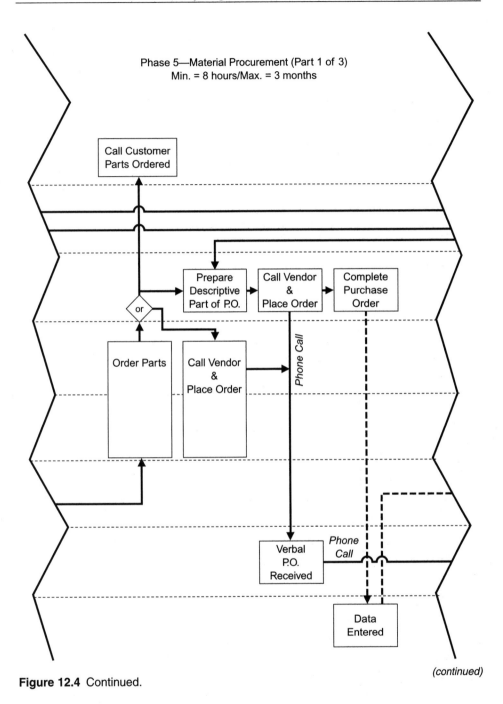

Phase 5—Material Procurement (Part 1 of 3)
Min. = 8 hours/Max. = 3 months

Figure 12.4 Continued.

(continued)

For 90 percent of the work requests, parts were needed. This is the *locating material* phase of the map. When parts were needed, about 60 percent of the time they were available inside the company; about half of the time, they were on the service truck; and about half of the time, they were in inventory at the area office. If the parts were on the truck, the technician completed the job. Thus, for less than half of all work requests (40 percent), the

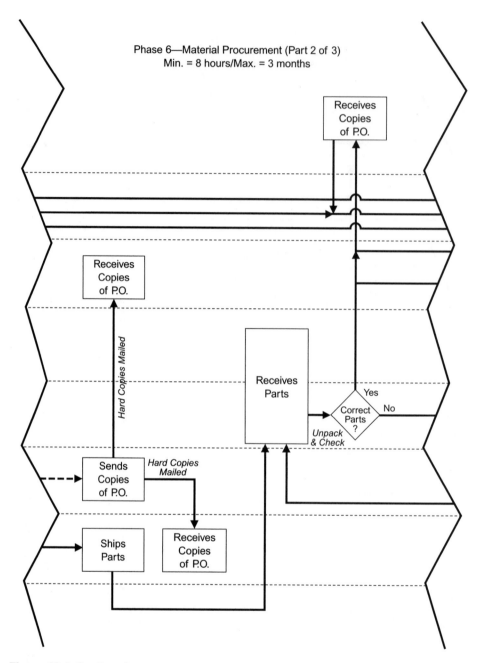

Phase 6—Material Procurement (Part 2 of 3)
Min. = 8 hours/Max. = 3 months

Figure 12.4 Continued.

work could be completed on one stop. This is the 10 percent of work requests requiring no parts and the 30 percent of work requests for which parts are available on the truck.

If the parts were available in the local inventory, the technician would drive to the warehouse, find the parts, and return to the customer's house. The technician would then complete the job. But, on average, it took 45 minutes to drive to the warehouse and return.

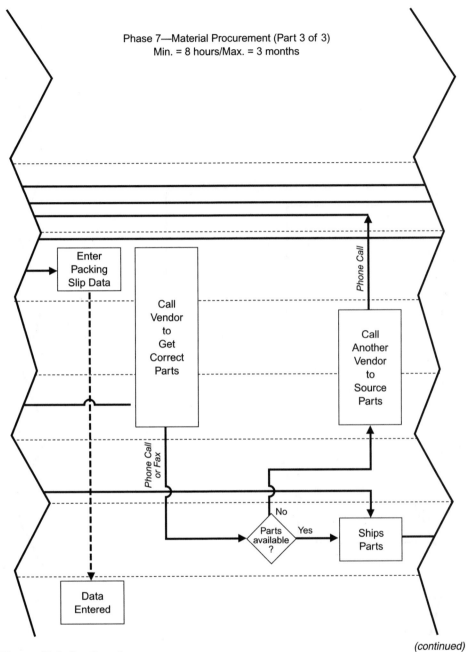

Phase 7—Material Procurement (Part 3 of 3)
Min. = 8 hours/Max. = 3 months

Figure 12.4 Continued.

(continued)

For 30 percent of the work requests, parts were needed but not available within the company. There were two categories within this 30 percent. For 5 percent of work requests, the parts were available with a local vendor. But this required the technician to drive to various vendors searching for the correct part and often paying full retail price. For 25 percent of work requests, the parts had to be special ordered from the manufacturer or from a distributor.

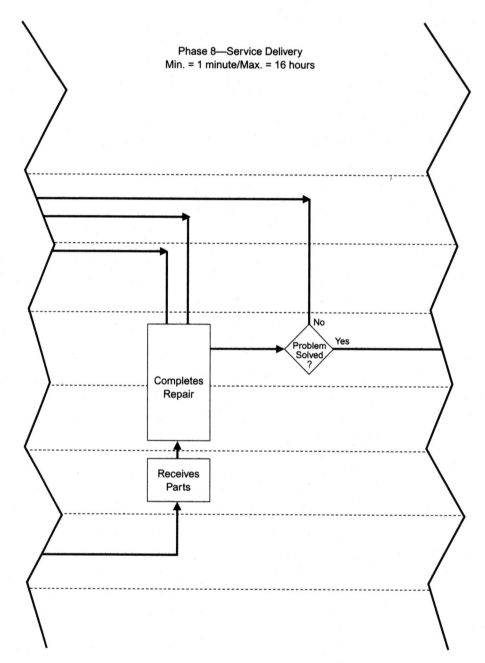

Figure 12.4 Continued.

As is obvious on the map, the materials procurement phase was time-consuming and costly. Vendors had to be sourced; purchase orders developed; orders placed; parts shipped, received, and inspected; and another service call scheduled with the customer. And, 95 percent of the time, the work was then completed. But, for 5 percent of the service calls, the parts were wrong or did not correct the initial problem, and the whole materials procurement phase started over again. The incorrect parts had to be returned and credited.

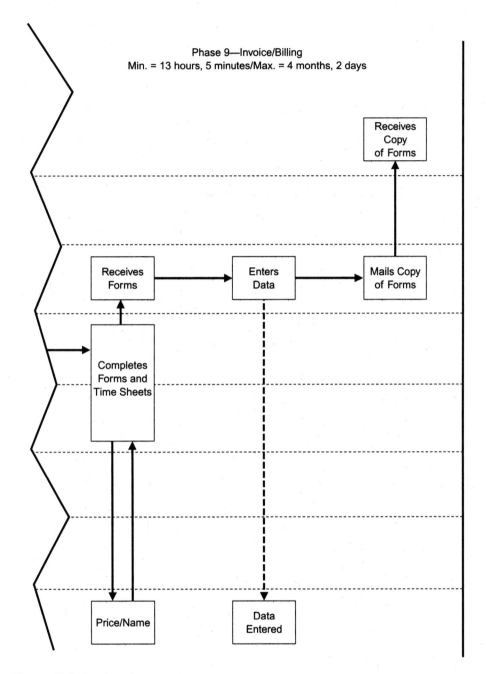

Figure 12.4 Continued.

Finally, at the end of each day, the technician completed all of the required paperwork. This was typically done after the technician returned to the area office. The paperwork was turned in to the office associate who developed an invoice and sent an invoice to the customer.

Once the map was completed, cycle times for each activity were calculated. The decision rule was that any activity that consumed one minute or more must be on the map. For example, receiving the work request from the customer took, on average, 2 minutes. Entering the information into the database took, on average, 2 minutes. For each activity, the minimum cycle time, the average cycle time, and the maximum cycle time were calculated. The three cycle times were totaled for all activities within each phase. Then the cycle times for all phases were totaled.

For each decision box represented by the diamond shape, the proportion of each alternative was determined. For example, the service technicians estimated that parts were not needed for 10 percent of the work requests and needed for 90 percent. This was subsequently confirmed through a study of 200 work requests.

By determining both the frequency of each alternative occurring and the cycle time for each activity, the total cycle time for completing a work request could be determined. For this repair process, a *no parts* work request consumed about 2 hours of time from beginning to end. However, when parts were required, depending on the situation, 3 to 4 hours were required to complete the job. Since 90 percent of the work requests required parts, the fully allocated marginal cost would total nearly 4 hours of labor plus the materials. This does not include any of the overhead costs for trucks, travel, warehousing, computer systems, or support functions.

The bulk of the labor was performed by the service technician, service foreman, and the office associate. However, there was also labor provided by the call center personnel, inventory personnel, and information technology personnel.

At this point, the process mapping was nearly complete. While there may have been a few discrepancies from actual practice, such as the travel issue, most were eventually corrected by the team. Since there were 10 area offices that had a fair amount of autonomy, there were minor variances in activities from area to area. However, the differences from area to area were viewed as relatively minor. Once there was consensus among the team that the "As-Is" map depicted the way the process actually worked, the next step was to identify the problems within the process.

Problem Identification

After the activities were mapped in detail, cycle times calculated, and the frequency of each alternative determined, the team identified all actual or potential problems. Using a nominal group technique, the team critically analyzed each activity. Each team member, and especially those that performed an activity, wrote down all of the problems associated with the way things were being done. This analysis included both the activities themselves and the interrelationships and work flows.

The problems were captured by a team member on a flip chart. A team normally begins with the first activity and works its way through the map so that every activity and interrelationship is carefully evaluated. For analysis purposes, it is often helpful to group the problems by phases of the process. This is illustrated in Table 12.1.

The team was able to identify 60 problems or disconnects in the service order process. There were 9 problems in the order-processing phase, 4 in dispatching, 6 in troubleshooting, 8 in locating materials, 25 in materials procurement, 4 in service delivery, and 4 in invoice/billing. Over half of all problems (32) dealt with locating material or material procurement. Since 90 percent of repair calls required parts, the material issue was quite significant, particularly since a no parts situation consumed about 2 hours of total labor and a parts required consumed about 4 hours of labor.

The issue of materials and parts was so significant that the repair process team gave birth to a new team. The focus of the new team was to resolve all of the materials problems. The team ultimately entered into a partnership with a supplier who assisted in improving the activities.

For the nonmaterials issues, the team identified what the cause of each problem was. In actual practice, a second, vertical column would be added to Table 12.1 that captured the causal factors. It is important to identify a root cause for every problem so that the corrective actions treat the true causes and not the symptoms. By identifying the root causes individually, the most major causal factors quickly emerged.

For example, in the order-processing phase, one of the problems was a 100 percent turnover rate of call center part-time staff. The company had made a decision to have only

---

Order Processing
- Phone lines—recording comes on, not a live person at peak times.
- Incomplete and inaccurate work order information.
- Incomplete information from customer.
- Call center personnel need to be oriented in field processes.
- Lack of communications concerning emergency calls.
- Service technician/foreman initiates service without computer information system.
- Bypass of computer information system causes schedule conflicts.
- 100% turnover of call center part-time staff.
- Part-time employees reduce efficiency.

Dispatching
- Double scheduling of service technicians.
- Correct information on location of service technicians (after hours and normal working hours).
- Communication equipment does not work in certain areas.
- After hours, difficult to reach service technicians (Internet being used at home).

Troubleshooting
- Inadequate tools for service technicians.
- Service technician may not have correct tools.
- Inability to determine the problem.
- No backup technician available to assist when needed.
- Being able to get to job site.
- Callbacks are not measured.

Locating Material
- Vendor stocking agreement ineffective.
- Location of parts inappropriate for usage.
- Stock levels not maintained in warehouse.
- Inconsistent pricing and/or noncompetitive prices.
- Supplier quality/pricing not measured.
- Lack of inventory system for jobbing material.
- Inconsistent parts inventory on trucks.
- Locating materials—too many people taking materials off the warehouse shelves.

Material Procurement
- Too many suppliers.
- Not sure which supplier to use.

(continued)

Table 12.1 Problems/Disconnects for Service Order Process.

Material Procurement—Continued
- Service technician/foreman not familiar with suppliers.
- Delay in shipment.
- Billing & shipping addresses get confused.
- Suppliers do not call and inform of a delay in shipment.
- No performance measurement in place for jobbing material.
- No consistent process in place for returning materials.
- Parts, numbers, and descriptions not being updated in system.
- Inconsistency in the amount that generates a purchase order.
- Service technician does not include name, address, and account number on invoice receipt.
- Shipper damages parts.
- No one responsible for receiving parts.
- Quantities and conditions not always checked in a timely manner.
- Shipping claims are denied because shipment not inspected in a timely manner.
- Do not track cost, time, and frequency of receiving wrong parts.
- Customer not always contacted that parts are on order.
- Too many different people ordering parts.
- Supplier ships to wrong area office.
- Supply order takers not always available.
- Central warehousing has difficulties in determining where shipments go.
- Parts procurement reduces productivity, employee satisfaction, and customer satisfaction.
- Incorrect parts received, impacts schedule.
- Customer satisfaction is reduced due to extended wait time for parts.

Service Delivery
- Callbacks are not measured.
- Schedule lacks flexibility to return for repairs.
- Pulled off jobs to assist elsewhere.
- Troubleshooting misdiagnosed (callback).

Invoice/Billing
- Cannot complete paperwork.
- Too many service order forms to prepare.
- Paperwork completed at end of day so technician estimates information.
- No standard approach to billing procedures for travel time, callbacks, material procurement.

Table 12.1 Continued.

a few full-time, permanent call center personnel and to staff predominantly with part-time employees. The reason for this was to save costs. Part-timers had a lower wage rate and had no fringe benefits. But, with the high turnover rate, the inexperienced call center personnel caused problems for other people in the organization, reducing overall productivity and efficiency. After analysis, it was determined that the problems caused far outweighed the labor savings. The solution to this problem was to staff with full-time personnel who would gain experience about the service repair process.

In the trouble order phase, one of the problems was *inadequate tools for service technicians*. In the locating material phase, one of the problems was *inconsistent parts inventory on the trucks.* Both of these problems had similar causes. The service technicians each had their own service trucks. Each technician had the responsibility to stock it with tools and parts as he (they were all male) saw fit. The cause of both problems was the lack of a standardized list of tools and parts.

After discussion, the team decided that there needed to be two parts lists, one for winter and one for summer. In the winter, furnace repair was a significant portion of service calls. Conversely, in the summer, air conditioner repair was quite common. The result was that the team developed a standardized parts and tools list based on seasonality.

After the problems and causes were identified, the team then looked for common patterns among the root causes. It was not unusual for a root cause to be manifested in several ways throughout a process. But the root causes are the issues that must be resolved by the team.

Many of the problems occurred because the people performing activities lacked complete information about the repair request. Information was either captured incorrectly initially or was inaccessible when needed. Therefore, many of the root causes revolved around database design, management, and quick, easy access. Other issues dealt with lack of training for new personnel, causing greater variability.

SUMMARY

Accurate, detailed process mapping is absolutely critical to virtually all Six Sigma process improvement efforts. The most common error is to not provide sufficient detail when describing the individual activities. If the "As-Is" process map lacks detail, all subsequent activities such as the calculation of cycle times, interrelationships, and disconnects are less effective.

Once a process is mapped, the individuals performing the activities must identify all of the actual or potential problems. Each activity, interrelationship, and phase should be critically evaluated. Once the problems are detailed, the root cause of each problem must be identified. The approach provides a very organized framework for understanding how work actually gets done and can identify why problems occur.

CASE STUDY

ANALYZING PROCESSES AND IDENTIFYING PROBLEMS

The Controls Business of Johnson Controls, Inc., has implemented a process-focused environment that permeates throughout the organization. This environment has been the backbone for its continuous improvement initiative, which is one of its core values. This strong process management focus also permeates to its system used for ISO 9000 compliance and makes it easier for assessing process performance and compliance. The case study at the end of chapter 14 discusses the fact that over 40 Sigma teams identified and improved over 52 processes using sophisticated Six Sigma tools in 1999. The results of these efforts had a significant positive impact on business and customer results. For instance, customer satisfaction improved about 3 percentage points, warranty expenses improved about 26 percent, and outgoing quality level from the factories improved 35 percent.

As part of its process management methodology, the Controls Business of Johnson Controls, Inc., employed the Rummler-Brache methodology for documenting both "As-Is" and "Should-Be" process maps. This was an initial step in its continuous improvement journey and preceded the application of Six Sigma tools to analyze and improve process performance. Over 50 facilitators helped the organization map over 75 key processes over the course of one year. This insight provided valuable knowledge to the organization on improving overall performance and also helped align processes and process parameters with customer requirements and customer satisfaction results. The fact that the key processes had been mapped was instrumental in the deployment and relatively quick results achieved with Six Sigma efforts that were launched in 1999.

An example of a process map that was derived from the initial analysis using Rummler-Brache methods is shown in Figure 12.5, which is the customer dissatisfaction alert (CDA) process used for contacting customers when low survey scores are found or a request for contact is made.

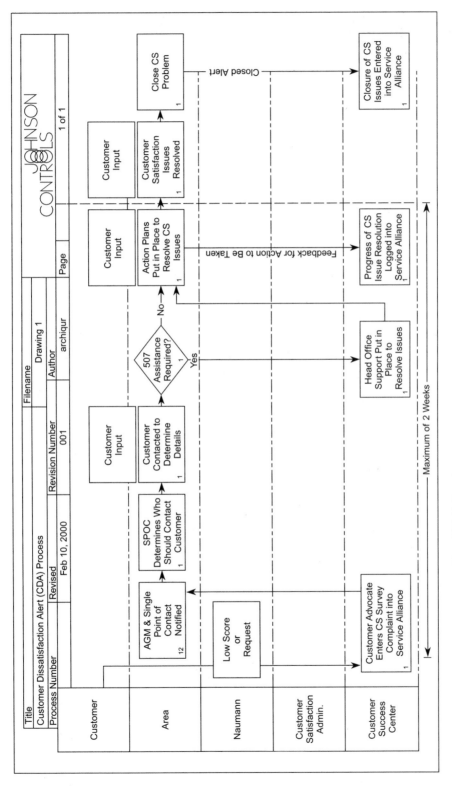

Figure 12.5 Customer Dissatisfaction Alert (CDA) Process.

13

Problem Solving

The first step in problem solving is to have a clear understanding of the nature of the problem and its causes. The previous chapter presented several "As-Is" maps and showed how a Six Sigma team critically analyzed the activities and their interrelationships. A list of problems was developed, along with an initial identification of the cause of each problem.

Unfortunately, analyzing problems can get much more complex than a simple *one problem–one cause* situation. The purpose of this chapter is to present a variety of tools that can be used to analyze problems that are more complex. In essence, all problem-solving approaches pursue the *five whys* concept. Observed problems are typically symptoms of an underlying root cause. The root cause may lead to a variety of problem manifestations. By asking *why* 5 times, the problem is peeled back until the root cause is finally exposed.

There are many specific tools that could be used for problem solving. These include brainstorming, designed experiments, developing Pareto charts and/or histograms, statistical process control, process capability studies, and multivariate statistical analysis. Discussing all of these techniques is well beyond the scope of this chapter. However, some of the techniques are discussed elsewhere in this book. This chapter focuses on five of the more commonly used tools.

The first tools are graphic techniques that are useful for identifying and organizing the root causes of actual or potential problems. These are *cause-effect (or fishbone) diagrams* and *tree diagrams*. Next, there is a discussion of *affinity diagrams*. Finally, there is a discussion of *failure mode effects analysis (FMEA)* that shows how to prioritize problems in order of importance, based on their impact on the organization or the customer.

The first four tools discussed in this chapter help to clarify problems and their causes. The fifth tool, benchmarking, focuses on how to solve a problem. By using some or all of the first tools, a Six Sigma team knows exactly what issues to address in a benchmarking effort.

The last part of the chapter shows how the recommendations to solve the problems can be converted into a *"Should-Be" map*. The "Should-Be" map is a graphical representation of how the redesigned process should work. This includes a clear statement of all recommendations, assumptions, and expected benefits.

CAUSE-EFFECT DIAGRAMS

A *cause-and-effect diagram* is similar to an affinity diagram in that it solicits inputs and possible causes for a problem from a group or team. A cause-and-effect diagram demonstrates natural relationships between the effects on an output due to a series of causes. Cause-and-effect diagrams have often been referred to as *fishbone diagrams* because the output from this technique resembles the bones in a fish. It is also sometimes referred to as an *Ishikawa diagram,* named after Dr. Kaoru Ishikawa of the University of Tokyo who first formalized its use in the mid 1940s. There are four steps to constructing a cause-and-effect diagram:

1. It is first necessary to identify the quality characteristic or performance measurement for which a cause-and-effect relationship is to be established. Let us say that we would like to determine the cause of not resolving customer complaints within a specified time period, say 24 days. We would like to resolve all complaints in 24 days or less. This desired outcome is written in a box to the right of the major horizontal axis shown in Figure 13.1 and forms the *head* of the fish. The major axis serves as the *backbone* of the fish, in which are fed major cause classifications described in Step 2.

2. Using structured brainstorming and the experience of knowledgeable people, including employees, customers, and suppliers, several major classifications of variables are generated that can affect the ability to resolve a customer's complaint within 24 days. Most cause-and-effect diagrams end up with many of the same major classifications and include methods, materials, measurements, machines or equipment, people, and environment. However, the group may define its own set of major classifications and is not restricted to the use of any of these six. The categories that the group define are placed above and/or below the major axis drawn in Step 1, with the vertical relationship lines drawn to the major axis as shown in Figure 13.1. These relationship lines form the major *fishbones* off the major axis or *backbone.*

3. For each of the major categories, the group identifies the variables or causes that fall within that category and inserts these into the diagram using horizontal lines feeding into the category relationship lines drawn in Step 2. For example, Figure 13.2 identifies one of the causes of not being able to resolve customer complaints within 24 days as *lack of training,* which is placed within the *people* category. Further breakout of causes may be possible such as under the major category of *people* and under the cause of *short personnel,* which has been further delineated as being caused by *high turnover* and *absence due to flu season.* The finer the delineation, the better, as this forces the group to get to the root cause of the problem rather than the symptom. Once the cause has been identified for each category, the group can move on to Step 4.

4. In Step 4, the group reviews each step in the associated process flow diagram to ensure that the brainstorming session has exhausted all possible variables and causes of the problem. The team leader may want to validate the list of causes with another group or team to get the best list of all possible causes.

In its use by a Six Sigma improvement team, the cause-and-effect diagram is a living document that, along with a process flow diagram, is included as part of the total

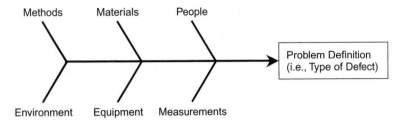

Figure 13.1 Cause-Effect Diagram (Part 1).

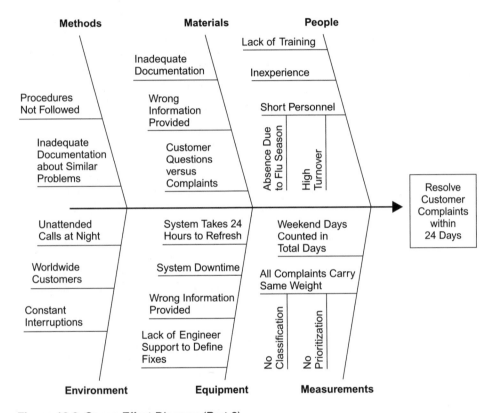

Figure 13.2 Cause-Effect Diagram (Part 2).

process documentation. The final document identifies every possible cause of a problem or poor process performance. If new variables or causes are discovered, they are added to the cause-and-effect diagram. The team reviews the cause-and-effect diagram and determines which variables have the biggest impact on the problem or on process performance. A Six Sigma team provides its attention only to those variables or causes that are considered key to process performance or delivering the desired outcome described by the *head of the fish*. Information from cause-and-effects diagrams is often used as input for use in failure mode effects analysis (FMEA), a problem-solving technique to be discussed subsequently.

TREE DIAGRAMS

A *tree diagram,* also referred to as a *systematic diagram,* identifies actions to solve a problem or implement a solution in a structured, logical progression. This method moves one's thinking logically from broad goals to more specifics. The tree diagram systematically maps the task that needs to be accomplished in order to solve a problem or achieve a goal. It translates general, universal objectives into the appropriate level of detail. The advantage of a tree diagram is that it details in a logical manner the sequence of tasks that need to be completed to fully address the problem. All the component parts of the problem that need to be addressed are identified, which helps define and develop implementation of a solution. Figure 13.3 shows a tree diagram.

An *opportunity box* is drawn on the left-hand side of the paper that describes the problem to be resolved or the goal to be achieved. Then, as in the creation of an organization chart, two or more boxes are drawn to the right of the opportunity box and connected by relationship lines. These boxes are created through brainstorming by asking the question "How can this problem be resolved?" or "How can this opportunity be accomplished?" Each of these new ideas then becomes a new opportunity box, and the same technique is applied to these. Additional boxes and relationship lines are identified and drawn in progression across the paper, moving to the right, until all possible tasks that affect the problem or goal have been identified. The process does not stop until specific actions to address the opportunity statement can be identified.

The tree diagram can be used to uncover multiple causes for a problem, until the root cause is revealed. Structured brainstorming with a Six Sigma improvement team could lead to identification of root causes of the problem, then to evaluation and prioritization, and then to identification of possible solutions.

The tree diagram in Figure 13.3 presents a problem faced by many people in the United States and, to a lesser degree, people from other industrialized countries. As industrialized economies have evolved, there is less physical effort and more mental effort required for most jobs. The result of a more sedentary work environment is that an increasing portion of the society is overweight. This problem is compounded by an aging population in the industrialized countries. We can do little about aging (although recent research does indicate there are things that can be done to extend our lives, possibly to age 120), but we can all do something about our weight. So, let us assume that our problem statement is that we are overweight and our goal is to correct that situation by losing weight. The desired state is to lose weight, the trunk of the tree.

There are two factors that result in weight loss. Weight loss is nothing more than an input-output ratio, which is, unfortunately, unique for each person. If you input more food than you burn off, you gain weight. If you input less food than you burn off, you lose weight. Losing weight is easier for some than others, but the fundamental, input-output principle still applies. However, to diet or to exercise, one must have a proper mental attitude. Both actions require self-discipline. Therefore, each branch contains some common elements dealing with reinforcing the desired behavior.

Each of the factors, or branches, can be explored further. Following a diet means that you must decide which diet is the most appropriate for you, personally. This could be recommended by a doctor, a book, or a class. Perhaps a person already has a low calorie intake. In this situation, exercise may be the needed alternative. Research suggests that lack of exercise is more of a problem for people in the United States than the actual calorie intake.

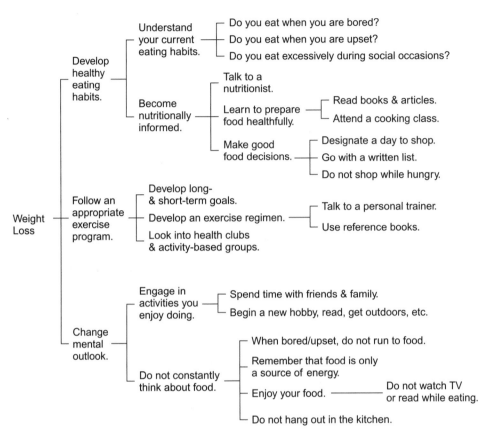

Figure 13.3 Tree Diagram.

This is obviously not a diet book. However, the use of a tree diagram is helpful to organize the possible causes of a problem, regardless of what the problem might be. The following technique, an affinity diagram, is also useful in the organization of an array of data into logical groupings.

AFFINITY DIAGRAMS

An *affinity diagram* clusters related items into more general groupings. You might say that an affinity diagram is used to organize verbal information into a visual pattern. It starts with specific ideas and works toward broader categories, each of which contains several of the more specific ideas. It is a way of clustering data into categories so that the data is more manageable. Affinity diagrams are usually generated from groups or teams that are formed to solve a problem. Using brainstorming or other forms of team participation techniques, the group tries to identify all the facets of the problem. These ideas are usually written down and posted for all group members to review. Sometimes the ideas are written on note cards, on a flip chart or white board, or on Post-it® notes. Then the ideas are clustered into

Possible Performance Indicators for Monitoring XX Manufacturing Operation	
• Number of Customer Returns • Machine Utilization • Number of Accidents • Hours Worked per Employee • Overtime Hours • Yield • Scrap • Customer Complaints • Color • Overtime Costs • Cost of Products Produced • Number of Units Rejected	• Age of Equipment • OSHA Cases/Incidents • Maintenance Costs • Material Costs • Percent Rework • Quality of Incoming Material • Machine Speed • Lost Time Injuries • Number of Units Produced • Utility Costs • Percent Capacity • Amount of Time Since Last Tooling Change

Table 13.1 List of Performance Metrics.

major categories. The group is asked to cluster similar ideas or thoughts together. The clusters of ideas are then defined in a broader category by the group. The resulting affinity diagram provides a hierarchical structure that provides valuable insight into the problem.

Affinity diagrams are most useful when analyzing written comments, such as those obtained from a customer satisfaction or employee satisfaction survey. The comments are clustered around common themes. For instance, there could be a host of comments related to each of the major attributes in the customer value models shown in chapter 11. The comments could be sorted by positive and negative comments related to the attribute. A series of metrics that were developed through a brainstorming session to determine appropriate performance indicators to use when monitoring performance of a manufacturing operation are shown in Table 13.1. These comments were then categorized by the group as shown in Table 13.2.

The use of an affinity diagram is a good way to organize the ideas and thoughts of many individuals. Its use and results are similar to cause-and-effect diagrams.

FAILURE MODE EFFECTS ANALYSIS

Failure mode effects analysis (FMEA) is a technique that meshes quite well with root cause analysis, QFD, and process mapping. FMEA is a structured approach to quantifying the effects of failures so that priorities for corrective action can be set. More frequent and costly problems are corrected first. The initial application of FMEA tended to focus on both actual failures and tangible products.

Gradually, the FMEA concept has broadened to include processes and services. The focus on failures has broadened to include potential failures and operating inefficiencies as well. In essence, FMEA is now a technique that can be used proactively to anticipate potential and actual problems in the design and delivery of products and services.

FMEA is a proactive extension of a QFD house of quality (HOQ). In the HOQ, each customer requirement or expectation was matched with a corresponding performance characteristic or metric. Both customer perceptions and internal design evaluations could be examined. With FMEA, each performance characteristic is evaluated by answering a

Costs/Expenses	Quality	Utilization	Maintenance	Safety
Hours Worked per Employee	Quality of Incoming Materials	Percent Capacity	Maintenance Costs	Number of Accidents
Overtime Costs	Percent Rework	Hours Worked per Employee	Amount of Time Since Last Tooling Change	OSHA Cases/ Incidents
Yield	Yield	Yield	Machine Speed	
Maintenance Costs	Number of Customer Returns	Overtime Hours	Age of Equipment	
Utility Costs	Color	Machine Utilization		
Number of Units Produced	Number of Units Rejected	Overtime Hours		
Overtime Costs	Customer Complaints			
Cost of Products Produced	Scrap			
Material Costs				
Scrap				

Table 13.2 Natural Groupings of Performance Indicators.

series of questions. The questions are intended to identify what could or does go wrong, what the resultant impact is, and what should be done to improve. In Six Sigma terminology, this is *mistake proofing* the process.

For tangible products, or a design FMEA, the product characteristics are usually of primary interest. However, the causes of product failure could lie with the design of the product, the system inputs such as materials or components, or process inefficiencies. Thus, the solution or recommendations to correct a problem could take various forms. Design FMEAs benefit directly from the House of Quality (HOQ), which becomes a coordinating mechanism.

For process FMEAs, the primary focus is on the activities that comprise the specific process. Thus, process mapping identifies the critical activities in a process. FMEA attempts to identify what could/does go wrong with each activity or, at the least, the major activities in the process. A process FMEA also examines the interrelationships or handoffs between activities. An example may better illustrate the application of FMEA.

The order fulfillment "As-Is" process map (Figure 12.5) in the previous chapter consisted of a variety of activities. While FMEAs could be done for all activities, only *order pulling* will be illustrated. Order pulling is performed in the warehouse by warehouse personnel. Therefore, the warehouse manager responsible for this activity is indicated at the top of Figure 13.4. The Six Sigma team completes this figure based on its analysis.

Process FMEA—Order Fulfillment

Process/Activity/Product: Order Fulfillment
Team: Six Sigma #3

Responsible: Warehouse
Critical Date: _____

Subprocess/ Activity	Failure Mode	Effect of the Failure	Severity	Cause of Failure Mode	Occurrence	Present Detection Systems	Detection	RPN*	Recommended Action(s)	Responsibility and Due Date	Action(s) Taken	Results				
												Severity	Occurrence	Detection	RPN*
1	2	3	4	5	6	7	8	9	10	11	12	13	14	15	16
Order Pulling	Incorrect Order Pulled	Dissatisfied Customer	6	Order Puller's Error	6	Packaging Review	5	180	New Form	Warehouses 12/98	OK	6	2	2	24
Order Input	Incorrect Order	Dissatisfied Customer	6	Incorrect Order Input	4	Order Confirmation	3	72	New Sales Order Input Procedures	Sales 12/98	OK	6	1	4	24

*RPN = Risk Priority Number

Figure 13.4 Process FMEA-Order Fulfillment.

Severity of Impact	Ranking
Will hardly be noticeable. Very low to negligible impact on the customer.	1–2
Noncompliance with operating policy. Low to very low impact on the customer.	3–4
Noncompliance with customer requirements and possible damage to the reputation of the company.	5–6
Major product/service problems. Very noticeable to customer. Serious damage to the reputation of the company.	7–8
Complete product/service failure.	9–10

Table 13.3 Scoring Guidelines for Severity.

For order pulling, the failure mode is an incorrect order. When an incorrect order is sent to the customer, there are a series of effects. The customer is dissatisfied. If an incorrect item has been shipped, it must be returned, restocked, and the customer account credited. If the order was incomplete, the deleted item must be pulled, packaged, and probably expedited because the order is now late, and invoice errors must be reconciled. Because of all these effects, and the fact that many customers will leave after several occurrences, an incorrect order is moderately severe. Therefore, the severity rating, Column 4, would be a six.

For consistency across FMEAs, there should be standard scoring guidelines for each of the scored components in an FMEA. These are the severity of the failure, the likelihood of occurrence, and the probability of detection. An example of a severity scoring guideline is presented in Table 13.3. A low score indicates a positive situation, whereas a high score indicates a negative situation.

The cause of the failure is identified in Column 5 of Figure 13.4. An incorrect order could be caused by several things. One cause could be an error by the warehouse order puller. Another cause could be incorrect order input. In the order fulfillment process map, there were three alternatives that were available to the customer for placing an order: with a salesperson, by phone, or over the Internet. Identifying the cause of incorrect order input may require further research before developing solutions. The likelihood of the cause occurring is scored in Column 6 of Figure 13.4. As with severity, scoring guidelines for the occurrence are presented in Table 13.4. Order puller error was much more likely to occur than incorrect order input. Therefore, the occurrence was rated as moderate and scored a 6. Incorrect order input was less likely due to confirmation procedures already in place and was scored a 4.

The present detection systems are listed in Column 7 for each cause. For order puller error, the only control system was the order review by packaging personnel. This works well for small orders of only a few items but is difficult for large orders requiring several pallets. For incorrect order input, the order entry personnel repeat the order back to the customer, and the Internet order requires the customer to confirm the product and quantity before allowing it to be sent. However, there are no controls on the input of orders by sales personnel. Therefore, the detection score for order puller error is a 5. The incorrect order input is scored a 3. Scoring guidelines for detection are presented in Table 13.5.

Occurrence of Condition	Estimated Chance	Ranking
Remote. Highly unlikely condition will ever occur.	Less than 1 in 1,000,000	1–2
Low. The condition occurs in isolated cases, but chances are low.	1 in 20,000 to 1 in 2,000	3–4
Moderate. The condition has a reasonable chance to occur (could be startup and shutdown).	1 in 80 to 1 in 2,000	5–6
High. The condition occurs very regularly and/or during a reasonable amount of time.	1 in 8 to 1 in 80	7–8
Very High. The condition will inevitably occur during long periods (typical for normal operating conditions).	± 1 in 2	9–10

Table 13.4. Scoring Guidelines for Occurrence of Condition.

Detection of Aspect	Ranking
The current controls will almost certainly immediately detect the aspect, and reaction can be instantaneous.	1–2
Chances are high that the aspect will be detected shortly after occurrence, and a quick reaction is possible.	3–4
There is a moderate chance the aspect will be detected in a reasonable time frame, and/or it will take some time to react.	5–6
It is unlikely the aspect will be detected, or it will take a fairly long time before action can be taken and results are seen.	7–8
The aspect will not be detected in any reasonable time frame, or there is no reaction possible (normal operating conditions).	9–10

Table 13.5 Scoring Guidelines for Detection.

Each of the failure modes and effects can now be quantified. An incorrect order has a severity rating of 6, regardless of the cause. Multiplying 6 times the order puller's error occurrence of 6, times the order puller's detection score of 5, produces a *risk priority number (RPN)* of 180, which is quite high. For incorrect order input, the severity score is still 6, the occurrence score is 4, and the detection score is 3, producing an RPN of 72. Thus, solving the order puller error problem is much more important than incorrect order input.

After much discussion and research, the Six Sigma team in this example developed a new order puller form that required individuals to double-check their own work. Also, a new sales order input procedure was developed. These are presented in Column 10 of Figure 13.4. The areas of responsibility and implementation dates are presented in

Column 11. The new scores, given after the changes have been implemented, are presented in Columns 13 to 16.

The real key to the success of FMEA is to have the right people involved. For design FMEAs, the right people are usually the engineers who convert the customer requirements into product characteristics. For process FMEAs, the right people are the individuals who perform the activities under review. These individuals should be, at the least, ad hoc members of the Six Sigma process improvement team.

BEST-IN-CLASS BENCHMARKING

Benchmarking is clearly one of the most important business concepts to emerge in the later part of the 1980s. The concept is diametrically opposed to the mentality of "If it's not invented here, it can't be any good." The concept of benchmarking is a part of and a supplement to continuous improvement efforts. Most benchmarking efforts are an attempt to identify *best practices* that will provide solutions to critical problems. Thus, benchmarking is fundamental to quality improvement efforts of all types. But, despite its popularity, benchmarking is still shrouded in ambiguity.

Benchmarking means different things to different people. This ambiguity exists because there are three types of benchmarking; internal, competitive, and best in class. Each type of benchmarking is conceptually different from the others, and each requires a different methodology to implement.

The choice of which type of benchmarking to pursue is not an either-or proposition. Each is essential to continuous improvement in a different way, so firms should simultaneously pursue all three approaches to benchmarking. The purpose of this section is to pierce the ambiguous fog that surrounds benchmarking and show how each type can be successfully implemented.

Internal benchmarking is concerned with consistent improvement over some time period, and the primary focus is internal; "How much have we improved?" *Competitive benchmarking* is an equal blend of internal and external focus; "How are we doing compared to the competition?" *Best-in-class benchmarking* adopts a predominantly external focus by trying to identify the best business practices that exist anywhere, within the same industry, in a different industry, in the United States, or elsewhere in the world.

Best-in-class (BIC) benchmarking ideally is an ongoing process that analyzes the best processes in other organizations with the intent of improving an organization's own processes. BIC benchmarking is a continuous, ongoing effort that attempts to bring new ideas, information, and innovations into the company. A Six Sigma team may use a BIC approach to solve a particular problem, however.

BIC benchmarking was applied successfully by firms such as Xerox and Motorola in the early 1980s. During the mid-to-late 1980s, many other firms such as AT&T, DuPont, Boeing, 3M, IBM Rochester, and Hewlett-Packard applied the concept widely. Robert Camp, a Xerox engineer, wrote *Benchmarking: The Search for Industry Best Practices That Lead to Superior Performance* in 1989.[27] Camp's book describes Xerox's benchmarking experiences and has become the standard reference on the subject.

More recently, consulting firms such as PricewaterhouseCoopers have created benchmarking networks. The most popular networking organization appears to be the International Benchmarking Clearinghouse (IBC), a division of the American Productivity and

Quality Center in Houston, Texas. The IBC serves as a sort of repository for best practices, coordinating networking contacts among members and producing a variety of materials on benchmarking.

Since BIC benchmarking often requires radical organizational change involving the redeployment or reallocation of resources, top management commitment is essential. Some innovative firms refuse to allow benchmarking site visits unless a CEO, president, Chief Operating Officer (COO), or vice president level is part of the team. Other organizations assess the benchmarking maturity of the visiting team to see if enough skill is present to make the benchmarking visit worthwhile.

Because benchmarking is oriented toward process improvement, the individuals involved in the Six Sigma process improvement are usually part of the benchmarking team. One measure of benchmarking maturity, in addition to top management commitment, is employee involvement in the change process. The presence of cross-functional empowered work teams is a common benchmarking characteristic.

A third indication of benchmarking maturity is the presence of a coordinating point or mechanism in an organization. Rather than have three or four different people all attempting to contact the same firm with a request to benchmark, there should be some centralized conduit for both inbound and outbound requests. When a benchmarking visit is completed, a brief summary report with the names of the benchmarking team should be collected. Some firms such as Kodak and IBM have all benchmarking data fed into a database that can be accessed by the firm visited, practice benchmarked, or individuals involved.

Another indication of benchmarking maturity is the presence of training and materials. There is a variety of background, internal analyses that should be done before a benchmarking site visit. There is a variety of materials, questions, and questionnaires that should be developed before a site visit. After the site visit, there are issues of data analysis, implementation, and communicating the results that need to be addressed. All of these can be improved by training the benchmarking team.

BIC benchmarking should, therefore, have top management commitment, involve an empowered Six Sigma team, and be a coordinated organizational effort involving explicit training. Without achieving some degree of benchmarking maturity, the whole effort may be of little value. If some degree of benchmarking maturity does exist, however, then embarking on the benchmarking process can be very fruitful.

Camp (see note 27) described Xerox's benchmarking effort as a 10-step process (see Figure 13.5). The real purpose of the process is to establish goals and objectives consistent with those of world-class firms. Since this method is quite different than the incremental, marginal improvement from year to year that most firms use, attaining the goals may require significant organizational stretch, leading to a major redesign of processes. For example, Motorola, instead of a 10 percent to 20 percent reduction in defects, established a 100 times quality improvement goal. This obviously meant rethinking the whole approach to quality.

The 10 steps were grouped into four phases of planning, analysis, integration, and action. Once the initial goals are achieved, a fifth phase, maturity, is also evident. It should be noted that BIC benchmarking should only be pursued for relatively major process improvement efforts.

Once the root causes of problems have been identified through the techniques discussed previously in this chapter, best-in-class benchmarking provides a very good way to solve problems. The use of benchmarking helps reduce the chance that all organizations

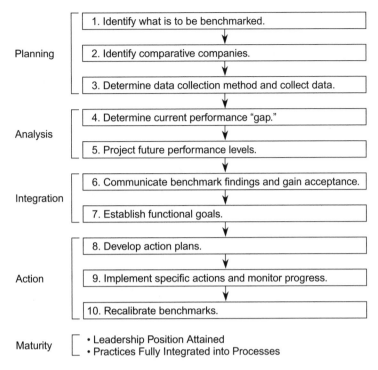

Figure 13.5 Xerox's 10-Step Benchmarking Process.

will keep reinventing the same wheel. In a very real way, benchmarking speeds the rate of innovation in industrialized economies. But, in some way, the goal of benchmarking is to determine how other firms have solved a problem facing a Six Sigma team, specifically, or an organization, more broadly.

The previous portions of this chapter have focused on how to identify, organize, and solve problems associated with activities within a process. At this point, the assumption is made that recommendations have been developed that will solve the problem or problems that a Six Sigma team is addressing. Now a transition will be made from an "As-Is" map to a "Should-Be" map that incorporates all of the recommendations.

"SHOULD-BE" MAPS

For each of the problems that resulted from the "As-Is" map, a detailed recommendation should be developed that corrects the root cause. The recommendations could take many forms. In the repair process "As-Is" map discussed in the previous chapter, there were over 60 problems identified. The Six Sigma team identified 30 recommendations that would resolve the 60 problems. A *"Should-Be" map* is simply a graphical representation of how the process *should* work after the recommendations are implemented.

Before developing a "Should-Be" map, all of the supporting assumptions necessary to implement the recommendations should be identified. This is necessary as a reality check to make sure that the recommendations are realistic and capable of being implemented. An example of a list of assumptions is presented in Table 13.6 for the repair process.

Assumptions
• All technicians have cell phones to call vendors rather than drive.
• Standardized truck and warehouse inventory for tools and high volume parts.
• 70% of calls can be completed from truck parts inventory if properly planned.
• All stock items have working barcode system for accurate inventory control and pricing.
• Vendors are precertified.
• Vendors will locate parts for us.
• Have a company-wide call list.
• Appropriate manpower on staff for service call volume.
• Everyone scheduled, including floaters.
• Paperwork is completed electronically, customer is invoiced at completion of job, and inventory receives information at same time.
• IT can develop/maintain appropriate database modules.
• All technicians had a laptop computer with relevant software.

Table 13.6 "Should-Be" Assumptions.

One assumption was that service technicians would have cellular phones so that they could call vendors to locate parts. Driving to locate or secure parts consumed almost 2 hours a day of service technician time. Using a cellular phone could reduce that time by at least half. Another assumption was that all service trucks would have a standard set of tools and replacement parts. By standardizing both tools and parts carried on the service trucks, it was estimated that 70 percent of service calls could be completed on the first visit, up substantially from current practice. Every proposed recommendation must be analyzed to determine all underlying assumptions. Very often, these assumptions require resource allocation.

Once the supporting assumptions have been identified, the team develops the "Should-Be" map that incorporates all of the recommendations and assumptions. An example of a "Should-Be" map for the repair process is presented in Figure 13.6. This map has some differences from the "As-Is" map that commonly emerge in most situations.

First, there are fewer activity boxes on the "Should-Be" map than on the as is map. This implies that individuals complete more activities at one time and, therefore, have fewer handoffs to other people. In essence, employees perform a wider range of tasks and have more responsibility than with the old process. This job expansion and enrichment typically results in higher levels of employee satisfaction and, ultimately, customer satisfaction.

A second major change in this map is the increased use of databases and technology. By maintaining and using databases for customer information, the efficiency of order entry and scheduling is enhanced. By using a centralized scheduling or work management database, the availability of technicians is easily determined. By using an inventory database, the stock levels of parts inventory are quickly determined as well as pricing information. And, by having a computer linkage with a key supplier, the location and procurement of parts are greatly enhanced. The increased use of information technology is quite common.

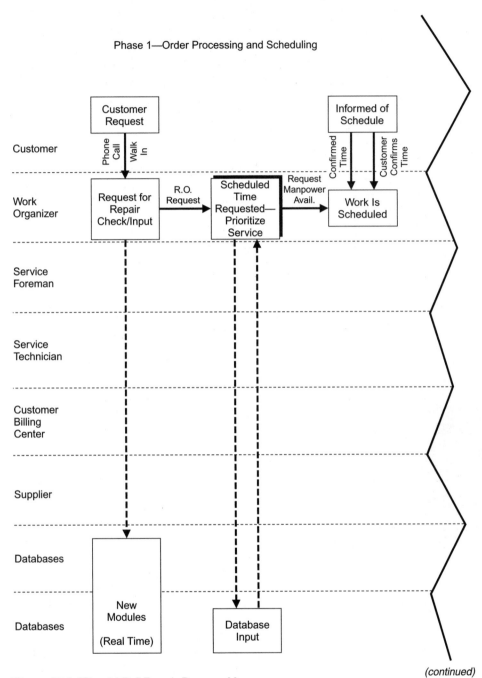

Figure 13.6 "Should-Be" Repair Process Map.

(continued)

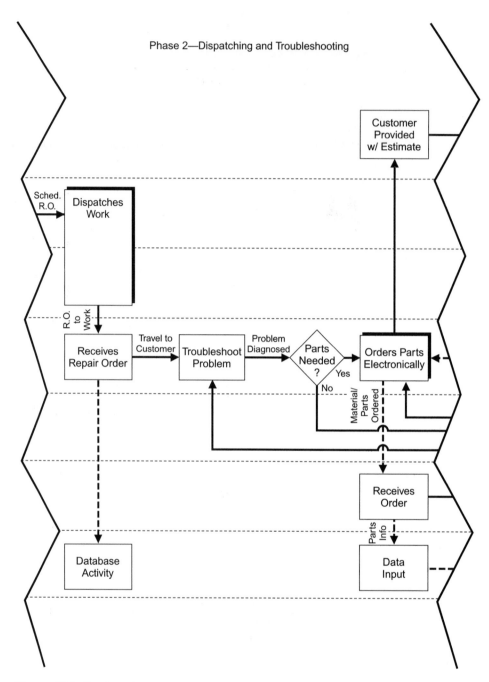

Figure 13.6 Continued.

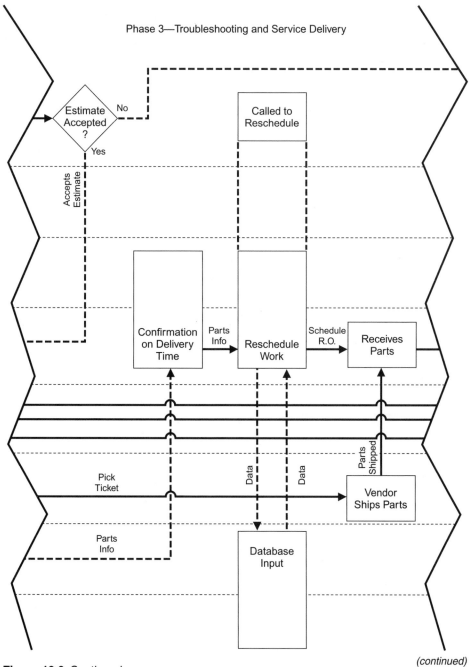

Figure 13.6 Continued.

(continued)

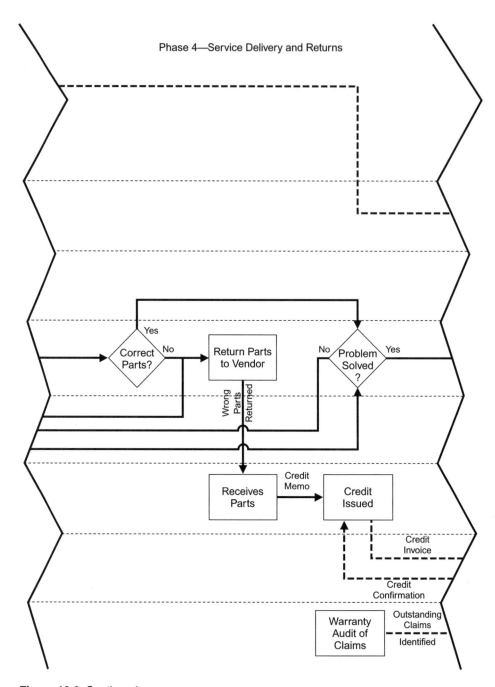

Figure 13.6 Continued.

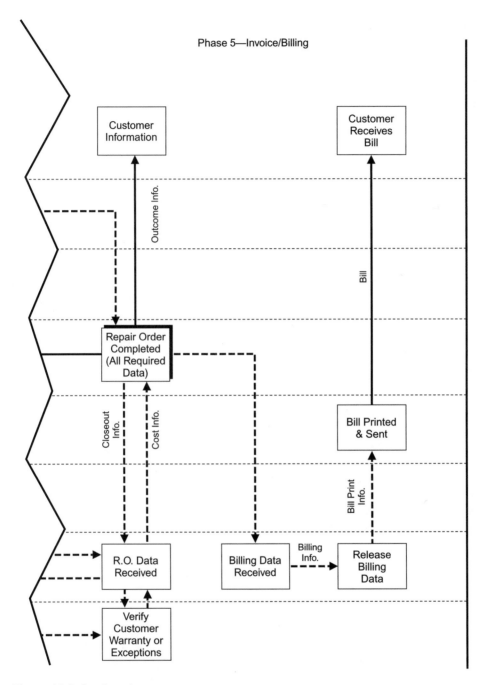

Figure 13.6 Continued.

Benefits
• Central dispatch—all information is entered into system.
• Provide more free time/billable time for the foreman.
• Real time status report (specific information to customer).
• Wide accessibility to status information.
• Eliminates handoff and makes more available time.
• Availability 24 hours a day.
• Increase billable time.
• Fast completion of service order.
• Increases employee & customer satisfaction.
• Major timesaving measure when technician is able to order parts electronically.
• Eliminate accounting functions.
• Creates ownership for completing the job.
• Orders received will go to specific tech and referenced to particular job.
• Free up foreman's time.

Table 13.7 Benefits of Redesigned Process.

After the "Should-Be" map is completed, the benefits of the redesigned process are determined. A sample list of benefits is included in Table 13.7. While all of these are clearly benefits, they are stated rather generally. The more specific the benefits are stated, the easier it is to calculate projected cost savings.

When the actual cost savings for labor and materials are calculated, the total value of the improvement effort becomes more apparent. An example of a more detailed approach that includes cost data is presented in Table 13.8. When the senior management became aware of the financial magnitude of the Six Sigma efforts presented in this summary, they became strong supporters.

The procedure for developing the "Should-Be" map is precisely the same as for an "As-Is" map. All functional roles must be identified and represented as a swim lane. All activities must be carefully mapped so that all interrelationships are identified. A common decision rule is to be sure that all activities that consume one one minute or more are on the map. Once the "Should-Be" map has been developed, the challenge for the Six Sigma team is how to get from the "As-Is" map to the "Should-Be" map in real life. That is the subject of a subsequent chapter.

SUMMARY

There are many approaches and tools that can be used for problem solving. This chapter addressed only a few of the more commonly applied techniques. However, it is important to note that, for every problem identified in a process, a root cause must also be identified. Then, the Six Sigma team makes a recommendation for every root cause that will correct the situation. The recommendations are incorporated into a "Should-Be" map that graphically represents how a process works. All assumptions that are necessary to implement the recommendations must be identified so that a cost of implementation can be calculated. Finally, the expected benefits, both behavioral and financial, from the improved process must be calculated so that a cost-benefit analysis can be completed.

1. Identified that key times of nonbillable activities are 8:00–8:30 A.M., 1:00–1:30 P.M., and 4:30–5:00 P.M. The total of 1 1/2 hours is enough time to complete one more service call per day with a potential revenue of $1.2 million (if demand exists).
2. Identified that parts procurement takes 1 to 2 hours per day per service tech, which is currently not billed in most cases.
3. Better managing #1 & #2 means that more service calls could be made by the existing workforce or the existing workforce could be downsized by about 25 percent.
4. Identified that if customers are billed an average of 15 minutes for travel to the job as most firms do, repair revenue would increase $250,000–$300,000 annually at no increase in cost.
5. Identified that if customers are billed an average of 15 minutes for paperwork related to their job that repair revenue would increase $250,000–$300,000 annually and customer associate labor ($180,000–$270,000) would decrease significantly.
6. Identified that standardized parts and tools on each service truck would increase the percentage of service calls completed on the first visit.
7. Identified that there are no consistent procedures across area offices for billing for travel, paperwork, parts procurement, and second or more service calls to complete a job. Everything is left to the discretion of the service techs in most cases.
8. Identified that average cycle time for billing the customer for repair work is over a month, resulting in reduced cash flow.
9. Identified that 90 percent of repair orders require parts and that from 15 minutes to 2 hours is spent sourcing parts per repair order.
10. Identified that 30 percent of repair orders require special order parts and sourcing parts in this situation requires 1–2 hours and a second visit.
11. Identified that supplier partnerships could reduce the cost of parts and reduce the labor required to source parts.
12. Identified that about one labor hour could be saved per special order situation by having a cell phone to contact supply partner at an annual savings of $288,000 (30,000 S.O. × 30% × 1 hour × 32.00 = $288,000).
13. Identified that current service parts and merchandise costs are between $650,000 and $1,000,000. By entering into a partnership, 15 percent to 20 percent could be reduced, saving between $97,000 to $200,000 annually.
14. Identified that a supplier certification process is needed to objectively evaluate supplier performance levels.

Table 13.8 More Detailed Benefits.

CASE STUDY

PROBLEM SOLVING

As mentioned numerous times in previous case studies, the Controls Business of Johnson Controls, Inc., embarked on a Six Sigma initiative in 1999. The intent was to identify major areas of variation, thus eliminating waste, scrap, and rework. The concept of Six Sigma was included as part of the overall continuous improvement methodology. Problem-solving tools, along with other basic and advanced statistical tools and techniques, were used by Sigma teams to identify, select, and prioritize improvement opportunities.

Problem-solving tools are taught to and used by Sigma specialists and Sigma teams. Proficiency in the application of problem-solving tools, including the advantages and disadvantages of their use in unique situations, is taught as part of Sigma specialist training. Sigma specialists, in turn, teach Sigma teams on the use of these tools.

Problem-solving tools were also taught as part of the Rummler-Brache process management course, that was used as a preamble to the launch of the Six Sigma initiative. The use of the Rummler-Brache methodology as part of process management resulted in mapping over 75 key processes across the Controls Business of Johnson Controls, Inc.

Problem-solving techniques are still offered as part of training curriculum offered to all employees. Training on specific techniques such as the use of affinity diagrams and failure mode effects analysis are offered to employees as courses, and these techniques are also included in broader process management training courses such as Rummler-Brache.

Sigma teams use problem-solving tools and techniques to help them through all four major steps of sigma projects. Problem-solving tools are used in the *prioritize* step to help identify root causes of problems and to characterize the opportunity of the problem. These tools are also used in the *characterize* step to help identify viable solutions. The *optimization* step uses problem resolution tools to help implement process improvements. They are also used in the *realize* step to verify that the process improvements have resulted in the expected outcomes.

It is safe to say that the use of formal problem-solving tools throughout the Controls Business of Johnson Controls, Inc., is pervasive and a natural outcome of the focus on process management and continuous improvement. These tools fit naturally with the Six Sigma initiative. One tool that is used the most and asked for by executives and champions is failure mode effects analysis for prioritization of opportunities.

14

Securing Management Support for Changes and Implementation

Gaining management support and commitment for changes, as well as implementation, is one of the biggest challenges for a Six Sigma team when first starting out. Once results are consistently demonstrated, management support is simply a routine approval in most cases. However, until that time, presenting the team's work and recommendations to senior management for approval is extremely important. This is most often accomplished through a well-planned, formal presentation.

Often, processes and projects selected for improvement cross functional boundaries or, in the most extreme case, reside in an organization that is totally separate from the process change leader. Until Six Sigma becomes integrated as part of the company's culture and continuous improvement philosophy, project team leaders have the task of selling the benefits of a Six Sigma project to an organization that may not welcome the "help." The outcome of the project may involve a reduction of head count in the area that is being analyzed. Clearly, the thought of identifying a better way of doing things also implies a level of incompetence on the immediate management team. The politics of these turf battles need to be carefully considered.

Once a Six Sigma philosophy is institutionalized in the organization and true benefits can be witnessed, organizations and management ask process improvement specialists and team leaders to help identify and make improvements in their areas. It becomes a *pull* environment rather than a *push* environment. This is a true sign of the value and benefit of Six Sigma in the company. But, until that point is reached, the Six Sigma team is essentially selling the recommendations to senior management.

Team leaders have a number of presentation tools available to assist them with securing management support for changes. A team leader with a good knowledge of the business, the organization, and business financials will be the most successful. The most effective sales issue is the financial impact of the recommendations. The presentation to management should discuss the need for change, the financial benefit associated with the change, and the scope of what needs to be changed. The presenter needs to really address the *WIIFM* factor—*what's in it for me*. Facts and figures should be used to support the proposed change, not just opinions and hunches. Management is often surprised to learn that employees in the organization have been complaining or dissatisfied with wasted effort in a certain area for a long time and would welcome a change. The discussion should be kept on a positive note and use positive language. The project should be viewed as an opportunity instead of fixing a previous mistake. Each member of the Six Sigma team should be involved in the presentation, although the team leader is usually the moderator. For example, one person might present the "As-Is" map, another would discuss the disconnects, another would discuss the assumptions and recommendations, and another would present the "Should-Be" map. Finally, someone should present the business case with financial results.

THE USE OF "AS-IS" PROCESS MAPS

Chapter 12 presented information on process mapping and the development of the *"As-Is" process map.* Process maps are also used to secure management support for changes and implementation. The use of this tool yields two revelations for management. First, management will view the efforts as having a process, rather than a people, focus. This takes the personal impact out of the equation and lets the process team leader focus on the true issues. Second, management will probably be quite surprised to learn how a process actually performs as opposed to how they think or would like the process to perform. Management will be able to offer some specific suggestions on how they think the process could be improved, which will greatly assist in gaining their commitment to the changes.

Once the "As-Is" map has been presented, the existing problems, disconnects, and inefficiencies are presented and discussed. Since a large number of disconnects can often be identified, the disconnects are grouped into categories for summary discussions. The groupings are usually collections of activities or phases in the process. The disconnects are presented in an objective manner with no finger-pointing. Along with the disconnects, the root causes are also usually presented at this point. Tables presented in earlier chapters actually were used in presentations to senior management.

After the disconnects are presented, the recommendations are presented along with the supporting assumptions. It is important to discuss how the recommendations were reached. This may require summarizing background research or benchmarking visits. The goal is to make sure that management has a clear understanding of exactly how the recommendations were developed. Management should realize the amount of time and effort expended by the Six Sigma team to reach the recommendations.

Once the recommendations have been presented, a new "Should-Be" map is presented. The "Should-Be" map is simply a comprehensive demonstration of how the new process should work. The "Should-Be" process map also takes into consideration competitive and world-class process models that the team aspires to emulate. The "Should-Be" process map comparison to competition and world-class companies also works as a significant selling point in securing management commitment for proposed changes. The team wants to be better than the competition and, in many cases, be considered the world-class process leader.

Once the "Should-Be" map has been presented, a comparison of the "As-Is" and "Should-Be" maps is made that highlights the major differences. This is typically done by first comparing cycle times.

CYCLE TIME ANALYSIS

As part of the "As-Is" and "Should-Be" process mapping, *cycle time analysis* is performed for each activity, phase, and the process as a whole. This cycle time analysis should be a true reflection of the time it takes to perform the process. The cycle times for an "As-Is" map are usually accurate. This accuracy is often the result of actual work sampling. Unfortunately, the cycle times for a "Should-Be" map are usually estimates since the new process is not in place yet.

Too often, cycle time analysis ignores the impact that it has on customers. For instance, cycle time mapping may consider an average time to produce a product in a large production order run, resulting in an average time to produce a product. However, customers may have to wait a long time to receive product because the product they order is in the middle of the production run. Let us assume that a manufacturing organization has determined that it is most efficient if it runs production lots of 40. This prevents multiple, nonproductive machine setups every time a different type of product is produced. Let us say that a lot of 40 parts can be run in one week, so that the average cycle time to produce one product is one hour (this assumes an 8-hour workday and a 5-day workweek). If you placed the order for the fifth product, it would not be available to be shipped to you for one week, even though it was conceivably produced on the first day of production. The average production time would be one hour, but the customer would view the production time as one week.

The actual "As-Is" cycle time of each process step and the process as a whole needs to be determined, and it should reflect minimum, maximum, and average times, as discussed previously. By adding up the maximum times for each process step and comparing this against the cumulative total for the minimum times, the process improvement team can determine the amount of improvement that is possible with the process. The minimum cycle time is referred to as the *entitlement* time, or the amount of time the process is entitled to assuming it is running optimally. The difference between the maximum and minimum process cycle times can be used to gain management commitment.

The average process cycle time can be compared against benchmarks of competition or other world-class companies to also gain management commitment to improve the process to the "Should-Be" state. By analyzing cycle times, the process improvement team can also determine areas of wasted or non-value-added effort that should be eliminated in the "Should-Be" state. These wasted or non-value-added times might include material movement from one operation to the next, waiting for input from previous process steps because of cycle time imbalances, or rework because of defective outputs. In all cases, however, the ultimate goal is to reduce process cycle times and process steps from the "As-Is" to the "Should-Be" process models.

The cycle times can be converted into actual costs. Fully allocated labor costs that include hourly wages, benefits, and overhead charges can be multiplied times the cycle times to determine labor costs. Direct and indirect materials costs can be identified for each activity and the process as a whole. Total capital investment for the process can be determined and allocated to process activities. The point is that cycle time analysis is converted into cost figures so that objective comparisons can be made.

COST/BENEFIT ANALYSIS

As pointed out in the beginning of this chapter, one of the best ways to secure management commitment for changes and implementation is to determine the financial impact of making the changes. This is often the responsibility of the Six Sigma team leader. The analysis must be based upon factual data, with a minimal amount of assumptions. Management expects to see the associated benefits, so these need to be accurate estimates of what will transpire once the change is made. A cost/benefit analysis is performed by the improvement team and reflects true costs and benefits expected.

Costs need to assume all direct, indirect, and ancillary expenses associated with making the change. The change may require efforts of several team members, whose labor time is reflected as an implementation cost. The change may involve the creation or improvement of an existing computer database or system, and these costs are reflected in the overall equation. The change could involve the addition of equipment or have an impact on another part of the organization. The changes could require training for employees to learn new skills. These costs all need to be reflected in the overall cost analysis. Obtaining the assistance of the finance or cost accounting department is most beneficial for the team or project leader. The project leader needs to take extreme care to prevent the inclusion or avoidance of costs and/or expenses that management may perceive as important. For instance, team members may be working on the project part-time, and this extra effort is expected of them. Therefore, their labor costs may not be considered as part of the improvement effort directly.

Similar to determining the costs associated with implementing an improvement project, benefits or savings also need to be determined. Benefits can take on many forms but are the backbone of any improvement project. Benefits need to be portrayed to gain management commitment and need to address the WIIFM factor. From a financial perspective, savings can be expressed as both hard and soft savings. *Hard savings* are those that have a direct impact to the bottom-line results, the company's overall financial performance. Hard savings may include things such as a reduction in head count due to shorter cycle times or fewer process steps, reduction in scrap or rework expenses due to improved yields, reduction in warranty expenses due to improved quality, lower overtime hours due to less rework or inspection steps, and so on. Hard savings are quantifiable and reflect a true reduction in expenses that can be witnessed on the bottom line. Mikel J. Harry, head of the Six Sigma Academy, is quick to point out that the typical return on a Six Sigma project is $250,000 in cost savings, with the average time for project completion of 6 months.[28] There is no more productive use of a person's time or one that yields more substantial financial returns than working directly on an improvement project. Figure 14.1 shows an example of how the scope, duration, and cost/benefit of a Six Sigma improvement project is formatted for presentation to management.

If the savings are reapplied elsewhere, they are not true savings and are reflected as soft savings. *Soft savings* may include things such as cost avoidance due to not purchasing an additional piece of equipment because of improved line capacity, reduction but reapplication of inspectors to assemblers, improvements to customer satisfaction due to improved product/service quality, and so on. While soft savings discussions should not be avoided, their impact on the cost/benefit analysis needs to be carefully projected and weighed accordingly. Typically, soft savings are the most controversial when presenting the cost/benefit analysis to management.

The cost/benefit analysis should reflect not only expense reductions but also potential or real increases to sales and revenues. These are not necessarily difficult to determine but are sometimes difficult to prove. For instance, if the organization has determined that there is a direct correlation between improvements in customer satisfaction and revenue, then this fact is presented as soft savings for projects in which one of the benefits is defined as an improvement to customer satisfaction. As an example, if a company has determined that an improvement of one percentage point in customer satisfaction yields $10 million in additional revenue as Johnson Controls, Inc., has, then a project that

Project Number: 991201-52-2

Project Name: Warranty Expense Improvement

Champion: VP of Manufacturing

Black Belt: John Doe, Hardware Warranty Engineer (full-time)

Opportunity: The trend for warranty expense has been climbing (adverse) the past 5 years and current warranty expenses are 50% above (worse) than levels 5 years ago.

Scope: Identify the top 10 contributors to warranty claims and improve each by 50%.

Financial Impact: Improve overall warranty expense by $2 million (50%).

Time Frame (Duration): 6 Months

Team Members: One full time member from engineering. One full time member from field service. Part time members from manufacturing, quality, and marketing.

Supporting documentation: Show 5-year warranty expense trend (graph)
Show Pareto analysis of warranty expense contributors

Benefits: Improvement in warranty expense, reduction in service calls, reduction in service call personnel, improvement in factory line yield, improved customer satisfaction

Cost/Benefit Analysis: Total expenses are unknown until implementation actions can be defined, but they are expected to be minimal, remaining under $100,000.00. John Doe has been assign full-time to this project for six months at a cost of $50,000.00. Warranty expenses are expected to be improved by at least $2 million, with actual results reflected as follows: $300,000.00 savings realized this calendar year due to the lag time associated with improvements made to field stock, and $1.7 million in the next calendar year. Savings each year thereafter will be $2 million. Although additional ancillary benefits are noted above, these are not reflected in the cost/benefit analysis. ROI = 2000% ($2M/$100K) in 2 years.

Figure 14.1 Six Sigma Project Description (Example).

expects to yield an improvement in customer satisfaction, say two percentage points, should show an associated increase in revenue as one of its benefits—$20 million more in revenue in this case. However, if company revenues increase over the next year or two, it will be difficult to prove that a certain dollar amount was attributable to the project improvements made.

In keeping with the WIIFM concept, the cost/benefit analysis should reflect additional benefits to the organization that may be difficult to quantify. These might include things such as improvements in a company's or product's image or associated benefits to another organization such as a supplier, which may be difficult to measure. For example, in the repair order process maps presented earlier in this book, the cycle time for completing a service call was reduced significantly. On average, a service technician was completing four service calls a day. With an improved process, the technicians should be able to complete five service calls per day, on average. This would result in an increased revenue of $1.2 million annually. But, this $1.2 million would only be realized if there were market demand for the service. If there were no additional demand, there would be no additional revenue.

The final step in the cost/benefit analysis is to determine and demonstrate the payback period or return on investment (ROI) of the project. This analysis compares the total expense and total benefits of the improvement over some duration of time. For instance, a project may cost $250,000 to implement but yield $1 million in true savings over the next two years. The return on investment would be 400 percent over two years. Management can use ROI numbers to compare against other planned investments to maximize expense allocation and investments.

IMPLEMENTATION PLAN

No matter how good a job the team does in determining potential opportunity associated with a change, unless an implementation plan is developed and accepted, the change becomes only an idea or a plan, never a reality. This fact demonstrates the need for securing management's support for the change. It also points out the need for involvement and commitment on the part of the affected organization for the change. The implementation plan should include all the steps and resources involved to make the change. It should include time frames associated with each step and be formally managed as any other project management opportunity. The team that proposed the original changes should be either personally involved or available to assist with any implementation questions or difficulties. Figure 14.2 shows an example of an implementation plan and many of the steps that should be considered.

The next chapter discusses implementation plans and strategies in detail. While the Six Sigma team may not have all of the implementation details worked out, a rough overview of the implementation plan should be part of the presentation. This allows management to see who will be responsible for changes, how the changes will be implemented, and the approximate time schedule. There is no point in developing a detailed implementation plan until management support is secured. For example, management may conceptually approve of projected changes in a process, but management may also have financial constraints. Therefore, management may allocate a budget of $100,000 out of the current fiscal year to begin the changes. The balance of the implementation costs may come out of the following year's budget. Therefore, the implementation plan has to reflect the constraint of a $100,000 budget.

SUMMARY

The formal presentation to senior management is particularly important when an organization is beginning its Six Sigma effort. The initial improvement efforts are often under the microscope and scrutinized very closely, particularly by skeptics with the organization. Therefore, the presentation should be thorough and well choreographed. Most Six Sigma teams actually conduct practice presentations as dress rehearsals before presenting to senior management. The framework for the presentation presented in this chapter has been used very effectively to sell senior management on the results of Six Sigma projects.

Date	What	Who	Duration	Implementation Costs	Other Comments/ Progress
January 15	Present Change Proposal to Production Operators	VP of Manufacturing presents to Production Operators	1 Day, 1 hour per session	January 15th production reduced to half due to interrupt	Completed as planned on January 15
January 15–22	Feedback from operators on changes	Operators provide feedback to team leader on proposed change	1 week	None	On track
January 22–31	Project leader adjusts project plan and "Should-Be" map	Project leader	1 week	None	
January 22–31	Process engineers create process and operation documentation to reflect changes	Process engineers	1 week	None	
February 1–15	Operators are trained on new process	Project leader and production supervisor train employees on new process	4 hour training session per operator spread over 2 weeks	Production interrupts by 10%	
February 15–22	Pilot Run on new process	Project leader supervises pilot run with production supervisor and process engineers	1 week, 5 consecutive process passes	All output to be inspected and scrapped until production is certified	

Figure 14.2 Six Sigma Implementation Plan (Example).

(continued)

249

Date	What	Who	Duration	Implementation Costs	Other Comments/Progress
February 22–28	Engineering analysis on output from new process	Engineering	1 week	None	
February 22–28	Customer trial of output from new process	Sales organization with customer	1 week		
March 1–8	Adjust process and documentation to reflect any additional changes from engineering and customer analysis	Project leader, Process engineers, and engineering	1 week	None	
March 9	New process becomes practice	Production supervisor	Immediately	20% impact on yield for month of March	
March 9–31	Monitor process performance against plans	Process engineers, production operators	1 month	None	
April 1	Present results to management	Process engineers and project leader present results to VP of Manufacturing, production supervisors, and production operators	1 day	None	

Figure 14.2 Continued.

CASE STUDY

SECURING MANAGEMENT SUPPORT
FOR CHANGES AND IMPLEMENTATION

The six-panel chart shown in Figure 14.3 is an example of a Six Sigma project presentation tool that was completed in 1999 at Johnson Controls, Inc., Controls Business. The chart has been altered to remove any confidential information. The project was undertaken to identify and eliminate the major cause(s) for a part (actuator) being rejected by one of Johnson Controls, Inc.'s, major customers. The customer had complained about, and rejected parts due to noise. This caused engineering to create a specification for noise that was ultimately inspected for at the end of the production line. Product was rejected at the end of the production line for noise, impacting yield. Inspectors were also added at the customer's location, and the customer rejected additional product for noise as well. The team identified the manufacturing process used by the gear supplier as the cause of noise. The process was modified to prevent gear damage.

Six Sigma Six-Panel Chart

Panel 1	Panel 2
Panel 3	Panel 4
Panel 5	Panel 6

Figure 14.3 Six Sigma Six-Panel Chart.

Panel 1

Six Sigma Project: Actuator Gear Noise

Problem Description:
• The largest customer for Actuators identified noise as their top Pareto item for defects found in recieving inspection.
• Actuator "noise" has been identifed as a production failure, which has reduced production yield.

Scope: M9108, M9116, M9124, M9216 Actuators

Champion: VP of Manufacturing
Black Belt: Process Engineer

Team: Process Engineer, Gear Supplier

Strategy:
Prioritize: Identify root cause of noise.
Characterize: Identify viable solutions to minimize noise.
Optimize: Implementation process improvements.
Realize: Verify process capability improvements.

Sigma Tools Applied: PF, CE, SOP, MSA, CP, CPK,
Pareto Analysis, DPPM

Panel 2

RESULTS

Customer Satisfaction
• Customer is very satisfied with the improvement and has eliminated quality inspection for noise defects in actuators.

Cost Savings = $43,370/Year

Hard Savings/Year
• Returned Material Costs $10,870/Year
• Internal Scrap & Reworks $7500/Year
• Line Yield Improved to 97%
• Appraisal/Inspection $25,000/Year
• Eliminated Part-Time Inspector

Soft Savings/Year*
• Improved Outgoing Quality Level from 5% to 0.1% Defective
• Improved Rolled Yield from 92% to 97%
• Customer Satisfaction Improved from 85% to 95% Satisfied

* Not Included in Total Cost Savings

Figure 14.3 Continued.

Panel 3
Process Before

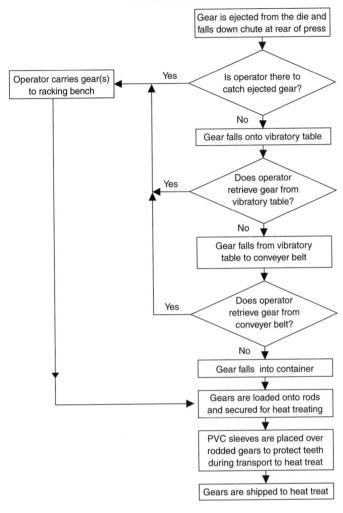

Panel 4
Process After

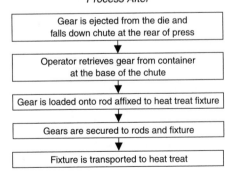

(continued)

Figure 14.3 Continued.

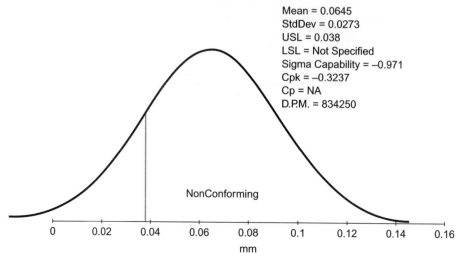

Panel 5

Process Capability *Before*

Mean = 0.0645
StdDev = 0.0273
USL = 0.038
LSL = Not Specified
Sigma Capability = –0.971
Cpk = –0.3237
Cp = NA
D.P.M. = 834250

NonConforming

mm

Tooth-to-Tooth Error Capability

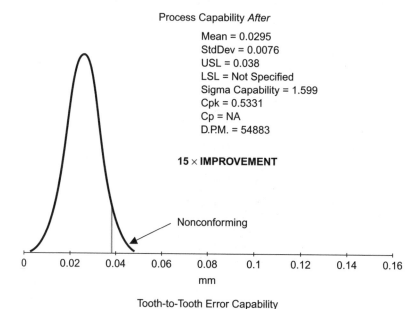

Panel 6

Process Capability *After*

Mean = 0.0295
StdDev = 0.0076
USL = 0.038
LSL = Not Specified
Sigma Capability = 1.599
Cpk = 0.5331
Cp = NA
D.P.M. = 54883

15 × IMPROVEMENT

Nonconforming

mm

Tooth-to-Tooth Error Capability

Figure 14.3 Continued.

15

Implementation

A high-level Six Sigma implementation plan was discussed in the previous chapter. When the Six Sigma team makes the presentation to management for approval, a summary of the planned implementation strategy is included. However, the summary is intended only to show management approximately what needs to happen. The actual implementation plan must be much more detailed and specific than the overview.

The reason for waiting until after the management presentation to develop a detailed implementation plan is quite simple. Management may not immediately approve all recommendations. For example, some recommendations could require a significant capital investment. In many organizations, this would require waiting for the next budget cycle to secure funding. Management may suggest that some recommendations be delayed to minimize the disruptions to operations during periods of high demand. There is no point in investing a lot of time and effort in developing an implementation plan until it is clear which recommendations will be implemented.

MANAGING CHANGE

The organizational behavior textbooks usually have a very simple behavior change model that suggests, to achieve change, a manager must *unfreeze* old behaviors, *move* to new behaviors, and *refreeze* the new behaviors. Obviously, such an approach implies periodic step changes rather than continuous improvement. But there is also merit in the concept.

An assessment of the organization must be done to identify the readiness for change. This goes well beyond the specific process issues addressed by the team. There must be alignment at all levels of the organization to achieve change. Therefore, the team must assess all aspects of the organization. There are five broad categories that should always be considered.

Vision

There must be a clearly stated *vision* statement that supports Six Sigma or continuous improvement. At the highest levels, this implies that strategy, structure, and goals are aligned and reinforce the continuous improvement, in general, or achieving Six Sigma performance, more specifically. As stated in previous chapters, senior leadership must be present. Without clear leadership, there will be confusion about what should be done.

Resources

Most change efforts require *resources* of some type. At the extreme, changes could require significant capital investment. Or, the required resources could be more modest for training employees in new skills. The allocation of resources is usually a good indicator of management commitment to continuous improvement. Unless a team has adequate resources with which to work, there will be frustration.

Skills

If employees are asked to change their behavior as part of a process change, the employees must have the *skills* necessary to carry out the new behaviors. This implies that a detailed assessment of the new skills has been completed. The results of the assessment would be compared to existing skill sets to identify training and development needs. As an example, major drivers of training at Solectron are the future needs of the customers. An organization must be strongly committed to the training and development of employees to achieve continuous improvement and Six Sigma performance levels.

Incentives

It is a well-known axiom that *what gets measured gets managed.* Equally logical is the axiom, *what gets rewarded gets done.* As discussed previously, many organizations are now using a balanced scorecard that usually includes financial, market, customer, and employee indicators that measure and reward senior management for balanced performance. Jack Welch, CEO at General Electric, was well known for asking executives two things for each performance indicator: "What is your current performance level?" and "What are you doing to improve?" (see note 20). The *incentives* should not be restricted to senior management.

Some organizations use the skill sets of employees to drive pay increases. The more skills that an employee possesses, the more valuable that employee is to the organization. The more rapidly an employee gains new skills, the faster the organization can achieve continuous improvement. Hence, the number of skills and the rate of increase can be key drivers of merit pay increases and other types of rewards. If incentives for change are not present, the rate of change is slower, much more gradual.

Action Plans

The fifth element that must be present is an *action plan*—a formalized approach to change. If a CEO commands that all employees should improve their performance, little will happen unless there are formal plans to support the imperative. Perhaps the greatest benefit of the concept of Six Sigma is that it is a formalized approach to high-level continuous improvement and innovation in products, services, processes, and employee behavior. But even without the pursuit of Six Sigma, an organization must develop detailed action plans that provide a road map to a better organization. The balance of this chapter is devoted to developing an implementation plan.

IMPLEMENTATION PLANS

A Six Sigma team that is pursuing process improvement undoubtedly has studied the process. The team probably has developed an "As-Is" process map, and all of the problems or disconnects have been identified. Recommendations have been developed and translated into a "Should-Be" map. The next step is implementation, where a broader organizational assessment occurs. This assessment extends well beyond just the process. The first decision is to decide who is responsible for developing the implementation plan.

Implementation Team

The implementation team may or may not have the same composition as the Six Sigma process improvement team. If the changes are not terribly complex, it is entirely possible that the Six Sigma team naturally evolves into the implementation team. But, the more comprehensive and complex the changes become, the more likely the implementation team will need to include new members. For example, some of the recommendations in a "Should-Be" map may require significant training. This may suggest that a training director or representative from training be on the implementation team. Or, perhaps, the recommendations require new database interfaces. This might imply that the information technology department be represented on the implementation team.

While the implementation team usually includes new members, it should not have a completely different composition than the Six Sigma team. The reason for this is to maintain an organizational, or team, memory. This memory is necessary so that the history behind each recommendation is maintained. Once the team has been formulated, the team can begin the organizational assessment.

Organization Assessments

The primary purpose of the assessment is to identify the strengths and weaknesses of the organization with respect to making significant changes. A good starting point is a critical evaluation of previous change efforts. If there are previous Six Sigma teams, evaluating their effectiveness is helpful. Identifying what went well or went wrong helps a team to avoid previous mistakes.

As the first part of this chapter suggested, the initial assessment starts with an honest evaluation of the senior leadership's support. This extends to corporate strategies, strategic initiatives, goals or objectives, organization structure, and management systems. For some process changes, the assessment may extend to the supply chain or to downstream channel members such as distributors. A sample organizational assessment form is presented in Table 15.1.

The goal of the initial assessment is to identify those factors that will constrain the implementation of the recommendations. If the implementation issues are narrowly focused around a specific performance area, the broader cultural context of the organization may not be a major factor. But when the change is major and affects several functional areas and important processes, the broader context of the organization will have a significant impact on the implementation success. In these situations, the implementation should develop an explicit strategy to overcome the constraints.

Characteristic	Readiness for Change			Recommended Actions
	Low	*Moderate*	*High*	
Senior Leadership				
Corporate Strategies				
Annual Goals, Objectives				
Organization Structure				
Financial Resources				
Information Technology				
Accounting Systems				
Human Resources				
Functional Area Managers				
—Employees, Workforce				
—Unions				
Supply Chain				
Downstream Channel Members				

Table 15.1 Organizational Assessment of Readiness for Change.

Project Assessment

Once the broader assessment is complete, the team must focus on the process improvement project. Every recommendation must be assessed. A sample project assessment form is presented in Table 15.2. This is more easily used if the recommendations were clustered together during the problem-solving phase.

Resource Requirements. One of the first issues to be addressed is usually resources. This would include any necessary capital investment for equipment, hardware, or software. All direct expenses, such as software training and travel, are included. Expenses such as labor are also included. For example, many process improvement efforts require the increased use of databases. To modify databases, an information technology individual must be on the implementation team so that the issues are well understood. The time devoted to team meetings has a cost. Likewise, the modification of databases can require significant labor costs. These must be estimated and included in the resource assessment. If a support area, perhaps already understaffed, is required to contribute labor to a new project, resistance to the project is likely.

When evaluating the resource requirements of recommendations, grouping the recommendations into categories is beneficial. One category typically consists of these recommendations that have no or negligible resource requirements. These recommendations can often be implemented quickly. A second category consists of recommendations that have moderate resource requirements. These may fall within existing approval limits of

Characteristic	Recommendation #	Support for Process Changes			Recommended Actions
		Low	*Moderate*	*High*	
Resource Allocation					
—Capital Investment					
—Team Expenses					
—Implementation Expenses					
—Direct & Indirect Labor					
Complexity					
—Localized Projects					
—Moderate Projects					
—Large Projects					
Time Line					
—Short-Term					
—Moderate-Term					
—Long-Term					
Area of Responsibility					
—Team					
—Individual					
—Functional Manager					
Rollout Strategy					
—Full Rollout					
—Phase In					
Action Plan Developed					

Table 15.2 Project Assessment of Recommendation Requirements.

managers. In these cases, a budget request must be made, but approval can be obtained quickly. The third category consists of recommendations that require significant capital expenditures. In most organizations, these require formal submission to a budget process. This may be the annual budgeting cycle in many organizations. These three categories help the implementation team to identify the recommendations for immediate implementation.

Complexity. Once the resource requirements are assessed, the complexity of the implementation is addressed. As with resources, every recommendation must be evaluated. A complex change may require significant resources and touch many functional areas and support systems. Highly complex changes that cause a good deal of disruption to the organization are often phased in.

Changes that cause little disruption can be the starting point for implementation. This allows for a sense of progress for the team and organization. This also implies that there is some logical sequence among recommendations. Some recommendations, such as a simple change in behavior, could be implemented independent of other recommendations. Other recommendations may require budgetary approval, new training courses, and database modifications before implementation.

The sequence and interrelationships among recommendations for a single project must be evaluated by the implementation team. However, the implementation team also evaluates the progress and recommendations of other Six Sigma teams. This is particularly important when changes to support systems (accounting, information technology, etc) are anticipated. In an organization with a well-established Six Sigma culture, this coordination is often achieved by a Six Sigma steering committee that tracks the progress of each team and ensures communication between teams occurs when relevant.

Time Line. A time line for initial and complete implementation for each recommendation must be developed by the implementation team. Simple recommendations may have a very short implementation duration. Some recommendations may have a very significant implementation duration. For example, a process change may require training for employees. If formal courses are necessary, the course content would need to be designed and a trainer trained. Then, there may be a period of time allowed for getting all employees trained.

For a large, complex change, the time line may include intermediate milestone points in addition to the starting and ending points. For some projects, time needs to be allowed for generating support among managers and employees. For some projects, there needs to be a communication period through newsletters, Intranet websites, or meetings. For some projects, there need to be supplier visits and evaluations. Each of these activities must have a planned time line.

In addition to the planned time line for implementation, there should be a time line for expected benefits. The cycle time, labor, or materials savings should be projected for initial phases as well as ultimate targets. This will allow a payback period and return on investment to be calculated.

Areas of Responsibility. Once the resources, complexity, and time line have been assessed, the areas of responsibility must be determined. Essentially, this identifies who is responsible for making each change. The responsibility could rest with a Six Sigma executive champion who has responsibility for cascading changes throughout the organization; or responsibility for implementing recommendations could rest with process owners; or the responsibility could rest with functional area managers such as marketing, human resources, accounting, or information technology for implementing recommendation clusters; or the responsibility for implementation could rest with the Six Sigma team itself, although this is less common.

Regardless of who assumes responsibility, every recommendation must be owned by an individual or a team. That individual or team is ultimately evaluated and rewarded on the effectiveness of the implementation. Recommendations that are not owned often drift into the black hole of the status quo. Specifically, any recommendations that are not the responsibility of someone are seldom implemented.

Rollout Strategy. Project recommendations can be immediately implemented or phased in somehow. Immediate implementation is typical for changes that have a small effect on the entire organization. These are often changes that primarily impact one, or a few, functional areas. Or, the changes may affect relatively minor processes. In some cases, even major changes can be implemented immediately when there is a high level of urgency, such as a competitive threat. An immediate full-scale rollout may still consist of sequential phases.

A phased rollout strategy implies that the recommendations are implemented on a trial basis. A plant, area office, or geographical region could be used for a trial, for example. A trial is often used to demonstrate the feasibility or effectiveness of recommendations. Or, in some organizations, a phased rollout is used to spread implementation costs over several years.

When a phased approach is used, there are typically two types of comparisons that are made. One comparison is a *before-after* comparison of process performance. This requires that data be gathered before the changes and then compared to subsequent process performance. The other comparison is *horizontal*. Performance at one plant is compared to performance at a different plant, for example.

A major benefit of a phased rollout strategy is that the recommendations and implementation plan can be modified and fine-tuned. This is like using a beta site to debug software. Unforeseen errors can be corrected before everyone in the company experiences them.

A phased rollout is very much like a large-scale design of experiment (DOE). Most applications of DOE examine the impact of one or a few changes in a product or activity. Rigorous statistical techniques can be used to examine the impact of various factors. Unfortunately, most Six Sigma process improvement projects generate a large number of recommendations. The magnitude of recommendations would make the technical use of DOE very difficult or impossible. For example, a factorial design with 50 changes is unworkable. However, the fundamental logic of DOE applies well at an overall, aggregate level. Specifically, rather than focusing on the impact of one or two changes, the focus is on the aggregate output of the process. This is usually the before-after or horizontal comparison.

Action Plans

The final part of the implementation plan is a detailed action plan. This is really an integration of the preceding discussions of resources, complexity, time line, areas of responsibility, and rollout strategy—with one addition. The additional component is the development of performance metrics.

The performance metric could simply be a completion date for an activity or recommendation. However, the performance metric could be a measure of cycle time, productivity increase, cost savings of some type, or annualized failure rate. Or, the performance metric might be linked back to customer perceptions or behavior. For example, the change in top box, top two, or mean score for overall satisfaction could be tracked. Or, perhaps, customer loyalty could be monitored through the percentage of contract renewals.

The performance metrics are clearly stated so that those responsible know precisely how the success of the implementation will be measured. It should be noted that there are two types of performance metrics to be addressed in the action plan. One indicates whether all of the recommendations were properly implemented. The other metric indicates the result of the recommendation. A recommendation may be properly implemented but yield no benefits.

As part of the action plan, the implementation team reconvenes periodically to evaluate both the implementation progress and the results of the recommendations. The periodic review allows for modification of both the implementation plan and the recommendations themselves.

SUMMARY

The implementation phase of a Six Sigma project is every bit as important as the other phases. The implementation is where "the rubber meets the road." A poorly planned implementation can destroy otherwise excellent recommendations. Therefore, it is important to conduct a thorough implementation assessment.

At the highest level, the assessment examines the overall cultural context of the organization to determine the likelihood of support for or resistance to changes. More specifically, the assessment evaluates the project recommendations for resources, complexity, time lines, areas of responsibility, and rollout strategy. All of this is integrated into an action plan that will serve as a road map for implementation.

CASE STUDY

IMPLEMENTATION

Various examples of the implementation of a Six Sigma initiative in 1999 within the Controls Business of Johnson Controls, Inc., have been discussed as part of case studies at the end of chapters in this book.

Chapter 15 discusses the implementation phase for Six Sigma and discusses the use of design of experiments, potential problem analysis, project management, action plans, and performance metrics. All these techniques are employed by Sigma teams within the Controls Business of Johnson Controls, Inc. The use of design of experiments is a key input asked of executives and champions as part of Sigma project status reviews. Project management, a key asset within the Controls Business of Johnson Controls, Inc., is almost an overall requirement of the company, simply due to the nature of the industry and business.

In order to provide commonality and consistency in the application of statistical tools, a formal procedure was written for their use across the organization. This procedure defines the measurement methodology to be employed for all product and process quality performance measurements. It also identifies minimum performance standards for short- and long-term process and design capability. The creation of this formal procedure has assisted the deployment of the Six Sigma initiative across the organization by providing definition, consistency, commonality, and performance standards to key performance metrics. This procedure is shown in Figure 15.1.

Procedure Number: 09-0001
Page: 1 of 12
Issue Date: 11/09/98
Owner:
Supersedes: None–NEW

Systems Products Worldwide

Product and Process Quality Performance Measurement

I. Summary

This standard defines the methods to be used to measure the performance of a process or product and identify and quantify improvement projects. Included are: Cp, Cpk, sigma, defects per unit (DPU), defects per million opportunities (DPMO), total defects per unit (TDU), first time yield (FTY), rolled yield, outgoing quality level (OQL).

II. Requirements

A. Minimum Performance
The safety and key characteristics of all new products must meet or exceed 4.5 Sigma performance requirements (<1350 DPPM) , or a deviation (Reference Process #08-2001) **must be approved.**
1. Short-term capability (applies to pilot, preproduction runs): Cp $\geq$ 1.5 and Cpk $\geq$ 1.33
2. Long-term capability: Cp $\geq$ 1.5 and Cpk $\geq$ 1.00
3. All measurement systems used to measure safety and key characteristics will comply to SP policies and standards.

B. Performance Measurement

1. Cp and Cpk

When the quality characteristics of interest are measurable, the type of information obtained is continuous/measurable data. Measurable quality characteristics are specified by designers as a target and maximum range. If only random variation is present in a process, the observed variation of measurable quality characteristics, in most cases, will approximate a normal distribution.
Assumptions:
1. Quality characteristics are measurable.
2. Only random variation is present; there are no assignable causes of variation; process is stable. SPC charts are used to verify the presence of only random causes of variation.

Cp is used to measure the robustness of a design by comparing manufacturing variation of a quality characteristic to its design specification tolerance. Cp measures the theoretical capability of the product and process.

$$Cp = \frac{\text{Allowable spread}}{\text{Actual spread}} = \frac{USL - LSL}{6\sigma} \quad \dots\dots\dots\dots\dots\dots\dots\dots\dots.(1)$$

(continued)

Figure 15.1   Product and Process Quality Performance Measurement Procedure.

Cpk is used to measure the capability of a process by comparing variation of quality characteristics to design specification. Cpk measures the actual capability of the process by combining information about process spread with information about the position of the mean with respect to target.

$$\text{Cpk} = (1 - k)\, \text{Cp} \quad\dots\dots\dots\dots\dots\dots\dots\dots\dots\dots\dots\dots\dots\dots\dots\dots \quad (2)$$

where

$$k = \frac{\text{Deviation from target}}{1/2 \text{ Allowable spread}} = \frac{T - X}{(\text{USL} - \text{LSL})/2}$$

For practical purposes, we calculate Cp and Cpk as follows:
Cpu = (USL − X)/3σ
Cpl = (X − LSL)/3σ
Cp = (Cpu + Cpl)/2
Cpk = Minimum of Cpu or Cpl $\dots\dots\dots\dots\dots\dots\dots\dots\dots\dots\dots\dots\dots$ (3)

Average (*X*) and standard deviation(s^2) are the only statistics used to calculate capability. When the average and standard deviation are calculated using prototype (built in the lab) data, the capability index is said to be *prototype capability index.* When the average and standard deviation are calculated using short-run production data, then the capability index is said to be *short-term capability.*

2. **Sigma Capability**

Definition: Sigma is used to measure both attribute and variable (continuous) data. The advantage of using Sigma as a measure of performance is that both variable and attribute data can be converted to a comparable sigma value.

Estimating Sigma for Measurable or Continuous Data:
For measurable data, Sigma as a measure of performance tells us how many sigma we can have within a tolerance width.
Sigma = Cp × 3

Estimating Sigma for Attribute Data:
For attribute data, Sigma is calculated by using the fraction defective as the tail area of the normal distribution outside the specification limits.

Steps:
• Find first-time yield and fraction defective from the data.
• The area at both tails of standard normal curve is represented by fraction defective.
• In standard normal table, find the *Z* value that relates to the area at the tail.
• To find the sigma value for attribute data, find the defect rate and look under the standard normal table to find the comparable *Z* value.
• Sigma = *Z* + 1.5
• 1.5 is added because the average is expected to shift by 1.5 sigma over a long period of time.

Figure 15.1 Continued.

Therefore

Sigma = Z + 1. 5 . . . .(4)

Also note that

Sigma = 3 $\times$ Cp = Z + 1. 5

Therefore, Cp (for variable data) and fraction defective (for attribute data) are related.

Note: Sigma and Cp are related and can be calculated for both attribute and measurable characteristics and data types. Appendix Z shows the relationship between sigma and parts per million. Appendix Z shows the impact of 1.5 sigma shifts.

For practical purposes, another formula that can be used to reach the same result is: Sigma capability = 0.8406 + 29.37 – 2.221 in (DPPM) . . . .(5)

3. **Defects per Unit (DPU)**

For a process or step the average number of defects observed per unit (DPU) is calculated by taking the total number of defects found or created by the process on *n* units and dividing it by the total number of units built, including scrap.

Therefore,

DPU = Total number of defects on *n* units/*n* . . . .(6)

4. **First-Time Yield and DPU**

Definition: First-time yield (FTY) is the number of units expected to go through the process the first time without any defect.

Assumptions: If defects are found on a unit in a random order, then the probability of finding *x* number defects is expected to have a Poisson distribution with an average defect of DPU.

Therefore, the probability of having exactly *x* defects per unit is P(x) where

$$P(x) = \frac{(DPU)X.e^{-(DPU)}}{x!}$$ . . . .(7)

First-time yield (FTY) = Probability of finding zero defects = P(O) and P(O) for Poisson distribution with mean of DPU is $e^{-(DPU)}$

Therefore:

FTY = $e^{-(DPU)}$ . . . .(8)

or DPU = – In FTY . . . .(9)

Another formula for first-time yield is:

$$\text{First-time yield} = \frac{\text{Number of units passed first time or inspection}}{\text{Number of units checked or inspected first time}}$$ . . . .(10)

(continued)

Figure 15.1 Continued.

For example, let a = Number of units without defects,
b = Number of units reworked, and
c = Number of units scrapped

$$FTY = \frac{a}{a+b+c}$$

Example

If the DPU for the soldering process is found to be 0.20 per unit, the first-time test yield for the process is

$FTY = e^{-(DPU)} = e^{-(0.20)} = 0.82$

or 82 percent of the products go through the process without any touchup or rework.

5. Total Defects per Unit (TDU)

If there is more than one process or step, then the total defects per unit (TDU) is the sum of DPUs at each process or step.

Therefore:

$TDU = \Sigma\ DPU$ . . . .(11)

Example

Step 1	Step 2	Step 3	
(0.3. DPU) ----	(0.2 DPU) ----	(0.1 DPU)	(0.6)
			Overall Observed TDU

6. Rolled Yield and TDU

Definition: Rolled yield is the expected proportion of products with zero defects while the product is manufactured or assembled through a series of processes.

Therefore:

Rolled Yield = $e^{-(TDU)}$ . . . .(12)

Another formula for rolled yield is :

$$Rolled\ yield = \frac{Number\ of\ units\ completing\ all\ processes\ without\ any\ defects}{Number\ of\ units\ processed\ or\ started\ with}$$ . . . .(13)

Example

Step 1	Step 2	Step 3	
(0.3. DPU) ----	(0.2 DPU) ----	(0.1 DPU)	(0.6)
			Overall Observed TDU

For the preceding product line or series of processes, the total observed TDU and rolled yield is:

$TDU = \Sigma\ DPU = 0.3 + 0.2 + 0.1 = 0.6$

Rolled yield = $e^{-(TDU)} = e^{-(0.6)} = 0.55$, or 55% rolled yield

Figure 15.1   Continued.

Defects per Million Opportunities (DPMO)

Defects per million opportunities (DPMO) is the expected number defects found per million opportunities. The formula for DPMO is:

$$DPMO = \frac{DPU \times 1,000,000}{\text{Average opportunity for error in one unit}} \quad \dots\dots\dots\dots\dots(14)$$

NOTE: Use DPMO only when there is compelling need to compare different products or processes or to evaluate a process running products of very different kind.

7. **Other Yields**

The following definitions are used to define Yield in general:

$$\text{Process gross yield} = \frac{\text{Number of units completed (not scrapped)}}{\text{Number of units started}} \quad \dots\dots\dots\dots\dots(15)$$

$$\text{First-time test or inspection yield} = \frac{\text{Number of units passed test / inspection first time}}{\text{Number of units tested / inspected first time}} \quad \dots\dots\dots\dots\dots(16)$$

Defect: A fault that causes an item or part to fail to meet specification requirements is called a defect. Each instance of an item's or part's lack of conformity to specification is a defect.

8. **Outgoing Quality Level (OQL)**

Definition: OQL is measured in terms of defective parts per million (DPPM).

$$OQL\ (DPPM) = \frac{\text{Quantity of defective units} \times 1,000,000}{\text{Total quantity of units audited}} \quad \dots\dots\dots\dots\dots(17)$$

Assumptions/Conditions:
- OQL audit is in random order on finished *in-the-box,* ready-to-ship products.
- Audit includes visual inspection and functional testing to engineering audit specifications and correct literature, labeling, and shipping paperwork.
- A defective product includes failure at final functional, final audit, visual quality standard, labeling, packing, quantity, and proper literature.
- A product having more than one nonconformance will be counted as a single defective product.
- Calculation of OQL is the cumulative sum of monthly and month rolling average results reported as DPPM.
- OQL values are calculated for product families. This measures cell performance by determining how many products within a cell do not meet minimum requirements.
- For attribute quality characteristics use the Attribute Sampling Plan outline in Systems Products Process Handbook
- Defective unit is a unit with one or more defects; which means a unit with any nonconformities will be considered as defective unit.

(continued)

Figure 15.1 Continued.

9. Return Rate

Return rate will be calculated for core product families as follows:

$$\text{Current return rate} = \frac{12 \text{ months' return}}{\substack{12 \text{ months' sales with} \\ 3 \text{ month lag}}} \qquad \dots\dots\dots\dots\dots\dots(18)$$

$$\text{Annualized warranty return rate} = \frac{12 \text{ months return}}{36 \text{ months sales}} \qquad \dots\dots\dots\dots\dots(19)$$

Returned units are units returned because of the defect codes 01100–01500 only.

10. Reliability

Reliability is the ability of an item to perform its required functions for the duration of specified time (such as one year).

Assumptions
- Product failure in random order.
- All failures are reported.

The following formulas are used to calculate reliability of a product based on product returns:

a. Mean time between failure (MTBF) = T / r ....(20)
where:

- T = Total accumulated operating hours (estimated) of assemblies under warranty (assumes an average 3-month lag from ship date to start of operation)
- r = Total number of warranty failures

b. One year reliability = $R - e^{-(8760 / MTBF)}$ ....(21)
There are 8760 hours in one year.

c. One year failure probability = $1 - R$ ....(22)

One year failure probability gives us the probability of a random failure occurring for a given product over a time period of one year.

C. Symbols & Definitions

X	= Arithmetic mean = $\Sigma (x)$
σ	= Standard deviation
USL	= Upper specification limit
LSL	= Lower specification limit
T	= A target value with preferred performance within the specification limit
DPU	= Defects per unit
DPMO	= Defects per million opportunities

Figure 15.1 Continued.

TDU   = Total defects per unit

OQL   = Outgoing quality level

Z   = A value found from standard normal distribution table. It represents number of sigmas (distance) away from the average.

Defect = A fault that causes an item or part to fail to meet specification requirements is called a defect. Each instance of an item's or part's lack of conformity to specification is a defect.

Defective = A part or unit with one or more defects is a defective part.

D. References

1. Continuous Improvement through Process Characterization: A Method of Identifying and Reducing Variation, (Motorola University Press, 1997).

2. Motorola University Course ENG 123, Design for Manufacturability.

3. Dr. Mickel Harry, *The Nature of Six Sigma* (Motorola University Press, 1997).

4. Robert A Dovich, *Reliability Statistics* (American Society for Quality Control, 1990).

5. Davis R. Bothe, *Measuring Process Characteristics* (New York: McGraw-Hill, 1997).

6. Attribute Sampling Plan, JCI Systems and Products Process Hand Book 08–6203.

APPENDIX Z—Relationship between Sigma and DPPM

Sigma	Cp	DPPM without Shift	DPPM with + 1.5 σ Shift
2	0.67	45,500	308,733
3	1.00	2,200	66,810
3.5	1.17	466	22,700
4	1.33	63	6,210
4.5	1.50	6.8	1,350
4.75	1.58	2.04	580
5	1.67	0.57	233
6	2.00	0.002	3.4

Figure 15.1 Continued.

16

Determining Process Capability

TRACKING THE PERFORMANCE METRICS

The identification of performance metrics was discussed in chapter 15. It is important to harmonize process performance parameters and product and service attributes that are important to customers. Process parameters that are *critical to quality (CTQs)* should be developed so that they support the parameters that are *critical to satisfaction (CTSs)*. This would imply a direct linkage between process control parameters and customer satisfaction attributes. Once the process performance metrics have been defined and aligned with customer expectations, they need to be tracked and monitored over time.

There are a number of methods that can be used to track and monitor performance metrics, but, regardless of the method chosen, the data should be easy to collect. Automation is often built into manufacturing processes that makes it easy to track, monitor, and analyze data. The type of data collected or that the process step is capable of producing affects the type of analysis, tools, and controls chart used. Data is either *attribute* (go or no go, yes or no, right or wrong, etc.) or *variable* (continuous measurements such as heights, weights, times, etc.). No matter what type of data is collected, it can be used for statistical process control and to determine process capability.

The first step involved in statistically analyzing performance begins with the collection of data from process performance metrics. The process is run, and the data for the characteristic being studied is gathered and converted into a form that can be plotted on a graph, often referred to as a run chart. The second step, which is discussed in the next section, is determining control limits. Trial control limits are calculated based upon data from the output of the process, reflecting the amount of variation that can be expected if only variation from common causes is present. Control limits are not specification limits or objectives but are reflections of the natural variability of the process. The ongoing data is compared against the control limits to see whether the variation is stable and appears to come only from common causes. If special causes of variation are evident, process activities and other performance metrics are studied to determine what is affecting the process. After corrective actions have been taken, further data is collected, control limits are recalculated, and additional special causes are studied and corrected.

The third step is calculating process capability, which is discussed in greater detail subsequently. After all the special causes have been corrected and the process is running in statistical control, then process capability can be determined. If the variation from common causes is extreme, the process will not produce output that consistently meets customer requirements or specifications. The process itself must be investigated and corrective actions taken to improve the system.

For continuous process improvement, these three steps are repeated over and over. More data on performance metrics is gathered as appropriate, work is done to reduce process variation, and ways to improve the capability of the process are explored and implemented. The subsequent sections of this chapter discuss the concepts of statistical process control, variation, and process capability in more detail.

STATISTICAL PROCESS CONTROL

The underlying goal of Six Sigma is to reduce variation in processes, thus reducing defects, eliminating waste, reducing rework, and improving the predictability of the final product, service offering, or process outcome. There are numerous textbooks written describing statistical tools and techniques, and the intent of this book is not to introduce every aspect of statistical process control or Six Sigma. Rather, the intent is to provide a high-level overview so that the concepts, tools, and techniques can be broadly understood.

Chapter 1 introduced the concept that almost every activity or process is subject to variation. To briefly summarize the earlier discussion, there are a few, fundamental statistical principles:

- A population is the total of all units being studied, such as invoices sent to customers, products being produced, or customer inquiries for technical support.

- A population's central tendency is called a population mean (μ), which is an average of the total population, and the amount of variation in the population is called the standard deviation.

- A sample is a subset of the population that is used to determine a sample mean and a sample standard deviation, which are estimates of the population mean and population standard deviation.

Statistical process control (SPC) employs a number of basic and advanced statistical tools to monitor and control variation within a process. The seven basic quality tools are presented in Table 16.1, but most deal with a sample mean and standard deviation in some way. Many of the tools employed under the umbrella of SPC have been discussed in previous chapters. Our focus here is primarily on the last tool.

Although control charts are often associated with SPC, the analysis of any data that results in a reduction in process variation is SPC. To explore the concept of Six Sigma, that is, reducing variation to a level that results in no more than 3.4 defects per million opportunities, a higher level of analysis is required than the first six basic quality tools can offer. The use of SPC applies to processes, a series of inputs manipulated by a set or sequence of actions and activities, which results in various outputs that can be measured.

In a manufacturing environment, inputs may consist of raw materials such as a set of parts or components. The actions or activities might be a set of assembly steps or activities, including tests. The output is a completely assembled product. In a service environment, input may consist of a phone call for service from a customer. The actions or activities might be answering the phone, dispatching a service person, or answering a question. The measurable outputs might be the time it takes to respond or the accuracy of the

> - **Check Sheets** (to Organize Data)
> - **Pareto Diagrams** (to Prioritize and Categorize Data)
> - **Histograms** (to Display the Shape and Behavior of the Data)
> - **Flow Diagrams** (to Identify Sequence of Steps or Activities)
> - **Cause-and-Effect Diagrams** (to Determine Relationships of Parameters)
> - **Scatter Diagrams** (to Determine Dependence of One Variable on Another)
> - **Control Charts** (to Monitor Performance)

Table 16.1 The Seven Basic Quality Tools.

response. Outputs should always be described in terms of what the internal or external customer expects, has contracted for, or is willing to pay for.

The performance of a process and key activities within the process need to be measured and tracked over time to understand how the process is behaving and to determine variability. Normal behavior suggests that process outputs, those areas that the customer experiences, are the prime candidates for the application of SPC. However, SPC tools can be applied to any step in the process to reduce variation and to move the process mean closer to the target value. Indeed, in most complex processes, there are typically a series of intermediate performance metrics that should be tracked.

Variation

It is important to understand the concept of *variation* in order to evaluate process control measurement data. The concept of normal variation in a population suggests that no two things are exactly alike. The differences among members of a population may be quite noticeable, or they may be almost unmeasurable, but differences are almost always present. In order to detect and reduce variation, outputs must be measured, differences noted, and variations traced back to their source. As discussed earlier, there are two types of variation, common cause and special cause. Common causes are those sources that produce natural variation in a process. Special causes are those factors causing variation that is not normal variation in the process. Special causes cause a process or output to be unpredictable and behave in ways that one would not expect.

Special and common causes can be seen in the distribution of process performance. Distributions can be described by three factors:

- Location within the specification limits

- Spread, or the distance between the highest and lowest distribution points

- Shape, or the pattern of the distribution

The concept of location, spread, and shape of distributions is presented in Figure 16.1. Location refers to the mean of a population. If a population's mean shifts, it can cause an output that is defective or unacceptable to customers. The spread of a population is an indication of a population's homogeneity. A very homogenous population (one with a small variation) has a very *tight* spread. A diverse population (one with a large variation) is wide and flat. The shape of a population indicates if the population is normally distributed and symmetrical or has some other shape, such as skewness.

Very generally, the goal of Six Sigma is to ensure that the mean of a population is on or very close to the desired target and that the spread of the distribution is very small. The

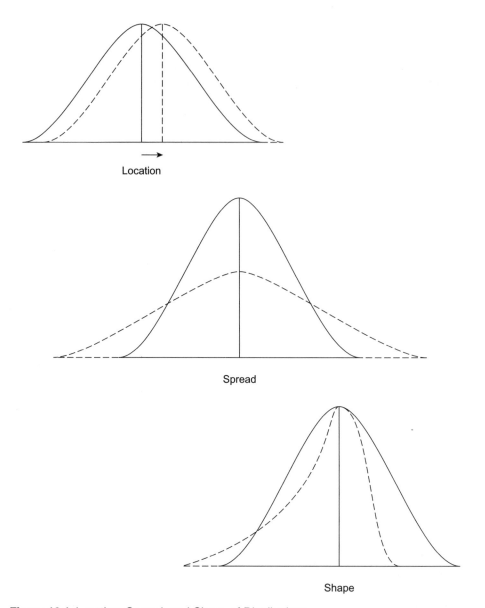

Figure 16.1 Location, Spread, and Shape of Distributions.

location and spread of a population are relevant to common-cause and special-cause variation. The most common indication of special-cause variation is the sudden and consistent shift of a population mean. The most common indication of common-cause variation is the spread of the population.

   If only common-cause variation is present, the mean of a population remains essentially constant, hopefully on target. Because the population mean is constant, the population is said to be stable and predictable. But, being stable and predictable does not mean the process performance is good. As indicated by the distributions at the top of Figure 16.2,

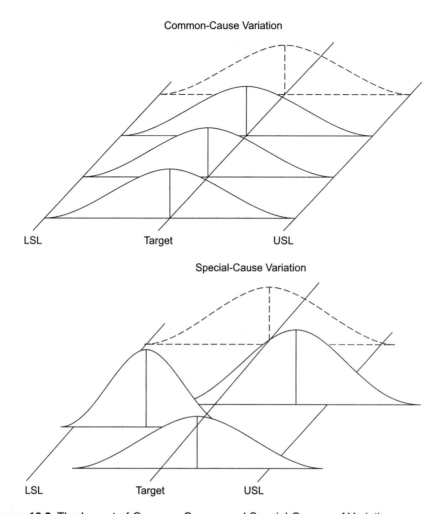

Figure 16.2 The Impact of Common Causes and Special Causes of Variation.

the population means are constant, but the distribution is very flat. This indicates a relatively large amount of variation in the population.

The impact of special-cause variation is indicated at the bottom of Figure 16.2. The mean of the population varies both above and below the target value. There is no clear pattern in the distributions. Therefore, the population is both unstable and unpredictable.

A process is said to be operating in a state of statistical control when variation in the process is at an acceptable level and the mean is near the target. The process output is predictable over time. This is not to say that it is operating as you would like it to. Perhaps reducing the amount of common-cause variation would be desirable. Reducing common-cause variation is achieved by reducing variation in the process activities. In other words, this is a process design and improvement issue. Special-cause variation is detected through the use of statistical process control. By tracking the process mean and variation within a population, a shift in the mean or the magnitude of variation can be detected. Subsequent adjustments in the process can be made to bring the population back on target.

Observation	Number of Days to Resolve Customer Complaints	Observation	Number of Days to Resolve Customer Complaints
1	21	11	18
2	20	12	19
3	20	13	20
4	18	14	22
5	20	15	21
6	19	16	22
7	21	17	19
8	20	18	21
9	22	19	18
10	19	20	20

Total observations in the sample = 20
Cumulative total of days to resolve a complaint of all observations = 400
Sample mean ($\bar{x}$) = 400/20 = 20 days

Table 16.2 Data from Customer Complaint Resolution Process.

For the purposes of explaining the concepts of statistical process control, the following situation is used as an example. Let us say we want to determine whether or not the process of resolving customer complaints is in or out of control. For simplistic purposes, let us say that the critical process parameter we want to measure and control is the amount of time (days) it takes to resolve a customer complaint. Table 16.2 shows the data for this example where we have gathered a sample of 20 complaints. The sample procedure was to randomly select one complaint each day for 20 days.

Control charts are used to determine if a process is in control. The first step in generating a control chart is to construct a run chart. A run chart is shown in Figure 16.3 and is simply a plot of data points over some period of time. A minimum of about 20 data points should be gathered before determining control limits, and a sample of 30 is much better. Computing the average time to resolve a complaint gives us some indication of how long we can expect it to take us in the future. The average ($\bar{x}$) is found for a single sample as follows:

$$\bar{x} = \text{Sum of the sample divided by the sample size}$$

$$\bar{x} = \left\{ \frac{\begin{array}{c} 21 + 20 + 20 + 18 + 20 + \\ 19 + 21 + 20 + 22 + 19 + \\ 18 + 19 + 20 + 22 + 21 + \\ 22 + 19 + 18 + 21 + 20 \end{array}}{20} \right\} = \frac{400 \text{ days}}{20 \text{ observations}} = 20$$

To determine the variability in the number of days it takes to resolve a complaint, we must estimate the variance of the population. The variance is the actual amount of variation in a population. To determine a variance for a population, it would be necessary to

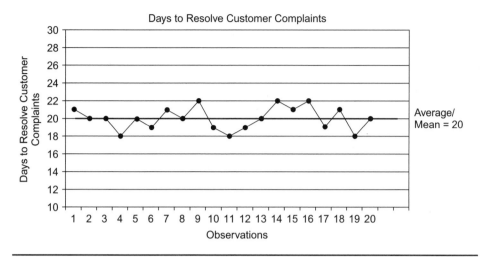

Observations	Number of Days to Resolve Customer Complaints	Observations	Number of Days to Resolve Customer Complaints
1	21	11	18
2	20	12	19
3	20	13	20
4	18	14	22
5	20	15	21
6	19	16	22
7	21	17	19
8	20	18	21
9	22	19	18
10	19	20	20

Total Observations in the Sample = 20
Cumulative Total Number of Days of All Observations in the Sample = 400
Sample Mean ($\bar{x}$) = 400/20 = 20 Days to Resolve a Complaint

Figure 16.3 Run Chart of the Data for a Sample of 20 Complaints (Presented in Table 16.2).

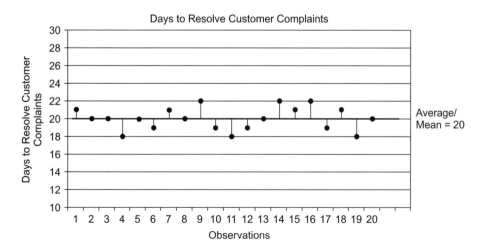

Figure 16.4 Deviation of the Individual Observations Identified in Table 16.2, from the Sample Mean ($\bar{x}$).

measure every unit in a population. In most cases, that is unrealistic. However, just as a sample mean provides an estimate of a population mean, a sample variance provides an estimate of a population variance. The sample variance S^2 is the sum of the squared deviations from the mean for each observation in a sample, all divided by the sample size minus one $(n - 1)$. The deviations from the mean for each observation are shown in Figure 16.4. The sample variance is computed as follows:

$$S^2 \sum \frac{(x - \bar{x})^2}{n - 1} = \frac{32}{19} = 1.684$$

Since the variance figure is technically the squared number of days, it is conceptually difficult to understand. Therefore, the sample standard deviation is typically used. The sample standard deviation S_x is simply the square root of the sample variance. In our example, the sample variance was 1.684.

Since

$$S_x = S^2_x$$

then

$$S_x = 1.684 = 1.298$$

Hence, the standard deviation, or σ, is 1.298 days. For simplicity, this has been rounded to 1.3 days. This sample standard deviation can then be used for our run chart.

From our data, we can now plot our upper and lower control limits. Most control charts establish upper and lower control limits at plus or minus 3 standard deviations from the centerline or the mean. The upper control limit (UCL) is computed by adding 3 standard deviations to the mean or is described as:

$$\text{UCL} = \bar{x} + 3\ (S_x) = 20 + 3(1.3) = 20 + 3.9 = 23.9 \text{ days}$$

The lower control limit (LCL) is computed by subtracting 3 standard deviations from the mean or is described as:

$$\text{LCL} = \bar{x} - 3\ (S_x) = 20 - 3(1.3) = 20 - 3.9 = 16.1 \text{ days}$$

If the population is normally distributed, statistical theory suggests that 99.73 percent of all the values associated with resolving a customer complaint should fall within the range of 16.1 to 23.9 days. Figure 16.5 shows the percent of a population that falls within a range of plus or minus 1, 2, and 3 standard deviations around a population mean. Please note that the terms *standard deviation* and *sigma* are used interchangeably. A sigma (σ) is actually the Greek symbol used to represent a population standard deviation. The sample standard deviation is an estimate of the population sigma.

Figure 16.6 shows the upper and lower control limits added to the previous run plot. Now that we have computed this data, we can monitor future performance and determine if the process is in control. The upper and lower control limits that we computed from the actual data represent the natural behavior of the process. The process can now be monitored for the purpose of detecting any special causes of variation. If the next or future value we measure is 17 days, we are within our control limits and the process is in control. If one of our future measurements is 26 days, then our process has gone out of control. The cause for an out-of-control situation needs to be determined. This is where some of the other quality tools such as cause-and-effect or flow diagrams can be used.

There are a number of SPC rules that apply to the determination of an out-of-control process besides just data points that fall outside the control limits. The occurrence of any

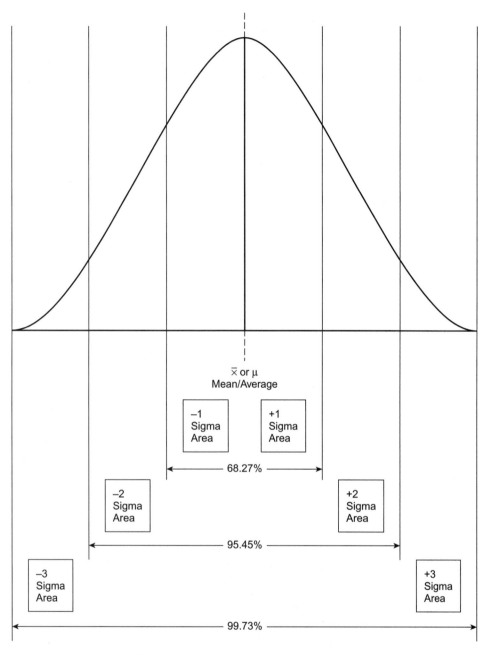

Figure 16.5 Percent of a Population That Falls within a Range of Plus or Minus 1, 2, or 3 Standard Deviations of the Mean.

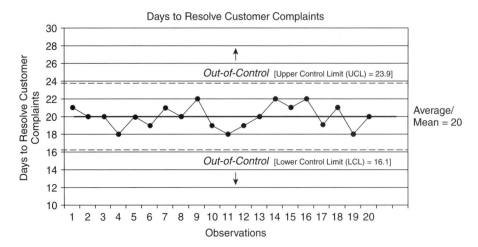

Figure 16.6 Upper and Lower Control Limits Added to the Run Chart Identified in Figure 16.3.

of the situations in Table 16.3 suggests that there is a problem with the process. Most likely, there is a special-cause problem that has developed.

Again, the idea is not to explore all the concepts of statistics in detail but to present the general concepts. A further explanation of process control behaviors can be examined in Juran's *Quality Handbook.*[29]

Figure 16.6 depicts a process that is in control. However, just because a process is operating in control does not mean that it is good. It may not be meeting required specifications. For instance, even though the UCL for resolving complaints is 23.9 days, customers may expect complaints to be handled in 21 days or less.

The mean time for resolving a complaint was determined to be 20 days, based on actual data. Around this value, both upper and lower control limits were established. A complaint that took 26 days to complete would indicate an out-of-control situation. Likewise, a complaint that took 14 days would indicate an out-of-control situation. Obviously, resolving a complaint *too fast* is not going to bother a customer. Only resolving a complaint too slow will irritate the customer. This is referred to statistically as a *one-tailed test.* But, when a complaint is resolved quickly, we would want to find out why. This information could help us in process redesign. This demonstrated level of good performance is referred to as *entitlement* and could indicate a performance level that a Six Sigma team may want to eventually establish.

In a one-tailed test, the control limit is single sided. With complaint resolution, we are concerned only about being too slow. In a *go–no go* or *good-bad* situation, we are concerned only about the unacceptable performance. A run chart is very effective when only a single control limit is plotted.

When a two-tailed situation is present, there are unacceptable performance levels on both sides of the population mean. For example, a cereal box might have a target fill weight of 16.0 ounces. Perhaps a fill weight of less than 16.0 ounces is unacceptable to customers. Anything less than 16.0 ounces would cause customers to feel that they are not getting their money's worth. The customers are not at all concerned with getting more than 16.0 ounces. But management might be very concerned if the actual fill weight exceeded

• One or more points are outside the control limits. • Seven consecutive points are on the same side of the centerline. • Seven consecutive intervals are either increasing or decreasing (trend). • Two out of three consecutive points are in the range of 2 to 3 standard deviations from the mean. • Four out of five consecutive points are in the range of 1 to 2 standard deviations from the mean. • Fourteen consecutive points alternate up or down repeatedly in a sawtooth fashion.

Table 16.3 Indicators of Out-of-Control Situations.

17.0 ounces, since they would be giving away an extra ounce in every box of cereal. As a result, control limits set by management preferences should always be compared to customer expectations. Thus, the control limits and specification limits should be aligned.

The implication is that individuals must decide if they are dealing with a one-tailed or two-tailed situation. Then, they must decide if the control limits, always calculated statistically, match up with customer expectations.

PROCESS CAPABILITY

The concepts of process control and process capability are often confused. *Process control* represents the *voice of the process* and only requires data from the process itself to determine if it is control. Customer specifications are not needed to determine if a process is in control. Control charts, as already explained, are used to determine if a process is in control.

Just because a process is in control does not mean that is performing as one would prefer. It may be operating as predicted but not meeting specifications or customer requirements. *Process capability* indicates how well a process is achieving its specification limits. It is a measurement of the performance of a process when it is being operated in a state of statistical control. Process capability is the measurement of total variation associated with common causes. Since a process in statistical control has a predictable outcome as depicted by its distribution curve, it will produce approximately the same results time and time again. If the process is only capable of producing 50 percent good parts, or completing a service call within 50 minutes, then this is the predictable outcome of the process. Specific management actions, as suggested in chapter 1, are required to improve the ability of the process to meet specifications. This could mean purchasing different assembly equipment that is more predictable, hiring more service call personnel, or convincing the customer to change required specification limits.

Process capability is a measure of how good or how bad the actual process performance is. Process capability takes into consideration specifications and customer requirements. From this perspective, it can be said that process capability represents the *voice of the customer.* Simply put, process capability means comparing the voice of the process with the voice of the customer.

Measuring how well a process matches up with specifications is the essence of process capability. The discussion of SPC demonstrated how the control limits for an in-control process are determined, but we need to explore a few more terms before we can delve into a determination of process capability. We need to first understand and define the upper and lower specification limits. Specification limits can be expressed as a stated requirement by management, a stated requirement by the customer, or a value identified by an engineering design. We also need to determine the specification width, which is the distance, or tolerance, between the upper and lower specification limits. Finally, we need to identify the target value, which the customer wants. The reason for differentiating the target value from the specification limits is to ensure that our process and the instructions accompanying the process, such as engineering specifications, allow our process to meet the customers' expectations or requirements. These terms are summarized as follows:

- *Upper specification limit* (USL) is the maximum allowable measurement of a characteristic. For a Six Sigma performance level, the USL would be six standard deviations above the target value.

- *Lower specification limit* (LSL) is the minimum allowable measurement of a characteristic. For a Six Sigma performance level, the LSL would be six standard deviations below the target value.

- *Specification width* (tolerance) is the difference between the USL and the LSL, or USL – LSL. For a Six Sigma performance level, the specification width is 12 standard deviations wide.

- *Target value* (T) is the absolute measurement that the customer wants and is the midpoint between the upper and lower specification limits for a two-tailed situation.

Now that common terms and specifications have been defined, the capability of the process can now be determined. There are two major calculations that are commonly used to assess process capability. These are the process potential index and the process capability index.

The *process potential index* (Cp) is used to assess the ability or potential ability of a process to satisfy specifications. Specifically, this index is the ratio of the specification width to the actual process width. It does not depend on the location of the center, average, or mean of the population. The Cp index should only be calculated after verifying that the process is in a state of statistical control. For example, if a process had an actual performance width of ±3 standard deviations, which is quite common, the process width would be six standard deviations. The process potential index (Cp) for a process width of ±3 sigma would be calculated as follows:

$$Cp = \frac{\text{Specification width}}{\text{Process width}} = \frac{\text{USL} - \text{LSL}}{6\sigma}$$

A process potential index of less than 1.0 means that the process performance is not capable of meeting the specification limits 100 percent of the time, even if the process mean is exactly on target. There is simply too much common-cause variation in the process. This situation is depicted in distribution *a* at the top of Figure 16.7.

A process potential index of exactly 1.0 means that the process performance will be within the specification limits only as long as the process mean is exactly on target. Should the process mean shift even slightly, a portion of the process output will be unacceptable. This is depicted by distribution *b* in Figure 16.7.

A process potential index of greater than 1.0 means that the process is capable of meeting the specification limits, even if the process mean shifts somewhat. This is depicted by distribution *c* at the bottom of Figure 16.7. Obviously, the preferred situation is to have

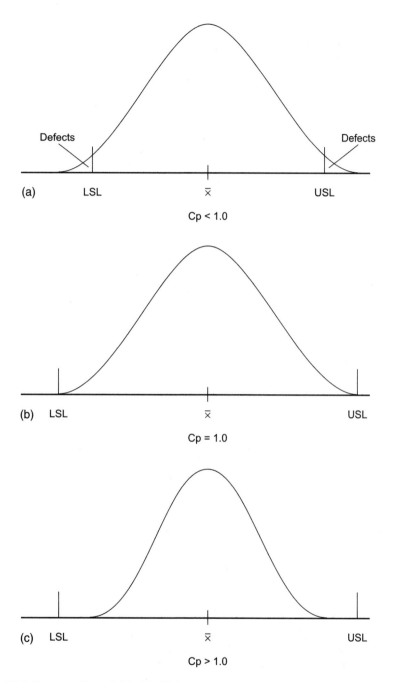

Figure 16.7 Process Potential Index (Cp).

a process potential greater than 1.0. For Six Sigma performance levels, the goal is to have a Cp of 2.0 or greater. This means that the process is designed to accept twice the normal variation and perform within the specification limits.

There are two ways to achieve a large (around 2.0) process potential index. One way is to simply relax the specification limits. This requires that the specification width is very large. As an example, assume that the target weight of a can of fruit is 16.0 ounces. A sample was taken, and the standard deviation of the sample was 0.4 ounces. To achieve a Six Sigma performance level, the specification limits would be 16.0 ounces ±6 standard deviations. Thus, the lower specification limit would be 13.6 ounces

$$16.0 - (6)(0.4) = 13.6$$

and the upper specification limit would be 18.4 ounces

$$16.0 + (6)(0.4)$$

This situation is presented in Figure 16.8. The process performance is not any better; we have just decided to tolerate more variation.

The second way to achieve a large process potential index is to reduce variation in actual process performance. If the standard deviation were reduced from 0.4 ounces to 0.2 ounces, the specification limits for a Six Sigma performance level would be an LSL of 14.8 ounces

$$16.0 - (6)(0.2)$$

and a USL of 17.2 ounces

$$16.0 + (6)(0.2)$$

This is obviously a much better situation. But it would be even better if the standard deviation were reduced to 0.1 ounces. This is indicated in Figure 16.9.

The LSL would be 15.4 ounces, and the USL would be 16.6 ounces. This is a relatively narrow distribution caused by reducing the standard deviation by a substantial amount. It may have required a significant improvement in the process design to achieve the reduction, however. When the process potential index is large, the process mean can shift somewhat, and the process will still produce nearly defect-free outputs.

The *process capability index* (Cpk) indicates how much a process mean can shift and still meet the specification limits. The process capability index depends on both the process spread and the proximity of the process center to the specification limits and, therefore, the target. Specifically, this index is the distance from the center or target of the distribution of the sample population to the closest specification limit, measured in units of standard deviations. The process capability index should only be calculated after verifying that the process is in a state of statistical control.

The process capability index (Cpk) can be expressed in its relationship to the process potential index, (Cp). The relationship is calculated as follows:

$$Cpk = Cp\ (1 - k)$$

where

$$k = \frac{\text{Process shift}}{\text{Design specification width } / 2}$$

When a process is designed for Six Sigma performance, the design specification width is 12 standard deviations wide (i.e., $+ 6\sigma$ and $- 6\sigma$). If the process potential index is 2.0,

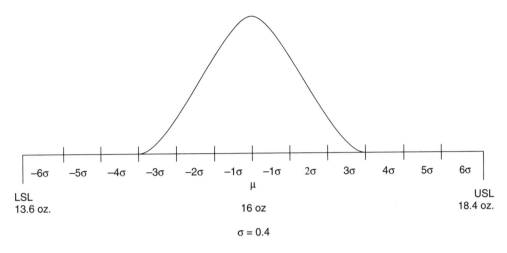

Figure 16.8 Process Potential Index (Example).

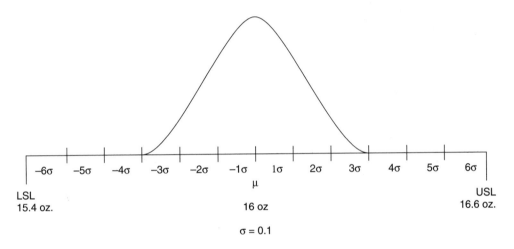

Figure 16.9 Process Potential Index (Example).

the process capability index will be 1.5σ at Six Sigma performance levels. This indicates that a process mean can shift by 1.5σ away from the target and still produce virtually defect-free products.

Cpk is the *capability* measurement and is dependent upon both the center or mean and the standard deviation of the process performance distribution. Cp is considered a process *potential* measure rather than a *capability* measure and is dependent only upon the standard deviation and spread of the process. Cp and Cpk are the same value whenever the process is centered on the target value or, simply put, the capability of the process matches its potential. Whenever the process is not centered, the Cpk value will be less than the Cp value. In these cases, the capability of the process is less than its potential. Therefore, Cp is the limiting factor for Cpk whenever the standard deviation is fixed.

The complaint resolution example used earlier described these concepts. Figure 16.10 shows a histogram of the data plotted in a bell-shaped curve, depicting a normal distribution. The upper and lower control limits (23.9 and 16.1 days, respectively) have been

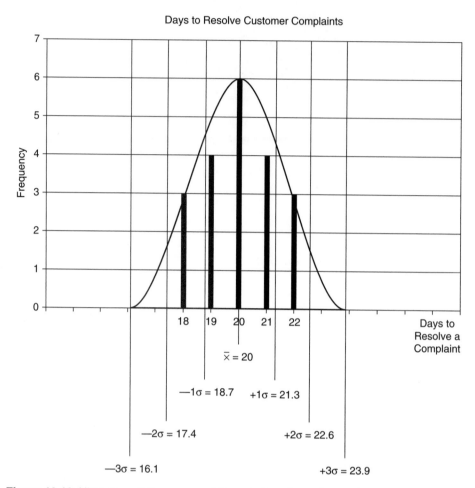

Figure 16.10 Histogram of Frequency of Days to Resolve a Complaint, Depicting a Normal Distribution, with the Upper and Lower Control Limits Included on the Chart.

included on the chart. For the purposes of this example, let us assume that our internal goal is to resolve customer complaints between 14 days and 28 days. Our customers have told us that, except for extreme emergencies, they understand the time it takes to investigate a problem and will accept resolution between 2 and 4 weeks. Figure 16.11 shows the data plotted with the upper and lower control limits and the average of the population. It also shows the data in relationship to the upper and lower specification limits and the target value. Cp is 1.79, and the Cpk is 1.5. This shows a process that is capable of delivering results most of the time. A Cp value of 2.0 or greater would indicate a process that is operating at a six sigma level of performance because the control limits of the process are well within the specification limits. A Cpk of 1.5 or better also indicates a process that is operating at a six sigma level of performance. However, both Cp and Cpk should be analyzed together since it is not just the spread of the actual process performance in relationship to the specification width (tolerance) that is important; it is also important to understand where the center of the population average ($\bar{x}$) lies in relationship to the center of the specification width or target value (*T*).

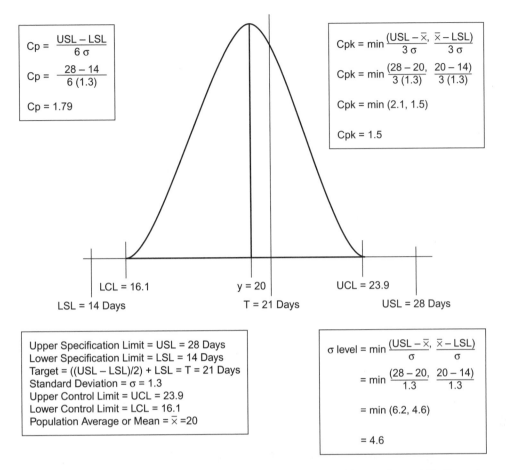

$$Cp = \frac{USL - LSL}{6\,\sigma}$$

$$Cp = \frac{28 - 14}{6\,(1.3)}$$

$$Cp = 1.79$$

$$Cpk = \min \frac{(USL - \bar{x},\ \bar{x} - LSL)}{3\,\sigma \qquad 3\,\sigma}$$

$$Cpk = \min \frac{(28 - 20,\ 20 - 14)}{3\,(1.3) \qquad 3\,(1.3)}$$

$$Cpk = \min\,(2.1,\ 1.5)$$

$$Cpk = 1.5$$

LCL = 16.1   y = 20   UCL = 23.9
LSL = 14 Days   T = 21 Days   USL = 28 Days

Upper Specification Limit = USL = 28 Days
Lower Specification Limit = LSL = 14 Days
Target = ((USL – LSL)/2) + LSL = T = 21 Days
Standard Deviation = σ = 1.3
Upper Control Limit = UCL = 23.9
Lower Control Limit = LCL = 16.1
Population Average or Mean = $\bar{x}$ = 20

$$\sigma\text{ level} = \min \frac{(USL - \bar{x},\ \bar{x} - LSL)}{\sigma \qquad \sigma}$$

$$= \min \frac{(28 - 20,\ 20 - 14)}{1.3 \qquad 1.3}$$

$$= \min\,(6.2,\ 4.6)$$

$$= 4.6$$

Figure 16.11 Data from Table 16.1 Plotted with the Upper and Lower Control Limits and the Average of the Population. Also Shows the Data in Relationship to the Upper and Lower Specification Limits and the Target Value.

Two other measurements should be considered. First is *defective parts per million* (DPPM), which measures the total number of defects that fall outside the specification limits, out of one million opportunities. These are the values that fall above or below the specification limits. DPPM is the area under the curve outside the specification limits multiplied by 1,000,000.

The other measurement is the *sigma level* (σ_{level}), which is the number of standard deviations (σ) between the center of the process ($\bar{x}$) and the specification limit nearest the center. This is referred to as a *Z value*. The formula for computing the sigma level is

$$\sigma_{level} = \text{Minimum of} \left(\frac{ULS - \bar{x}}{\sigma}\ \text{or}\ \frac{\bar{x} - LSL}{\sigma} \right)$$

In the case of the example shown, the sigma level is 3.

Table 16.4 shows the relationship between sigma levels (σ), process potential index (Cp), and defective parts per million (DPPM). The table shows the DPPM levels with and without a natural shift of 1.5 sigma. As explained in chapter 1, the concept of Six Sigma

Sigma	Cp	DPPM without Shift	DPPM with + 1.5 σ Shift
2	0.67	45,500	308,733
3	1.00	2,200	66,810
3.5	1.17	466	22,700
4	1.33	63	6,210
4.5	1.50	6.8	1,350
4.75	1.58	2.04	580
5	1.67	0.57	233
6	2.00	0.002	3.4

Table 16.4 Relationship between Sigma Levels (σ_{level}), Process Potential Index (Cp), and Defective Parts per Million (DPPM).

as defined by Motorola research shows that a process has a natural tendency to shift over the longer term and go undetected, but the shift rarely will exceed 1.5σ.

By definition, a six sigma capable process will have a Cp = 2.0, Cpk = 1.5, and DPPM = 3.4. Six Sigma focuses on centering process performance first and then on reducing the causes of variation. Lower DPPMs are better, while bigger σ_{level}'s, Cpk's, and Cp's are better. All of these are improved by reducing the variation in a process or activities within the process.

SUMMARY

The concept of Six Sigma is to reduce variation. Statistical process control uses a number of basic and advanced statistical tools to monitor, control, and reduce variation within a process. Control limits are computed from actual data about the process. Run charts and histograms with control limits applied provide visual information as to whether or not a process is in control. These controls charts can then be used to monitor future process performance.

Once it has been determined that a process is in control, it is then necessary to determine if a process is capable of performing to specifications that have been defined from inputs such as engineering, manufacturing, marketing requirements, part prints, and customer requirements. Process control and process capability are often confused. Just because a process is in control does not necessarily mean that it is good and is capable of delivering output that meets specifications. Process capability means comparing the voice of the process with the voice of the customer.

With information determined from process control parameters and process capability values (Cpk), including process potential (Cp), additional information concerning defective parts per million (DPPM) and sigma levels (σ_{level}) can be calculated. This information provides a total assessment of how well a process performs and how well a process performs in meeting specifications, including customer requirements. A six sigma capable process is one in which Cp = 2.0, Cpk = 1.5, and DPPM = 3.4. The capability of an in-control process is crucial to meeting customer requirements.

CASE STUDY

DETERMINING PROCESS CAPABILITY

As stated in case studies from earlier chapters, the Controls Business of Johnson Controls, Inc., initiated a Six Sigma strategy in 1999. The previous case studies presented the overall quality strategy and discussed the need to align a robust quality strategy with the company's overall strategy, as well as cascading goals and objectives throughout the organization through Hoshin Planning. Figure 16.12 shows the overall quality strategy for the Controls Business of Johnson Controls, Inc. The quality strategy identifies Six Sigma performance as one key initiative. Key objectives to support this initiative include minimizing variation to prevent defect occurrence, achieving Six Sigma performance levels for key characteristics of core products and processes, and eliminating special-cause failures. Specific strategies to support these objectives include developing robust designs and capable processes with specific sigma performance levels for *new product development,* prioritizing and improving existing core products and processes with demonstrated sigma performance levels for *manufacturing and delivery of products,* measuring and improving field performance and application for *post-sales support,* and requiring and validating sigma performance levels of suppliers as part of the *supplier management* process. Although specific sigma performance levels and goals have been identified to support these strategies, they have not been identified here due to the confidentiality of their nature.

An example of one formal procedure that has been put in place at the Controls Business of Johnson Controls, Inc., to define measurement philosophies for product and process quality performance was shown in Figure 15.1, and will not be repeated here. The procedure defines the measurements to be used and provides for consistent application and interpretation of all data. It also identifies the minimum performance standards for short- and long-term capability. It is important to note that the creation of a formal procedure allows for easier deployment of Six Sigma within the organization.

Johnson Controls, Inc., Controls Business—Quality Strategy

Quality Policy
We, individually and as a team, will deliver products and services that consistently conform to our customers' requirements and exceed their increasing expectations.

Quality Strategy
We will achieve a *step change* in quality performance. A fundamental change in our quality culture and a strengthening of discipline will be achieved to realize a sustained improvement in quality performance.

Initiatives
Three major initiatives will drive our change:
- Six Sigma Performance
- Software Process Improvement (SPI) to achieve SEI CMM Level 5
- Process and Systems Globalization

Objectives
1. Excellence in customer satisfaction
   - Achieve *top box* survey ratings for the three most important customer satisfaction attributes.

2. Consistent conformance to customer requirements
   - Minimize variation to prevent defect occurrence.
   - Achieve Six Sigma performance levels for key characteristics of core products and processes.

3. Achieve SEI CMM level 5 performance capability in software engineering and development.

4. Eliminate *special-cause* failures (field recalls, updates).

Strategies
1. Rigorously apply accepted best practices that are defined by our ISO 9000-certified quality system.
2. Globalize core processes (best practices) and systems; continuously improve.
3. Employ common metrics to direct performance improvement efforts.
4. New Product Development
   - Accurate, complete market requirements will drive hardware, software, and system specifications.
   - Apply advanced project/program management methods.
   - Develop robust designs and capable processes; demonstrate their sigma performance levels.
5. Manufacturing and Delivery of Products
   - Prioritize and improve existing core products and processes, demonstrating sigma performance.
   - Apply advanced order management, advanced material planning, and demand-flow technology.
   - Complete global PDM system for component, part, and product data management and change control.

Figure 16.12 Controls Business, Johnson Controls, Inc., Quality Strategy.

6. Post-Sales Support
   - Measure and improve product field performance and application, employing Six Sigma methods.
   - Ensure timely, thorough handling of product problems and complaints.
7. Supplier Management
   - Rigorously select, develop, and manage key suppliers; require and validate their sigma performance.

Performance Goals

Specific performance goals have been developed but are not shown here due to the confidentiality of their nature.

Figure 16.12 Continued.

17
Summary and the Future

It is difficult, if not impossible, to predict the future. It is interesting to note the accuracy of predictions made by others once the future becomes the present. As was presented in chapter 16, statistical process control can be used to predict the future behavior of a process, assuming all things remain constant. This prediction is based upon past performance. However, many scenarios impact the future viability or existence of an organization; focusing on the past will provide few clues about the future. The importance and need for a vision and integrated strategies and objectives to guide an organization were discussed previously. A company's vision should paint a picture of what the company needs to be in the future.

This chapter focuses primarily on the new roles for leaders as significant changes around the world impact nearly all aspects of commerce and business as it exists today. The preceding chapters discussed technical changes required of an organization in order to implement Six Sigma continuous improvement and to become more customer focused. This chapter discusses how leaders also need to change to coincide with both environmental and organizational changes.

There are a number of forums and articles that can be used to predict the future of commerce as well as the role quality will play in these new environments. Most professional and trade organizations have means for gathering predictions about the future. For example, the American Society for Quality devoted an entire *Quality Progress* publication in December 1999 to discussions on the future role of quality. The need for rapid change within an organization has never been more important. This chapter discusses four aspects associated with how the future needs to be explored and examined to keep the competitive edge. Knowing that change is inevitable, the first topic, addresses how change needs to be institutionalized within the organization—in people, products, and processes. The next two topics are somewhat related and discuss the need for understanding and addressing knowledge obsolescence and the need for organizational learning to combat knowledge obsolescence. The final topic discusses the need for leadership changes required of an organization and the new role of leaders as coaches, facilitators, and supporters.

INSTITUTIONALIZING CHANGE IN PEOPLE, PRODUCTS, AND PROCESSES

It is necessary for an organization to understand the dynamics that produce and institutionalize change within its structure. Changing an organization's culture can be a daunting undertaking that requires stamina, commitment, desire, and strong leadership. Institutionalizing change in an organization needs to identify the benefit or value to all major stakeholders. An organization needs to understand the value the change will have to the company as a whole and to its future. The organization needs to understand the value the change will have to its shareholders. The organization needs to understand and communicate the value or benefits the change will have on employees. Finally, the organization needs to understand the value the change will have on customers.

Regardless of what has been taught over time, business is all about money. The biggest changes in the advancement of quality the past decade have been the linkage of quality results with financial performance. Focusing on quality for the sake of quality because it is believed to be good for the organization is no longer accepted. Although the quality function might be about defect reduction, the impact to the bottom line, such as a decrease in warranty expense, needs to be portrayed. Although quality may take on different connotations in the future, as it has in the past, it should never lose its association with financial performance as was instilled the past decade. So, one of the keys to institutionalizing change within an organization is to tie results of changes to financial performance. One technique that is a major part of institutionalizing change in people is to modify their behavior and, ultimately, the organization's culture through financial incentives.

An organization needs to put quality at par with other financial performance measures. The linkage between quality results and financial performance was discussed previously in chapter 2. Six Sigma strategies at companies such as Motorola and GE have contributed billions of dollars to their bottom line. The Baldrige Winners Stock Index demonstrates where a strategic and systematic focus toward quality management yields significantly higher returns for stockholders (see note 12). Organizations need to understand that there is a return on investment involved with quality and customer satisfaction, and they need to exploit this within the culture.

The second major change in quality the past decade has been the view of quality from a holistic, systems, or strategic perspective. In other words, an organization's focus on quality should be integrated with the way in which it conducts its business and makes decisions and not a separate activity. There have been a number of quality *programs* introduced over time, each seeming to build upon the next. What has emerged is quality as a strategy and an integrated part of business. So, in order to institutionalize changes within an organization's processes, the focus needs to take an integrated approach. This implies that the quality function will become less distinct and evolve more toward the customer.

In the future, markets and customers will define the new standards or measurements associated with quality such as we have seen in the past decade. The ISO 9000-2000 standards, introduction of AS 9000, and CE Mark in Europe are examples of where the marketplace has invoked its standards. Information from a government accounting survey conducted in 1999 revealed that *quality* moved up to the top of the list as a primary purchasing requirement of U.S. consumers from a fifth place position 10 years prior. Quality is now just as important as price when consumers make their purchasing decisions. A new paradigm has been formed where quality is expected and price is seldom discussed between negotiations of customers and suppliers. This is very evident within the automotive industry, where standards such as QS 9000 have been imposed on suppliers as a condition of business.

Another major change that has occurred the past decade is the concept of the customer or market being the one to define what *quality* means. Some organizations have continued to focus on quality in its traditional sense as meaning a reduction of defects in products, processes, and services and have even publicized advancements they have made over time. However, customers have translated quality to mean *value*.

With changes in the way commerce is now conducted over the Internet, the quality of the entire value chain has or will soon become the new measure of customer quality in the future. This means that factors such as ease of ordering, ease of service, ease of getting information, ease of use, and speed of delivery are now just as important to a customer's perception of quality as is the defect level of the product or service. A recent survey has identified requirements of Internet shoppers as being faster delivery, reduced cycle times, competitive price, and guaranteed quality. Therefore, an organization needs to focus on customer and market needs to institutionalize changes within its culture and processes. For instance, an organization's customer satisfaction strategy needs to focus on objectives for enhancing value and customer perceptions, not merely reacting to defect reduction as customer satisfiers. This new approach is precisely why this book has included significant discussions of becoming customer centered.

KNOWLEDGE OBSOLESCENCE

Winston Chen, CEO of Selectron Corporation, has stated that technology changes so fast that it is estimated that 20 percent of an engineer's knowledge becomes obsolete every year. Steve Appleton, CEO of Micron Technology, feels that the rate is closer to 30 percent each year. The rapid changes not only in technology but in society as a whole cause the notion of knowledge obsolescence to play a significant role in an organization's strategies and plans for the future. Knowledge obsolescence can be the Achilles' heel of an organization.

There are numerous examples of technology having caused dramatic changes that have made old skills obsolete. For instance, most computer programs that one used five years ago are no longer in use, are not accepted as the norm, or are incompatible with versions or programs in use today. An organization needs to realize the impact that knowledge obsolescence will have on the organization, its employees, and its culture and plan accordingly. IBM Rochester has implemented an initiative that focuses on skill requirements needed to support strategic objectives.[30] Measurements of skill gaps then become the most important metric of education, training, and skills, as opposed to number of hours and dollars spent on education per employee. If the strategy supports the longer term and is all-encompassing of the organization's resources, then it should reflect the future predictions for the organization and the industry. If skill requirements can be projected to support the strategy, then skill needs can be planned for and met. Closing skill gaps and ensuring the right skills will be available when needed can then take on many forms, including training or retraining the current workforce, recruiting and hiring needed skills, or developing curriculum with educational institutions through partnerships.

Rapid changes in the marketplace will also cause the need for new skills and technology, making an organization's focus on knowledge obsolescence important for survival. The advent of the Internet and E-commerce has created a whole new way for customers to interact with organizations for goods and services. Customers have information available to them to help them make choices and comparisons. It is easier for customers to compare one product, service, or feature against another. A customer no longer has to go from one store to another and then back to compare products before purchasing. The pervasive use of the Internet and companies focused on E-commerce solutions has introduced a whole new line of competitors into the field. For example, on-line auction companies offer a service to consumers that helps them locate a particular product or service they wish to purchase. The on-line auction companies never handle or see the goods and services that others purchase through their service. Customers and the workforce today are not just better informed; they are also more educated.

Traditional sales and distribution methods are falling by the wayside. This change in the way goods and services are offered to customers also means that a paradigm shift is occurring that impacts the manufacturing processes. Individual customization is causing a focus on lot sizes of one. The desire for goods is moving away from *one size fits all* to personalization, *built exclusively for you.* These radical changes in purchasing habits of customers are causing dramatic changes in technology and processes. Old, tried-and-true, or traditional methods no longer fit these scenarios. Knowledge obsolescence, then, extends itself to methods, processes, and the collective learning of the organization. Identifying current customer and market needs and defining processes to deliver these have never been so important as they are today. Six Sigma teams get the opportunity to define solutions that are fundamentally different than those of today. The teams need to think *outside the box* and identify a whole new way of doing things. Rapid changes in process technologies and innovation are also causing the need for an organization to consider knowledge obsolescence as a strategic imperative.

An organization cannot wait for the future to happen; it has to be there when it happens or cause it to happen. If an organization waits, the competition will be there first.

Organizational Learning

An old Chinese proverb reads, "Wise men learn more from fools than fools from wise men." The need for an organization to develop a strategy or strategic imperatives that address an environment that is focused on continuous learning is imperative if it hopes to prevent the impact of knowledge obsolescence. Continuous learning needs to apply to all facets impacting an organization, including continual learning about customers, about markets, about industry, about competitors, about employees, and about the organization itself. An organization needs to learn about new or future technologies and trends that will have an impact on its goods, services, and offerings, as well as its processes. Sometimes it is necessary to relearn old tricks but reapply these to new situations and scenarios. For example, many have stated that the use of Six Sigma is nothing new and that most of these techniques and tools have been around forever. However, as presented in chapter 1, the sudden interest in Six Sigma is caused by taking these tools and techniques and applying them to nontraditional areas of the organization. Six Sigma is being converted into a business strategy that supports an environment of continuous improvement and breakthrough strategies, which allows an organization to become significantly better and much faster.

Continuous learning applies to all areas of the organization and becomes the backbone for initiatives such as innovation, research and development, breakthrough strategies, process management, and continuous improvement. As the organization's culture changes, the organization needs to learn how to behave in this new environment. IBM Rochester implemented an educational program for managers entitled *Managing in New Blue* after several fundamental changes were made to the way in which IBM conducted its business (see note 30). Traditional ways of managing employees no longer worked in a new environment of empowerment and teamwork.

Continuous learning helps employees to be better prepared to face the future and to contribute to the organization. Some companies are in the business of hiring specialized skills for the short term, and employees that benefit from this process quickly learn the need for keeping their skills current. These employees can also command a premium for their skills or specialties. The IBM Rochester correlation study that is discussed in Appendix A identified that a major contributor to an employee's satisfaction level was having the right skills (see note 3). This in turn positively impacts productivity, cost of quality, customer satisfaction, and market share. So, continuous learning has a direct impact on the financial performance of an organization, as well as employee morale.

Rapid changes in the marketplace will also cause the need to acquire new skills and knowledge. Major changes in the recent past that will have a significant impact on skill requirements and the need for organizational learning in the future include globalization of markets and competitors, demographics of the workforce, demographics of customers and markets, and rapid changes in technology. These factors alone indicate an urgent need to learn more about the factors influencing one's business in today's environment.

Based upon current estimates, the current global economic system has about one billion out of about five billion people in the world integrated through products and services primarily in industrialized countries. As E-commerce grows, a global system of over two billion consumers will be even more diverse, and this increase will occur in the next few years. This will cause the need to learn even more about global customers and global markets.

As was suggested earlier, one factor that can cause an organization and its culture to focus on continuous learning is financial rewards or incentives offered to those that acquire new skills. An example of this might be providing rewards for individuals that become certified in a certain skill base after they have demonstrated their competence. Retention or acquisition of skills can also be included as part of an individual's development or performance expectations to further reinforce the behavior and incorporate a continuous learning environment into the culture of the organization.

Continuous learning is not just about formal education and training or skills. It is also about learning from one's experiences and mistakes. An organization's culture needs to allow individuals and teams the opportunity to take calculated risks and then learn from these experiences, whether successful or not. An organization does not want to instill a culture in which risk taking is not allowed or in which failure means sudden doom. This will hamper most attempts at continuous learning, empowerment, and risk taking.

THE NEW ROLES OF LEADERS AS COACHES, FACILITATORS, AND SUPPORTERS

Change requires leadership. More change requires more leadership. One feeds the other, but it can become a feeding frenzy with the rapid changes that are taking place today. Just as major changes in the world have caused organizations to change processes and cultures, these changes also require leaders to change the way they lead. As was mentioned earlier, IBM Rochester implemented a new management education course entitled *Managing in New Blue* to address new ways to manage and lead the organization based upon significant changes that had been made to its culture and the way business was now conducted. The first imperative for changing an organization is that leaders need to lead the way, becoming role models and, ultimately, its agents of change.

The attitude toward leadership is not about style, nor is it about management. Both of these can be taught through formal education. Leadership is about a mind-set, a culture, or a behavior that causes others to rally around a common set of goals and objectives with a burning desire to win, not just individually but collectively. Leaders in an organization need to define the vision and a common set of objectives that the organization can relate to. This organizational direction needs to be understood by every individual within the organization. The new paradigm in leadership is one in which leaders focus more on strategic direction for the organization and less on the tactical execution of strategies and initiatives. This new role for leaders, then, provides an environment where leaders guide or coach an organization toward common goals and facilitate and support the organization in achievement of these goals. The new role for leaders is to provide coaching to support employees' efforts to realize the vision and align their objectives with that of the organization. This allows the employees to be in control.

Like coaches, leaders need to be inspirational. Leaders need to help employees embrace learning. They need to be visionary. These are new skills for many. In the past, leaders were often selected for their knowledge about aspects that significantly impacted business performance. For instance, in the past, a vice president of quality was selected because of knowledge of quality practices and principles and, possibly, because of a proven track record on having developed and implemented a quality program. In today's environment, it is more important that this individual be able to predict changes that will influence the organization and provide a vision of what the organization needs to become to address these changes.

In addition to a leader's new role as coach, facilitator, and supporter, leadership for the next decade will be about balance. Leaders will need to learn how to create balance between the environment and business, professional and personal, busy and approachable, serious and humorous, and decisive yet empowering. Organizations today tend to be over-managed and underled. The balance needs to change from one of managing to one of leading, from one of controlling to one of motivating.

Managing is about order and consistency. Leadership is about planning and managing for change. It is more important for leaders to align people than organize them. Leaders take control from management and turn it over to the employees. This is a new definition of empowerment or delegation. Leaders need to delegate and streamline operations. Decisions will stack up and slow down the organization if they are all left up to leaders to make. A true leader will let the Six Sigma teams do their jobs and hold them responsible for results. Leaders set the vision, strategy, and direction. Setting short- and long-term plans is managing as opposed to leading and is no good if directional strategies are not set or understood by the organization.

It is also more important for leaders to establish relationships—both formal and informal—with customers, suppliers, and employees and nurture these relationships as opposed to trying to control them. Relationships cannot be controlled. But relationships with people can be strengthened through inspiring and motivating, which changes behaviors. Therefore, as coaches, facilitators, and supporters, leaders need to inspire and motivate, thus creating a culture that is governed by a sense of urgency, one team–one goal, one wins–all wins, passion for winning, and inspired behavior.

As change agents, leaders will understand that there will be resistance to change. The best way to overcome this resistance is through education and communication. This is where a leader's role as coach, facilitator, and supporter is most important. Participation and involvement of others with definition and deployment of the change will also help to overcome resistance.

SUMMARY

Global changes are having a significant impact on commerce, customers, markets, and the workforce. Drastic actions need to be taken by the organization in order to address these changes. Leaders as change agents need to ensure that a culture and an environment are created to support and institutionalize these changes, including prevention of knowledge obsolescence through continuous organizational learning. Leaders need to modify their roles to address this new environment, including the need to act as coaches, facilitators, and supporters.

CASE STUDY

SUMMARY AND THE FUTURE

The Controls Business of Johnson Controls, Inc., has taken a holistic and strategic view toward quality and customer satisfaction. A formal strategy to address changes occurring in the marketplace is discussed throughout the case studies at the end of the chapters. The financial impact of customer satisfaction and quality on the organization, including the cost of lost customers and the correlation between customer satisfaction and other key financial indicators such as customer renewals, has been calculated. This information serves as a catalyst to propose and implement required changes throughout the organization. Much of this data was derived using customer satisfaction survey and market research tools. Analysis and use of customer-related data by the organization, including lost customer analysis, have been used to change processes and procedures that are aligned with customer and market needs and requirements. Creation of a formal vision, including strategies, initiatives, and objectives, has led to creation of formal processes and procedures that actively encourage and support change at all levels.

Leaders at the Controls Group of Johnson Controls, Inc., have been personally involved in ensuring that a formal system and strategy exist to support a quality and customer-focused environment. Leaders have ensured that the quality strategy supports and is integrated with the overall strategy, and supports an environment of continuous improvement and leadership with the industry. Support for Six Sigma leaders and teams is a natural extension of this commitment and support. In addition to leaders offering their support in terms of resources (both people and money), they have been involved with the selection of team leaders, team members, and projects. In addition to communicating the importance of an environment focused on customers, markets, continuous improvement, leadership, and excellence, leaders play an active role in reviewing status and results that support this environment.

Appendix A

IBM Rochester Correlation on Measurements of Employee Satisfaction, Cost of Quality, Productivity, Customer Satisfaction, and Market Share

Customer Satisfaction and Market Share
An Empirical Case Study of IBM's AS/400 Division

Steven H. Hoisington
Tze-Hsi (Sam) Huang

THEORY VERSUS FACT

As a society, we are constantly bombarded by theories that we would like to believe are true. We are evolving into a society where managing based upon facts, rather than gut feelings, is becoming commonplace. The distinction between theory and fact is often a hard area to bridge. Take for instance the notion that happy employees produce fewer defects. Or, would one be comfortable allowing disgruntled employees handling customer service calls? We know in our hearts what is right, but how can we prove this?

A *Harvard Business Review* article outlines a profit chain theory suggesting a direct relationship between quality, employee satisfaction, employee productivity, customer satisfaction, and revenue growth.[31] Intuitively, the theory makes sense, but can it be proven? Contemplation of this may be why David L. Rivera, editor of *Continuity,* a publication by the Electronics Division Association of the American Society for Quality Control (ASQC), wrote in the Winter 1994 edition that ". . . if a story demonstrated a strong correlation between employee satisfaction and customer satisfaction, then that would be news."[32]

BUSINESS QUALITY AND PEOPLE-RELATED MEASUREMENTS

IBM's AS/400 Division in Rochester, Minnesota, winner of the 1990 Malcolm Baldrige National Quality Award, struggled with this same dilemma. Management is constantly bombarded with a wealth of information and a plethora of measurements. But which measurements have the greatest impact on overall business performance?

Armed with a fistful of theories and 10 years of data, we set about trying to determine if there were any relationships among the numerous measurements that the organization focuses on. The study was begun by interviewing AS/400 Division managers from various functional organizations. They were asked to identify which measurements they felt were most important. A list of over 50 key measurements was considered. This list includes traditional measurements such as market share, overall customer satisfaction, employee morale, job satisfaction, warranty costs, inventory costs, product scrap, and productivity. The list of key measurements can be defined in three general areas: business-related, such as revenue and productivity; quality-related, such as customer satisfaction and warranty cost; and people-related, such as employee satisfaction and morale.

MEASUREMENT CORRELATION PROVEN

Strong correlation has been demonstrated between the following measurements: market share, customer satisfaction, productivity, warranty cost, and employee satisfaction. Figure A.1 illustrates those measurements that have strong relationship between them as defined by a correlation factor equal to or greater than 0.7.

The following descriptions explain the sources for the measurements found to be strongly correlated:

- Customer satisfaction (Cs) data is derived from customer satisfaction surveys of AS/400® customers.[33] Cs represents the decimal fraction of the percentage of customers responding *satisfied* or *very satisfied* on the 5-point-scale surveys.

- Employee satisfaction (Es) data is derived from an annual survey of AS/400 Division employees. The indicator used is an unweighted index representing the decimal fraction of the percentage of employees responding favorably to a set of survey questions. These survey questions, among other things, address employees' satisfaction with their job, their immediate manager, and their level of skills.

- Productivity (P) is computed as the measurement of revenue produced per number of employees, calculated on an annual basis.

- Quality (Q) represents a measurement of the cost of quality. Although numerous measurements of the cost of quality exist such as scrap and rework expenses, *warranty costs* (expenses) had the highest correlation to the other measurements used in this study. Warranty costs include labor, parts, and service expended during the warranty period of an AS/400. An aggregate of both hardware and software maintenance and service is used in this calculation. This represents the total required costs associated with servicing an AS/400 at a customer's location, including replacement costs. Warranty cost per employee is calculated on an annual basis.

IBM AS/400 Division Data 1984–1994

	Market Share	Customer Sat.	Productivity	Cost of Quality	Employee Sat.	Job Sat.	Manager	Sat. w/ Right Skills
Market Share	1.00	0.71	0.97	-0.86	0.84	0.84	—	0.97
Customer Sat.	0.71	1.00	—	-0.79	0.70	—	—	0.72
Productivity	0.97	—	1.00	—	0.93	0.92	0.86	0.98
Cost of Quality	-0.86	-0.79	—	1.00	—	—	—	—
Employee Sat.	0.84	0.70	0.93	—	1.00	0.92	0.92	0.86
Job Sat.	0.84	—	0.92	—	0.92	1.00	0.70	0.84
Sat. with manager	—	—	0.86	—	0.92	0.70	1.00	0.92
Right Skills	0.97	0.72	0.98	—	0.86	0.84	0.92	1.00

Productivity (P) = Revenue per Employee
Cost of Quality (Q) = Hardware Warranty Cost
Employee Satisfaction (ES) = Index of Job Satisfaction, Satisfaction with Manager, and Satisfaction with Right Skills

- To improve **Employee Satisfaction**, focus on improving **Job Satisfaction** and **Satisfaction with Having the Right Skills for the Job.**
- To improve **Job Satisfaction**, focus on improving **Satisfaction with Manager**, and **Satisfaction with Having the Right Skills for the Job.**
- Improving **Satisfaction with having the Right Skills for the Job** will improve **Employee Satisfaction, Job Satisfaction,** and will directly impact **Productivity, Market Share,** and **Customer Satisfaction.**
- Improving **Employee Satisfaction** will directly impact **Productivity** and **Market Share.**
- To improve **Customer Satisfaction** and focus on improving **Productivity, Employee Satisfaction** and decrease the **Cost of Quality.**
- Decreasing the **Cost of Quality** will directly impact **Customer Satisfaction** and **Market Share.**
- Improving **Customer Satisfaction** will directly impact **Market Share.**

Figure A.1 illustrates those measurements that have a strong relationship between them as defined by a correlation factor equal to or greater than 0.7.

Figure A.1 Measurement Correlation.

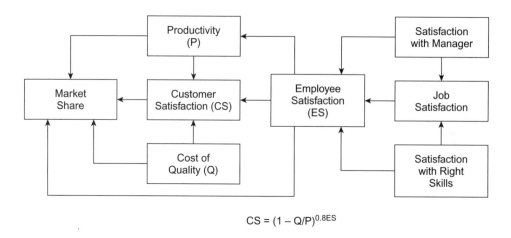

$$CS = (1 - Q/P)^{0.8ES}$$

Figure A.2 illustrates the relationship between Market Share, Customer Satisfaction, Productivity, Cost of Quality, and Employee Satisfaction.

Figure A.2 Relationship among Factors.

THEORIES PROVEN

Figure A.2 illustrates the relationship among the factors. Only those measurements with a correlation factor equal to or greater than 0.7 are shown. This study can be used to factually prove earlier theories. To improve employee satisfaction, a manager must focus on improving job satisfaction, satisfaction with management, and satisfaction with having the right skills for the job. To improve job satisfaction, a manager must focus on improving satisfaction with management and satisfaction with having the right skills for the job. Improving satisfaction with having the right skills for the job will improve employee satisfaction and job satisfaction and will positively impact productivity, market share, and customer satisfaction. Improving employee satisfaction will directly impact productivity and customer satisfaction and will decrease warranty costs. Decreasing warranty costs will directly impact customer satisfaction and market share. Improving customer satisfaction will directly impact market share.

In theory, these relationships make sense. Satisfied employees should have higher productivity and provide good service to customers. If warranty costs decrease, fewer defects are being passed on to customers, resulting in higher customer satisfaction. Employees that are satisfied are those that have the right skills for the job and are satisfied with the relationship they have with management. These employees should be more satisfied overall.

AN AGGREGATED APPROACH TO USING MEASUREMENTS

This study was not meant to explore every possible impact or relationship between operational measurements. However, a favorable outcome of this study suggests the need to take an enterprise view of measurements and understand the impact of one measurement or another. Most organizations are hierarchical and functionally oriented. Typically, customer satisfaction, employee satisfaction, quality, and productivity are each managed by a different group. Therefore, analyses and decisions are generally performed by each separate group without consideration for overall integration among these measurements. Additionally, reviews of these measurements are typically done through separate meetings or reports. A company needs to understand these relationships and review these measurements in aggregate. Otherwise, actions may be taken that have the opposite desired outcome on upstream results. For instance, if an action is taken that impacts employee satisfaction such as a layoff, the company must consider counteractions to prevent a decline in productivity, customer satisfaction, and market share.

Although the results of this study have proven useful for IBM's AS/400 Division, others should be wary of applying the absolute results to their businesses. The relationships between measurements will vary by industry. Different cost of quality measurements need to be tested. What is important, however, is for a company to use a systematic approach to understanding the relationship of key operational measurements and review these in aggregate.

Appendix B

Companies/Organizations That Comprise the American Customer Satisfaction Index (ACSI)

Company or Organization	Rank	Company or Organization	Rank
AETNA LIFE & CASUALTY	181	CAMPBELL SOUP	37
ALBERTSON'S	79	CENTRAL & SOUTH WEST	71
ALLSTATE	110	CHASE MANHATTAN	160
AMERICAN AIRLINES	187	CHEVROLET	72
AMERICAN ELECTRIC POWER	80	CHEVRON	81
		CHRYSLER	53
AMERICAN STORES	111	CITICORP	161
AMERITECH	125	CLAIBORNE (LIZ)	88
AMOCO	60	CLOROX	21
ANHEUSER-BUSCH	36	CMS ENERGY	99
APPLE COMPUTER	145	COCA-COLA	10
ARMY & AIR FORCE EXCHANGE SERVICE	151	COLGATE-PALMOLIVE personal care products	16
AT&T	51	COLGATE-PALMOLIVE pet foods	3
ATLANTIC RICHFIELD	112	COMPAQ COMPUTER	172
BANC ONE	152	CONAGRA	54
BANKAMERICA	178	CONSOLIDATED EDISON OF NEW YORK	137
BELL ATLANTIC	131		
BELLSOUTH	70	CONTINENTAL AIRLINES	182
BMW	52	COORS (ADOLPH)	50
BUICK	14	DAYTON HUDSON department stores	113
BURGER KING	171		
CADBURY SCHWEPPES	15	DAYTON HUDSON Target/Mervyn's	82
CADILLAC	8		

(continued)

Company or Organization	Rank	Company or Organization	Rank
DELL COMPUTER	132	JEEP EAGLE	116
DELTA AIR LINES	153	JVC AMERICA	63
DIAL	22	KELLOGG	39
DILLARD DEPARTMENT STORES	114	KEYCORP	148
		KFC	156
DODGE PLYMOUTH	83	KMART	134
DOLE FOOD	61	KRAFT FOODS	25
DOMINION RESOURCES	115	KROGER	122
DOMINO'S PIZZA	162	LINCOLN MERCURY	41
DTE ENERGY	100	LITTLE CEASARS	157
DUKE POWER	62	MARRIOTT hotels	96
EDISON INTERNATIONAL	73	MARS pet foods	42
ENTERGY	146	MARS food processing	5
EXXON	74	MAY DEPARTMENT STORES	107
FARMERS INSURANCE GROUP	133	MAYTAG	6
FEDERATED DEPARTMENT STORES	126	MAZDA	117
		MCDONALD'S	189
FEDEX	23	MCI COMMUNICATIONS	135
FIRST CHICAGO NBD	147	MEUER discount stores	103
FIRST UNION	138	MEUER grocery stores	89
FOOD LION	127	MERCEDES-BENZ	1
FORD	84	METROPOLITAN LIFE INSURANCE	118
FPL GROUP	154		
FRUIT OF THE LOOM	85	MILLER BREWING	43
GENERAL ELECTRIC	75	MITSUBISHI ELECTRIC	44
GENERAL MILLS	38	MOBIL	77
GENERAL PUBLIC UTILITIES	155	MONTGOMERY WARD	128
GMC	55	NATIONSBANK	167
GREAT ATLANTIC & PACIFIC TEA	163	NESTLÉ food processing	17
		NESTLÉ pet foods	18
GTE local service	164	NEW YORK LIFE INSURANCE	104
GTE long distance	86	NIAGARA MOHAWK POWER	179
HEINZ (H.J.) food processing	2	NIKE	119
HEINZ (H.J.) pet foods	4	NISSAN	64
HERSHEY FOODS	9	NORDSTROM	26
HEWLETT-PACKARD (HP)	101	NORTHEAST UTILITIES	173
HILTON HOTELS	102	NORTHWEST AIRLINES	183
HONDA MOTOR	24	NORWEST	140
HOUSTON INDUSTRIES	165	NYNEX	175
HYATT	87	OLDSMOBILE	27
HYNDAI MOTOR	166	PACIFIC TELESIS GROUP	136
INTERNAL REVENUE SERVICE	190	PACKARD BELL	176
		PANASONIC	19
INTERNATIONAL BUSINESS MACHINES (IBM)	139	PECO ENERGY	180
		PENNEY (J.C.)	76

Company or Organization	Rank	Company or Organization	Rank
PEPSICO	20	SONY	47
PG&E	141	SOUTHERN	95
PHILIP MORRIS	90	SOUTHWEST AIRLINES	97
PHILIPS	65	SPRINT	98
PHILLIPS PETROLEUM	28	STATE FARM INSURANCE	93
PILLSBURY	29	STRAUSS (LEVI)	40
PNC BANK	158	SUBARU	68
POLICE central cities	186	SUPERVALU	106
POLICE suburban	174	TACO BELL	177
PONTIAC	78	TEXACO	94
PROCTER & GAMBLE	48	TEXAS UTILITIES	149
PROMUS	91	TOYOTA	11
PRUDENTIAL INSURANCE OF AMERICA	168	TYSON FOODS	59
		UNICOM	188
PUBLIC SERVICE ENTERPRISE GROUP	105	UNILEVER	33
		UNITED AIRLINES	169
PUBLIX SUPER MARKETS	56	UNITED PARCEL SERVICE	34
QUAKER OATS	7	US AIRWAYS	170
RALSTON PURINA pet foods	30	U.S. POSTAL SERVICE mail, counter service	159
RAMADA	184		
RCA	66	U.S. POSTAL SERVICE packages, express mail	150
REEBOK INTERNATIONAL	120		
RJR NABISCO	57	US WEST	143
RJR REYNOLDS TOBACCO	67	VF	49
SAFEWAY	129	VOLKSWAGEN	69
SANYO FISHER	31	VOLVO	12
SARA LEE apparel	58	WAL-MART STORES discount stores	123
SARA LEE food processing	45		
SATURN	32	WAL-MART STORES Sam's Club	108
SBC COMMUNICATIONS	142		
SEARS ROEBUCK	121	WELLS FARGO	181
SHELL	46	WENDY'S INTERNATIONAL	144
SOLID WASTE DISPOSAL central cities	130	WHIRLPOOL	109
		ZENITH ELECTRONICS	13
SOLID WASTE DISPOSAL suburban	92		

Appendix C

Johnson Controls Lost Customers Survey

Hello, my name is _____ with Naumann & Associates, Inc., a Boise, Idaho-based consulting firm calling on behalf of Johnson Controls. May I please speak with:

YES—PRESS "1" TO CONTINUE
NO—When would be a good time to call back? SCHEDULE CALLBACK

Hello, my name is _____ with Naumann & Associates, Inc., a Boise, Idaho-based consulting firm calling on behalf of Johnson Controls. Our records indicate that you are a former Johnson Controls customer. We are calling you to determine the areas of performance that were inadequate for your needs. We would like to ask a few questions about your former relationship with Johnson Controls and Johnson Controls' current competitors. This should only take about 10 minutes.

In the competitive Building Systems market, there are a number of factors that contribute to overall customer value. This first sequence of questions asks about Johnson Controls and their key competition.

1. Thinking about your overall experience with your current Building Systems products and services provider, how satisfied are you in doing business with that provider?

   [READ LIST]

   5 Very Satisfied
   4 Satisfied
   3 Neither Satisfied Nor Dissatisfied
   2 Dissatisfied
   1 Very Dissatisfied
   0 DON'T KNOW/REFUSED

2. Who would you say is JCI's key competitor?

   _____Code as <COMPETITOR>

3. Is <COMPETITOR> your current Building Systems products and services provider?

   If "Yes": Code <COMPETITOR> as <CURRENT PROVIDER>

   If "No": Who is? _____ Code as <CURRENT PROVIDER>

311

Please answer the questions in this section using a 1 to 5 scale (5 = excellent, 4 = very good, 3 = good, 2 = fair, 1 = poor).

4. How would you rate JCI on value for the money?

    [READ LIST]
    5 Excellent
    4 Very Good
    3 Good
    2 Fair
    1 Poor
    0 DON'T KNOW/REFUSED

5. How would you rate <COMPETITOR> on value for the money?

    [READ LIST]
    5 Excellent
    4 Very Good
    3 Good
    2 Fair
    1 Poor
    0 DON'T KNOW/REFUSED

6. How would you rate Johnson Controls on planning support (for example, planning for your long-term needs for products and services)?

    [READ LIST]
    5 Excellent
    4 Very Good
    3 Good
    2 Fair
    1 Poor
    0 DON'T KNOW/REFUSED

7. How would you rate <COMPETITOR> on planning support?

    [READ LIST]
    5 Excellent
    4 Very Good
    3 Good
    2 Fair
    1 Poor
    0 DON'T KNOW/REFUSED

8. How would you rate Johnson Controls on ordering (for example, procedures, communications, status reports)?

    [READ LIST]
    5 Excellent
    4 Very Good
    3 Good
    2 Fair
    1 Poor
    0 DON'T KNOW/REFUSED

9. How would you rate <COMPETITOR> on ordering?

[READ LIST]
5 Excellent
4 Very Good
3 Good
2 Fair
1 Poor
0 DON'T KNOW/REFUSED

10. How would you rate Johnson Controls on personnel performance (for example, accessibility, knowledge, follow-up)?

[READ LIST]
5 Excellent
4 Very Good
3 Good
2 Fair
1 Poor
0 DON'T KNOW/REFUSED

11. How would you rate <COMPETITOR> on personnel performance?

[READ LIST]
5 Excellent
4 Very Good
3 Good
2 Fair
1 Poor
0 DON'T KNOW/REFUSED

12. How would you rate Johnson Controls on product delivery (for example, availability, timeliness, completeness)?

[READ LIST]
5 Excellent
4 Very Good
3 Good
2 Fair
1 Poor
0 DON'T KNOW/REFUSED

13. How would you rate <COMPETITOR> on product delivery?

[READ LIST]
5 Excellent
4 Very Good
3 Good
2 Fair
1 Poor
0 DON'T KNOW/REFUSED

14. How would you rate Johnson Controls on engineering services (for example, system configuration, accuracy, responsiveness to your needs)?

    [READ LIST]
    5 Excellent
    4 Very Good
    3 Good
    2 Fair
    1 Poor
    0 DON'T KNOW/REFUSED

15. How would you rate <COMPETITOR> on engineering services?

    [READ LIST]
    5 Excellent
    4 Very Good
    3 Good
    2 Fair
    1 Poor
    0 DON'T KNOW/REFUSED

16. How would you rate JCI on maintenance and repair (for example, responsiveness, problem resolution, timeliness)?

    [READ LIST]
    5 Excellent
    4 Very Good
    3 Good
    2 Fair
    1 Poor
    0 DON'T KNOW/REFUSED

17. How would you rate <COMPETITOR> on maintenance and repair?

    [READ LIST]
    5 Excellent
    4 Very Good
    3 Good
    2 Fair
    1 Poor
    0 DON'T KNOW/REFUSED

18. How would you rate Johnson Controls on post-sales support (for example, follow-up after the sale, customer care)?

    [READ LIST]
    5 Excellent
    4 Very Good
    3 Good
    2 Fair
    1 Poor
    0 DON'T KNOW/REFUSED

19. How would you rate <COMPETITOR> on post-sales support?

    [READ LIST]
    5 Excellent
    4 Very Good
    3 Good
    2 Fair
    1 Poor
    0 DON'T KNOW/REFUSED

20. How would you rate Johnson Controls for training (for example; on-site training, detail, professionalism, completeness)?

    [READ LIST]
    5 Excellent
    4 Very Good
    3 Good
    2 Fair
    1 Poor
    0 DON'T KNOW/REFUSED

21. How would you rate <COMPETITOR> for training?

    [READ LIST]
    5 Excellent
    4 Very Good
    3 Good
    2 Fair
    1 Poor
    0 DON'T KNOW/REFUSED

22. How would you rate Johnson Controls for technical support (for example, ability to address product related issues, product knowledge)?

    [READ LIST]
    5 Excellent
    4 Very Good
    3 Good
    2 Fair
    1 Poor
    0 DON'T KNOW/REFUSED

23. How would you rate <COMPETITOR> for technical support?

    [READ LIST]
    5 Excellent
    4 Very Good
    3 Good
    2 Fair
    1 Poor
    0 DON'T KNOW/REFUSED

24. How would you rate Johnson Controls for sales support (for example, understanding customer needs, responsiveness, pro-active problem solving)?

[READ LIST]
5 Excellent
4 Very Good
3 Good
2 Fair
1 Poor
0 DON'T KNOW/REFUSED

25. How would you rate <COMPETITOR> for sales support?

[READ LIST]
5 Excellent
4 Very Good
3 Good
2 Fair
1 Poor
0 DON'T KNOW/REFUSED

In this section, there are just four questions about your relationship with Johnson Controls and about your current service provider.

26. How likely would you be to recommend <CURRENT PROVIDER> as a Building Systems products and services provider?

[READ LIST]
5 Definitely Would Recommend
4 Would Recommend
3 Might or Might Not Recommend
2 Would Not Recommend
1 Definitely Would Not Recommend
0 DON'T KNOW/REFUSED

27. Considering your total Building Systems expenditures, approximately what percentage of your budget is spent with <CURRENT PROVIDER>?

_____ Code as <PERCENT>

28. What term best describes your current level of commitment to <CURRENT PROVIDER> (Johnson Controls' replacement)?

[READ LIST]
4 Definitely Committed
3 Moderately Committed
2 Slightly Committed
1 Not Committed
0 DON'T KNOW/REFUSED

29. If Johnson Controls' performance improved, what term best describes your possibility of becoming a Johnson Controls customer again?

    [READ LIST]
    5 Very Likely
    4 Somewhat Likely
    3 Equally Likely (50/50 chance)
    2 Somewhat Unlikely
    1 Very Unlikely
    0 DON'T KNOW/REFUSED

These last questions are open-ended. I would like to simply record your answers so I can get your exact words. The only purpose of the recording is to ensure an accurate transcript. May I turn on the recorder now?

1 YES, PERMISSION IS GIVEN TO AUDIO RECORD—TURN ON RECORDER.

2 NO, DO NOT AUDIO RECORD—TYPE IN ANSWERS ONLY.

IF PERMISSION IS GIVEN, BEGIN RECORDING NOW.

Thank you for your permission to audio record, Mr./Mrs. _____.

30. Was there a specific incident or event that caused you to discontinue your relationship with Johnson Controls? If yes, please describe:

31. How far in advance of your contract expiration would you begin to consider new proposals?

32. What factors do you consider to be Johnson Controls' strengths?

33. What two things could Johnson Controls do to win you back as a valued customer?

34. Would you like to add anything else that has not been mentioned?

Those are all the questions. On behalf of Johnson Controls, thank you for your help.

Appendix D

Vision 2000—Total Customer Satisfaction

FOREWORD

Our vision is to be recognized as being among the best companies in the world. We must acknowledge, of course, that a complex array of factors will influence our success in pursuing this vision. Some might even argue that the conditions confronting our company in coming years are so complex and so unpredictable that we cannot hope to chart a clear path to our goals.

I disagree. As I look ahead, I, too, see change and uncertainty. But within that volatile business landscape lies one constant, and one factor that above all others will determine our success—the customer.

Customers are the reason there is a _____ Corporation. We exist because we have customers. Without customers we would cease to exist. It is that simple. To excel, we must satisfy our customers better than anyone else. And believe me, there are many competitors who would love the opportunity to satisfy our customers.

If we are wise enough to keep this fundamental reality foremost in our thoughts—that customers are why _____ Corporation exists—then there will always be a _____ Corporation. We will grow. We will prosper. And we will achieve our vision of being the very best at everything we do.

That is why we have implemented Six Sigma, our company-wide quality management process. We have defined a clear pathway toward our vision and our goals. In fact, we are now two years into the Six Sigma process. And the results we have achieved in that time clearly show that we are moving in the right direction.

By the end of this year, all employees will have been trained in Six Sigma concepts, which builds quality awareness, teaches fundamental quality concepts, and helps all of us to know and understand our internal and external customers. We are also providing company-wide training to Six Sigma Action Teams, which arms our people with the structured problem-solving techniques they need to prevent and overcome obstacles to customer satisfaction.

We have already made significant improvements in work processes and in some specific problem areas. And we are all beginning to speak a new language—one that stresses continuous improvement—in doing right things right the first time and every time. Most of all, we are achieving a universal understanding that the quality of our work is defined by our customers.

Many of our divisions have received quality awards from our customers. Such recognition is impressive and gratifying. But rather than rest on our laurels, we will build on them. We will continue to work harder and work smarter. We will seek new breakthroughs. And we will strive for continuous improvement through consistent and comprehensive—Six Sigma—that reaches every group, every division, every department, and every employee in _____ Corporation.

This document details our Six Sigma goals and game plan for the next five years. It spells out in clear terms the specific actions we will take in all divisions to continue and increase the momentum of Six Sigma. This is a living document. From time to time, additions, deletions and clarifications will be made to keep us on course toward our goal of *total customer satisfaction.*

The journey ahead will not be easy, but nothing worthwhile ever is. I am confident that we can achieve our vision, and I am counting on all of you to make it happen.

Chairman, CEO

1—INTRODUCTION

The goals of Six Sigma, as articulated when we launched the process two years ago, and which are the foundation for all of our quality efforts, are:

- *Focus on the Customer.* Create an increased emphasis on the customer and responsiveness to customer needs.

- *Emphasize Leadership.* Define our corporate values, goals, and objectives. Stimulate active leadership among our responsible people by example, by involvement, and by demonstrated commitment.

- *Make Six Sigma a Way of Life.* Encourage a culture in which we do right things right the first time and every time. Avoid crises and strive for continuous improvement.

- *Streamline Our Processes.* Simplify our decision-making process and our operating procedures.

- *Enhance Communications.* Improve communications within the company—share more information and encourage reaction and participation.

- *Recognize and Reward Employees.* Concentrate on recognition, reward and performance appraisal to foster a sense of achievement and to reinforce the idea that this is our company and each of us has a stake in its success.

The Corporation is proceeding through five distinct phases in implementing Six Sigma in order to attain our goals:

1. Start up—calendar year 1994

2. Awareness—calendar years 1995 & 1996

3. Transition—calendar year 1997

4. Significant results—calendar years 1998 & 1999

5. Approaching world class—calendar years 2000 & 2001

The *Vision 2000* document was prepared specifically to help all parts of the corporation move ahead through Six Sigma implementation phases three, four, and five in calendar years 1997–2001. Vision 2000 contains a statement of work requirements, a master schedule, data requirements, and a review and audit plan. Each division/organization is expected to plan, organize and take whatever actions may be necessary to achieve the requirements presented herein.

These requirements and associated schedules may only be revised via the Corporate Quality Council. All requests for changes, revisions, or clarifications must be brought, in writing, to the attention of the Chairman of the Corporate Quality Council.

Approved revisions and all clarifications will be issued to each division/organization in an expedited manner no later than two (2) weeks after said request.

These quantifiable outcomes are to be achieved through Six Sigma between now and the end of calendar year 1998:

- *Reduce Total Cycle Time* by 25 percent in our critical work processes by the end of calendar year 1998, and by another 25 percent by the end of calendar year

1999. We will initiate this effort by identifying, flowcharting and benchmarking the critical work processes outlined in the accompanying work requirements section.

- *Defect Elimination* in all of our operations—engineering, manufacturing, testing, estimating, pricing, accounts receivable, billing, etc. We will gather data, apply measurements, and eliminate the causes of defects in a systematic way. Our interim goals are a 25 percent reduction in defects by the end of calendar year 1999, and another 25 percent reduction in defects by the end of calendar year 2000.

- *Achieve Scores of 800 or More in Malcolm Baldrige Criteria* by the end of calendar year 2000. The Baldrige Criteria provide a useful framework for shaping total quality strategy and plans, as well as an existing mechanism for measuring progress against widely accepted, customer-focused standards of success. Each division has completed a self-assessment in accordance with the Baldrige criteria and is in the process of preparing/implementing an enhancement/action plan. Yearly incremental improvements must be made so that all divisions score equal to or greater than 800 (out of 1000), which is world-class level, by 2000.

2—REQUIREMENTS

2.1 Organization

To more effectively pursue our original quality goals and achieve the three quantifiable outcomes by the end of calendar year 2000, a change in the quality infrastructure is required as follows:

- All divisions/organizations shall appoint a quality executive for Six Sigma. This position will carry the title of *vice president* or *director,* as appropriate. The executive for Six Sigma will report directly to the division's/organization's leader. It shall be the responsibility of the executive to provide the leadership within the division/organization to ensure that requirements and associated schedules contained in Vision 2000 *total customer satisfaction* are successfully achieved

- Division/organization steering committees shall be restructured, as appropriate. They shall have as members the division/organization leader, the Six Sigma executive, the process shepherds of the critical work processes and others as may be required. The chairperson of the steering committee shall be the Six Sigma executive.

- The Corporate Quality Council shall continue to establish corporate policy for Six Sigma and stimulate active leadership among our people by example, by involvement, and by demonstrated commitment. In addition, the Council shall review on a regular and formal basis the progress being made by all divisions/organizations in meeting Vision 2000 requirements and associated schedules.

2.2 Training

2.2.1 Facilitator and Advanced Facilitator. Each division/organization shall continue to identify and have trained and certified the number of facilitators and Six Sigma team leaders necessary to accomplish the requirements outlined herein. Each division/organization shall be responsible for their pro rata share of the total cost of such training and certification.

2.2.2 The Six Sigma Advantage. Each division/organization is expected to have delivered the Six Sigma Advantage training to all employees by the end of calendar year 1996. It shall be the responsibility of each division/organization to train all new hires no later than three (3) months subsequent to the satisfactory completion of their probationary period. Subsequent to the Six Sigma Advantage training, each individual shall be encouraged to meet with his/her internal customer and begin to initiate improvements in their customer supplier chain. Techniques such as specific assignments with positive feedback to the individual's supervisor or holding "class reunions" to review progress are recommended.

2.2.3 Quality Action Teams. Each division/organization shall continue to establish Six Sigma action teams (SSATs) to improve work processes and shall continue to train all members of SSATs in structured problem solving and associated tools such as Pareto diagrams, selection grids, fishbone diagrams, QFD, FEMA, process capability, etc.

2.2.4 Team Leader Training. Each division/organization shall provide team leader training to all management personnel and all others who are/will be Six Sigma Team Leaders in accordance with the established curriculum.

2.2.5 Six Sigma Quality Institute & Training Center. A Six Sigma Quality Institute and Training Center is hereby established. The Institute will be initially located at headquarters. The Institute will consist of 12 fully equipped training classrooms, a resource/media center, several conference rooms, and sufficient office space to house a small staff of permanent training specialists.

2.3 Work Process Management

2.3.1 Identification. Each division/organization shall develop and implement a system to identify its critical work processes and attendant subwork processes. It is expected that while many features will be similar to other division/organization processes, the uniqueness of critical processes/subprocesses will require individualized efforts by each division/organization.

For consistency among divisions/organizations, a work process is defined as any process that has customers (internal and/or external) and suppliers (internal and/or external) and produces a product or service.

In identifying critical work processes, begin to gather data from external customers, internal processes, and employees. Analyze the data against criteria important to your division/organization such as:

- Customer satisfaction

- Cycle time

- Defects

- Cost

- Strategic plan/business objectives

Then have the division/organization steering committee decide which processes are critical and focus on continuous improvement as defined herein.

2.3.2 Flowcharting. Each division/organization will map their unique critical work processes. For consistency among divisions/organizations, a process map is defined as a pictorial representation that shows all the steps involved in a work process. The symbols to be used in constructing a flowchart are:

- Box—activities

- Diamond—decision points

- Arrow—direction of flow from one activity to the next

2.3.3 Benchmarking. Each division/organization shall develop and implement a system of measuring its products, services, and practices against its competition or those companies considered to be world class. After measurements are obtained, analyzed, and compared to your present state, look at how the other companies operate and, where appropriate, adapt and modify their practices for your own use. The intent of this effort shall be to specifically improve those critical work processes identified and flowcharted in accordance with the requirements of paragraphs 2.3.1 and 2.3.2.

2.4 Supplier Involvement

Each division/organization shall develop and implement a system to involve its suppliers in a quality improvement process. The goal of this initial involvement will be to find areas of interaction with critical vendors in which both companies have a significant opportunity to mutually benefit. Our role will be to help and assist our vendors in whatever capacity we can so we will receive higher quality products or services, at the lowest possible cost, on or ahead of schedule.

2.5 External Customer Involvement

Each division/organization shall develop and implement a system to initiate involvement with its key external customer(s) in a Six Sigma process. This is clearly a high-risk/high-gain situation in that we may expose some weaknesses in how we are accomplishing our work. This involvement could take many forms, such as participating in the customers' training, having the customer participate in our training, and utilizing surveys or face-to-face interviews to determine, via customer-approved measurements, if we are meeting customer needs and expectations. The formation of joint partnership teams initially targeted to improve specific initiatives mutually beneficial to both parties, and ultimately with the super-ordinate goal of satisfying the end-user, shall be initiated.

2.6 Policy Deployment

Each division/organization shall develop and implement a system to deploy their goals and business objectives down through the organization to each employee. This effort requires each division/organization to establish objectives and measurements that will support achievement of our quality goals and our three quantifiable outcomes. The manager and his/her direct reports will then set more detailed objectives and measures to support the division/organization goals and objectives. The format for this process will be at the discretion of each division/organization.

It is expected that all managers shall review the progress being made with his/her direct reports on a regular basis but at least twice a year as a minimum. The results of these reviews shall be included as an integral part of each individual's annual performance appraisal.

2.7 Statistical Process Control

Each division/organization shall develop and implement a statistical process control (SPC) system. SPC means using statistical methods to monitor and control the steps in a process. While the processes most commonly referred to in implementing SPC are manufacturing processes, most efforts that have a beginning, steps to be followed, and end; cost money to perform; and have an output can benefit from statistical monitoring.

In applying SPC within your division/organization, the following hints may be useful:

- Employees need only a working knowledge of SPC, not an in-depth statistical education.

- Generate only the quantity of data your division/organization can reasonably manage.

- Concentrate on the areas with the largest cost benefit.

- Realize that statistics are a tool and not corrective action.

2.8 Employee Suggestion System

Each division/organization shall continue to implement an employee suggestion system in accordance with the corporate requirements.

2.9 Awards—External

Awards are not ends unto themselves, but, rather, the award process provides a learning environment for continuous quality improvement. Receiving an award recognizes superior quality achievements, will enhance our quality efforts, and will renew our commitment to quality by receiving due recognition.

2.9.1 Malcolm Baldrige National Quality Award.   Each division/organization shall utilize the Baldrige criteria as a framework for shaping detailed quality plans and as a mechanism for measuring progress against widely accepted, customer-focused standards of success. Our initial thrust was to have each division/organization conduct a self-assessment and score itself against this criteria. Yearly incremental improvements must now be made so that all divisions score equal to or greater than 800 (out of 1000), which is world-class level, by the end of calendar year 2000.

Each division/organization shall prepare a Malcolm Baldrige National Quality Award enhancement/action plan in its own format. This plan shall be in sufficient detail so that yearly incremental improvements can be made from the score associated with the initial self-assessment completed in calendar year 1995, to scores as follows:

- >675 end of calendar year 1998

- >750 end of calendar year 1999

- ≥800 end of calendar year 2000

Each division/organization shall include in the enhancement/action plan the requirements for additional formal self-assessments in calendar years 1998 and 2000. If desired, more frequent self-assessments may be conducted at the discretion of the division/organization. These two formal self-assessments, however, will be reviewed, analyzed, and validated by an outside consultant to be retained by the Corporate Quality Council. It is desired to have one or more divisions make formal application in calendar year 2001. If, in the opinion of the Corporate Quality Council, a division is *ready* to make formal application before this date, said division will be encouraged to do so.

2.10 Recognition, Reward, and Performance Appraisal

One of the original goals was to "concentrate on recognition, reward and performance appraisal to foster a sense of achievement and to reinforce the idea that is our company and each of us has a stake in its success." Each division/organization shall adhere to the requirements of the following subparagraphs, as appropriate:

2.10.1 Recognition.   A cross-organizational Six Sigma quality action team was formed to determine the process, procedure, and method to be used to recognize the exemplary efforts of all of our employees involved in Six Sigma. The solution of this Six Sigma quality action team shall establish the minimum means of employee recognition. Each division/organization shall implement the solution of this action team, when available, and in addition is encouraged to implement other means of recognizing employee efforts that complement the corporate requirement(s).

2.10.2 Reward.   A corporate steering committee was formed to more fully understand broad-based incentive programs, how they work, and inherent advantages and disadvantages. A report of this committee's findings will be made available to all divisions/organizations.

2.10.3 Performance Appraisal.   Each division/organization shall ensure that performance appraisals are completed for all employees in accordance with corporate procedure. In addition, all employees shall be evaluated on their contribution to Six Sigma as individuals or as members of Six Sigma quality action teams.

2.11 Communications

Another of the original goals was to improve communications within the company—share more information and encourage reaction and participation.

2.11.1 Internal Communications.   Communication of Six Sigma successes, lessons learned, future plans, and simple "How's it going?" is vital to the attainment of our quality goals and quantifiable outcomes. Employee dialogue sessions, job shadowing, walk-arounds, one-on-one discussions, breakfast gatherings, and others are all effective techniques that can be used to supplement more formal means of communication such as staff meetings, memos, and audiovisual briefings. The use of articles in the company magazine, newsletter, and the Intranet newsboard are encouraged.

  Each division/organization shall make maximum effective use of the communication techniques described herein, is encouraged to publish a quarterly quality management report to all employees, and shall implement other innovative means of communicating with its employees.

2.11.2 External Communications.   We must let our customers, suppliers, neighbors, and the general public know who we are and what we are doing. Six Sigma quality must be our message. Obviously, the most effective means of communication would be to continue to supply our customers with the products and services they expect, on time, at the most affordable price.

Additionally, however, we must target certain newspapers and periodicals and utilize radio and television to promulgate our message that the corporate image is synonymous with quality. Each division, in conjunction with the corporation's public affairs department, shall prepare an external communication plan.

2.12 Quality Techniques

- Quality function deployment
- Concurrent (simultaneous) engineering
- Design of experiments
- Variability reduction
- Just-in-time
- Process capability
- FEMA

These techniques are very powerful tools that are best used in specific, unique circumstances particularly in a mature quality environment—an environment where critical processes are fully understood, all employees have been trained in the Six Sigma advantage (awareness), several quality action teams using structured problem-solving techniques have implemented *successful* solutions, and where all members of management are fully committed to continuous improvement through the Six Sigma process. It would be best to prototype (pilot) these techniques and gain experience with them prior to widespread application within a project or division. Each of these techniques provides benefits through its use, in and of itself, but used together (except for just-in-time) in an integrated manner will provide innovative breakthroughs through synergistic actions.

3—SCHEDULE

This section contains a Master Schedule (Figure D.1, four parts) for Vision 2000 efforts and covers each requirement specified in Section 2. The Master Schedule also contains efforts scheduled in prior years and the completion status of such efforts, which have been used as the foundation for our Vision 2000 planning. Achievement of these schedule milestones will help ensure that our quality goals and quantifiable outcomes are attained.

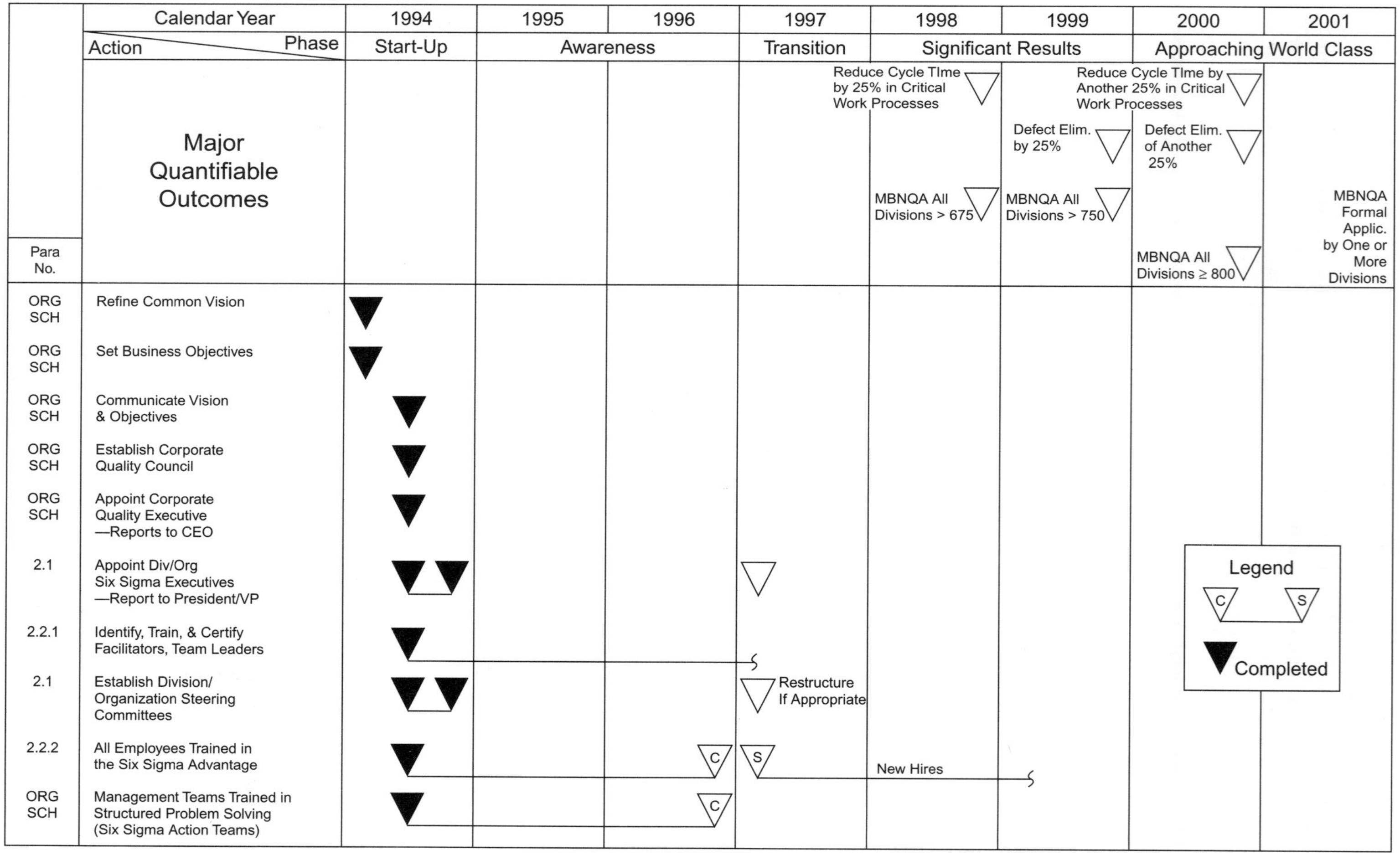

Figure D.1 Vision 2000 Master Schedule (1 of 4).

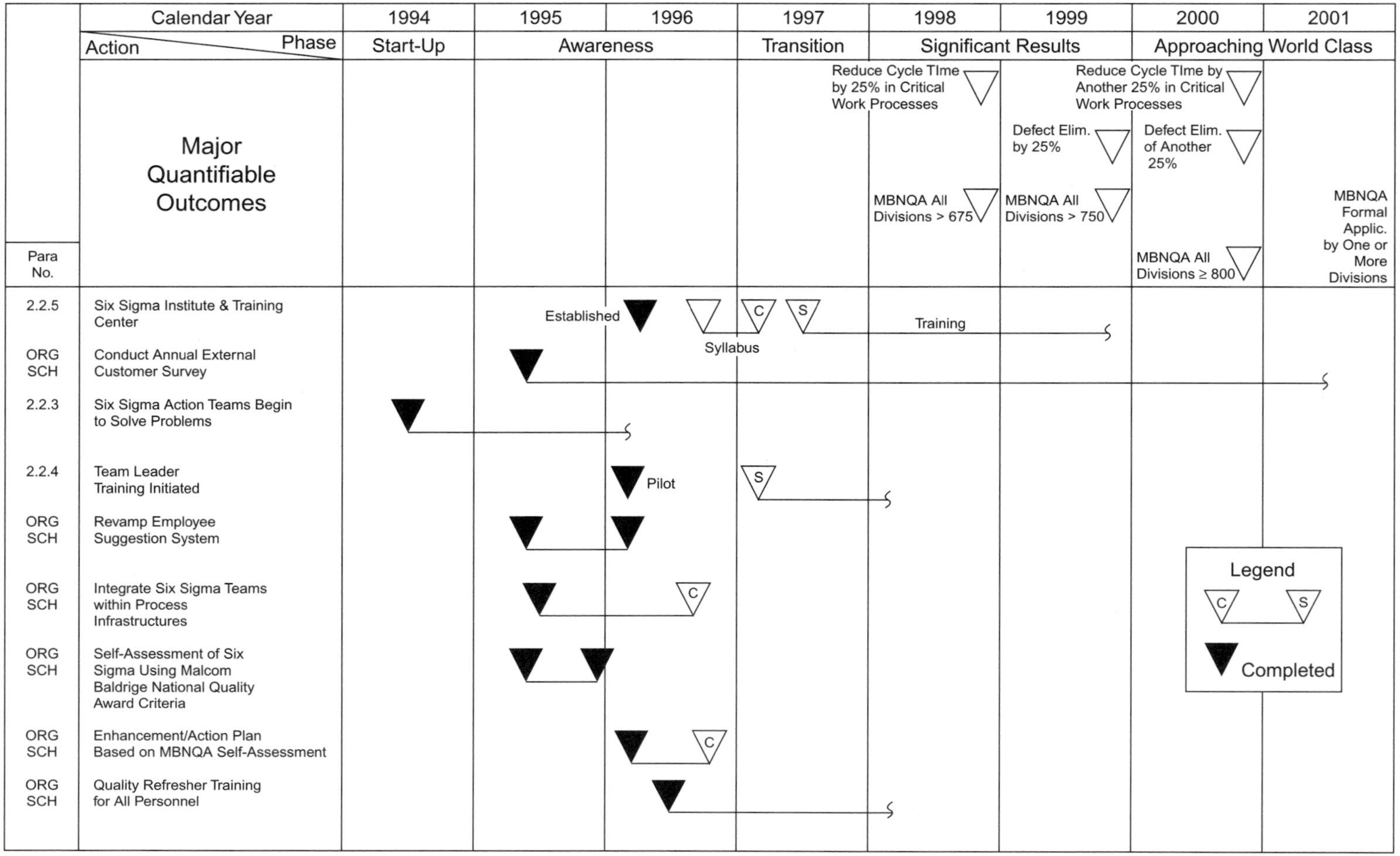

Calendar Year	1994	1995	1996	1997	1998	1999	2000	2001
Phase	Start-Up	Awareness		Transition	Significant Results		Approaching World Class	
Major Quantifiable Outcomes					Reduce Cycle Time by 25% in Critical Work Processes	Reduce Cycle Time by Another 25% in Critical Work Processes		
						Defect Elim. by 25%	Defect Elim. of Another 25%	
								MBNQA Formal Applic. by One or More Divisions
					MBNQA All Divisions > 675	MBNQA All Divisions > 750	MBNQA All Divisions ≥ 800	

Para No.	Action	
2.2.5	Six Sigma Institute & Training Center	Established — Syllabus
ORG SCH	Conduct Annual External Customer Survey	
2.2.3	Six Sigma Action Teams Begin to Solve Problems	Pilot
2.2.4	Team Leader Training Initiated	
ORG SCH	Revamp Employee Suggestion System	
ORG SCH	Integrate Six Sigma Teams within Process Infrastructures	
ORG SCH	Self-Assessment of Six Sigma Using Malcom Baldrige National Quality Award Criteria	
ORG SCH	Enhancement/Action Plan Based on MBNQA Self-Assessment	
ORG SCH	Quality Refresher Training for All Personnel	

Legend
C | S | ▶ Completed

Figure D.1 Vision 2000 Master Schedule (2 of 4).

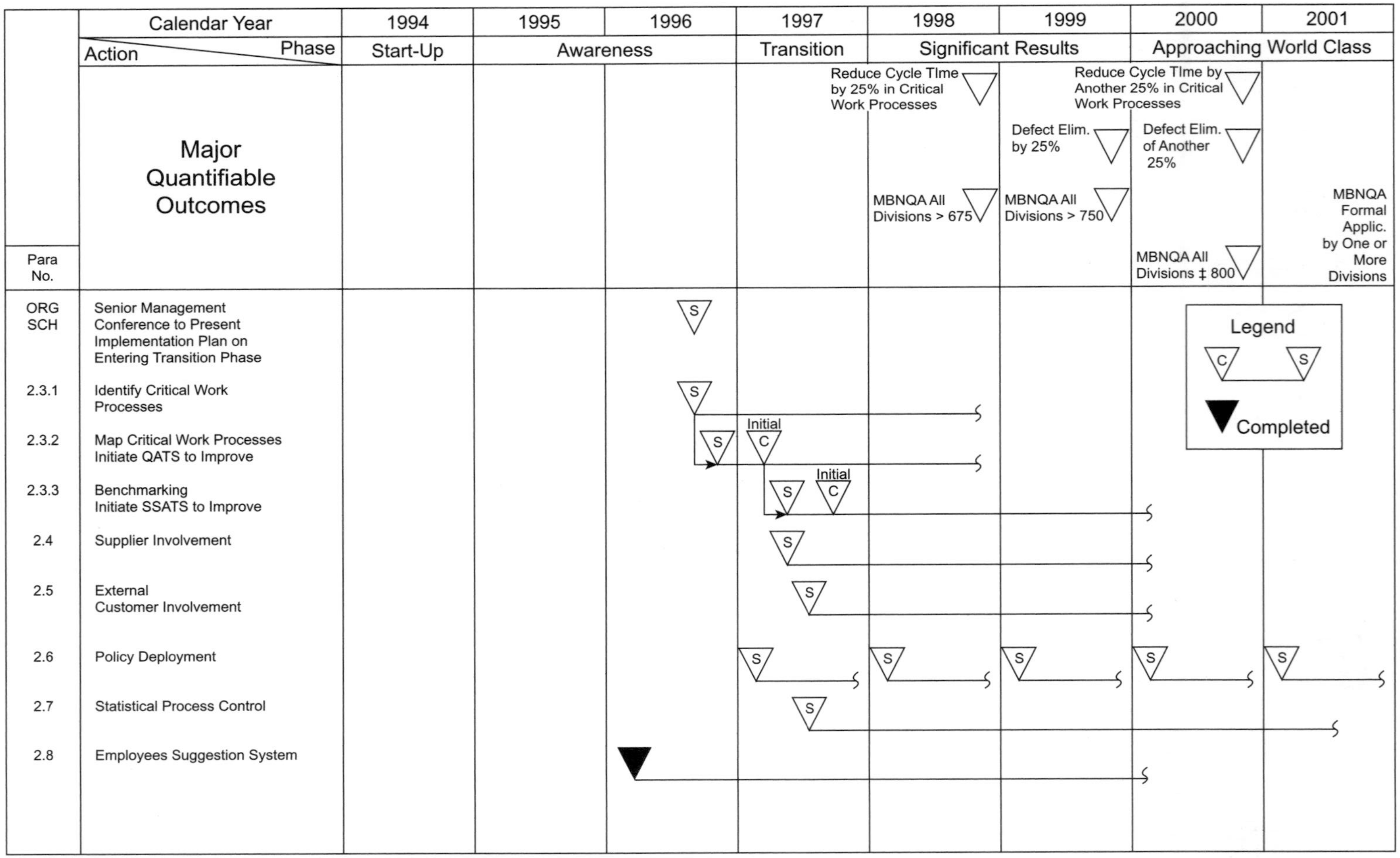

Figure D.1 Vision 2000 Master Schedule (3 of 4).

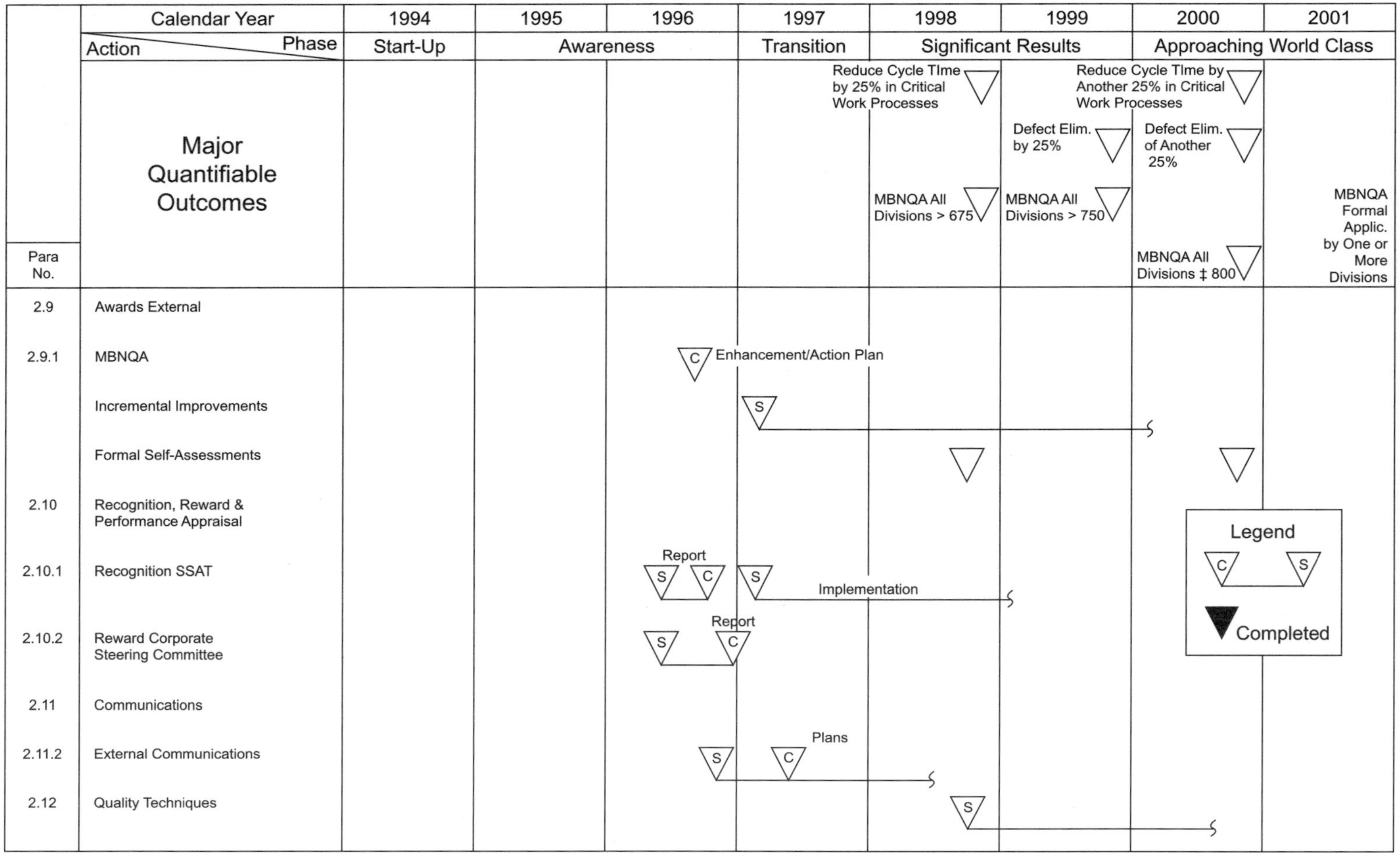

Figure D.1 Vision 2000 Master Schedule (4 of 4).

References

1. Robert Slater, *Jack Welch and the GE Way* (New York: McGraw-Hill, 1999).
2. Steve Hoisington, "Information and Analysis at IBM's AS/400 Division" (published in proceedings from the Celebrating Quality, the 10th Annual Minnesota Quality Conference, Saint Paul, MN, October 14, 1998).
3. Victor Tang and Roy Bauer, *Competitive Dominance: Beyond Strategic Advantage and Total Quality Management* (New York: Van Nostrand Reinhold, a Division of International Thompson Publishing, 1995), 55–57.
4. Steve Hoisington, "Information and Analysis at IBM's AS/400 Divison" (published in the proceedings from the Celebrating Quality, the 10th Annual Minnesota Quality Conference, Saint Paul, October 14, 1998).
5. Elizabeth R. Larsen, "GE Reports Record Earnings with Six Sigma," *Quality Digest* (Chico, CA: QCI International, December 1999).
6. Claes Fornell, Christopher D. Ittner, and David Larcker, "Understanding and Using the American Customer Satisfaction Index (ACSI): Assessing the Financial Impact of Quality Initiatives" (Juran Institute's Conference on Managing for Total Quality, December 1995).
7. Contact the American Society for Quality (ASQ) on information regarding various ACSI studies (1-800-248-1946, www.asq.org).
8. *United States Department of Commerce News* (February 1999, United States Department of Commerce, Technology Administration, National Institute of Standards and Technology, Baldrige National Quality Award Program, Administration Building, Room A635, 100 Bureau Drive, Stop 1020, Gaithersburg, MD 20899-1020, www.nist.gov).
9. "Investing in Quality Managed Companies" (advertisement for Robinson Capital Management, Craig H. Robinson, president), ASQ *Quality Progress* (Milwaukee, WI: American Society for Quality, January 2000), 82.
10. Kevin B. Hendricks and Vinod Singhall, "Don't Count TQM Out," ASQ *Quality Progress* (Milwaukee, WI: American Society for Quality, April 1999).
11. Steve Hoisington, "Information and Analysis at IBM's AS/400 Division" (published in proceedings from the Celebrating Quality, the 10th Annual Minnesota Quality Conference, Saint Paul, MN, October 14, 1998).
12. *United States Department of Commerce News* (February 1999, U.S. Department of Commerce, Technology Administration, National Institute of Standards and Technology, Baldrige National Quality Award Program, Administration Building, Room A635, 100 Bureau Drive, Stop 1020, Gaithersburg, MD 20899-1020, www.nist.gov).
13. Robert C. Camp, *Business Process Benchmarking: Finding and Implementing Best Practices* (Milwaukee, WI: ASQC Quality Press, 1995).

14. Steve Hoisington, "Information and Analysis at IBM's AS/400 Division" (published in proceedings from the Celebrating Quality, the 10th Annual Minnesota Quality Conference, Saint Paul, MN, October 14, 1998).

15. Steve Hoisington, "Information and Analysis at IBM's AS/400 Division" (published in proceedings from the Celebrating Quality, the 10th Annual Minnesota Quality Conference, Saint Paul, MN, October 14, 1998).

16. Technical Assistance Research Program (TARP), Washington, D.C. In Michael Le Boeuf, *How to Win Customers and Keep Them for Life,* (New York: G.P. Putnam's Sons, 1987).

17. Steve Hoisington, "Information and Analysis at IBM's AS/400 Division" (published in proceedings from the Celebrating Quality, the 10th Annual Minnesota Quality Conference, Saint Paul, MN, October 14, 1998).

18. Steve Hoisington, "Information and Analysis at IBM's AS/400 Division" (published in proceedings from the Celebrating Quality, the 10th Annual Minnesota Quality Conference, Saint Paul, MN, October 14, 1998).

19. Roy A. Bauer, Emilio Collar, and Victor Tang, *The Silver Lake Project: Transformation at IBM* (New York: Oxford University Press, Inc., 1992).

20. Robert Slater, *Jack Welch and the GE Way* (New York: McGraw-Hill, 1999).

21. Steve Hoisington, "Information and Analysis at IBM's AS/400 Division" (Published in proceedings from the Celebrating Quality, the 10th Annual Minnesota Quality Conference, Saint Paul, MN, October 14, 1998).

22. *1998 General Electric (GE) Annual Report* (GE Corporate Investor Communications, 3135 Easton Turnpike, Fairfield, CT 06431).

23. Robert S. Kaplan and David P. Norton, "The Balanced Scorecard—Measures That Drive Performance," *Harvard Business Review* (Boston, MA: Harvard Business School Publishing Corporation, January–February 1992).

24. Steve Hoisington, "Information and Analysis at IBM's AS/400 Division" (published in proceedings from the Celebrating Quality, the 10th Annual Minnesota Quality Conference, Saint Paul, MN, October 14, 1998).

25. Mikel J. Harry, Ph.D., *The Vision of Six Sigma: A Roadmap for Breakthrough* (Phoenix, AZ: Tri Star Publishing, 1997).

26. Robert Slater, *Jack Welch and the GE Way* (New York: McGraw-Hill, 1999).

27. Robert C. Camp, "Benchmarking: The Search for Industry Best Practices That Lead to Superior Performance," ASQC *Quality Progress* (February 1989):70–75.

28. Mikel J. Harry, Ph.D., *The Vision of Six Sigma: A Roadmap for Breakthrough* (Phoenix, AZ: Tri Star Publishing, 1997).

29. J.M. Juran and Frank M. Gryna, *Juran's Quality Handbook,* 4th ed. (New York: McGraw-Hill, Inc., 1988).

30. Steve Hoisington, "Information and Analysis at IBM's AS/400 Division" (published in proceedings from the Celebrating Quality, the 10th Annual Minnesota Quality Conference, Saint Paul, MN, October 14, 1998).

31. James L. Heskett, Thomas O. Jones, Gary W. Loveman, W. Earl Sasser, Jr., and Leonard A. Schlesinger, "Putting the Service-Profit Chain to Work," *Harvard Business Review* (March–April 1994).

32. David L. Rivera, "Customer Satisfaction," *Continuity* (ASQC Electronics Division, Winter 1994).

33. AS/400® is a registered trademark of IBM. Application System/400 and Advanced Series/400 are commercial computers developed and manufactured by IBM's AS/400 Division in Rochester, MN.

Index